Managing Information Singularity

Boris Kantsepolsky • Lev Topor

Managing Information Singularity

AI, Quantum Technologies, and the Future of Information Systems

palgrave
macmillan

Boris Kantsepolsky
The Academic College of Tel Aviv-Yaffo
Tel Aviv-Yaffo, Israel

Lev Topor
Institute for the Study of Global Antisemitism and Policy (ISGAP)
Cambridge, UK

ISBN 978-3-032-26222-6 ISBN 978-3-032-26223-3 (eBook)
https://doi.org/10.1007/978-3-032-26223-3

Cover image: BlackJack3D | Getty Images

This Palgrave Macmillan imprint is published by the registered company Springer Nature Switzerland AG
The registered company address is: Gewerbestrasse 11, 6330 Cham, Switzerland

This book is dedicated to our families, whose love, unwavering support, and encouragement sustained us throughout this journey.
Boris Kantsepolsky
Lev Topor

Foreword

There are moments when a field must admit that its familiar vocabulary is no longer enough. Information Systems is at such a moment now, not because we lack theories or methods, but because the object of our study is mutating. Systems that once stored, processed, and reported information are rapidly evolving to systems that infer, recommend, persuade, and decide. They do not simply support information processing and flow through an organization; they shape what counts as information in the first place.

This is the intellectual wager of *Managing Information Singularity: AI, Quantum Technologies and the Future of Information Systems*. The authors argue that we are approaching a threshold where the defining challenge is no longer "digital transformation" in the managerial sense, but epistemic transformation: who produces knowledge, how it is validated, how it flows, and how it is contested. In practical terms, this is already visible. Generative models draft reports and essays (in fact, this very foreword was co-authored with such a model), write code, summarize intelligence, generate synthetic media, and provide decision support at speed and scale. Recommender systems curate attention and, with it, public discourse. Automated agents execute tasks across workflows. The informational environment becomes less like a database and more like a continuously updated hypothesis about the world—useful, powerful, and sometimes dangerously wrong.

What makes this book particularly timely is its multidimensional analysis; rather than treating artificial intelligence (AI) as a standalone topic and quantum information science as a separate scientific and technological advancement, the authors place both within the core of IS: the design, governance, and consequences of socio-technical systems that mediate work, markets, and institutions. AI changes the *logic* of information systems as it blurs the lines between data and interpretation, and between reporting and reasoning, between assistance and delegation. Quantum technologies change the *assumptions* underlying information systems, as they enable us to reimagine security, trust, and computational advantage. Along with the strategic asymmetries that will emerge as quantum capabilities will become unevenly distributed across states and firms, together, AI and quantum information systems (QIS) will manage both the production and the trustworthiness of knowledge.

Readers will find that the authors do not romanticize this shift. They acknowledge what many of us have observed in our own research and practice: that the benefits of advanced systems are inseparable from new forms of fragility. When systems generate outputs that appear authoritative, using confident language, plausible citations, and compelling imagery, the burden of validation shifts from the system to the user and the institution. This shift can take place in a gradual and unnoticeable manner, rendering the users unaware of their new responsibility. Furthermore, when automation accelerates action, it also accelerates error. When decision support becomes decision shaping, accountability becomes harder to locate, especially across supply chains of models, platforms, data brokers, and outsourced analytics. And when information becomes abundant, the scarce resource is no longer access, it is trust.

It is precisely here that the book makes a contribution beyond technical forecasting. It treats governance as part of system design rather than an afterthought. Regulation, standards, auditing, procurement rules, professional norms, and institutional ethics are not external constraints imposed upon technology; they are components of the socio-technical architecture that determine the extent of both the public value and the potential harm they introduce. In the coming years, organizations will be expected to justify not only what their systems do, but how they were trained, what data they relied upon, what risks were assessed, what safeguards were implemented, and how failures will be detected and corrected. The future of Information Systems will be shaped as much by ethics and accountability as by performance.

As a discipline, Information Systems has lived through waves of technological change that promised rupture from mainframes and time-sharing, personal computing, enterprise integration, to the web, platforms, cloud, and mobile. Each wave altered organizational life, but it also forced Information Systems scholars to clarify what we study and why it matters. This book continues in these lines; beyond discussing new tools and technologies, it asks what kinds of systems we are building, what kinds of organizations these systems shape, and what kinds of societies these organizations sustain.

The authors' ambition to speak across audiences is noteworthy as well. Scholars will recognize core disciplinary concerns, related to data, infrastructure, organizational routines, decision processes, and the politics of technology, reframed for an era of AI-mediated knowledge and emerging quantum capabilities. Policymakers and regulators will encounter a nuanced account of why simplistic solutions, whether total permissiveness or blanket bans, fail to address the realities of complex socio-technical systems. Practitioners will find terminology extended for expressing what they are already experiencing: accelerating automation, expanding vendor ecosystems, mounting compliance expectations, and risk landscapes that no longer fit legacy governance structures.

On the note of terminology, the term "information singularity" can sound dramatic. In this book, it is carefully handled, serving for naming a convergence of forces that compresses time, amplifies scale, and destabilizes the traditional relationship between information, expertise, and authority. Whether we embrace this term or choose another, the underlying question remains: how do we design and govern information systems when the system is no longer a mere conduit of information, but a producer of meaning?

While we all hold our own perspectives on the questions explored in the book, and some may differ with the authors' specific analyses, one thing is certain: regardless of your background, this book will challenge you to reconsider your assumptions and reevaluate your vision of the future.

Professor Irit Hadar, Director, Center for Cyber, Law and Policy, University of Haifa.

Haifa, Israel
March 1st, 2026

Contents

1 Introduction **1**
- 1.1 About the Book 1
- 1.2 The Challenges of Technological Progress 3
- 1.3 Methodology and Book Structure 5
- 1.4 Book Audience and Contribution 6
- 1.5 Debating on Information Singularity 7

2 A Brief History of Information Systems **9**
- 2.1 Introduction 9
- 2.2 Capturing, Storing, Processing, and Disseminating Information 10
- 2.3 The Birth of Hardware, Software, and Communication 13
- 2.4 The Rise of Information Systems 21
- 2.5 Conclusions 26

3 The Current State of Information Systems **33**
- 3.1 Introduction 33
- 3.2 Common Types of Information Systems 34
- 3.3 Emerging Technologies and Innovations (2000–2025) 42
- 3.4 Digital Transformation 46
- 3.5 Academic Perspectives 52
- 3.6 Conclusions 57

4 Challenges and Abuses of Information Systems **65**
4.1 Introduction 65
4.2 Vulnerabilities of Information Systems 68
4.3 The Main Dilemmas/Challenges of Information Systems 70
4.4 Conclusions 86

5 Legal and Regulatory Frameworks for Information Systems **93**
5.1 Introduction 93
5.2 Understanding Domestic and International Law 95
5.3 Overview of Major Legal Frameworks Governing IS 97
5.4 Regulatory Compliance, Standards, and Risk Management 118
5.5 Ethical and Social Considerations in IS Law 120
5.6 International and Cross-Border Regulatory Issues 123
5.7 Conclusions 127

6 Implications of Artificial Intelligence for Information Systems **135**
6.1 Introduction 135
6.2 Artificial Intelligence: Evolution, Types, Functions, and Approaches 137
6.3 AI Agents and Agentic AI in Information Systems 149
6.4 AI Use Cases and Applications in Information Systems 152
6.5 How AI Enhances Information Systems 154
6.6 Challenges and Negative Implications 159
6.7 Conclusions 175

7 Introduction to Quantum Information Science **187**
7.1 Introduction 187
7.2 Introduction to Quantum Theory 188
7.3 Quantum Information Science 194
7.4 The Second Quantum Revolution 198
7.5 Conclusions 213

8 Toward Information Singularity **225**
8.1 Introduction 225
8.2 Defining Singularity 226
8.3 How AI Might Lead to Information Singularity 231
8.4 The Role of QIS 234
8.5 Are We Ready? 240
8.6 The Way Ahead: Future Trends and Applications 246
8.7 Conclusions 247

Index **255**

List of Abbreviations

AGI	Artificial General Intelligence
AI	Artificial Intelligence
AIS	Association for Information Systems
ANI	Artificial Narrow Intelligence
APPI	Act on the Protection of Personal Information
ASI	Artificial Superintelligence
ATT	App Tracking Transparency
AWS	Amazon Web Services
BBS	Bulletin Board Systems
BCPL	Basic Combined Programming Language
BI	Business Intelligence
BIS	Bureau of Industry and Security
BYOD	Bring Your Own Device
C2PA	Coalition for Content Provenance and Authenticity
CAC	Cyberspace Administration of China
CBPR	Cross-Border Privacy Rules
CCDCOE	Cooperative Cyber Defense Centre of Excellence
CCL	Commerce Control List
CCPA	California Consumer Privacy Act
CDO	Chief Digital Officer
CFO	Chief Financial Officer
CFPB	Consumer Financial Protection Bureau
CGA	Color Graphics Adapter
CIA	Confidentiality, Integrity, and Availability
CLOUD	Clarifying Lawful Overseas Use of Data

CMMC	Cybersecurity Maturity Model Certification
CMS	Content Management Systems
CNN	Convolutional Neural Network
COBOL	Common Business-Oriented Language
COPPA	Children's Online Privacy Protection Act
CPL	Combined Programming Language
CPRA	California Privacy Rights Act
CRM	Customer Relationship Management
CSL	Cybersecurity Law
CTSS	Compatible Time-Sharing System
CV	Computer Vision
DE-CIX	Frankfurt Internet Exchange
DMA	Digital Markets Act
DOE	Department of Energy
DOS	Disk Operating System
DPC	Data Protection Commission
DSA	Digital Services Act
DSL	Data Security Law
DSR	Design Science Research
DSS	Decision Support Systems
EAR	Export Administration Regulations
EC2	Elastic Compute Cloud
ECIS	European Conference on Information Systems
EDPB	European Data Protection Board
EDVAC	Electronic Discrete Variable Automatic Computer
EIS	Executive Information Systems
ENIAC	Electronic Numerical Integrator and Computer
ENISA	European Union Agency for Cybersecurity
ERP	Enterprise Resource Planning
ESS	Executive Support Systems
ETHICS	Effective Technical and Human Implementation of Computer-based Systems
EU	European Union
FAR	Federal Acquisition Regulation
FCA	Financial Conduct Authority
FHE	Fully Homomorphic Encryption
FISMA	Federal Information Security Management Act
FORTRAN	Formula Translation
FTC	Federal Trade Commission
FTQC	Fault-Tolerant Quantum Computing
GDPR	General Data Protection Regulation
GIGO	Garbage In, Garbage Out
GLBA	Gramm-Leach-Bliley Act

GPS	Global Positioning System
GRC	Governance, Risk, and Compliance
GSP	Golden Shield Project
GUI	Graphical User Interface
HBS	Harvard Business School
HHS	Health and Human Services
HIPAA	Health Insurance Portability and Accountability Act
HTAP	Hybrid Transactional and Analytical Processing
HTML	Hypertext Markup Language
HTTP	Hypertext Transfer Protocol
IBP	Integrated Business Planning
ICIS	International Conference on Information Systems
ICO	Information Commissioner's Office
ICS	Industrial Control Systems
IEC	International Electrotechnical Commission
IFIP	International Federation for Information Processing
IRS	Internal Revenue Service
IS	Information Systems
ISACA	Information Systems Audit and Control Association
ISMS	Information Security Management Systems
ISO	International Organization for Standardization
IT	Information Technology
ITU	International Telecommunication Union
IYQ	Year of Quantum Science and Technology
KMS	Knowledge Management Systems
LGPD	Lei Geral de Proteção de Dados
LSE	London School of Economics
MAXC	Multiple Access Xerox Computer
MDM	Mobile Device Management
MIS	Management Information Systems
ML	Machine Learning
MRI	Magnetic Resonance Imaging
NERC	North American Electric Reliability Corporation
NIN	National Information Network
NIS	Network and Information Security
NISQ	Noisy Intermediate-Scale Quantum
NIST	National Institute of Standards and Technology
NLP	Natural Language Processing
NSF	National Science Foundation
OECD	Organization for Economic Cooperation and Development
OES	Operators of Essential Services
OS	Operating System
OT	Operational Technology

PARC	Palo Alto Research Center
PC	Personal Computer
PIPEDA	Personal Information Protection and Electronic Documents Act
PIPL	Personal Information Protection Law
PPML	Privacy-Preserving Machine Learning
PPP	Public-Private Partnership
PQC	Post-Quantum Cryptography
PSD2	Payment Services Directive 2
QAI	Quantum Artificial Intelligence
QIS	Quantum Information Science
QKD	Quantum Key Distribution
QNN	Quantum Neural Networks
RAI	Responsible AI
RE	Requirements Engineering
RLS	Row-Level Security
RPS	Requests Per Second
RSI	Recursive Self-Improvement
SBU	Security Service of Ukraine
SCC	Supreme Council of Cyberspace
SCM	Supply Chain Management
SI	International System of Units
SSM	Soft Systems Methodology
TAM	Technology Acceptance Model
TIA	Transfer Impact Assessment
TPS	Transaction Processing Systems
TRADIC	Transistorized Airborne Digital Computer
TTF	Task-Technology Fit
UN	United Nations
UNCLOS	United Nations Convention on the Law of the Sea
UTAUT	Unified Theory of Acceptance and Use of Technology
UX	User Experience
WEEE	Waste Electrical and Electronic Equipment
WWII	World War II
WWW	World Wide Web
XAI	Explainable AI

List of Tables

Table 4.1	Main threats for information systems (A conceptual model)	68
Table 6.1	AI in Information Systems	176
Table 7.1	Common quantum sensing types: representative performance	210
Table 8.1	The Information Singularity Readiness Maturity Model (ISRMM)	245

1

Introduction

1.1 About the Book

Throughout modern human history, Information Systems (IS) have always been both mirrors and engines of change. They reflect the organization of knowledge, labor, and power at any given time, while simultaneously shaping new modes of coordination and decision-making, serving as enhancers and enablers of work. Today, however, IS stands at a juncture that demands more than incremental adaptation. The accelerating fusion of Artificial Intelligence (AI) and Quantum Information Science (QIS) is not merely adding computational horsepower to existing infrastructures, but it is altering the very fabric of how information is produced and managed. These two forces, AI and QIS, form the twin engines of what we term in this book as Information Singularity, a phase in which the velocity and autonomy of information processing exceed the capacities of human oversight and institutional control.

The central argument of this book is that AI and QIS together compress the information cycle: the span between input, inference, output, and, of course, decision. As information loops tighten and decisions become increasingly automated, the boundaries between data/information, knowledge, and action begin to blur. Traditional architectures of governance, audits, regulations, and ethical reviews operate too slowly to keep pace. Managing this compression responsibly requires a reimagined discipline of IS that integrates technical, organizational, and regulatory design—a socio-technical approach or alignment. Information Singularity, therefore, denotes not a distant

B. Kantsepolsky, L. Topor, *Managing Information Singularity*,
https://doi.org/10.1007/978-3-032-26223-3_1

science-fiction event but a concrete managerial threshold: the point at which the tempo and complexity of information flows demand continuous verification, adaptive control, and cross-disciplinary governance and regulation. This book proposes a roadmap for reaching that threshold deliberately rather than stumbling into it. Of course, we cannot predict how this might develop, but we can plausibly and probably assume this stage is coming in the twenty-first century, and perhaps, we are already in its beginning.

Our book begins with history, because history offers both caution and guidance. The discipline of IS was built, layer by layer, at the intersection of computing, management, operations research, and social science. Each technological wave, from mainframes to client-server, from the Web to cloud and mobile, reconfigured the relationship between data and decision. Scholars such as Heinz K. Klein and Rudy Hirschheim have shown that IS evolved through multiple overlapping eras characterized by shifts in governance structures, research themes, and educational institutions. IS became pluralistic by necessity as it absorbed insights from engineering, sociology, even psychology and behavior, and management science because no single discipline could explain or manage the socio-technical complexity it confronted. This pluralism is the field's greatest strength and its enduring challenge. It allows IS to adapt, but it also demands constant negotiation of boundaries and purposes. That is, there is no point in computing power or complex systems if we, the people, cannot use them for our benefit, and, thus, IS can also be considered as a problem solver.

Revisiting the field's intellectual history is not an antiquarian exercise. Understanding how earlier generations defined the *information problem* helps us recognize our own blind spots. The transition from data processing to information management in the 1960s mirrored industrial modernization; the move toward decision support in the 1980s reflected the rise of strategic management; the subsequent turn to enterprise systems and business intelligence paralleled globalization and digitization, especially with the rise of the internet. Each stage carried its own assumptions about human judgment, organizational control, and technological determinism. Today's fascination with AI and automation revives similar hopes and anxieties, only now amplified by scale, speed, and even depth. By recovering the field's earlier debates about systems thinking along with the balance between design science and interpretive inquiry, we arm ourselves against the amnesia that often accompanies technological enthusiasm.

What, then, distinguishes IS as a discipline in the mid-2020s? Above all, it is its action-orientation, or usability. Unlike computer science, which focuses on the properties of artifacts, or management science, which often abstracts from the materiality of technology, IS studies the intertwined integration of people, processes, data, and machines in real contexts. It produces knowledge that is both descriptive and prescriptive, grounded in practice yet theoretically aware. Hirschheim's and Klein's call for bridging the gap between disciplines and communities remains relevant precisely because it encourages the codification of process knowledge, the reusable insights about how systems are conceived, developed, implemented, and governed. Codifying such knowledge does not constrain pluralism, but rather channels it into patterns that practitioners and educators can use. This book continues that effort by articulating patterns and capabilities for AI-native and quantum-aware IS design.

In the context of product design, the present moment can be characterized as one of compressed complexity, meaning we now see a visible part with a hidden backend. Cloud computing, data pipelines, MLOps, and, generally, platform ecosystems have made organizations simultaneously more powerful and more fragile. Information now flows across global infrastructures with latency measured in milliseconds, yet governance mechanisms often lag by months or years. The GDPR, for example, was adopted only in 2016 and became effective in 2018, decades after the internet raised privacy-related issues. Now, IS professionals are tasked not only with implementing technologies but also with ensuring that they remain transparent, secure, and ethically aligned, which is a whole contested topic of its own.

Education must evolve accordingly, and now we see the beginning of effective programs that integrate technical proficiency with socio-technical awareness, teaching students not just how to build systems but how to anticipate their organizational and ethical consequences. We can attest to this firsthand, as Dr. Kantsepolsky is a scholar-practitioner and seasoned executive with over 30 years of experience leading strategy, business development, product innovation, and the development of Information and Communication Technologies (ICT) in multinational corporations. Dr. Topor served as the Head of Cybersecurity Studies at the School of Information Systems at the Academic College of Tel Aviv-Yaffo, where both are currently educating the next generation of IS specialists. While working on this book, we applied the logic of professional practice—every technical decision embeds a governance decision.

1.2 The Challenges of Technological Progress

Technological progress has always been a double-edged sword, where every leap in efficiency is shadowed by a growing "pathology" of security debt and algorithmic bias. The automation of information flows often outpaces the automation of accountability. Machine-learning models trained on biased or low-quality data produce inequitable outcomes that undermine trust. Data pipelines designed for efficiency frequently sacrifice traceability, making post-hoc audits difficult. Organizational incentives, meanwhile, can encourage speed over safety. The result is a growing mismatch between the complexity of systems and the maturity of the institutions that rely on them. The financial aspect of IS is still premature in mid-2020, but this issue is outside of our research scope. One of the book's core claims is that governance itself must be treated as architecture—just like the concept of security by design, or objectivity by design. Legal obligations and ethical principles must be translated into system properties like auditability, explainability, and resilience, rather than appended as afterthoughts, just as software code should be written securely, and not patched afterward.

AI-enhanced IS is already well underway. AI reshapes every classical system type. For instance, transaction systems become self-monitoring and anomaly-detecting; management information systems evolve into predictive dashboards; decision support systems employ ensemble models to simulate strategic outcomes; executive systems ingest near-real-time intelligence from global data streams; and enterprise resource planning, customer relationship management, and supply-chain management platforms now incorporate generative and prescriptive analytics that automate planning and interaction. These capabilities expand organizational intelligence but also magnify risk. Bias, model drift, and lack of interpretability can undermine decisions at scale. The challenge is to integrate intelligence without losing control.

Still emergent but already influential are quantum technologies. Quantum Information Science promises revolutionary breakthroughs in optimization, simulation, sensing, communications, and cryptography. Even before these systems reach widespread practical advantage, their implications are immediate: classical cryptography will need to be replaced or augmented with post-quantum algorithms, demanding years of migration work across digital infrastructures. The governance dimension of this transition is critical. Asset inventories, key-management policies, and cryptographic agility must be treated as continuous capabilities, not one-time projects. Moreover, quantum-inspired and hybrid quantum-classical algorithms may soon redefine what is computationally feasible in machine learning, creating new opportunities for pattern discovery but also new challenges for verification. The prudent approach is scenario-based, where we should plan multiple options, define decision checkpoints, and maintain adaptability.

From these dynamics emerge three guiding questions. First, how do AI and QIS reconfigure classical IS types at the levels of architecture, workflow, and control? Second, what design and governance patterns make AI/QIS-ready systems trustworthy and compliant in practice, or not? Third, what transition pathways allow organizations to capture the benefits of acceleration while minimizing technical and regulatory debt? Each question connects to a corresponding set of working propositions. We suggest, for example, that organizations embedding auditability-by-design will outperform those that rely on post-hoc audits in both incident response and regulatory exposure. We argue that human-in-the-loop oversight must evolve into human-on-the-loop governance, where people supervise systems rather than micromanage them. And we also suggest that crypto-agility, the ability to change cryptographic primitives rapidly, is the best leading indicator of quantum readiness, in the context of security.

1.3 Methodology and Book Structure

This book adopts a multidimensional, pragmatic framework to bridge the gap between technical complexity and regulatory oversight. The evidence base spans peer-reviewed IS scholarship, standards such as those from NIST and ISO/IEC, industry white papers, incident analyses, and regulatory documents. The approach combines literature synthesis, comparative case studies, design-science pattern mining, legal-doctrinal analysis, and scenario planning. The synthesis identifies convergences and divergences across IS, security, and policy research. Case studies, drawn from multiple sectors, are used to surface repeatable problem-solution patterns, each articulated with context, forces, and consequences. Legal and regulatory analysis translates obligations, such as transparency, robustness, and accountability, into technical requirements. Finally, scenario planning tests these patterns under varying technological and regulatory futures, ensuring that the recommendations remain robust amid uncertainty. We also avoid vendor-specific prescriptions and focus on capabilities, those architectural and managerial competencies that remain valid even as specific technologies evolve.

The eight chapters that follow are arranged as a coherent arc. The present introduction establishes the conceptual frame, definitions, guiding questions, and methodology. Chapter 2 revisits the history of IS, tracing its evolution through successive technological and organizational paradigms and examining how its pluralistic identity took shape. Chapter 3 surveys the current landscape, describing dominant technologies, industry practices, and educational trends. Chapter 4 examines the dark side, security debt, bias, disinformation, and other abuses that test the limits of governance. Chapter 5 analyzes the often too many and too complex legal and regulatory frameworks that define what responsible practice means, translating their demands into system properties. Chapter 6 explores the concrete implications of AI for traditional IS types, identifying both opportunities and systemic risks. Chapter 7 introduces QIS, explaining its technical foundations and governance ramifications. Finally, Chapter 8 synthesizes these thematic threads into a strategic roadmap toward the information singularity. By introducing the Information Singularity Readiness Maturity Model (ISRMM), the chapter provides a robust framework for capability assessment and a targeted research agenda. ISRMM may serve as a planning utility for both scholars and practitioners, facilitating the design of transition sequences for governing AI-enabled autonomy and navigating quantum-era security shifts.

1.4 Book Audience and Contribution

Designed as a bridge between technical and strategic disciplines, this book speaks to the diverse stakeholders tasked with building and regulating our digital future. Executives and architects will find actionable guidance for designing and governing next-generation systems. Policymakers will gain a translation layer between technical feasibility and legal obligation. Educators and researchers will encounter a conceptual framework that links historical foundations to emerging challenges. Each chapter is self-contained yet interdependent, allowing readers to enter through the pathway most relevant to their roles. For this reason, we include chapter introductions, conclusions, and some recurring examples. The style is deliberately integrative, where technical detail is paired with conceptual clarity, and theoretical discussion is grounded in practice.

The contribution of this work lies in four interlocking achievements. First, it offers a unified conceptual framework for understanding the convergence of AI and QIS as a single socio-technical phenomenon: the compression of information cycles that constitutes information singularity. Second, it suggests actionable design patterns for AI-native and quantum-aware IS, giving practitioners tools for building systems that are explainable, auditable, and resilient. Third, it advances the notion of compliance-as-architecture, demonstrating how legal and ethical obligations can be embedded into the technical and organizational layers of IS. Fourth, it proposes a research and education agenda that redefines what it means to teach and study IS in the age of AI and QIS, ensuring that future professionals are equipped not only to build systems but also to govern them.

The book's scope is ambitious but bounded. It does not aim to teach quantum mechanics or to catalog every AI algorithm or every possible risk and bias. Its focus is on implications, architectures, and governance—on the managerial and institutional challenges of integrating these technologies into the infrastructures of society. Where we generalize, we do so cautiously, acknowledging the diversity of organizational contexts and legal regimes. Where we prescribe, we label our guidance as design-and-action, open to empirical refinement. The pace of technological change guarantees that some details will age, but the underlying principles—responsibility, transparency, and adaptability—will remain.

1.5 Debating on Information Singularity

To understand the systems of tomorrow, we must first acknowledge the dual heritage of IS as a field built on the rigid feedback loops of early systems theory and the nuanced, even interpretivist, perspectives that followed. IS has always balanced the technical and the human. Early systems thinkers emphasized feedback and control; later waves incorporated interpretivist approaches that valued meaning and context. The coexistence of these paradigms, sometimes contentious, ultimately enriched the field. Pluralism, rather than fragmentation, is what allows IS to address complex real-world problems. The field's ongoing efforts to establish a coherent body of knowledge, seen in the IS literature and in comparative education studies, reflect its maturing professional identity. Meanwhile, contemporary research on IS education emphasizes the triad of learner, environment, and curriculum. Understanding who learns, where they learn, and what they learn in a digital age shaped by AI can indicate a lot. The same triad guides how institutions must now adapt their own IS to the coming quantum horizon.

From this vantage point, the integration of AI and QIS appears not as a rupture but as the next logical evolution in the co-development of technology and governance. Architecture and compliance emerge as the twin pillars of this evolution. Architecture determines where intelligence resides, at the edge, in the service layer, or in the enterprise core, and how it connects to data sources and human oversight. Compliance ensures that these architectures remain accountable to the societies that depend on them—somewhat of a social contract. Together, they define a new professional ethic, which means that technical design is a form of governance.

Skeptics may question whether talk of information singularity exaggerates near-term change. They may argue that both AI and QIS are still constrained by technical and economic limits. Such caution is healthy, but it misses the point. The singularity, as used here, is not a prediction of runaway intelligence; it is a description of accelerating interdependence between human and machine decision loops. Even if full quantum advantage remains decades away, the preparation window for governance and migration is already open. Cryptographic standards are being rewritten as these lines are being written as well, and regulators are integrating AI risk management into law. Delay carries a cost. Proactive design is the rational form of skepticism, and we must learn from past delays, as with previous technologies.

Others may fear that efforts to codify patterns and bodies of knowledge risk freezing a dynamic field. Yet codification, if done correctly, is not ossification. Patterns do not prescribe a single method; they record problem-solution relationships that can be adapted to context. Our aim is not to standardize thought but to make learning cumulative. Similarly, design-and-action guidance will inevitably age, but by embedding scenario planning and capability thinking, we ensure that organizations can adapt their implementations as technologies evolve.

In practical terms, the message of this introduction is straightforward. The acceleration of information cycles is real and measurable. The risk of institutional lag—legal, organizational, or ethical—is likewise real. The task ahead is to build systems and organizations that can keep pace without losing coherence or legitimacy. That means embedding governance into design, cultivating crypto-agility and auditability as core capabilities, and educating a generation of professionals who can think simultaneously in technical, managerial, and ethical terms.

The chapters that follow elaborate this agenda in detail, but the orientation is clear from the outset, and we advise that information singularity is not destiny—it is design. Whether societies experience it as empowerment or as disruption depends on how deliberately we manage the convergence of intelligence and information. IS, as both a discipline and a practice, holds the keys to that management. By revisiting our history, refining our methods, and expanding our imagination, we can ensure that the next transformation of information serves human purposes rather than eroding them. This book is written in that spirit.

2

A Brief History of Information Systems

2.1 Introduction

This chapter contains a historical exploration of information systems, briefly from ancient times and pre-industrialization and digitization, and mainly from the twentieth century onward until the year 2000, when it became clear that the world was headed toward more reliance on IS. In addition, the chapter charts IS's institutional maturation, conferences, journals, curricula, and its shift from tool appraisal to theory about adoption, value, alignment, and change. Our purpose is twofold. First, we show how successive waves of technology, mechanization, mainframes, personal computing, and the internet reconfigured the basic informational functions of collection, storage, processing, and communication. Second, we situate these changes within the maturation of IS as a discipline, highlighting how its questions, theories, and methods differentiated it from adjacent fields such as computer science and management while remaining deeply intertwined with them. In doing so, we treat IS as a socio-technical endeavor: systems that succeed only when technical architectures, organizational routines, and human practices evolve together.

This chapter is organized into three main sections. We begin with the history of information practices to illuminate how enduring informational needs of early humans developed through time up to the Industrial Revolution, which introduced the first communication and information processing methods and technologies. Then we provide historical perspectives on the birth

B. Kantsepolsky, L. Topor, *Managing Information Singularity*,
https://doi.org/10.1007/978-3-032-26223-3_2

of computers, and their deployment in organizations, along with the first managerial applications. This section also presents the development path and explains the information and communication technologies available by the late 1990s. Finally, we end with the internet's diffusion and the web's standardization to explain how, at the end of the twentieth century, formerly isolated applications became networked platforms serving global audiences, foreshadowing developments we cover in later chapters.

Following the explanations on the core technological components of IS, the last section deals with the rise and establishment of IS as a distinguished discipline. A part of this section, we present the initial IS schools of thought and academic programs of that time. The historical trajectory of IS reveals a field shaped by continuous technological advancements, shifting human, social, and organizational needs, and evolving academic perspectives. By examining IS as a socio-technical process, we set the stage for the subsequent chapters in this book, which also address human and technological factors.

2.2 Capturing, Storing, Processing, and Disseminating Information

2.2.1 Information Practices from Ancient Civilizations to the Middle Ages

The need to collect and share information has been fundamental to survival since the earliest days of human existence. Early humans used oral communication to transmit and share experiences and thus preserved vital knowledge about reaching food, survival strategies, and social hierarchies (Couch, 1989; Marlowe, 2005). The transition from oral to written communication constituted significant progress in social development. Writing as a method of information creation was used to record and document stories, laws, and economic activities. The literature and the archeological artifacts show that the Sumerians used cuneiform writing on clay tablets around 3200–3000 BCE (Kramer, 2010). Written records enabled the storage of information beyond the limitations of human memory and, consequently, its sharing across generations. Hence, cuneiform writing constitutes one of the earliest examples where information used for decision-making enabled advanced social structure development.

The importance of information in the governance and administration of ancient civilizations is often exemplified in the literature by referring to ancient Egypt. As part of their cultural tradition, Egyptians used temple walls, tombs, statues, and papyrus scrolls to describe and document everyday life routines, important events, and even religious beliefs (Teeter, 2011; Lichtheim, 2019; Galán, 1994). Ancient Egyptians are also often credited for establishing the first bureaucratic systems that relied on information to manage resources, labor, and trade. One example is the construction of monumental architecture, including pyramids (Bard, 2005). The writings in the form of hieroglyphics, along with the information-based decision-making management practices, were vital for organizing information to coordinate large-scale labor, materials, resources, and timelines (Kahl, 2022).

In addition to governance and administration, the economic prosperity of ancient civilizations was also dependent on trading. Since the role of information in trade and commerce cannot be overestimated, the ability to disseminate information during Egyptian times was critical. To allow trading operations, there was a need for information about trade routes and market conditions, along with record-keeping about transactions, goods, and prices (Vasiljević, 2013). With the time and development of trade networks, the influence of information management practices extended beyond Egypt, where similar systems emerged, and the need for information exchange continued to grow.

The first alphabet was developed about 2000 years later, approximately 1050 BCE, by the Phoenicians, significantly simplifying writing and improving communication across cultures (Elayi, 2018). The economic development and rise of empires, such as Greece and Rome, enhanced the importance of and dependence on information management. In the fields of philosophy and science, the Greeks developed early forms of data organization and classification. Greek philosophers of that time laid the basis for systematic thinking about information and knowledge (Chondros, 2017). In turn, the Romans' sophisticated administrative systems for governing territories relied on written rules and protocols and served as the basis for hierarchical management practices with an emphasis on documentation and record-keeping (Haighton, 2010; Zhang, 2022). As the organization and retrieval of information became increasingly important, this period of human history marked the beginning of a structured approach to information management.

The Antikythera Mechanism, dating to approximately the second century BCE, serves as a profound historical precursor to the human drive to mechanize calculation and systematize information. Often described as the world's first mechanical calculator, its intricate assembly of bronze gears demonstrates an early mastery of converting complex celestial data into predictable, physical outputs, hinting at the human desire to calculate and control information (Seiradakis & Edmunds, 2018).

The Middle Ages, followed by the epoch of the Renaissance, were remarkable moments in the history of information management. At a time when the monasteries' libraries and archives served as repositories of information, they also ensured continuity between generations (Araslanova, 2022; Giannachi, 2016). The invention of the printing press in the fifteenth century revolutionized the availability and distribution of information. Since printed documents were less expensive and more accessible, they facilitated information exchange. The number of books in circulation significantly increased, and the information became more accessible to a broader segment of society (Eisenstein, 1980). Moreover, since more books were published in vernacular languages rather than in Latin, more people were able to engage with literature and educational materials, causing the flourishing of educational institutions and collaboration among scholars, which contributed to an exchange of ideas that laid the basis for the scientific revolution.

2.2.2 The Industrial Revolution: A New Era in Communication and Information Processing

Started in the late eighteenth century, the Industrial Revolution began a new era in information processing. The mechanization, rise of factories, and mass production required principal changes in managing labor, raw materials, and inventory. These managerial challenges required the development and deployment of supporting organizational practices and information flows. In 1911, Frederick Winslow Taylor, the recognized father of scientific management, published his seminal work "The Principles of Scientific Management". By promoting systematic data collection and analysis, Taylor argued that observation and measurement of work processes are needed to identify the best way to perform them (Giannantonio & Hurley-Hanson, 2011). These data-driven management practices could be seen as a precursor to contemporary information management that leverages data analytics for business process optimization.

At a time when machinery led to increased productivity, it also catalyzed the invention of early information technologies for calculations and record-keeping (Dummer, 1983). Among examples of information technologies from that time are mechanical calculators and early computing devices, such as Charles Babbage's Analytical Engine. Babbage's machine, conceptual design published in 1837, was entirely mechanical, containing thousands of gears, levers, and other components. Nevertheless, this invention constitutes a remarkable milestone in the history of future computers and information management. The Analytical Engine was revolutionary not only for its intended computational capabilities but also for its architecture. The Analytical Engine presumed two principal elements of future computers—a unit called a mill for data processing and a separate memory store (Haecker, 2022). One could argue that the concept of the Analytical Engine became inspirational for the next generation of scientists and engineers, including Alan Turing, as described in the next section.

Additional remarkable inventions of that time were the telegraph and telephone. The telegraph, developed in the middle of the nineteenth century, became the first practical application of electrical communication. This type of communication greatly simplified and reduced the time of information flow between distant points and by the beginning of the twentieth century had become an integral part of the United States, linking people and businesses across the country (Blondheim, 2014). In turn, the invention of the telephone in 1876 constituted another level in the development of communication technologies. Through the first decades of the twentieth century, telephones became commonplace in urban areas, enabling people to communicate in real-time, thus further enhancing the immediacy of communication compared to the telegraph (Chou, 2013; Segal, 2014).

2.3 The Birth of Hardware, Software, and Communication

2.3.1 Data Processing during World War II

The beginning of World War II (WWII) catalyzed the development of information systems. It was mainly driven by the military's demand for efficient data processing and communication. The examples of the Bombe machine, developed to break the Enigma cipher, and its successor, the Colossus computer, designed to break the Lorenz cipher, became the cornerstones for the beginning of the computer epoch (Copeland, 2017). The Bombe was *an electromechanical machine* that could simulate the various settings of the Enigma device used by the German military to secure communication (Wright, 2017; Hu et al., 2022). The story of Bombe's development by Alan Turing, a British mathematician, and his colleagues inspired Andrew Hodges to write about Alan Turing's life and work. The biography called Alan Turing: The Enigma was published in 1983 and served as a basis for the blockbuster *The Imitation Game* released in 2014.

In turn, the Colossus is acknowledged as *the first special-purpose programmable digital computer*, which demonstrated the potential of electronic systems for complex data-processing tasks, and was designed specifically for cryptoanalysis. There were other programmable computers in 1944, but as far as it is known, none were electronic (Randell, 1980). The use of electronics permitted a thousandfold increase in internal speed over relay or electromechanical devices. Colossus could execute Boolean logic operations, representing a breakthrough in the evolution of computing technology (Sale, 2003). In the following years, the significance of the Colossus was acknowledged beyond its wartime applications and served as the foundation for future developments in computer architecture and programming (Haigh & Priestley, 2018). Colossus was an externally programmed computer that used gas tubes and hard valve trigger circuits as data stores (Randell, 1980). So, the final step required for the invention of the modern computer was the need for the development of high-speed storage, capable of holding a large number of binary digits.

At the same time, the military use of information systems spread beyond cryptography. For example, the U.S. military utilized data processing for logistics, troop movements, and supply chain management (Ohl, 2020). Although special-purpose machines were being developed at Bell Labs, IBM, and elsewhere in the States, it appears that these devices that pre-dated COLOSSUS were much simpler (Randell, 1980). Nevertheless, the evolution of military logistics during this period exemplified the need for reliable information management systems for coordination and operational success.

2.3.2 The First Computers

Advances in computing technology during WWII triggered postwar developments. One of the most well-known examples of that time is the Electronic Numerical Integrator and Computer (ENIAC), referred to as ***the first general-purpose electronic digital computer***. The ENIAC project was funded by the U.S. government, indicating substantial interest in computing technology driven by wartime experience and the quest for technological superiority. Developed at the University of Pennsylvania, ENIAC was publicly demonstrated on February 14, 1946 (Stuart, 2018). ENIAC was a massive machine that used over 18,000 vacuum tubes, took up about 1,800 square feet of area, and weighed roughly 30 tons, making it one of the biggest electrical devices of its time. It was able to perform a wide range of computations, including sophisticated mathematical operations required for military applications such as ballistic trajectory calculations and nuclear bomb simulations, while its architecture enabled it to perform hundreds of operations per second (Stuart, 2018).

However, programming the ENIAC was not a simple task. To set up the computations, one must manually connect cables and configure switches, which might take days or even weeks for particular workloads (Germann, 2021). This time-consuming process emphasized the importance of the development of more efficient programming techniques and sophisticated programming languages. ENIAC also pioneered the use of breakpoints for debugging (Fontana & Petrillo, 2021). As programmers attempted to find and fix errors in their code, the need for systematic debugging methodologies became apparent, resulting in practices that are still employed today. Until its retirement in 1955, the ENIAC operated as a national computing resource for uses other than military computations, including scientific research and engineering difficulties. Its architecture and operational principles influenced the design of future computers, such as the Electronic Discrete Variable Automatic Computer (EDVAC), which introduced the stored-program concept and influenced the design of the first commercial products, such as the Universal Automatic Computer (UNIVAC I) and IBM's early models (Williams, 1993; Regan, 2018).

The UNIVAC I and early IBM models such as IBM 701, IBM 704, and IBM 650 exemplify ***the first commercial computers*** that reached the market at the beginning of the 50es. The first UNIVAC I was delivered by Remington Rand in 1951 to the U.S. Census Bureau. It was the first commercial computer based on vacuum tubes and magnetic tape for storage. The UNIVAC I was capable of performing around 1,000 operations per second, processing both numerical and alphabetical data, and therefore considered a breakthrough at the time (Johnson, 2006).

Formally, IBM's entry into the commercial computer market started in the early 1950s. Their IBM 701 was introduced in 1952. It was *IBM's first stored-program computer* designed primarily for scientific computations that used vacuum tubes and was programmed using punch cards (Rosenheim, 1983). Despite its lack of commercial success, the IBM 701 played an important part in IBM's future growth. The IBM 650, launched in 1954, was IBM's first mass-produced computer, making it more accessible to businesses and educational institutions. Instead of punch cards, it used drum memory, which is slower but significantly faster than the prior method (Knuth, 1986).

As technology improved, the need for more advanced high-level programming languages became apparent. The IBM 704, launched in 1954, was among the earliest IBM computers to offer *Formula Translation (FORTRAN) programming language*. The IBM 704 was a scientific computer that used magnetic core memory and could do floating-point arithmetic, making it ideal for scientific computations and greatly simplifying the programming process for difficult numerical jobs (Backus et al., 1957). The IBM 7090, which debuted in 1960 with expanded capabilities of FORTRAN programming, gained widespread use in scientific research and engineering applications and reinforced FORTRAN's position as the leading programming language in these domains (Backus, 1978).

In turn, ***Common Business-Oriented Language (COBOL)*** was developed to address the more business-oriented programming needs. COBOL enabled users to write programs in a more human-readable form (Sammet, 1981). COBOL found its early implementations on IBM's 1401 that was introduced in 1959, and 7090 systems, while the first COBOL compilers were successfully used on the UNIVAC II and RCA 501 machines in 1960 showing for the first time in history that the same high-level language program was successfully compiled and executed on computers from two different manufacturers of COBOL demonstrating machine-independent portability across different systems (Lombardi, 1964).

The 1950s also saw the birth of transistor technology, which transformed computer hardware. This was a major step forward since utilizing transistors resulted in smaller, quicker, and more reliable computers with lower power consumption and heat generation. The Transistorized Airborne Digital Computer (TRADIC) was *the first computer to use transistors* delivered by Bell Labs to the U.S. Air Force in 1954 (Irvine, 2002). In turn, the first commercially available IBM product based on transistors was IBM 608, which was launched in 1957 (Garner & Dill, 2010).

2.3.2.1 From Mainframe to Workstation, Ethernet, and Distributed Computing

The first mainframe computers, such as the UNIVAC series, IBM701, and IBM650, were primarily used by large organizations for data processing. These systems were expensive and required specialized knowledge to operate. However, the introduction of a time and resource-sharing approach in 60es dedicated to allowing multiple users to access a single computer simultaneously enabled rare and expensive computing resources to become more accessible.

One notable example from that time is MIT's Project Compatible Time-Sharing System (CTSS). Initially, CTSS was a specially developed version of the operating system (OS) running on IBM 709. CTSS used tape drives to store the programs and files of the users of the four terminals. For the first time, a proof of concept was demonstrated in November 1961, showing that multiple users could interact with a computer concurrently, using terminals to share processing power in academic and practical applications. In 1962, the CTSS project development continued with the IBM7090, which by 1963 was upgraded to IBM7094. IBM's 7094 was one of the largest and fastest computers available, with a cost of about $3.5 million, which is equivalent to a purchasing power of over $36 million today. In the same year, Project MAC—an interdepartmental laboratory to explore the development of a brand-new idea of a time-shared computer started at MIT Computation Center. By 1965, most of the CTSS development group had moved over to Project MAC for the design of Multics—the next-generation time-sharing system that later served as the ancestor of the Unix shell. According to the literature, Multics influenced Unix as Bell engineers who worked on the Multics left the project and created Unix instead (Lee et al., 1992; Walden & Van Vleck, 2011).

While time-sharing systems answered the need to make rare and expensive computing resources more accessible, improvements in silicon and magnetic storage technologies formed the basis for further progress in the computer industry. Since 1972, when Intel introduced semiconductor memories, prices began to decline by a factor of four every three years, creating the cycle for new memory chip introductions and establishing the economic basis for different computer classes (Bell, 1988). At that time, one could determine roughly three levels of computer use: central (mainframe), departmental (minicomputer), and personal workstations—each according to performance, style of use, size, and price.

The appearance of personal workstations and distributed personal computing systems resulted from the evolution of computer usage, including how people and computers interact, by providing a level of responsiveness that timesharing systems could not achieve. In turn, the smaller machines required interconnecting, urging the need to create Local Area Networks (LANs). According to Bell (1988), an intriguing fact is that the workstation phenomenon is not well described or recorded, as most products originate from industry, where individuals are not rewarded for writing papers but for producing and selling machines. A notable exception was Xerox PARC, which published its work and was marginally successful.

The Xerox Palo Alto Research Center (PARC) was established in 1970 with the primary goal of creating office information systems to expand Xerox's traditional copier business so that it could include most of the functions performed in offices. Although it resulted in what is known as distributed personal computing, initially, the ambitions were much lower (Thacker, 1988). The implementation of the Alto began in November 1972. While the first machines did not contain Ethernet interfaces, already by the end of 1973, the Alto prototypes were exchanging data packets (Thacker, 1988). The name "Ethernet" was first introduced in May 1973 by Xerox engineers Bob Metcalfe and David Boggs. Their pioneering work, called "Ethernet: Distributed Packet Switching for Local Computer Networks" (Metcalfe & Boggs, 1976), established Ethernet as a LAN protocol, allowing multiple devices to communicate over a shared medium to use shared resources such as printers and file storage systems. Unlike time-sharing, Ethernet decentralized the computing environment by allowing individual devices to communicate directly over a shared medium (Wright, 2018).

The first Alto machines were delivered in September 1974. Their software consisted of the OS written in Basic Combined Programming Language (BCPL), the BCPL compiler, and a primitive text editor. BCPL takes its origins from the Combined Programming Language (CPL) that was first implemented in 1967 on an IBM 7094 computer running CTSS at MIT (Richards, 2012). In turn, the Multiple Access Xerox Computer (MAXC) time-sharing system served as a mainframe for electronic mail, file storage, and printing (Thacker, 1988).

After completing the workstations and the network that interconnects them, Xerox understood that, since some functions, such as high-quality printing, are very expensive, they must be shared for economic reasons. In 1974, the first printing server called EARS was deployed at PARC. As Thacker (1988) explained, EARS was named according to its components—Ethernet, Alto, RCG (research character generator), and SLOT—scanning laser output terminal. The file server development also took place at PARC, and the early prototypes were introduced already in 1975. According to Xerox, by 1979, approximately 1,500 Altos were built and used by the firm's engineers and scientists as personal workstations or servers.

By 1983, personal workstations, including those from Apollo and SUN, reached full-scale deployment use under the term JAWS—just another workstation (Bell, 1988). While many variations were possible, these machines satisfied essentially all the computational needs of a single corporate user. Having high-resolution displays with a highly interactive user interface, they were connected to the local networks typically within a single building to access capabilities that need to be shared, either for economic or logical reasons.

2.3.2.2 The Personal Computer

The introduction of the Personal Computer (PC) changed the world of information management. These machines became affordable and accessible, allowing individual users to perform tasks that were previously limited to mainframe or workstation environments. Starting from the mid-70s and the MIT's Altair 8800 (1975), through Apple I (1976) and Apple II (1977), and by the IBM PC (1981), conventional PCs became the de facto standard for running virtually all applications. The progress was not only in the PC's hardware but also in the software and the programming languages. Already in 1977, as part of the programming conference, the participants provided a detailed overview of over a dozen existing programming languages. The list contained Algol 60, APL, APT, BASIC, COBOL, FORTRAN, GPSS, JOSS, JOVIAL, LISp, PLIl, SIMULA, and SNOBOL (Wexelblat, 2014). For example, although it lacked a formal OS, Altair 8800 used the Control Program for Microcomputers and enabled code creation, which was leveraged by Bill Gates, Paul Allen, and Monte Davidoff for developing the first version of BASIC for Altair 8800 (Haigh & Ceruzzi, 2021). Similarly, Apple I had no built-in OS but used a simple monitor program for input/output and memory management. The Apple I supported Integer BASIC, written by Steve Wozniak. Released a year later, Apple II already had the Apple Disk Operating System (DOS) supporting floppy disk storage and enabled programming on Applesoft BASIC, Integer BASIC (built-in), and assembly language for more advanced development (Nooney, 2023).

The breakthrough happened with the introduction of the IBM 5150, launched on August 12, 1981. IBM 5150 was built on the Intel 8088 processor, had 16 to 256 KB of RAM, and supported floppy disk drives with 160 KB or 320 KB capacity for external storage (IBM, 1981). It had the possibility for connection with a monochrome monitor or a color graphics adapter (CGA) for basic graphics and five slots for add-on hardware cards, providing customization options. IBM 5150's open architecture allowed other companies to create compatible hardware and software, becoming the standard for PC architecture. From the software perspective, IBM 5150 was shipped with Microsoft PC-DOS 1.0, which later became the foundation of MS-DOS and supported alternative OSs such as CP/M-86 and UCSD p-System. It had preinstalled BASIC as part of the ROM, allowing users to write and run programs without a DOS, and supported high-level programming languages such as Pascal for system-level programming (IBM, 1985). Its preinstalled applications such as VisiCalc for financial or mathematical computations and EasyWrite for text editing, became widely popular among businesses. IBM's decision to use Microsoft for the OS and Intel for the processor created a third-party ecosystem that served the Wintel platform for decades. By the mid-80s, both Apple and Microsoft introduced a graphical user interface (GUI), significantly simplifying the operation of the PC. In particular, Microsoft Windows, launched in 1985, became the GUI on IBM-compatible PCs, eventually dominating the market (Campbell-Kelly et al., 2018).

By the 1990s, PCs were integrated into businesses and in use by private citizens who leveraged them for applications, networking, email, and more. Laptops further shrunk the PC form factor, gained popularity due to their portability, and became a favorite among business professionals. One example is the IBM ThinkPad, i.e., 700 series from 1992, which featured a sleek design and the TrackPoint pointing device. With the development of computer hardware, programming languages have also undergone significant advancements, reflecting the growing needs of developers. During the second programming languages conference that took place on April 20-23, 1993, in Cambridge, Massachusetts, the list of languages included Ada, ALGOL 68, C, C++, CLU, Concurrent Pascal, FORMAC, Forth, Icon, Lisp, Pascal, Prolog, Simulation languages, and Smalltalk (Bergin & Gibson, 1996).

2.3.2.3 The Development of the Internet and Its Impact on IS

The history of the Internet is entangled with the history of modern IS. Although computers had long been capable of processing data, their use was largely isolated within organizations and institutions until the creation of a global network enabled the global flow of information. Thus, one can argue that the Internet stands as the single most transformative infrastructure for IS since the invention of the computer itself. It provided the connectivity, scalability, and universality that allowed disparate systems to interoperate, thereby laying the foundations for the globally integrated digital economy of today (Leiner et al., 2009). Today's IS are scaled up and depend on connectivity, but modern IS will be discussed further on in this book.

Historically, the Internet's origins can be traced back to the late 1960s, with the creation of ARPANET, a U.S. Department of Defense project that pioneered packet-switching technology. Unlike traditional circuit-switched networks, which required a dedicated channel for communication, packet switching allowed data to be broken into smaller units and routed through multiple paths to reach its destination. This innovation dramatically increased efficiency, reliability, and resilience, especially in the context of Cold War anxieties about centralized vulnerabilities and about the resilience of circuit-switched networks (Kleinrock, 2010).

Equally significant was the adoption of Transmission Control Protocol/Internet Protocol (TCP/IP) in the early 1980s, which standardized how data was addressed, transmitted, and received. This created a common "language" for machines to communicate, ensuring that different networks could interconnect and exchange information. At this early stage, ISs consisted largely of email, file transfers, and experimental Bulletin Board Systems (BBS) or USENET forums, which served as primitive online communities. These systems, while limited in scale and functionality, introduced the notion that information could be shared and accessed across a network without the constraints of geography (Topor, 2024).

The next step came in the early 1990s with Tim Berners-Lee's invention of the World Wide Web (WWW). By introducing the Hypertext Transfer Protocol (HTTP), Hypertext Markup Language (HTML), and the first web browsers, Berners-Lee created a user-friendly interface for navigating and publishing information online. What had previously been the domain of technical experts became suddenly accessible to the broader public (Brügger, 2010; Topor, 2024).

With time, institutions ranging from universities to businesses adopted web technologies to disseminate information, conduct transactions, and manage records, and it was all made easily accessible through websites, which became very interactive and data-rich as years went by. E-commerce pioneers such as Amazon and eBay, established in 1995, demonstrated how online systems could fundamentally alter markets by enabling real-time transactions at scale (Swanson, 2020). The development of the Internet has propelled IS from isolated data processors to globally networked ecosystems of unprecedented scale and complexity. Each stage, ARPANET's technical experiments, the Web's democratization of access, broadband's expansion, social media's real-time interactivity, to today's AI-driven infrastructures, has reshaped how information is collected, stored, analyzed, and disseminated. It allows us all to communicate globally and for IS to thrive.

2.4 The Rise of Information Systems

One of the earliest references to information systems in literature can be found in Mann and Williams (1960), who analyzed the organizational change associated with implementing electronic data processing equipment (Bryant et al., 2013). At that time, this topic was typically referred to as "management information systems" that lay at the intersection of computer science, management, and organization theory (Hirschheim & Klein, 2012). While each of these disciplines dealt with a specific role of computers in organizations, the management of information systems emerged to provide a broader orientation. Thus, historically, since then and to our days, the focus of the information systems domain is different from computer science and other disciplines. For example, Börje Langefors (1980) introduced the concepts of datalogical and infological systems, distinguishing between data and information, data processing and the meaningful use of information. According to Langefors, data becomes information only when it is interpreted by a user with the appropriate semantic background.

For the understanding of how the IS field developed since the mid-60s and by the beginning of the twenty-first century, Hirschheim and Klein (2012) offered to distinguish several key periods in the historical development of the IS. Starting from the period covering the 1960s and 1970s, the epoch started with mainframe computers and went until the invention of Ethernet, which decentralized the computing environment by allowing individual devices to communicate directly over a shared medium. Then, the 1980s—the introduction of the personal computer and local networks. Finally, the 1990s instituted civil usage of the internet and mobile devices. Together with global interconnectivity enabled by the Internet and WWW, IS departments dealt with integrating automated solutions into organizational workflows for information-based decision-making processes. Driven by technological innovations and academic inquiry, the evolution of information systems became fundamental in shaping organizational management. By the late twentieth century, the academic study of IS had begun to mature, marked by the establishment of journals, conferences, and theoretical frameworks.

2.4.1 Information Systems' Schools of Thought

Since organizations increasingly rely on information technology to drive innovation and efficiency, it is imperative to understand how different schools of thought influence IS research, education, and practice. Over the decades, various schools of thought have evolved considerably, integrating diverse disciplines and methodologies, each contributing to the conceptual and practical evolution of IS. These schools offer distinct perspectives on the design, implementation, and analysis of IS, ranging from technical and computational methodologies to sociotechnical and organizational theories that incorporate human, social, and ethical considerations (Pereira & Baranauskas, 2017).

There are a few major Schools of Thought in IS, which could be characterized into how technology interacts with individuals, organizations, and societies. These can be categorized as technical, behavioral, and sociotechnical, each with its underlying theories and methodologies. The technical school of thought conceptualizes IS as a technical artifact, emphasizing optimization for efficiency, accuracy, and automation. Rooted in disciplines such as computer science, software engineering, and operations research, this approach focuses on developing robust information systems that ensure data integrity, scalability, and security (Baxter & Sommerville, 2011). The behavioral school of thought focuses on the interactions between individuals and IS, drawing from cognitive psychology, decision theory, and human-computer interaction. This perspective seeks to understand how users adopt, interact with, and derive value from information systems (Gregor, 2006; Lee, 2004).

Key theoretical frameworks within this school include the Technology Acceptance Model (TAM), which explains user acceptance of technology based on perceived usefulness and ease of use, and the Task-Technology Fit (TTF) theory, which examines how well technology aligns with user needs and job tasks (Howard & Hair, 2023; Nunamaker & Briggs, 2011). The behavioral perspective has also contributed to studies on digital transformation, exploring how organizations navigate technological change and the impact of IS on employee productivity and organizational culture (Bozkus, 2023).

There is a middle ground between the above-mentioned approaches. Scholars such as Rudy Hirschheim emphasized the importance of epistemology in IS research, highlighting that IS knowledge draws heavily from social sciences because information systems are fundamentally sociotechnical systems. The sociotechnical approach posits that IS should balance technical efficiency with social and organizational considerations. This school emerged as a critique of overly rigid, technology-centric IS designs, advocating for systems that account for human dynamics and workplace structures. Unlike purely technological determinism, which focuses on maximizing system efficiency, or social constructivism, which emphasizes human and organizational dynamics over technical constraints, the sociotechnical approach advocates for a holistic perspective. It acknowledges that technological advancements alone cannot drive success unless they are embedded within a well-structured social and operational environment. By fostering collaboration between system designers, end-users, and organizational stakeholders, this approach enhances both system usability and organizational effectiveness, leading to higher adoption rates and improved workplace integration (Khosroshahi et al., 2015; Patnayakuni & Ruppel, 2010).

The sociotechnical approach has significantly influenced fields such as enterprise systems implementation, digital workplace transformation, and IT governance, ensuring that technology is deployed in ways that enhance collaboration and organizational effectiveness (Checkland & Poulter, 2020; Ciborra, 2004). One methodology within this school is Soft Systems Methodology (SSM), which views IS as interpretative tools that help organizations structure complex problems rather than as mere computational solutions. Unlike traditional "hard" systems approaches that assume well-defined problems with technical solutions, SSM recognizes that in many real-world scenarios, problems are ill-defined, and stakeholders may have conflicting views.

The emphasis on SSM effectively nudges the need to consider end-users, who often do not have detailed guidelines and need a less restrictive system to work with. Exploring further the role of IS end-users, Enid Mumford's Effective Technical and Human Implementation of Computer-based Systems (ETHICS) method underscored the critical role of user participation in system design. Recognizing that technological solutions must align not only with organizational objectives but also with human values and workplace dynamics, Mumford advocated for a human-centered approach to IS development. Unlike traditional top-down, technology-driven approaches, ETHICS empowers employees and stakeholders by integrating their needs, concerns, and expectations into the design process. This participatory model enhances system acceptance, reduces resistance to change, and fosters greater job satisfaction and productivity (Mumford, 2017). Eventually, in the IS research schools of thought, the concept of the learning organization and systems thinking also played a crucial role in shaping IS as a discipline. Theories from cybernetics, general systems theory, and complex adaptive systems are often applied to understand and manage information flows within organizations (Senge, 2006).

2.4.2 Education in the Field

The formalization of IS education began in the 1960s, driven by pioneers such as Gordon Foster and Frank Land at the London School of Economics (LSE). The LSE played an important role in establishing IS as a research and teaching discipline, with a strong emphasis on the sociotechnical nature of information systems. Foster secured funding from the National Computing Centre in 1967, which led to the hiring of Land, who had worked on the Lyons Electronic Office computer, one of the first business computers. Their vision shaped the initial curriculum, which emphasized not just technical aspects but also the organizational and social implications of information systems. At LSE, the MSc in Analysis, Design, and Management of Information Systems (ADMIS) was introduced, offering a comprehensive approach to IS education that integrated technical, organizational, and strategic perspectives. The program attracted students from diverse backgrounds, reinforcing the interdisciplinary nature of IS. Additionally, PhD programs in IS gained prominence, producing research that shaped the field's theoretical foundations and practical applications (Bryant & Land, 2020; 2021).

In the 1970s, IS education expanded beyond LSE to other universities, driven by the increasing demand for professionals who could manage computer-based systems in organizations. During this period, scholars such as Ronald Stamper (1973) contributed to the theoretical development of IS, incorporating perspectives from semiotics and social systems theory into systems design. This decade saw the establishment of the first dedicated IS degree programs, differentiating IS from computer science and business studies by focusing on the interaction between technology, people, and organizations.

While LSE played a crucial role in establishing the field, other institutions like MIT and Harvard, across the United States and other regions, also contributed to the growth of IS as a discipline. Also, professional forums, such as the International Conference on Information Systems (ICIS), were founded in the 1980s to support the global IS academic community, with North American universities playing a dominant role in research and curriculum development (AIS, n.d.; Hirschheim & Klein, 2012). By the late 1980s, IS had emerged as a recognized academic discipline with dedicated programs and departments in universities worldwide. The rise of enterprise computing and the increasing adoption of management information systems (MIS) in organizations fueled the demand for IS professionals. As a result, universities developed structured curricula covering areas such as systems analysis and design, database management, human-computer interaction, and strategic IT management.

The European Conference on Information Systems (ECIS) was established in 1993 (Stein et al., 2016). In turn, the Association for Information Systems (AIS) was formally founded in 1994 to provide an umbrella professional association for the IS field, and it took over as the sponsoring body for ICIS and other conferences/journals (AIS, n.d.). These initiatives helped establish IS as a global academic field with shared research agendas and methodological approaches. Since then, IS scholars have played an active role in international collaborations, contributing to organizations such as the International Federation for Information Processing (IFIP), which was established in the 1960s under the auspices of UNESCO (Speiser, 1968).

Later innovations have brought significant changes to IS education, reflecting shifts in technology and organizational needs. As explained further in this book, cloud computing, big data analytics, cybersecurity, and artificial intelligence have become integral parts of IS curricula. Universities have adapted by offering specialized programs in data science, digital transformation, and IT governance, ensuring that graduates are equipped with the skills needed for today's digital economy.

2.5 Conclusions

The historical trajectory of IS reveals a field shaped by continuous technological advancements, shifting human, social, and organizational needs, and evolving academic perspectives. From ancient record-keeping, through mechanical tabulators to the rise of digital computing and global networking, IS has played a critical role in how information was captured, organized, managed, and disseminated. Across decades of change, the core insight of this chapter demonstrates that IS is never "just" technology. It constitutes an ongoing and permanent interaction between technology, system/business architectures, organizations, and people.

As we have seen, the development of IS has been influenced by both technological breakthroughs and human-centered considerations, demonstrating that successful IS must contain both efficiency and usability. By the late 1990s, this co-evolution had produced a recognizable IS field and an enterprise landscape no longer defined by isolated applications but by increasingly networked infrastructures. Three patterns recur throughout the history we have traced and remain relevant as the story continues. First, the pendulum between centralization and decentralization—from mainframes to client-server and PCs, and back to shared infrastructures. Second, the principle of layering infrastructures—new capabilities rarely replace the old; they sit atop them, inheriting their strengths and brittleness. Last, but not least important, the human factor as the decisive variable leads to a shift from data-logical to an info-logical approach.

Over time, these patterns were reflected in different schools of thought, ranging from purely technical and computational approaches to socio-technical and managerial perspectives, indicating the interdisciplinary nature of the field. The IS scholarship moved beyond tool evaluation to theory and method about adoption, alignment, value, and change, leading to more sophisticated and integrated digital ecosystems.

With this foundation, the next chapter, about the current state of information systems, builds upon this historical perspective to examine the present-day landscape of IS. It will explore the latest technological developments, digital transformation, and academic advancements to establish a structured understanding of how IS continues to evolve in response to emerging technological, organizational, and societal demands.

References

Araslanova, S. (2022). Library as a universe. Scientific Search: Personality, Education, Culture, (4), 70–72. https://doi.org/10.54348/scis.2022.4.13

Association for Information Systems [AIS]. (n.d.). AIS history. Retrieved September 12, 2025, from https://ishistory.aisnet.org/

Backus, J. (1978). The history of FORTRAN I, II, and III. ACM SIGPLAN Notices, 13(8), 165–180. https://doi.org/10.1145/960118.808380

Backus, J. W., Beeber, R. J., Best, S., Goldberg, R., Haibt, L. M., Herrick, H. L., ... Nutt, R. (1957, February). The FORTRAN automatic coding system. In Papers presented at the February 26–28, 1957, Western Joint Computer Conference: Techniques for reliability (pp. 188–198). ACM. https://doi.org/10.1145/1455567.1455599

Bard, K. A. (2005). Encyclopedia of the archaeology of ancient Egypt. Routledge. https://doi.org/10.4324/9780203982839

Baxter, G., & Sommerville, I. (2011). Socio-technical systems: From design methods to systems engineering. Interacting with Computers, 23(1), 4–17. https://doi.org/10.1016/j.intcom.2010.07.003

Bell, G. (1988). Keynote address: Toward a history of (personal) workstations. In A. Goldberg (Ed.), A history of personal workstations (pp. 1–50). ACM. https://dl.acm.org/doi/pdf/10.1145/61975.66913

Bergin, T. J., & Gibson, R. G. (1996). History of programming languages II. ACM Press.

Blondheim, M. (2014). The telegraph in America, 1832–1920. Journal of American History, 101(2), 601–602. https://doi.org/10.1093/jahist/jau361

Bozkus, K. (2023). Organizational culture change and technology: Navigating the digital transformation. In Organizational culture: Cultural change and technology. IntechOpen. https://doi.org/10.5772/intechopen.112903

Brügger, N. (Ed.). (2010). Web history (Vol. 56). Peter Lang.

Bryant, A., & Land, F. (2020). A "conversation" between Frank Land (FL) and Antony Bryant (AB): Part I. Journal of Information Technology, 35(4), 361–375. https://doi.org/10.1177/0268396220908274

Bryant, A., & Land, F. (2021). A "conversation" between Frank Land (FL) and Antony Bryant (AB): Part 2. Journal of Information Technology, 36(1), 39–55. https://doi.org/10.1177/0268396220908275

Bryant, A., Black, A., Land, F., & Porra, J. (2013). Information systems history: What is history? ...and why even bother with history? Journal of Information Technology, 28(1), 1–17. https://doi.org/10.1057/jit.2013.3
Campbell-Kelly, M., Aspray, W., Ensmenger, N., & Yost, J. R. (2018). Computer: A history of the information machine (3rd ed.). Routledge. https://doi.org/10.4324/9780429495373
Checkland, P., & Poulter, J. (2020). Soft systems methodology. In Systems approaches to making change: A practical guide (2nd ed., pp. 201–253). Springer. https://doi.org/10.1007/978-1-4471-7472-1_5
Chondros, T. G. (2017). Natural philosophy and the development of mechanics and engineering from the 5th century B.C. to the Middle Ages. FME Transactions, 45(4), 603–619. https://doi.org/10.5937/fmet1704603c
Chou, P. A. (2013). Advances in immersive communication. ACM Transactions on Multimedia Computing, Communications, and Applications, 9(1s), 1–4. https://doi.org/10.1145/2492704
Ciborra, C. (2004). The labyrinths of information: Challenging the wisdom of systems. Oxford University Press. https://doi.org/10.1093/acprof:oso/9780199275267.001.0001.
Copeland, J. G. (2017). At Bletchley Park. In The Turing guide. Oxford University Press. https://doi.org/10.1093/oso/9780198747826.003.0017
Couch, C. J. (1989). Oral technologies: A cornerstone of ancient civilizations? The Sociological Quarterly, 30(4), 587–602. https://doi.org/10.1111/j.1533-8525.1989.tb01536.x
Dummer, G. W. A. (1983). A concise history of computers, robotics and information technology. In *Electronic inventions and discoveries: Electronics from its earliest beginnings to the present day* (3rd ed., pp. 29–34). Pergamon Press. https://doi.org/10.1016/B978-0-08-029354-7.50013-8
Eisenstein, E. L. (1980). The printing press as an agent of change. Cambridge University Press. https://doi.org/10.1017/CBO9781107049963
Elayi, J. (2018). The history of Phoenicia. Lockwood Press. https://www.lockwoodpressonline.com/index.php/ebooks/catalog/book/6
Fontana, E. A., & Petrillo, F. (2021). Mapping breakpoint types: An exploratory study. In 2021 IEEE 21st International Conference on Software Quality, Reliability and Security (QRS) (pp. 1014–1023). IEEE. https://doi.org/10.1109/QRS54544.2021.00110
Galán, J. M. (1994). Bullfight scenes in ancient Egyptian tombs. Journal of Egyptian Archaeology, 80(1), 81–96. https://doi.org/10.1177/030751339408000107
Garner, R., & Dill, R. (2010). The legendary IBM 1401 data processing system. IEEE Solid-State Circuits Magazine, 2(1), 28–39. https://ibm-1401.info/IBM1401_IEEE_SSCS_Mag_Jan2010-100DPI.pdf
Germann, T. C. (2021). Co-design in the Exascale Computing Project. International Journal of High Performance Computing Applications, 35(6), 503–507. https://doi.org/10.1177/10943420211059380

Giannachi, G. (2016). Archive everything. MIT Press. https://doi.org/10.7551/mitpress/9780262035293.001.0001
Giannantonio, C. M., & Hurley-Hanson, A. E. (2011). Frederick Winslow Taylor: Reflections on the relevance of the principles of scientific management 100 years later. Journal of Business and Management, 17(1), 7–10.
Gregor, S. (2006). The nature of theory in information systems. MIS Quarterly, 30(3), 611–642. https://doi.org/10.2307/25148742
Haecker, R. (2022). Sacramental engines: The trinitarian ontology of computers in Charles Babbage's Analytical Engine. Religions, 13(8), 757. https://doi.org/10.3390/rel13080757
Haigh, T., & Ceruzzi, P. E. (2021). A new history of modern computing. MIT Press.
Haigh, T., & Priestley, M. (2018). Colossus and programmability. IEEE Annals of the History of Computing, 40(4), 5–27. https://doi.org/10.1109/MAHC.2018.2877912
Haighton, A. (2010). Roman methods of authentication in the first two centuries AD. Journal of the Society of Archivists, 31(1), 29–49. https://doi.org/10.1080/00379811003658484
Hirschheim, R., & Klein, H. (2012). A glorious and not-so-short history of the information systems field. Journal of the Association for Information Systems, 13(4), 188–235. https://doi.org/10.17705/1jais.00294
Howard, M. C., & Hair, J. F., Jr. (2023). Integrating the expanded task–technology fit theory and the technology acceptance model: A multi-wave empirical analysis. AIS Transactions on Human-Computer Interaction, 15(1), 83–110. https://doi.org/10.17705/1thci.00184
Hu, Z., Liu, B., Ren, X., & Tang, Y. (2022, January). Analysis and implementation of the Enigma machine. In 2022 International Conference on Big Data, Information and Computer Network (BDICN) (pp. 475–480). IEEE. https://doi.org/10.1109/BDICN55575.2022.00093
International Business Machines Corporation [IBM]. (1985, April). *A guide to IBM personal computers* (Publication No. GC20-8210-00). https://www.ardent-tool.com/docs/pdf/GC20-8210-00_A_Guide_to_IBM_Personal_Computers_Apr85.pdf
IBM Information Systems Division, Entry Systems Business. (1981, August 12). Personal computer announced by IBM [Press release]. https://doshistory.exp-soft.de/doc/infos/pcpressibm5150.pdf
Irvine, M. M. (2002). Early digital computers at Bell Telephone Laboratories. IEEE Annals of the History of Computing, 23(3), 22–42. https://doi.org/10.1109/85.948904
Johnson, L. (2006). Coming to grips with UNIVAC. IEEE Annals of the History of Computing, 28(2), 32–42. https://doi.org/10.1109/MAHC.2006.27
Kahl, J. (2022). Manuscripts and monuments: The ten contracts of Djefai-Hapi and economies of knowledge. Manuscript and Text Cultures, 1, 83–111. https://doi.org/10.56004/v1k83

Khosroshahi, P. A., Aier, S., Hauder, M., Roth, S., Matthes, F., & Winter, R. (2015). Success factors for federated enterprise architecture model management. In A. Persson & J. Stirna (Eds.), *Advanced information systems engineering workshops: CAiSE 2015 international workshops, Stockholm, Sweden, June 8–9, 2015, proceedings* (pp. 413–425). Springer. https://doi.org/10.1007/978-3-319-19243-7_38

Kleinrock, L. (2010). An early history of the internet. IEEE Communications Magazine, 48(8), 26–36. https://doi.org/10.1109/MCOM.2010.5534584

Knuth, D. E. (1986). The IBM 650: An appreciation from the field. IEEE Annals of the History of Computing, 8(1), 50–55. https://doi.org/10.1109/MAHC.1986.10010

Kramer, S. N. (2010). The Sumerians: Their history, culture, and character. University of Chicago Press.

Langefors, B. (1980). Infological models and information user views. Information Systems, 5(1), 17–32. https://doi.org/10.1016/0306-4379(80)90065-4

Lee, A. S. (2004). Thinking about social theory and philosophy for information systems. In L. Willcocks & J. Mingers (Eds.), Social theory and philosophy for information systems (pp. 1–26). John Wiley & Sons.

Lee, J., Fano, R., Scherr, A., Corbató, F., & Vyssotsky, V. (1992). Project MAC (time-sharing computing project). IEEE Annals of the History of Computing, 14(2), 9–13. https://doi.org/10.1109/85.150016

Leiner, B. M., Cerf, V. G., Clark, D. D., Kahn, R. E., Kleinrock, L., Lynch, D. C., ... Wolff, S. (2009). A brief history of the Internet. ACM SIGCOMM Computer Communication Review, 39(5), 22–31. https://doi.org/10.1145/1629607.1629613

Lichtheim, M. (2019). Ancient Egyptian literature (Vol. 1, The Old and Middle Kingdoms). University of California Press. https://doi.org/10.1525/9780520933057

Lombardi, L. A. (1964). A general business-oriented language based on decision expressions. Communications of the ACM, 7(2), 104–111. https://doi.org/10.1145/363921.363939

Mann, F. C., & Williams, L. K. (1960). Observations on the dynamics of a change to electronic data-processing equipment. Administrative Science Quarterly, 5(2), 217–256. https://doi.org/10.2307/2390779

Marlowe, F. W. (2005). Hunter–gatherers and human evolution. Evolutionary Anthropology: Issues, News, and Reviews, 14(2), 54–67. https://doi.org/10.1002/evan.20046

Metcalfe, R. M., & Boggs, D. R. (1976). Ethernet. Communications of the ACM, 19(7), 395–404. https://doi.org/10.1145/360248.360253

Mumford, E. (2017). The participation of users in systems design: An account of the origin, evolution, and use of the ETHICS method. In D. Schuler & A. Namioka (Eds.), Participatory design: Principles and practices (pp. 257–270). CRC Press.

Nooney, L. (2023). The Apple II age: How the computer became personal. University of Chicago Press. https://doi.org/10.7208/chicago/9780226816531.001.0001

Nunamaker, J., & Briggs, R. (2011). Toward a broader vision for information systems. ACM Transactions on Management Information Systems, 2(4), 1–12. https://doi.org/10.1145/2070710.2070711

Ohl, J. K. (2020). Supplying the troops: General Somervell and American logistics in World War II. Plunkett Lake Press/Cornell University Press.

Patnayakuni, R., & Ruppel, C. P. (2010). A socio-technical approach to improving the systems development process. Information Systems Frontiers, 12, 219–234. https://doi.org/10.1007/s10796-008-9093-4

Pereira, R., & Baranauskas, M. C. C. (2017). Systemic and socially aware perspective for information systems. In C. Boscarioli, R. M. de Araujo, & R. S. P. Maciel (Eds.), *I GranDSI-BR: Grand research challenges in information systems in Brazil 2016–2026* (pp. 148–160). Sociedade Brasileira de Computação. https://doi.org/10.5753/sbc.2884.0.12

Randell, B. (1980). The Colossus. In A history of computing in the twentieth century (pp. 47–92). Academic Press. https://edu.fmph.uniba.sk/~winczer/historia/2012/Colossus.pdf

Regan, G. (2018). EDVAC and ENIAC computers. In The innovation in computing companion (pp. 113–117). Springer. https://doi.org/10.1007/978-3-030-02619-6_23

Richards, M. (2012). How BCPL evolved from CPL. The Computer Journal, 56(5), 664–670. https://doi.org/10.1093/comjnl/bxs026

Rosenheim, D. (1983). Installation of the first production 701. IEEE Annals of the History of Computing, 5(2), 146–147. https://doi.org/10.1109/MAHC.1983.10029

Sale, T. (2003). Colossus. In A. Ralston, E. D. Reilly, & D. Hemmendinger (Eds.), *Encyclopedia of computer science* (4th ed., pp. 233–235). Wiley. https://dl.acm.org/doi/pdf/10.5555/1074100.1074222

Sammet, J. E. (1981). History of IBM's technical contributions to high-level programming languages. IBM Journal of Research and Development, 25(5), 520–534. https://doi.org/10.1147/rd.255.0520

Segal, H. P. (2014). Rewiring the history of the telegraph and the telephone. Reviews in American History, 42(3), 456–461. https://doi.org/10.1353/rah.2014.0063

Seiradakis, J. H., & Edmunds, M. G. (2018). Our current knowledge of the Antikythera Mechanism. Nature Astronomy, 2(1), 35–42. https://doi.org/10.1038/s41550-017-0347-2

Senge, P. M. (2006). The fifth discipline: The art and practice of the learning organization (Rev. and updated ed.). Doubleday/Currency.

Speiser, A. P. (1968). Scientific information: The IFIP, its structure and its aims. USSR Computational Mathematics and Mathematical Physics, 8(2), 369–374. https://doi.org/10.1016/0041-5553(68)90057-8

Stamper, R. (1973). Information in business and administrative systems. John Wiley & Sons.

Stein, M.-K., Galliers, R. D., & Whitley, E. A. (2016). Twenty years of the European Information Systems Academy at ECIS: Emergent trends and research topics. European Journal of Information Systems, 25(1), 1–15. https://doi.org/10.1057/ejis.2014.25

Stuart, B. L. (2018). Debugging the ENIAC [Scanning our past]. Proceedings of the IEEE, 106(12), 2331–2345. https://doi.org/10.1109/JPROC.2018.2878986

Swanson, E. B. (2020). How information systems came to rule the world: Reflections on the information systems field. The Information Society, 36(2), 109–123.

Teeter, E. (2011). Religion and ritual in ancient Egypt. Cambridge University Press. https://www.cambridge.org/core/books/religion-and-ritual-in-ancient-egypt/08AE3225E00D7332594F9DC083E94E12

Thacker, C. (1988). Personal distributed computing: The Alto and Ethernet hardware. In A. Goldberg (Ed.), A history of personal workstations (pp. 265–290). ACM. https://dl.acm.org/doi/10.1145/61975.66920

Topor, L. (2024). Cyber sovereignty. Springer Nature.

Vasiljević, V. (2013). Ancient Egypt in our cultural heritage? Issues in Ethnology and Anthropology, 8(3), 825–844. https://doi.org/10.21301/EAP.v8i3.10

Walden, D. C., & Van Vleck, T. (2011). The compatible time-sharing system (1961–1973): Fiftieth anniversary commemorative overview. IEEE Computer Society. https://history.computer.org/pubs/2011-06-ctss.pdf

Wexelblat, R. L. (2014). History of programming languages. Academic Press.

Williams, M. (1993). The origins, uses, and fate of the EDVAC. IEEE Annals of the History of Computing, 15(1), 22–38. https://doi.org/10.1109/85.194089

Wright, D. (2018). The history of the IEEE 802 standard. IEEE Communications Standards Magazine, 2(2), 4–11. https://doi.org/10.1109/MCOMSTD.2018.8412452

Wright, J. (2017). The Turing Bombe victory and the first naval Enigma decrypts. Cryptologia, 41(4), 295–328. https://doi.org/10.1080/01611194.2016.1219786

Zhang, X. (2022). Centralization and corruption: The political dilemma of the late Roman Empire. In A. Khalil & J. S. Zha (Eds.), *Proceedings of the 2022 8th International Conference on Humanities and Social Science Research (ICHSSR 2022)* (pp. 1481–1485). Atlantis Press. https://doi.org/10.2991/assehr.k.220504.268

3

The Current State of Information Systems

3.1 Introduction

Information systems have undergone profound changes between 2000 and 2025. Since the turn of the millennium, they have expanded dramatically in scope and impact, evolving from back-office data processing tools into core enablers of digital organizations and society. This period represents a transformative era in which emerging technologies like cloud computing, mobile devices, and artificial intelligence fundamentally reshaped how organizations collect, process, and use information as the strategic driver for creating and capturing value from global information access.

Through this chapter, we examine how IS has evolved since the beginning of the twenty-first century to our days. We begin by introducing the common system types and their roles in organizations. Next, we delve into emerging technologies that continue to shape the IS landscape. In the special section on digital transformation, we provide an in-depth analysis of its importance and challenges, as well as strategies and decision-making during global information accessibility. This chapter concludes with a discussion of how the IS transformation from 2000 through 2025 affected the workforce skills and IS education required to meet the changing industry demands.

B. Kantsepolsky, L. Topor, *Managing Information Singularity*,
https://doi.org/10.1007/978-3-032-26223-3_3

3.2 Common Types of Information Systems

The evolution of information systems from 2000 to 2025 can be characterized by increasing integration, intelligence, and strategic importance. What began as primarily support tools for operations and management has transformed into the backbone of virtually every business function and a driver of innovation. A variety of information system types have been developed to serve different organizational needs and levels of management. Understanding these classic categories and how they have evolved or converged is crucial to describing the current state of IS and is required to effectively collaborate with IT and IS professionals to discuss business needs and leverage technology strategically (Pearlson et al., 2024).

Traditionally, information systems have been classified into several types, including Transaction Processing Systems (TPS), Management Information Systems (MIS), Decision Support Systems (DSS), and Executive Support Systems (ESS), which are also referred to as Executive Information Systems (EIS). In addition, there are cross-functional enterprise applications such as Enterprise Resource Planning (ERP) systems, and specific functional systems such as Customer Relationship Management (CRM), Supply Chain Management (SCM), and Business Intelligence (BI) systems. In the next sections, we define and discuss each of them.

3.2.1 Transaction Processing Systems (TPS)

TPSs are the information systems that record the daily routine transactions necessary to conduct business, and constitute the data foundation of an organization's IS. A TPS is often a high-volume, mission-critical system that ensures tasks such as order entry, payroll, shipping, or inventory tracking are performed consistently and accurately (Laudon & Laudon, 2021). For example, a point-of-sale system in a retail store or an ATM network for a bank is TPS. TPSs capture transactional data such as sales, withdrawals, and deposits and update databases. The primary goal of TPS is to streamline operations by automating repetitive tasks and to provide reliable records of all transactions. In 2000, most organizations had multiple TPS—often one per major function or department (Wahsheh et al., 2023). Nowadays, many TPSs have been integrated into larger systems like ERP, but the function they serve remains indispensable. Modern TPSs are expected to operate in real-time, with near-instant processing and availability of data, as opposed to the batch processing modes of earlier decades. They also often feed into analytical systems, supplying the raw material for management reports and business intelligence.

An example of a TPS is *Stripe*, which is a cloud-based payment processing platform that executes thousands of financial transactions per second while maintaining correctness and durability. It handles end-to-end payment flows like card and wallet authorization, capture, settlement, refunds, chargebacks, and payouts, exposing them via Application Programming Interfaces (APIs) that enforce idempotency keys to prevent double charges and webhooks for real-time status updates. At its backend, Stripe combines online transaction processing databases with queues and event streams to meet latency and high availability targets, operates within PCI-DSS (Payment Card Industry Data Security Standard) compliance, and maintains a detailed audit trail so every transaction can be reconciled. Because each payment is a discrete, stateful event with legal and financial consequences, Stripe exemplifies a modern TPS: it records the sale as the system of record, triggers downstream processes (invoicing, ledger updates, fraud checks), and publishes transactional data to analytics and risk models without compromising the integrity of the original transaction (Markovich et al., 2017).

3.2.2 Management Information Systems (MIS)

Traditionally, MIS referred to systems that take data from TPS and other sources, aggregate it, and produce routine reports and summaries that help middle management monitor and control the business (Laudon & Laudon, 2021). An MIS typically provides answers to structured questions that are known in advance—for example, regular reports on monthly sales, inventory levels, or quarterly financial results. In the 2000s, MIS were often custom reporting systems or modules within enterprise software that managers could use to get periodic updates. These systems were geared toward operational and tactical decision-making by providing information on what has happened, e.g., sales figures, production output, and more. Many traditional MIS functions have been subsumed by more flexible BI tools and dashboards.

With time, the line between MIS and other systems has blurred. A modern dashboard might, in real-time, show key performance indicators (KPIs) to a manager, effectively serving the same purpose as an old-fashioned monthly report, but with live data. Although the concept of MIS as structured reporting for management is still a core need, the scope of MIS has expanded. Modern managers want not only internal data but also information from external sources, such as market trends or social media sentiment, integrated into their reports. Yet the mission of MIS remains similar—to support management by providing the right information at the right time in an understandable format.

An example of an enterprise CRM/MIS is *Salesforce*, which is a cloud-based customer relationship management platform that records and orchestrates day-to-day "customer transactions" such as lead captures, opportunity updates, quotes, orders, service cases, and support interactions. It serves operational teams through objects and workflows (e.g., Accounts, Contacts, Opportunities, Cases) with validation rules, approvals, and automation to ensure data integrity, while exposing APIs and platform events for real-time integration with other systems, such as TPSs. For managers, *Salesforce* acts as an MIS via built-in reports and executive dashboards that summarize pipeline, success rates, SLA (Service-Level Agreement) adherence, and agent productivity, supporting routine decisions and periodic reviews. Its multi-tenant architecture, field-level security, audit trails, and role-based access control protect sensitive customer data, and its AppExchange ecosystem (its marketplace) extends core CRM with configurations, prices, billing, and industry clouds, making *Salesforce* a representative example of a modern, integrated customer-centric information system (Koli et al., 2023).

3.2.3 Decision Support Systems (DSS)

These systems are designed to assist with semi-structured or unstructured decisions. DSSs typically offer analytical models, simulations, or data analysis tools that help middle managers and analysts explore data and "what-if" scenarios, including cases that may not have a clear procedure or routine. A DSS might combine data with a model, such as a statistical model or optimization algorithm, and an interactive interface (Power, 2002). In the early 2000s, a DSS was used for tasks such as forecasting, portfolio management, or supply chain optimization. Nowadays, sophisticated analytical models and artificial intelligence have significantly increased DSS capabilities.

Modern DSS might include predictive analytics using ML algorithms, data visualization tools, and even natural language query interfaces. They can handle much larger datasets, derived from both internal and external data sources, often termed "big data". The proliferation of self-service analytical platforms means that many end-users can perform some DSS functions themselves, e.g., using a tool like Tableau or Power BI to analyze data trends (Oliveira & Bernardino, 2020). Real-time data are frequently incorporated into contemporary DSS, allowing different stakeholders to work together to explore possibilities. Notwithstanding these improvements, DSS's primary goal is still to assist human decision-makers in imperfectly structured scenarios by offering insights rather than merely regular output.

An example of a DSS platform is *IBM Cognos Analytics*, which delivers governed operational reporting and self-service analysis for routine managerial decisions. With it, organizations model a consistent semantic layer over their warehouses/lakehouses, then build reports, dashboards, and explorations that track KPIs such as revenue, churn, SLA compliance, and inventory turns. Cognos supports enterprise needs such as row-level security (RLS), audit trails, scheduling, to thousands of recipients, versioned report packages, and reusable prompts, so monthly close packs and daily performance reports are consistent across departments. For exploratory/DSS use, analysts can join additional data, create ad-hoc visualizations, and use AI-assisted insights or natural-language queries to spot anomalies and drivers, while the platform also enables data export to downstream tools. Cognos exemplifies how a modern DSS system turns heterogeneous operational data into standardized, decision-ready information without sacrificing governance (Jadhav et al., 2024).

3.2.4 Executive Support Systems (ESS)

These systems, often also referred to as Executive Information Systems (EIS), are designed to meet the strategic information requirements of senior management, particularly executives at the chief and board levels. By concentrating on several KPIs, ESS offered a high-level perspective of the organization's performance. A typical ESS in the 2000s contained specially designed dashboards for CEOs that included certain intelligence, such as market trends, competition data, and economic indicators, along with internal data, such as financials and operations. One hallmark of ESS was the inclusion of information that was relevant to strategic decisions—for example, a balanced scorecard approach, which includes financial metrics, customer metrics, internal process metrics, and innovation/learning metrics, giving a balanced view of organizational health. Using charts and graphs to convey information understandably, ESS enabled executives to "drill down" for further information as needed (Laudon & Laudon, 2021).

Nowadays, ESS has transformed into extremely interactive executive command centers that are also available on tablets and mobile devices. Through an underlying data warehouse or enterprise performance management system, modern ESS combines data from the entire organization and may display insights into the future along with historical information (XDuce, 2025). Executives may also view predictive indications, such as AI-powered risk warnings or projected revenue, social media trends, or real-time news feeds. Despite these developments, literature indicates that executive decision-making is still primarily a judgment-based, human-driven process (Shepherd et al., 2024). Information systems are still less successful at supporting completely unstructured, novel decisions that require creativity and judgment beyond what data can provide. Hence, in the meantime, ESSs are here to stay and inform but not replace executive intuition.

Here, *IBM Cognos* can also be given as an example as it serves executives through board-level dashboards, scorecards, and briefing books that surface a focused set of KPIs (e.g., revenue growth, cash conversion, compliance). Executives can track thresholds, see curated explanations by region or product, and receive alerts on exceptions without wading through operational reports. When paired with IBM Planning Analytics, Cognos adds scenario and what-if modeling to compare plan with actual events and stress-test decisions, making it a practical ESS layer atop the governed MIS or a BI foundation.

3.2.5 Enterprise Applications (ERP, CRM, SCM)

Alongside the classic layered view of TPS→MIS→DSS→ESS, the 2000–2025 era has been dominated by large-scale enterprise information systems that integrate processes across functions. Enterprise Resource Planning (ERP) systems deserve special attention. ERP systems combine many TPS and MIS functions across different departments into one unified system with a common database, with modules such as finance, human resources, manufacturing, sales, and more (Pohludka, 2018). In the early 2000s, ERP implementations led by vendors like SAP, Oracle, and Microsoft were in full swing, aiming to substitute disparate functional systems that had difficulties "cannot easily share information to support cross-functional business processes" (Laudon & Laudon, 2021). By integrating data, ERP systems broke down information silos and enabled end-to-end processes, for example, order-to-cash, procure-to-pay, etc., to be managed in one system. Early ERP systems were often large, on-premises installations that were costly and complex to maintain. Over the last two decades, ERP vendors have evolved their offerings. Modern ERPs are often cloud-based or hybrid, more modular, and sometimes supplemented by specialized cloud applications. The key contribution of ERP to the current state of IS is that it established the expectation of real-time, enterprise-wide visibility into operations. If the ERP is fully adopted, managers at any level can, in principle, get up-to-date information on any aspect of the business. Many organizations have either implemented ERP or migrated to newer integrated suites or use a mix of systems that are connected via interfaces (Chinta, 2021). Regardless of the approach, integration of data remains a central requirement.

Closely related to ERP, Customer Relationship Management (CRM) and Supply Chain Management (SCM) systems also became prominent in the late 1990s and 2000s. CRM systems focus on managing a company's interactions with current and potential customers, from initial inquiries and sales calls to support tickets, to improve customer service, and enable targeted marketing (Dalili & Beheshtifar, 2018). In the 2000s, CRM was sometimes part of ERP or sometimes a separate system. Modern CRM systems have moved from simple contact management to sophisticated analytics, e.g., predicting churn, recommending the next best action for a salesperson, and are commonly delivered as a cloud service. For example, Salesforce is a notable example of a cloud CRM dominating the market (IDC, 2025). It is hard to underestimate the value of CRM. Companies realize that customer data are an asset, and personalized, data-driven customer engagement can drive loyalty and revenue.

In turn, SCM systems manage relationships with suppliers, distributors, and logistics. They help optimize the flow of materials, information, and finances in the supply chain. SCM functionality may include demand forecasting, procurement, inventory management, and logistics planning. The importance of SCM systems became evident when globalization made supply networks more complex. By integrating supply chain partners through information systems, companies in the 2000s aimed to reduce inventory levels with just-in-time strategies, improve forecast accuracy, and respond faster to changes in demand (Sujatmiko et al., 2024). Nowadays, SCM systems have incorporated IoT data, advanced analytics, and better integration with supplier systems—sometimes via cloud-based B2B networks or blockchain for traceability (Chukwunweike, 2025). The COVID-19 pandemic-related supply disruptions have further underscored the value of agile SCM systems that provide visibility and flexibility.

An example of an enterprise resource planning (ERP) system is *Microsoft Dynamics 365*, a cloud-native suite that integrates finance, supply chain, manufacturing, commerce, and human resources on a common data model with embedded analytics (Power BI) and extensibility through the Power Platform. In practice, large organizations adopt *Dynamics 365* Finance and Supply Chain Management for core transactional processes, general ledger, accounts payable/receivable, fixed assets, procure-to-pay, order-to-cash, materials requirements planning, and warehousing, while mid-market firms frequently employ Business Central as a unified alternative. The platform enforces internal controls via standardized workflows, role-based access, auditability, and jurisdiction-specific localizations, and it facilitates near-real-time interoperability through Business Events and Dataverse connectors to adjacent systems (e.g., CRM, e-commerce, and logistics). Extensibility is pursued primarily through configuration and low-code applications rather than bespoke customizations, thereby reducing technical debt, while embedded analytical capabilities and since 2023 AI "Copilot" features (e.g., cash-flow projections, demand forecasting, and anomaly detection) provide decision support within the ERP's operational context (Rizqy et al., 2022).

3.2.6 Business Intelligence (BI) and Analytics Systems

While not always listed alongside TPS/MIS/DSS in traditional taxonomies, the rise of BI systems in the 2000s was a crucial development in IS. BI systems are dedicated to analyzing data and presenting actionable information to help in decision-making. They often involve data warehousing—collecting data from various operational systems into a central repository, and tools for querying, reporting, and data mining (Vaish et al., 2020). Although BI partially overlaps with DSS in function, whereas DSS can be any ad-hoc or specialized analysis tool, BI usually refers to an enterprise-wide approach to analytics, standardizing data metrics, and providing a platform for everything from standard reports to advanced analysis. At the beginning of the 21st century, many organizations have had a BI team and platform that served as the analytical layer above their transactional systems (Watson and Wixom, 2007). Nowadays, BI has further merged into the concept of business analytics or, even broader, "data science" in organizations with updated in real-time, operational intelligence dashboards for all levels of management. Having machine learning and AI-driven insights, these systems are sometimes termed as augmented analytics (Petrova, 2021).

An example of a BI and analytics system is *Microsoft Power BI*, a cloud-based platform that supports the end-to-end analytical lifecycle from data ingestion to governed dissemination of insights. The service provides workspace governance, deployment pipelines, and lineage views to preserve consistency and auditability across development, test, and production. Analysts and managers consume interactive dashboards and paginated reports, employ AI-assisted features (natural-language, anomaly detection, automated insights), and monitor standardized KPIs through scorecards, while embedded analytics and APIs operationalize insights within line-of-business applications. Integration with the broader Microsoft data stack enables scalable storage and compute, and the platform's role-based access controls and endorsement mechanisms help align self-service exploration with enterprise data governance (Nabil et al., 2023).

3.2.7 A Single Integrated Platform

While the common types of information systems discussed in the previous sections can still exist in 2025, in many cases, a single integrated platform of a tightly integrated set of tools providing the described functionalities is emerging. According to the literature, many organizations pursue a unified information architecture where data flows from transactions to analytics to executive dashboards in a continuous, near-real-time manner (Schneider et al., 2024; Song et al., 2024). This integration is facilitated by technologies like enterprise data warehouses and cloud platforms that connect systems (Holdsworth et al., n.d.). In other words, nowadays we have a continuum of information capabilities, while the taxonomy of rigid tiers and systems is expanding and blurring. Nevertheless, the definitions and purposes outlined above still provide a useful framework for understanding how different information needs are met by different types of systems. Each has a role. Starting from TPS for handling the recording of events and MIS for providing structured summaries, to DSSs for analysis of complex questions, and up to ESSs for strategic oversight. The fundamental needs of each level—transaction processing, management reporting, decision support, and executive information persist, even if new technologies and integrated platforms now deliver these capabilities in unified ways (Pearlson et al., 2024). Understanding these classic system types is still necessary for managers and serves to understand the information flows and decisions throughout the enterprise.

To illustrate how the current state of IS in any large organization is typically an amalgamation of all these, often with one or more core platforms and many interconnected modules or services, let's consider an example of a bank in 2025. Its mobile app and online banking platform are the primary channels for customer interaction. AI algorithms decide credit limits and detect fraud. Data analytics systems drive personalized offers. The core banking TPS handles millions of real-time transactions reliably, and executives rely on dashboards, which are part of ESS, showing risk and performance indicators. The bank's strategy might include expanding into new markets via digital-only services, meaning the success of the business is essentially the success of its information systems.

In addition, during the last decades, new types of systems have appeared, such as knowledge management systems (KMS) to share organizational knowledge and support collaboration, and content management systems (CMS) to handle documents and digital content. These systems have become important, especially in knowledge-intensive industries. Collaboration platforms, e.g., Microsoft Teams, Slack, and more, can also be considered part of the IS ecosystem by enabling information sharing and group decision support (Laudon & Laudon, 2021). Once the systems are secure, reliable, and innovative, the business can thrive and grow. Otherwise, the business might be at risk. After decades of evolution, information systems are not just a support function, but the business itself in many cases.

3.3 Emerging Technologies and Innovations (2000–2025)

Technological progress between 2000 and 2025 had a significant impact on information systems. In this section, we discuss some of the major trends and technologies, including cloud computing, mobile computing, and the Internet of Things (IoT). Artificial intelligence (AI) and quantum information science (QIS) are covered separately in Chapters 6 and 7 because of their disruptive and revolutionary nature. Together, these technologies constitute a large portion of the "cutting edge" of information systems in the twenty-first century, each of which has brought new capabilities and challenges for the IS stakeholders.

3.3.1 Cloud Computing

One of the most significant shifts in how information systems are delivered and managed was caused by the rise of cloud computing. Cloud computing, as we know it today, did not emerge suddenly from a single inventor. It evolved over decades of advances in networking, virtualization, and distributed systems. By the early 2000s, most businesses operated their information systems on-site. Typically, software was installed on local computers after being licensed, and IT personnel controlled their own data centers. This started to change in 1999 with the introduction of the software-as-a-service (SaaS) model by Salesforce, which launched one of the first successful Software as a Service (SaaS) offerings, delivering CRM entirely through the web (Campbell-Kelly, 2009). In 2002, Amazon introduced Amazon Web Services (AWS) —a set of web-based services for storage, messaging, and computation, laying the groundwork for cloud infrastructure (Huawei, 2023). Finally, in 2006, AWS officially launched Elastic Compute Cloud (EC2), pioneering Infrastructure as a Service (IaaS), where developers could rent computing capacity on demand (Armbrust et al., 2010). This is widely regarded as the birth of commercial cloud computing. A few years later, Google and Microsoft joined with Platform as a Service (PaaS), cementing in 2010 cloud computing as the new paradigm (Huawei, 2023). Since then, organizations might obtain scalable, on-demand resources and outsource a large portion of the maintenance work by shifting their software and computer infrastructure to cloud providers, releasing budget and resources for creativity, cost flexibility, and agility.

Based on these developments, one could summarize three main types of cloud computing services as IaaS for renting servers, storage, and networking between them. PaaS is a platform for developing and deploying applications. Finally, SaaS—as complete applications hosted by a provider, e.g., email, CRM, ERP applications running in the cloud. In addition to full public cloud-based deployments, one could find hybrid cloud, defined as a combination of cloud and on-premise, along with private and multi-cloud architectures using multiple providers. strategies. For mature companies born in the twentieth century, one of the significant challenges was the gradual migration of legacy systems to the cloud or replacing them with cloud-native applications.

The deployment of commercial cloud farms enabled another emerging technological trend of software innovation through APIs and microservices, facilitated by cloud platforms that host these microservices and allow them to scale independently (Fowler & Lewis, 2014; Jamshidi et al., 2018). Cloud computing has also introduced new considerations for IS, such as data security in multi-tenant environments, compliance with regulations when data are stored globally, and the need for robust internet connectivity for access (Subashini & Kavitha, 2011). By 2025, the narrative has shifted from "should we move to the cloud?" to "how best can we leverage the cloud?" Enterprise strategists focus on optimizing cloud costs, preventing vendor lock-in, and architecting systems to be cloud-native, taking full advantage of cloud features such as auto-scaling, distributed architectures, and managed services. Thus, cloud computing has transformed IS from a product to a utility. Computing is seen as something you consume as a service, much like electricity, which fundamentally changes how IS departments operate and plan for capacity. Some scholars even defined delivering computing as the 5th utility, after water, electricity, gas, and telephony (Buyya et al., 2009).

3.3.2 Mobile Computing and Ubiquitous Access

Mobile devices became mainstream in the 2010s as the number of smartphone users worldwide experienced exponential growth. In 2023, there were an estimated 6.8 billion smartphone users globally, projected to reach over 7.3 billion by 2025 (Hooda, 2025). Considering the world's population, these numbers mean that any information system aimed at consumers or employees has to account for mobile access.

For customer-facing systems, mobile devices have become even more critical. Whether it is banking, shopping, or socializing, a large share of interactions occurs via mobile applications. This fact and customer preferences have led to the development of mobile commerce and omnichannel strategies where information systems must ensure a seamless experience across online, mobile, and physical channels. For example, retail IS integrating inventory and customer data so that a customer can check product availability on their phone, order online, and pick up in store, with all systems synchronized. Mobile devices generated new data streams, including location data, photos, voice input, and more, that can be leveraged by a variety of IS. Since usage patterns differ between mobile and desktop, many modern IS include features of mobile analytics for understanding how users are engaging via mobile.

In addition, mobile devices enable ubiquitous access, so that employees expect to be able to check email, use enterprise applications, and access analytics on their phones or tablets. Ubiquitous access to everything from anywhere belongs to the broader concept, often called pervasive computing (Satyanarayanan, 2001; Hansmann et al., 2013). People have come to expect continuous access to information everywhere, every time, and on every platform that is connected to the internet. Information systems should therefore be designed with high availability and user experience in mind to meet these expectations. Field workers use specialized mobile applications connected to central IS, such as a delivery driver using an application linked to the logistics system, or a maintenance technician recording service data on a tablet that feeds into the asset management system. However, from an IS management perspective, the mobile era introduced multiple challenges, including responsive design, device management, security, and more. Companies had to implement Mobile Device Management (MDM) solutions to secure corporate data on employee phones. One example is the concept of Bring Your Own Device (BYOD). Businesses were also required to invest in redesigning the user interfaces of legacy systems or adopting new platforms to ensure usability on small screens.

The current state is that mobile computing is so ingrained that many IS are simply assumed to include it. The distinction of a "mobile IS" versus a normal IS is fading, as nearly all systems have mobile interfaces or APIs that mobile apps can use. Moreover, many enterprise software vendors follow a "mobile-first" or "mobile-friendly" design principle. From the technological point of view, the synergy of mobile and cloud became a catalyst and facilitator of ubiquitous access, cloud computing facilitated a variety of mobile applications, and these applications, in turn, increased the demand for cloud computing services. As a result, when cloud services power mobile apps, the application serves as a front-end, while the heavy processing and data storage happen in cloud servers. This synergy further pushed organizations toward cloud-based backends for global accessibility and scale.

3.3.3 Internet of Things (IoT) and Cyber-Physical Systems

The Internet of Things (IoT) refers to the network of physical objects ("things") embedded with sensors, software, and connectivity, enabling them to collect and exchange data. The term IoT has been known since 2005 (ITU, 2005) and has extended information systems to the physical world on a massive scale. IoT started with RFID tags and sensor networks, and grew with the availability of ubiquitous wireless connectivity and cheap sensors such as accelerometers, temperature sensors, GPS, etc. As of 2025, IoT devices, including everything from smart home devices and wearables to industrial sensors and connected cars, already numbered in the billions, with estimates raptly ranging from 20 billion currently (IoT Analytics, 2024) to 40 billion by the end of the decade (Westervelt, 2020; Kumar, 2025). These devices generate continuous data streams that feed into enterprise IS, allowing for real-time monitoring and control of physical assets.

In industrial contexts, the Industrial IoT (IIoT) refers to manufacturing plants and energy grids that deploy sensors to monitor machine performance, implement predictive maintenance, and optimize operations. For example, a production line machine might report vibration and heat data to an analytics system, which can predict failure before it happens and schedule maintenance proactively (Jardine et al., 2006; Pech et al., 2021). Supply chains use IoT for end-to-end visibility, where items can be tracked in real time via GPS and environmental sensors. These types of applications are important for perishable goods like food or pharmaceuticals that need temperature control (Lamberty & Kreyenschmidt, 2025). Retailers experiment with IoT in stores with smart shelves that detect inventory levels (Jose et al., 2024). Cities adopt IoT for smart city initiatives, connecting traffic lights, surveillance cameras, and utility meters to central management systems (Zaman et al., 2024).

To reduce latency and bandwidth usage, the integration of IoT data into information systems requires advancements in handling high-velocity streaming data and edge computing for processing data closer to where it is generated. To do so, many IS architectures contain an edge layer and a cloud layer, where the edge devices do initial data processing or filtering, while aggregated data are sent to the cloud or data center for deeper analysis and storage.

Real-time data-driven decision-making related to the physical processes is one of the key benefits of IoT in information systems. This ability further blurs the borderline between operational technology (OT) and information technology (IT). Historically, factory floor machines and corporate IT systems were separate domains, but IoT and the drive for digital transformation in manufacturing, often referred to as Industry 4.0, have brought them together (Wan et al., 2022). Nowadays, the CIO and the plant manager share overlapping concerns, as sensor data flow into ERP systems and analytics results flow back to adjust machine settings.

However, together with the apparent advantages, IoT also introduces significant security and data management challenges. Every connected device constitutes a potential entry point for cyber-attacks, and IoT security incidents, such as the CyberAv3ngers attacks on water and gas systems (Greenberg, 2025), the breach exposing 2.7 billion IoT records (Infosecurity Magazine, 2025), and the Raptor Train botnet compromising over 200,000 IoT devices globally (Asimily, 2025), illustrate the severity of this vulnerability. As further discussed in Chapter 5, ensuring the confidentiality, integrity, and availability of IoT data constitutes one of the significant IS security domains. While in 2025, IoT is a mature field, it is still a growing aspect of IS since some businesses are still figuring out how to monetize and capture its value effectively (Deloitte, 2023b). The ongoing developments in standards, interoperability, and synergy of IoT data with AI are particularly promising for providing deeper analysis and support in decisions toward creating autonomous systems.

3.4 Digital Transformation

As discussed, at the beginning of the twenty-first century, organizations were dependent on information systems not just for efficiency, but also for agility, innovation, and competitive advantage. In the 2010s, the concept of digital transformation took hold as organizations recognized that incremental improvements were not enough to compete in an increasingly digital world. Digital transformation goes beyond simply digitizing existing processes and refers to the profound changes in business activities, processes, competencies, and models that are enabled by digital technologies (Vial, 2019).

Several factors converged in the 2010s to make digital transformation a central agenda. One was the maturation of the technologies discussed above, which, among others, enabled scalable computing power and SaaS business models. Another was the growth of big data analytics and BI, which allowed organizations to harness the massive streams of data. A third factor was the rise of social media and digitally empowered customers, which pressured companies to become more customer-centric and responsive. Finally, increased competition from digital-native firms, i.e., those that were born digital, such as Facebook, Google, Uber, Airbnb, Alibaba, and others, showed traditional industries that leveraging data and technology in innovative ways could disrupt entire markets. In the remaining sections, we discuss what digital transformation entails, its drivers and challenges, and how it has redefined the role of information systems in delivering business value.

3.4.1 Understanding Digital Transformation

A widely cited definition of Vial (2019) describes digital transformation as "a process where digital technologies create disruptions triggering strategic responses from organizations" (p. 118), which in turn leads to profound changes in business activities, processes, competencies, and models. The digital transformation moved to the center of corporate strategy in the 2010s (Teubner & Stockhinger, 2020). The drivers of digital transformation have been manifold. First, competitive pressure from digital natives and rapidly changing consumer expectations forced incumbents to adapt. Second, the availability of enabling technologies, as discussed earlier, made certain transformations feasible and economically attractive. Third, there were efficiency and agility gains to be had—companies saw digital processes as a way to reduce costs since automation can cut manual effort, digital channels can be cheaper than physical, and increase agility—respond faster to market changes with flexible systems. The 2020 COVID-19 pandemic then gave a clear external shock that underscored the importance of being digital. Academic research on IS strategy reflects these shifts as shown in the literature review by Teubner and Stockhinger (2020), who identified five developments in IT/IS strategy research over 2008–2018, all linked to digital transformation.

The first was the transaction of strategy-making *from an organizational to a supra-organizational perspective*, which means considering networks, ecosystems, and platforms that go beyond firm boundaries. Digital transformation, as engaging with partners and communities, was evident in, for instance, building a developer ecosystem around the firm's platform or integrating with supplier/customer systems. The second was *focused on accelerated environmental change.* The digital age's rapid technological changes require a more dynamic strategy. One example is changing from traditional multi-year

IT plans that were often quickly obsolete to agile approaches and continuous innovation in IT investments. Third, *IT as a Driver of Business Strategy.* Rather than aligning IT with a given business strategy, the researchers offered to explore new IT-enabled possibilities as a strategy. In other words, instead of being merely a support function, consider the IT/IS strategy as a corporate-wide business strategy. For example, businesses look for new value through technology, e.g., what can we do with AI that we couldn't before? Fourth, *resource-based view expansion.* A shift from focusing on IT resources like systems and infrastructure to IT-enabled business capabilities. In other words, instead of focusing on technology itself, ask what the organization can do with it, or how the development of digital capabilities, such as data analytics, can be co-specialized with business processes. For example, how to use IT capabilities to revolutionize marketing efforts? Finally, the *emergence of the digital business strategy concept.* Scholars and practitioners started using terms like "digital strategy" to denote an integrated approach that covers both business and IT dimensions. Some even argued to entirely replace the IS strategy term with digital business strategy, reflecting that in a digitally transformed organization, technology decisions are inseparable from business decisions (Bharadwaj et al., 2013).

These five points underline that digital transformation is not just an IT update. It is a strategic reorientation of the firm around digital capabilities and innovation. Essentially, digital transformation is the journey that involves redefining how value is delivered to customers, how operations are run, and even what the business's core is. However, changes in IS technology without corresponding changes in organizational processes and structures can lead to misalignment and unintended consequences. In effect, digital transformation blurs the distinction between "business" and "IT" strategy, requiring integrated planning. As stated by Pearlson et al. (2024), the Information Systems Strategy Triangle necessitates that business strategy, organizational strategy, and IS strategy must be designed in harmony and adjusted together for success. This alignment is discussed in the next section.

3.4.2 Challenges and Risks in Digital Transformation

Digital transformation is difficult and fraught with challenges. According to the literature, the following are common hurdles of the digital transformation journey. The first and primary challenge is *Legacy Systems and Technical Debt.* Many established companies have older core systems that are inflexible. Modernization or integration of these legacy systems can be costly and risky.

Balancing the need to renovate core IT with delivering new features is tough. Approaches like APIs and middleware were often used to wrap legacy systems with newer digital interfaces. But for the long term, many firms undertake core system replacement, which itself is a major project (Comella-Dorda et al., 2000).

Since new technologies require new expertise, the next challenge is the *Talent and Skills Gap*. Because of global competition for talent in areas like cybersecurity, data science, and AI, many organizations find that they need to upskill existing staff, which means not just hiring but also creating an environment that retains those skilled workers through an innovative, flexible, and mission-driven culture (Tamayo et al., 2023; Weddle et al., 2025). However, digital transformation often fundamentally changes how people work, e.g., using new tools, altering processes, and sometimes even reducing headcount due to automation. The problem is that people inherently resist change. Getting buy-in at all levels, communicating the vision, and managing change are essential. Cases of transformation failures often cite cultural resistance when employees don't adopt a new system or process. To overcome the third challenge of *Cultural Resistance*, change management and clear communication are as important as the technology itself (Cieślak & Valor, 2025; Kherrazi & Roquilly, 2025).

Transformation is not a one-time project with an end, but a continuous process. Some organizations experienced "transformation fatigue," where constant change causes stress and confusion. To manage the challenge of *Continuous Change and Fatigue*, KPMG advised that having an enterprise-level view and coordinating changes helps mitigate initiative overload (KPMG, 2024). By understanding that it is impossible to achieve everything at once, successful companies phase their transformations, focusing on areas of highest impact and building momentum. Finally, measuring ROI and early wins are important to justify further investment. Without evidence, executives or shareholders may pull back funding or lose faith. Deloitte (2023b) found that 73% of leaders struggle to measure digital transformation due to a lack of defined metrics, even as many recognize its enterprise value. In turn, organizations that adopt a broader KPI framework are 20% more likely to see medium-to-high value outcomes. This is why the "metrics that matter" research is so pertinent. Focusing on and communicating the right metrics can sustain the transformation effort. According to the BCG (2020), only 30% of digital transformations achieved or exceeded expected value. BCG emphasizes the importance of defining measurable outcomes (KPIs), adapting as progress unfolds, and securing executive buy-in as transformation scales.

As appears from the leading consulting firms' reports, the outcomes of digital transformation efforts range from spectacular success of companies that reinvented themselves and grew, to middling results that achieved some improvements but not game-changing, and to failures or stalls where money was spent with little return. Many organizations have learned that technology adoption must be accompanied by process redesign, cultural change, and upskilling—the socio-technical alignment long emphasized in IS theory. Hence, not surprisingly, Pearlson et al. (2024) underscore that technology and organizational change must go hand in hand since deploying new IT without appropriate changes in job expectations, processes, and incentives will likely fail.

3.4.3 The Impact of Digital Transformation on Value Creation

Leading consulting firms and researchers have tried to quantify or frame the value of digital transformation. For example, Deloitte's global study "Mapping Digital Transformation Value—The Metrics that Matter" investigated how organizations measure the outcomes of digital initiatives. They found that 68% of respondents believe digital transformation is the single most important investment for driving enterprise value, yet 73% struggle to define metrics to measure that value (Deloitte, 2023b). This measurement challenge means many firms undertake digital projects without clear KPIs, making it hard to prove success. The interesting finding was that companies using a holistic set of metrics across all these domains were up to 20% more likely to self-report achieving high value from digital transformation. Since customer satisfaction and employee productivity are crucial to long-term value, Deloitte recommended categorizing metrics into five domains—financial, customer/client, process, workforce, and purpose (social/environmental). This recommendation is dedicated to ensuring that the organization is focusing not only on financial KPIs.

Another Deloitte survey, "Digital Value and the Industry Context", found that the value of digital transformation can differ greatly by industry (Deloitte, 2023a). For example, what matters for a bank—e.g., customer digital engagement and trust, might differ from what matters for a manufacturing company—e.g., supply chain efficiency or product innovation rate. The survey also found variation in digital spend, focus, and barriers, which means that there is no one-size-fits-all metric—each sector finds digital value in different places. For example, life sciences might value R&D innovation from digital, government might value citizen satisfaction or inclusion via e-services.

However, a common barrier across industries was difficulty in securing funding and defining ROI, especially in newer areas like AI, where outcomes versus investment can be uncertain (Deloitte, 2023a).

KPMG's research also provides a perspective on the value and success of digital initiatives. Their consequential surveys from 2023 to 2024 show that around 80% of senior leaders said they were moderately to fully satisfied with the results of their transformations (KPMG, 2024). This suggests that after years of digital transformation experiences, organizations have gained experience and are starting to realize tangible benefits. KPMG identified that successful digital leaders are bolstering their data and technology foundations, improving transformation management through orchestration and alignment, building a resilient culture, and engaging their ecosystems. These are capabilities that develop through the transformation journey. While at the beginning, many companies struggled with integrating siloed initiatives or lacked the necessary talent and culture for digital, over time, they learned and adapted.

One key to success that was often cited is leadership. Digital transformation requires strong leadership to set a vision and allocate resources, and further alignment across the business and IT. KPMG notes that all parts of the senior team and every function need to align with the mission and goals, maintaining a unified view of the target state. If, for example, the marketing department digitizes customer touchpoints, but operations do not update back-end fulfillment processes, the transformation's value won't be realized fully. Coordination and avoiding fragmentation were recurring themes. Indeed, KPMG urges sequencing and managing initiatives with an enterprise-wide perspective to maximize value and minimize disruption. Many companies realized this the hard way—early on, one department might launch a mobile app, another invests in analytics, but if they weren't coordinated, the experience to customers or the data integration internally could suffer. Tech leaders are expected to do more with less in many cases. According to KPMG (2023), 67% of respondents reported budget pressures, which means making smart choices and demonstrating quick wins is important to keep support from the rest of the business.

Another factor in extracting value is addressing the cultural and workforce dimension. Digital transformation often demands new skills, e.g., data scientists, agile project managers, UX designers, and a mindset of continuous learning and experimentation. Organizations have had to invest in re-skilling programs and in fostering a culture where innovation is encouraged and failure is seen as a learning step. According to KPMG's report, 73% of digitally mature enterprises have high levels of trust in their leaders (KPMG, 2024), indicating that trust and leadership are correlated with transformation maturity.

Early in the decade, some firms created separate digital units to drive transformation, together with the trend of reintegrating digital into the core business once maturity grows. The ultimate goal became not to have a parallel "digital" organization, but to make the entire organization digitally enabled (Matt et al., 2015). In some organizations, it has become common to have roles like a Chief Digital Officer (CDO) or for the CIO to wear a "digital strategist" hat—the phenomenon is often referred to in the literature as digital transformation and IS strategy convergence (Haffke et al., 2016; Raković, 2022).

3.5 Academic Perspectives

Now, let's look at how these changes in practice and strategy have influenced information systems research and education. Since 2000, in light of new contexts, IS research has continuously adapted to study new phenomena such as virtual communities, digital platforms, social media, cloud computing, big data, AI adoption, etc., while reassessing older topics like IT productivity, user acceptance, and IS development methodologies. In this section, we outline some of the major research areas in IS and how they have developed from 2000 to 2025. We also discuss how IS education has changed to prepare students for the modern environment.

3.5.1 Major Research Streams and Theoretical Advances

IS, as a field, is inherently interdisciplinary, drawing from management science, computer science, psychology, sociology, economics, and more. One enduring school of thought in IS that discussed in Chapter 2, is the sociotechnical perspective—the view that optimal outcomes arise when both the social and technical systems are designed in harmony. Dates back serves as a reminder that technology implementations must consider human and organizational factors. As Trist and Bamforth (1951) showed with coal mining long ago, changes in technology affect social systems and vice versa. This principle applies to implementing an AI system in an office today. In practice, successful adoption of new technologies in organizations requires attention to people—building digital skills, fostering a culture open to change, and aligning incentives. The socio-technical approach reminds us that technology implementations succeed only when the social system, such as processes, roles, and culture are designed in tandem (Ali, 2023; Kantsepolsky, 2025). For example, simply installing a knowledge management system, such as an enterprise wiki, does not guarantee knowledge sharing—one also needs a culture of collaboration and trust. The academic community has contributed by studying user behavior, such as factors influencing technology acceptance (Rahimi et al., 2018), organizational change management (Phillips et al., 2022), and strategic alignment (Gede, 2023), offering frameworks and models that practitioners use to guide IS initiatives.

A central concern historically has been IS success and value. Early studies in the 1990s struggled to resolve the "productivity paradox", where investments in IT were not showing up in productivity statistics. However, by the 2000s, better data and methods started to identify conditions under which IT creates value, e.g., when complemented by organizational changes. The seminal IS Success Model of DeLone and McLean (1992, 2003) provided a framework with dimensions like system quality, information quality, usage, user satisfaction, and net benefits to evaluate how and why an information system yields benefits. From 2000 to 2025, that model has been applied in countless studies, expanded to consider things like service quality and contextual factors. The quest to link IT investments to firm performance, often termed the IT productivity or IT value research, also evolved. As we saw with digital transformation, measuring value remains a theme, now including intangibles like agility or customer experience.

Another major stream is technology adoption and diffusion. The Technology Acceptance Model (TAM) by Davis (1989) was foundational, positing that perceived usefulness and ease of use drive user adoption. This line of work extended into the Unified Theory of Acceptance and Use of Technology (UTAUT) by Venkatesh et al. (2003), incorporating factors like social influence and facilitating conditions. From 2000 onward, researchers applied these models to numerous new technologies, e.g., adoption of e-commerce, mobile banking, social media, enterprise systems, etc., often extending or modifying them to fit context by adding constructs like trust for online systems, or habit for mobile use. The rise of consumer IT and Bring Your Own Device (BYOD) trends even led to studying IT adoption outside work settings, blending with marketing research on consumer behavior. By 2025, with things like wearable devices and IoT in the home, the boundary of what is an IS has expanded, and user acceptance research covers a broad swath, from employees accepting an enterprise system to the public accepting algorithmic decisions or contact-tracing apps.

The IS development and project management area also progressed. The early 2000s saw a critical examination of why IS projects fail. One classic example from that time was a series of CHAOS reports showing software projects' high failure rates, with many projects either cancelled or severely challenged (The Standish Group International, 1995). These findings were widely cited in both industry and academia, reinforcing the importance of improving project management practices. Although some questioned the exact numbers reported in CHAOS reports, e.g., Eveleens and Verhoef (2009), the fact that the absolute majority of software projects had these issues was broadly discussed in the literature. This led to research on better methodologies, risk management, user involvement, and governance. The emergence of agile development methods, such as Scrum, Kanban, Lean, XP, and more around the early 2000s, coming from practitioners, garnered research interest—how agile methods compare to traditional waterfall, how they scale in large organizations, and so on (Dikert et al., 2016). Nowadays, agile and DevOps are mainstream in practice, and IS research has documented factors for success with agile, as well as new challenges like coordinating agile at enterprise scale and integrating with outsourced development. Another development was open-source software, which started as a niche and became a major phenomenon; researchers studied the motivations of open-source contributors, business models around open source, and how firms participate in open ecosystems (Li et al., 2024).

A very notable theoretical development in the 2000s was the growth of design science research (DSR) in IS. Spearheaded by a seminal paper by Hevner et al. (2004), design science positioned IS as not only analyzing existing phenomena (behavioral science) but also designing and evaluating new IT artifacts as a form of research contribution, e.g., creating a new decision support tool and demonstrating its utility. This legitimized studies that build novel systems or methods within IS research. Over the past two decades, DSR has become a well-established paradigm, with its own methodologies and venues. It resonates with practice as well since it often addresses concrete problems and provides innovative solutions.

Another conceptual shift was recognizing the role of materiality of technology—the sociomateriality perspective (Orlikowski & Scott, 2008), arguing that the social and material (technical) are inextricably entwined. This is a philosophical view that influenced qualitative studies of how people and tech enact each other in contexts like emergency response systems or hospital IS. It pushed researchers to consider how technology's material properties, e.g., a smartphone's portability, shape human action and organizational routines, rather than treating tech as just a neutral tool.

As discussed, information and cybersecurity, along with privacy research, also grew in importance given the rising threats. Topics include individual behavior related to security, e.g., why people fall for phishing, how to encourage better security practices, organizational policies and investment in cybersecurity, and factors affecting disclosure of personal info, privacy-by-design principles, and many more. See Chapter 4 for the dedicated discussion on the main challenges of IS, Chapter 5 dealing with legal and regulatory frameworks for IS for the intersection of IS with law and data protection regulations, and Chapter 6 for implications of AI on society in general, ethical and privacy concerns in particular.

Due to the permanently emerging innovations in the IS field, each new technology or social trend creates a research thread. For instance, e-commerce in the early 2000s spawned research on online consumer behavior, trust in e-commerce, website design, and electronic markets. Then, social media and virtual communities became hot topics. IS scholars studied knowledge sharing in communities of practice, the impact of social networks on work, and how firms should engage on social platforms. These and additional specialized research domains, such as *Global IS and Offshoring/Outsourcing* (Gunawan et al., 2024; Gambal et al., 2022), *Sustainability and Green IS* (Brendel & Börner, 2022), *Healthcare IS* (Milioris et al., 2022), and many more, continually spur research. Nowadays, IS research tackles cutting-edge questions, such as algorithmic decision-making and its fairness (Khademi et al., 2019; Gafni et al., 2025), human–AI collaboration (Hadar et al., 2025), and the impact of emerging technologies like quantum technologies. The field also increasingly uses advanced methods such as data analytics for research itself, experiments, and even NeuroIS, which uses biometric or neurophysiological measures to study technology use (Entezarian et al., 2025).

3.5.2 Evolution of IS Education and Skills for the Digital Age

The changes in technology and business have had reflective effects on IS education, the university programs and curricula that prepare future IS professionals, as well as ongoing professional development. Traditional MIS programs around 2000 might have focused on systems analysis and design, database management, some programming, and business fundamentals. While those fundamentals remain, the 2020s demand new topics and approaches to keep programs relevant.

For example, Saulnier (2016) addressed the need for aligning IS education with the skills employers seek in the modern workplace. Saulnier argues that because employers overwhelmingly value skills like critical thinking, problem-solving, communication, and the ability to drive innovation, academia must prepare students for a world of *permanent white water*—a continuous, turbulent change. This and many other studies suggest that IS education must go beyond technical knowledge. It must cultivate adaptive learners and thinkers who can apply technology strategically.

To meet these needs, IS programs have been incorporating High Impact Practices (HIPs) and Essential Learning Outcomes (ELOs) as described in the initiative of the Association of American Colleges and Universities (AAC&U). HIPs might include project-based learning, internships, collaborative assignments, and real-world problem solving in the curriculum. For example, many IS programs now have capstone projects with real industry clients, giving students hands-on experience with digital transformation projects or data analytics tasks (Sherman et al., 2022, Roth et al., 2025). Another trend is encouraging interdisciplinary learning. For instance, some IS programs allow or require minors in areas like UX, cybersecurity, analytics, or double majors, recognizing that IS professionals often sit at the intersection with other domains. Conversely, many business students outside IS now learn some IS concepts, e.g., a marketing major learns digital marketing analytics, which is essentially an IS application. Consequently, curriculum content has also evolved to include, among others, the disciplines of data analytics and business intelligence, cybersecurity, enterprise systems/ERP, programming with the focus on relevant languages like Python and Java, user experience (UX), design thinking, cloud computing, DevOps, AI, and machine learning basics, digital innovation and strategy.

In light of the above, it is evident that IS education has shifted to produce graduates who are technically competent, business savvy, and agile learners. The aim is someone who can not only build or manage a system, but also understand business needs, communicate with stakeholders, and continually adapt as new technologies emerge. This vision aligns with what employers stated—critical thinking, communication, and innovation capacity are key. The best programs incorporate real-world practice and emphasize problem-solving to ensure students can apply what they learn. Given the field's rapid change, educators also instill the importance of continuous learning. Students are taught how to learn new technologies and paradigms so they remain relevant throughout their careers.

3.6 Conclusions

From 2000 to 2025, the field of Information Systems has undergone a remarkable transformation. While at the turn of the millennium, IS was often viewed as a support function for automating transactions, producing reports, and keeping records, by 2025, IS is widely recognized as a strategic driver of innovation, integral to every aspect of business and daily life. The IS journey from 2000 to 2025 shows an arc of greater integration, democratization, and innovation. Information is more integrated across systems and accessible to more stakeholders. Nowadays, when approximately 5.56 billion people, which is nearly 68% of the global population, are internet users (Kemp, 2025), IS has penetrated deeply into every aspect of human activities.

Because technology is democratized, even small businesses or individuals can leverage capabilities such as cloud services and open-source tools that were once available only to large enterprises. At a time when innovation is relentless, and each year brings new technology to incorporate, the field of IS has never been more relevant or exciting. The ongoing task for IS practitioners and scholars is to guide this evolution in ways that maximize benefits such as efficiency, knowledge, connectivity, and opportunity, while minimizing risks like inequity, security threats, and ethical pitfalls. Undoubtedly, the story of IS from 2000 to 2025 is one of impressive achievements that sits at the intersection of technological potential and human ambition. For the decades to come, information systems will continue to shape our economic, organizational, and social future, setting the stage for new inventions and challenges.

References

Ali, M. (2023). *Information systems research: Foundations, design and theory.* Springer Nature. https://doi.org/10.1007/978-3-031-25470-3

Armbrust, M., Fox, A., Griffith, R., Joseph, A. D., Katz, R., Konwinski, A., Zaharia, M., et al. (2010). A view of cloud computing. *Communications of the ACM, 53*(4), 50–58. https://doi.org/10.1145/1721654.1721672

Asimily. (2025). *The top Internet of Things (IoT) cybersecurity breaches in 2025.* https://asimily.com/blog/the-top-internet-of-things-iot-cybersecurity-breaches-in-2025

Bharadwaj, A., El Sawy, O. A., Pavlou, P. A., & Venkatraman, N. V. (2013). Digital business strategy: Toward a next generation of insights. *MIS Quarterly, 37*(2), 471–482. https://doi.org/10.25300/MISQ/2013/37.2.03

Boston Consulting Group. (2020, October 27). *Flipping the odds of digital transformation success.* https://web-assets.bcg.com/c7/20/907821344bbb8ade98cbe10fc2b8/bcg-flipping-the-odds-of-digital-transformation-success-oct-2020.pdf

Brendel, A. B., & Börner, K. (2022). Review of design-oriented Green Information Systems research: Artifacts, evaluation, and future directions. *Sustainability, 14*(8), Article 4650. https://doi.org/10.3390/su14084650

Buyya, R., Yeo, C. S., Venugopal, S., Broberg, J., & Brandic, I. (2009). Cloud computing and emerging IT platforms: Vision, hype, and reality for delivering computing as the fifth utility. *Future Generation Computer Systems, 25*(6), 599–616. https://doi.org/10.1016/j.future.2008.12.001

Campbell-Kelly, M. (2009). The rise, fall, and resurrection of software as a service. *Communications of the ACM, 52*(5), 28–30. https://doi.org/10.1145/1506409.1506419

Chinta, S. (2021). Evaluating the impact of ERP cloud integration on organizational agility and decision-making. *International Journal of Creative Research Thoughts,* 9(6), h619–h631. https://doi.org/10.2139/ssrn.5046557

Choudhury, M., & Trimi, S. (2023, September). Reskilling in the age of AI. *Harvard Business Review*. https://hbr.org/2023/09/reskilling-in-the-age-of-ai

Chukwunweike, S. O. (2025). *Bridging the gap: Innovations in supply chain technology through ERP integration and intelligent automation.* Pennsylvania State University. https://www.researchgate.net/publication/386423768_Bridging_the_Gap_Innovations_in_Supply_Chain_Technology_Through_ERP_Integration_and_Intelligent_Automation

Cieślak, V., & Valor, C. (2025). An integrative review of employee resistance to digital transformation. *Cogent Business & Management, 12*(1), Article 2442550. https://doi.org/10.1080/23311975.2024.2442550

Comella Dorda, S., Wallnau, K., Seacord, R. C., & Robert, J. (2000, April 1). *A survey of legacy system modernization approaches* (Technical Note CMU/SEI-2000-TN-003). Software Engineering Institute, Carnegie Mellon University. https://www.sei.cmu.edu/library/a-survey-of-legacy-system-modernization-approaches/

Dalili, A., & Beheshtifar, M. (2018). Exploring the benefits of customer relationship management. *Specialty Journal of Knowledge Management, 3*(3), 10–16. https://sciarena.com/article/exploring-the-benefits-of-customer-relationship-management

Davis, F. D. (1989). Perceived usefulness, perceived ease of use, and user acceptance of information technology. *MIS Quarterly, 13*(3), 319–340. https://doi.org/10.2307/249008

Deloitte. (2023a, November 17). *Digital value and the industry context: Prioritizing digital investments and measures of success across industries.* https://www.deloitte.com/global/en/issues/digital/how-industry-orientation-informs-digital-transformation-in-business.html

Deloitte. (2023b, November 17). *Mapping digital transformation value: The metrics that matter.* https://www.deloitte.com/global/en/issues/digital/measurements-that-matter-for-calculation-digital-transformation-roi.html

DeLone, W. H., & McLean, E. R. (1992). Information systems success: The quest for the dependent variable. *Information Systems Research, 3*(1), 60–95. https://doi.org/10.1287/isre.3.1.60

DeLone, W. H., & McLean, E. R. (2003). The DeLone and McLean model of information systems success: A ten-year update. *Journal of Management Information Systems, 19*(4), 9–30. https://doi.org/10.1080/07421222.2003.11045748

Dikert, K., Paasivaara, M., & Lassenius, C. (2016). Challenges and success factors for large-scale agile transformations: A systematic literature review. *Journal of Systems and Software, 119*, 87–108. https://doi.org/10.1016/j.jss.2016.06.013

Entezarian, N., Bagheri, R., Rezazadeh, J., & Ayoade, J. (2025). NeuroIS: A systematic review of NeuroIS through bibliometric analysis. *Metrics, 2*(1), Article 4. https://doi.org/10.3390/metrics2010004

Eveleens, J., & Verhoef, C. (2009). The rise and fall of the CHAOS report figures. *IEEE Software, 27*(1), 30–36. https://doi.org/10.1109/MS.2009.154

Fowler, M., & Lewis, J. (2014). *Microservices: A definition of this new architectural term.* https://martinfowler.com/articles/microservices.html

Gafni, R., Kantsepolsky, B., & Sherman, S. (2025). Understanding and mitigating biases in AI systems: Insights and recommendations. In I. Venezia & R. Calipha (Eds.), *Behavioral finance: Beyond the basics* (pp. 1–26). World Scientific. https://doi.org/10.1142/9789811290633_0013

Gambal, M. J., Asatiani, A., & Kotlarsky, J. (2022). *Strategic innovation through outsourcing: A theoretical review.* arXiv. https://doi.org/10.48550/arXiv.2206.00982

Gede, D. U. (2023). The impact of strategic alignment on organizational performance: A study of functional area strategy fit. *Cogent Business & Management, 10*(1), Article 2247873. https://doi.org/10.1080/23311975.2023.2247873

Greenberg, A. (2024, April 14). *CyberAv3ngers: The Iranian saboteurs hacking water and gas systems worldwide. WIRED.* https://www.wired.com/story/cyberav3ngers-iran-hacking-water-and-gas-industrial-systems

Gunawan, A. I., Dewi, A. S., & Azis, E. (2024). Conceptual review of global outsourcing–offshoring in the last 20 years: Notes on systematic literature review. *Asian Management and Business Review, 4*(1), 16–31. https://doi.org/10.20885/AMBR.vol4.iss1.art2

Hadar, I., Kantsepolsky, B., Sadovski, E., & Sherman, S. (2025). Requirements engineering for accountable and conscious human-centered AI. In *Proceedings of the 33rd IEEE International Requirements Engineering Conference.* Valencia, Spain.

Haffke, I., Kalgovas, B., & Benlian, A. (2016, December). The role of the CIO and the CDO in an organization's digital transformation. In *Proceedings of the 37th International Conference on Information Systems (ICIS 2016).* Association for Information Systems. https://www.researchgate.net/publication/311653140

Hansmann, U., Merk, L., Nicklous, M. S., & Stober, T. (2013). *Pervasive computing handbook*. Springer.

Hevner, A. R., March, S. T., Park, J., & Ram, S. (2004). Design science in information systems research. *MIS Quarterly, 28*(1), 75–105. https://doi.org/10.2307/25148625

Holdsworth, J., Kosinski, M., & Jonker, A. (n.d.). What is a data warehouse? IBM. Retrieved October 11, 2025, from https://www.ibm.com/think/topics/data-warehouse

Hooda, K., & Mansukhani, A. (2025, March 12). *50 top smartphone usage stats to know in 2025*. Keywords Everywhere. https://keywordseverywhere.com/blog/smartphone-usage-stats/

Huawei Technologies Co., Ltd. (2023). Introduction to cloud computing. In *Cloud computing technology* (pp. 1–58). Springer. https://doi.org/10.1007/978-981-19-3026-3_1

IDC. (2025, May 16). *Salesforce named #1 CRM provider by IDC market share* [Press release]. Salesforce News. https://www.salesforce.com/news/stories/idc-crm-market-share-ranking-2025/

Infosecurity Magazine. (2025, February 12). *IoT data breach exposes 2.7 billion records*. https://www.infosecurity-magazine.com/news/iot-data-breach-exposes-27-billion

International Telecommunication Union [ITU]. (2005, November). *The Internet of Things: The Internet of Things*. https://www.itu.int/net/wsis/tunis/newsroom/stats/The-Internet-of-Things-2005.pdf

IoT Analytics. (2024, September 3). *State of IoT 2024: Number of connected IoT devices*. https://iot-analytics.com/number-connected-iot-devices/

Jadhav, P., Padalkar, K., Talokar, S., Gode, R., & Agme, R. (2024, June). Supplier selection analytics and visualization using IBM Cognos: An important step in procurement decision making and supply chain finance management. In *International Conference on Intelligent Computing and Big Data Analytics* (pp. 14–29). Springer Nature.

Jamshidi, P., Pahl, C., Mendonça, N. C., Lewis, J., & Tilkov, S. (2018). Microservices: The journey so far and challenges ahead. *IEEE Software, 35*(3), 24–35. https://doi.org/10.1109/MS.2018.2141039

Jardine, A. K. S., Lin, D., & Banjevic, D. (2006). A review on machinery diagnostics and prognostics implementing condition-based maintenance. *Mechanical Systems and Signal Processing, 20*(7), 1483–1510. https://doi.org/10.1016/j.ymssp.2005.09.012

Jose, J. A. C., et al. (2024). Smart shelf system for customer behavior tracking in retail. *Sensors, 24*(2), Article 367. https://doi.org/10.3390/s24020367

Kantsepolsky, B. (2025). Quantum transformation of electrical systems: The potential for decentralization of infrastructures, governance, and organizational structures. In S. Sareen, T. H. Jackson Inderberg, & P. O. Eikeland (Eds.), *Are low-carbon futures decentralized? Visions and praxis in governing collective electric systems* (pp. 38–49). Edward Elgar. https://doi.org/10.4337/9781035355198.00009

Kemp, S. (2025). *Digital 2025: Global overview report.* DataReportal. https://datareportal.com/global-digital-overview

Khademi, A., Foley, D., Lee, S., & Honavar, V. (2019). Fairness in algorithmic decision making: An excursion through the lens of causality. In *Proceedings of the 2019 World Wide Web Conference (WWW '19)* (pp. 2907–2914). Association for Computing Machinery. https://doi.org/10.1145/3308558.3313559

Kherrazi, S., & Roquilly, C. (2025). Managing digital transformation in contemporary contexts: Are classical change management frameworks still relevant? *Journal of Change Management, 25*(2), 85–115. https://doi.org/10.1080/14697017.2025.2494508

Koli, S., Singh, R., Rana, P., Aggarwal, A., & Dumka, A. (2023, February). Salesforce technology: A complete CRM solution on the cloud. In *2023 2nd Edition of IEEE Delhi Section Flagship Conference (DELCON)* (pp. 1–5). IEEE. https://doi.org/10.1109/DELCON57910.2023.10127497

KPMG. (2023). *Global tech report 2023: Secure value by navigating uncertainty with confidence.* KPMG International. https://kpmg.com/xx/en/our-insights/ai-and-technology/kpmg-global-tech-report-2023.html

KPMG. (2024, June). *Transforming the enterprise of the future: The new champions in a digital era* (Global Transformation Study). KPMG International. https://assets.kpmg.com/content/dam/kpmg/xx/pdf/2024/06/Transforming-the-enterprise-of-the-future.pdf

Kumar, N. (2025, July 5). *Internet of Things (IoT) statistics: Market & growth data.* DemandSage. https://www.demandsage.com/internet-of-things-statistics/

Lamberty, A., & Kreyenschmidt, J. (2025). Technical, process-related, and sustainability requirements for IoT-based temperature monitoring in fruit and vegetable supply chains. *Discover Food, 5*, Article 151. https://doi.org/10.1007/s44187-025-00427-1

Laudon, K. C., & Laudon, J. P. (2021). *Management information systems: Managing the digital firm* (17th ed.). Pearson.

Li, X., Zhang, Y., Osborne, C., Zhou, M., Jin, Z., & Liu, H. (2024). *Systematic literature review of commercial participation in open source software.* arXiv. https://doi.org/10.48550/arXiv.2405.16880

Markovich, S., Achwal, N., & Queathem, E. (2017, October 10). *Stripe: Helping money move on the internet* (Kellogg School of Management Case No. 5-416-756 [KE1042]). Kellogg School of Management, Northwestern University. https://www.kellogg.northwestern.edu/academics-research/research/detail/2017/stripe-helpingmoney-move-on-the-internet/

Matt, C., Hess, T., & Benlian, A. (2015). Digital transformation strategies. *Business & Information Systems Engineering, 57*(5), 339–343. https://doi.org/10.1007/s12599-015-0401-5

McKinsey & Company. (2025, July 14). *We're all techies now: Digital skill building for the future.* McKinsey & Company. Retrieved August 26, 2025, from https://www.

mckinsey.com/capabilities/people-and-organizational-performance/our-insights/we-are-all-techies-now-digital-skill-building-for-the-future

Milioris, K., Konstantopoulos, C., Papageorgiou, K., & Skordoulis, M. (2022). The use of healthcare information systems: A research study about health professionals' needs. *International Journal of Healthcare Technology and Management, 19*(1), 77–89. https://doi.org/10.1504/IJHTM.2022.123580

Nabil, D. H., Rahman, M. H., Chowdhury, A. H., & Menezes, B. C. (2023). Managing supply chain performance using a real-time Microsoft Power BI dashboard by action design research (ADR) method. *Cogent Engineering, 10*(2), Article 2257924. https://doi.org/10.1080/23311916.2023.2257924

Oliveira, A., & Bernardino, J. (2020). Evaluating self-service BI and analytics tools for SMEs. In *Proceedings of the 17th International Joint Conference on e-Business and Telecommunications (ICETE 2020)* (Vol. 3, pp. 89–97). SCITEPRESS. https://doi.org/10.5220/0009820400890097

Orlikowski, W. J., & Scott, S. V. (2008). Sociomateriality: Challenging the separation of technology, work, and organization. *Academy of Management Annals, 2*(1), 433–474. https://doi.org/10.1080/19416520802211644

Pearlson, K. E., Saunders, C. S., & Galletta, D. F. (2024). *Managing and using information systems: A strategic approach* (8th ed.). Wiley.

Pech, M., Vrchota, J., & Bednář, J. (2021). Predictive maintenance and intelligent sensors in smart factories: A review. *Sensors, 21*(4), 1470. https://doi.org/10.3390/s21041470

Petrova, B. (2021, November 17). *Augmented analytics guide: Definition, examples & use cases*. Reveal. https://www.revealbi.io/blog/augmented-analytics-definition examples-use-cases

Phillips, J., & Klein, J. D. (2022). Change management: From theory to practice. *TechTrends, 67*(1), 189–197. https://doi.org/10.1007/s11528-022-00775-0

Pohludka, M. (2018). Implementation and unification of the ERP system in a company: ERP systems as integrated applications. *Sustainability, 10*(8), 2916. https://doi.org/10.3390/su10082916

Power, D. J. (2002). *Decision support systems: Concepts and resources for managers*. Faculty Book Gallery. https://scholarworks.uni.edu/facbook/67

Rahimi, B., Nadri, H., Lotfnezhad Afshar, H., & Timpka, T. (2018). A systematic review of the Technology Acceptance Model in health informatics. *Applied Clinical Informatics, 9*(3), 604–634. https://doi.org/10.1055/s-0038-1668091

Raković, L. (2022). What about the chief digital officer? A literature review. *Sustainability, 14*(8), 4696. https://doi.org/10.3390/su14084696

RevealBI. (2025, February 10). *What is augmented analytics? Definition, examples & use cases*. Reveal. https://www.revealbi.io/blog/articles/augmented-analytics-definition-examples-use-

Rizqy, A. A., Puspitasari, W., & Saputra, M. (2022). An empirical evaluation of IT adoption for Microsoft Dynamics 365: A case study in the manufacturing industry. In *2022 International Conference on Advancement in Data Science, E-learning and Information Systems (ICADEIS)* (pp. 1–4). IEEE. https://doi.org/10.1109/ICADEIS56544.2022.10037501

Roth, I., Kantsepolsky, B., & Sherman, S. (2025). Jumping into deep waters: The impact of industry experience on student motivation. *Eurasia Journal of Mathematics, Science and Technology Education, 21*(11), em2737. https://doi.org/10.29333/ejmste/17389

Satyanarayanan, M. (2001). Pervasive computing: Vision and challenges. *IEEE Personal Communications, 8*(4), 10–17. https://doi.org/10.1109/98.943998

Saulnier, B. M. (2016). Towards a 21st-century information systems education: High-impact practices and essential learning outcomes. *Issues in Information Systems, 17*(1), 168–177. https://doi.org/10.48009/1_iis_2016_168-177

Schneider, J., Jung, S., & Shareef, A. (2024). The lakehouse: State of the art on concepts and technologies. *SN Computer Science, 5*, 449. https://doi.org/10.1007/s42979-024-02737-0

Shepherd, N. G., Lou, B., & Rudd, J. M. (2024). Going with the gut: Exploring top management team intuition in strategic decision-making. *Journal of Business Research, 181*, Article 114740. https://doi.org/10.1016/j.jbusres.2024.114740

Sherman, S., Kantsepolsky, B., & Roth, I. (2022). Teamwork skills: The case of a practical course. *Issues in Information Systems, 23*(2), 20–28. https://doi.org/10.48009/2_iis_2022_102

Song, H., Ren, K., Chen, C., & Jensen, C. S. (2024). A survey on hybrid transactional and analytical processing (HTAP). *The VLDB Journal*. https://doi.org/10.1007/s00778-024-00858-9

Standish Group. (1994). *The CHAOS report: Project outcomes and success rates*. Standish Group International. https://www.csus.edu/indiv/v/velianitis/161/chaosreport.pdf

Standish Group. (2012). *CHAOS manifesto 2012*. Standish Group International. https://cs.calvin.edu/courses/cs/262/kvlinden/resources/CHAOSManifesto2012.pdf

Subashini, S., & Kavitha, V. (2011). A survey on security issues in service delivery models of cloud computing. *Journal of Network and Computer Applications, 34*(1), 1–11. https://doi.org/10.1016/j.jnca.2010.07.006

Sujatmiko, S., Krisnanto, B., & Sasmita, H. (2024). Global supply chain management: Trends, challenges, and strategies. *Vifada Management and Digital Business, 1*(2), 20–38. https://doi.org/10.70184/bwafw902

Tamayo, J., Doumi, L., Goel, S., Kovács-Ondrejkovic, O., & Sadun, R. (2023, September–October). Reskilling in the age of AI. *Harvard Business Review*. https://hbr.org/2023/09/reskilling-in-the-age-of-ai

Teubner, R. A., & Stockhinger, J. (2020). Understanding information systems strategy in the digital age: A literature review. *Journal of Strategic Information Systems, 29*(4), Article 101642. https://doi.org/10.1016/j.jsis.2020.101642

The Standish Group International, Inc. (1995). *The CHAOS report*. https://www.classes.cs.uchicago.edu/archive/2014/fall/51210-1/required.reading/Standish.Group.ChaosReport.pdf

Trist, E. L., & Bamforth, K. W. (1951). Some social and psychological consequences of the longwall method of coal-getting. *Human Relations, 4*(1), 3–38. https://doi.org/10.1177/001872675100400101

Vaish, P., Shrivastava, S., & Sen, S. (2020). Business intelligence: Escalation of data warehousing and data mining for effective decision making. *International Journal of Advanced Science and Technology, 29*(5), 1377–1388.

Venkatesh, V., Morris, M. G., Davis, G. B., & Davis, F. D. (2003). User acceptance of information technology: Toward a unified view. *MIS Quarterly, 27*(3), 425–478. https://doi.org/10.2307/30036540

Vial, G. (2019). Understanding digital transformation: A review and a research agenda. *Journal of Strategic Information Systems, 28*(2), 118–144. https://doi.org/10.1016/j.jsis.2019.01.003

Wahsheh, F. R., Marie, Z., Farea, M. M., Al-Haithami, W. A., Mohamad, F. S., & Bisht, N. (2023, October). Operational level system: Transaction processing system and decision making. In *2023 International Conference on Computer Science and Emerging Technologies (CSET)* (pp. 1–7). IEEE. https://doi.org/10.1109/CSET58993.2023.10346773

Wan, Z., Gao, Z., Di Renzo, M., & Hanzo, L. (2022). The road to Industry 4.0 and beyond: A communications-, information-, and operation technology collaboration perspective. *IEEE Network, 36*(6), 157–164. https://doi.org/10.1109/MNET.008.2100484

Watson, H. J., & Wixom, B. H. (2007). The current state of business intelligence. *Computer, 40*(9), 96–99. https://doi.org/10.1109/MC.2007.331

Weddle, B., Hancock, B., Stefanski, H., & Glover, M. (2025, July 14). *We're all techies now: Digital skill building for the future.* McKinsey & Company. https://www.mckinsey.com/capabilities/people-and-organizational-performance/our-insights/we-are-all-techies-now-digital-skill-building-for-the-future

Westervelt, R. (2020, July). *IoT device security risks prompt manufacturers to adopt PKI security, provisioning certificates during production* (IDC Report No. US46704620). DigiCert. Retrieved August 26, 2025, from https://www.digicert.com/content/dam/digicert/pdfs/idc-iot-device-security-paper.pdf

Wixom, B. H. (2007). *Key components of business intelligence systems: Data warehouses, ETL tools, OLAP, and data mining.* Decision Support Study, University of Oregon. https://scholarsbank.uoregon.edu/xmlui/bitstream/handle/1794/9527/BIComponents.pdf

XDuce. (2025, March 7). *Interactive executive dashboard for real-time financial insights.* https://xduce.com/case-studies/interactive-executive-dashboard-for-real-time-financial-insights/

Zaman, M., Puryear, N., Abdelwahed, S., & Zohrabi, N. (2024). A review of IoT-based smart city development and management. *Smart Cities, 7*(3), 1462–1501. https://doi.org/10.3390/smartcities7030061

4

Challenges and Abuses of Information Systems

4.1 Introduction

The twenty-first century is characterized by an unprecedented growth of, and reliance on, information systems. From the complex algorithms driving social media platforms to the intricate networks powering critical infrastructure, these systems have revolutionized our lives. How else can we store, filter, manipulate, and analyze the vast amounts of information affecting our daily lives? Humanity has created an ever-evolving living mechanism of information management. However, this reliance comes with a dark underbelly—a multitude of challenges and abuses that threaten the very foundations of our *digital* society. This chapter delves into the labyrinth of regulatory, ethical, privacy, security, and data authenticity challenges and abuses that affect and infect information systems. To focus on exploring the impact and potential solutions for each of the challenges and abuses, and to discuss future challenges related to AI and QIS, we present them separately. In practice, they are interconnected, and a single element cannot be addressed without affecting the others.

Information systems, as we have defined previously in this book, are any combination of hardware, software, data, networking, people, and procedures that collect, store, process, and disseminate information. While the vast majority of information systems are interconnected, some are independent or air-gapped from global cyberspace due to regulatory or security concerns. In

B. Kantsepolsky, L. Topor, *Managing Information Singularity*,
https://doi.org/10.1007/978-3-032-26223-3_4

this chapter, we mainly address the interconnected systems that have a greater impact on society. These information systems have multiple vulnerabilities, which we refer to as challenges and abuses. While it is possible to address sole vulnerabilities of hardware, software, networking, and procedures, and those of collection, storage, process, and dissemination of information, we refer to the vulnerabilities of information systems as a whole. This holistic systemic perspective approach contributes to the novelty and applicability of the study and is used for setting the scene for the concluding chapters of the book, discussing the future of IS. Some of these challenges and abuses can be dealt with. That is, vulnerabilities can be tackled and "fixed" with relatively little compromise and without making systems more complex and less efficient. Yet, other challenges and abuses also hold core philosophical dilemmas—Catch-22s—that make it harder to address them. We elaborate on this issue throughout this chapter.

There are five primary challenges and abuses we have identified while applying a holistic systemic vision to information systems. The first challenge deals with ethical dilemmas of technology companies, such as ethical responsibility, liability, accountability, algorithmic biases and discrimination, privacy, surveillance concerns, and the digital divide. The latter is especially true for less developed countries, which have either stayed or will stay behind in the global IS race. We present and elaborate on several cases, including the Cambridge Analytica scandal, algorithmic bias in tenant screening, price discrimination, and predictive policing. Chained to this first challenge is also a policy challenge.

The second challenge we address is regulation and derived policies. These challenges stem from differences between state policies, international business policies, and individual rights and desires. We present and discuss privacy regulations like the DSA (Digital Services Act) and the DMA (Digital Markets Act).

Third, we address privacy-related challenges, assuming information is privately owned by an individual or a company. Information, as was suggested by Topor, is harder to block or facilitate than flu or Coronaviruses (Topor, 2024). This is further complicated due to the global nature of the internet and information systems. Using the European Union's GDPR (General Data Protection Regulation) as a model, we present cases of private information abuse by governments, corporations, and individuals and discuss whether they should be regarded as intentional abuse or a mistake. Of course, privacy-related challenges overlap with ethical and policy-oriented challenges. Rather than dealing with the question of whether our private information is fully ours and do we, the people, have a right to own and control it, we focus on the issue of whether, when, and how a company or a government can own and use it.

Fourth, we address security challenges. Regulatory and privacy-related issues tremendously affect security challenges. For instance, complete isolation of a system and fewer privileges is a more secure policy, although less comfortable than an open and trust-oriented one. Without having a goal of surveying the entire field of information and cybersecurity, we focus on and analyze cases of cybercrime and espionage, including theft of information by foreign adversaries of a country.

The fifth and final challenge we address is data authenticity. Assuming we have a system that collects, stores, processes, and disseminates information, how can one know if the information we have collected is real and authentic? In this part, we discuss the J.P. Morgan Chase lawsuit against Charlie Javice, the creator of *Frank*, who is accused of manipulating customer information to gather funding, as well as the case of Brexit and the suggested influence of fake accounts on it. We also discuss the issue of scientific misconduct and data fabrication. Emerging technologies like Generative AI and deepfake make the topic of data authenticity even more intriguing. Further, AI systems like ChatGPT have been "inventing" new data, histories, and even fake publications, which were often given as references (Moran, 2023). The danger is not just fake references but the supercharged creation and dissemination of disinformation. For instance, both neo-Nazis and radical Islamists create and spread antisemitic material to supercharge hatred against Jews. They use AI tools to generate text for fake conspiracy theories and use graphical AI tools to spread images and memes (Topor, 2025; Stenzler & Klempner, 2024).

The challenges and abuses of information systems in the twenty-first century are complex, multifaceted, and therefore exciting for policymakers, businesses, citizens, and, of course, the IS community. Addressing them effectively requires a holistic approach that combines ethical considerations, sound regulatory and policy frameworks, robust privacy and security measures, and all stakeholders' commitment to data authenticity. By fostering collaboration between governments, industry, civil society, and individuals, we offer a systemic approach to navigate this labyrinth, better understand vulnerabilities in the existing systems, and design more sane and robust information systems in the future. We further address these challenges in the concluding chapter of this book in the context of future developments in AI (Artificial Intelligence) and QIS (Quantum Information Science).

4.2 Vulnerabilities of Information Systems

Information systems, as defined in the introduction to this chapter, are any combination of hardware, software, data, networking, people, and procedures that collect, store, process, and disseminate information. All these building blocks and actions can be manipulated and abused by malicious users, whether cybercriminals or state agents of a foreign adversary. Similar to the vulnerabilities of networking within cyberspace, the vulnerabilities of information systems can be related to technical aspects, processes, and procedures, as well as social engineering. As defined by Timothy Casey (2007), the main threats to information/data include copying, destruction, manipulation, and theft of it (Casey, 2007; Dobrovoljc et al., 2017). This definition was accepted by the *Tallinn Manual on the international law applicable to cyber warfare (2017),* which refers to cyber warfare and the abuse of information. According to the manual, the main threats of cyber warfare—cyber-attacks—are espionage, propaganda, denial of service (DoS), data modification, and infrastructure manipulation or sabotage (Schmitt, 2017; Geers, 2008).

Some IS vulnerabilities can be exploited by ordinary system users, while others can be created by an external actor; some are intentional, and some are not; some may create minimal damage, while others may cause a devastating impact. Interestingly, some vulnerabilities can be considered as more legal than others. Once vulnerabilities are exploited, they may have an immediate impact, while in many cases, the impact could remain delayed or even undetected. Further, some of the vulnerabilities can be exploited by those with minimal skills, while in other cases, a more professional set of skills is required. In Table 4.1 below, we summarize, based on the Tallinn Manual and

Table 4.1 Main threats for information systems (A conceptual model)

		Threats			
		Copy	Theft	Destruction	Manipulation
Information System Components	Hardware		+	+	+
	Software	+	+	+	+
	People				+
	Data	+	+	+	+
	Procedures				+
	Network			+	+
Actions Made with Information Systems	Collect				+
	Store	+	+	+	
	Process	+			+
	Disseminate				+

Casey's White Paper, the main threats to information systems. This summary is conceptual and not exhaustive. However, it is important to note that many of these categories are interconnected. Based on our systemic vision approach, we further analyze case studies based on this mapping. Hereafter, we refer to these vulnerabilities as challenges and abuses.

Information systems should be designed to manage information in an ethical, legal, secure, and efficient manner. A conceptual review of each information system component, as presented in Table 4.1, suggests that this design is difficult to develop and implement. The first component of information systems is hardware, and it can be stolen, damaged, or destroyed (or copied, but we refer to information only). Manipulations can also be done to adjust its usability, for instance, actual measurements taken by hardware can be manipulated, as was done in the infamous Stuxnet virus. Second, software can be stolen, destroyed, or manipulated. Third, people can be manipulated so that their behavior will not be compliant with the predefined procedures, input to the system, or processing of the system's output will vary, sometimes in a way not initially intended by the design of an information system. As a result, data can be stolen, destroyed, or manipulated. Finally, networking can be manipulated or halted altogether, and others could eavesdrop on it.

In real-world scenarios, while taking a holistic approach, these seemingly "fixable" threats translate into more complex challenges and abuses. The growing interconnectedness and complexity of systems make them harder to secure and manage, increasing the attack surface for malicious actors but also opening these systems to abuse by mistake or by actions that are short of abuse, like adaptive pricing or biases (while these two examples are abuse, they can be executed legally). There are, of course, more concerns. For instance, aspects of information privacy and ownership vary by jurisdiction. That is, while information may be private, countries like Russia, China, Iran, North Korea, Saudi Arabia, and many others seek to control it for monitoring and regulation. Other countries allow regulating the data-driven market less, which often allows for the abuse of information, like in the case of the United States (Topor, 2024).

Interestingly, though, some regulations like the Provisions on Regulating and Facilitating Cross-Border Data Flow (a draft for comments in September 2023), suggested by the Chinese Cyberspace Administration of China (CAC), are aimed to protect private information as CAC seeks to restrict and regulate the private information of Chinese citizens. This approach is similar to the European approach to information privacy, as expressed and implemented in the renowned GDPR (Li et al., 2019). Thus, the European and Chinese approaches to information privacy, as an example, are much closer than they are to the American approach to information privacy, which is regulated by the market but not so by Uncle Sam (however, some states have initiated a process to change their privacy approach) (Bellamy, 2023; O'Connor, 2018).

4.3 The Main Dilemmas/Challenges of Information Systems

The vulnerabilities and threats to information systems, as presented in Table 4.1, are opportunities for abusers. This raises five main dilemmas, or challenges, about ethics, regulation and policies, privacy, security, and data authenticity. The first dilemma concerns ethics. The pervasive use of information systems raises profound ethical questions. Algorithmic bias, for example, can perpetuate discrimination in areas like employment, housing, loan applications, court rulings, policing, intellectual property, and much more. For instance, facial recognition technology, combined with AI, while touted for security purposes, raises concerns about mass surveillance and the potential for profiling and targeting individuals. The collection and use of personal data often fall into ethical gray areas, blurring the lines between individual autonomy and the need for data-driven solutions, like in the cases of using biometric information for security, from biometric passports to AI-driven street cameras for domestic security (Sham et al., 2023; Almeida et al., 2022; Michael et al., 2022). Addressing these ethical dilemmas requires a multipronged approach. Firstly, robust ethical frameworks need to be developed and implemented, guiding the design, development, and use of information systems. Secondly, transparency and accountability are crucial. Individuals should be informed about how their data is collected and used, and have control over it. Public discourse and engagement are essential to foster responsible innovation and ensure that technology serves humanity, not the other way around, especially in liberal democracies. This ethical dilemma brings us to the next one—regulation and policy (Gafni et al., 2025).

The second dilemma is regulation and policy. The rapid evolution of information systems often outpaces existing regulatory and policy frameworks. This creates gaps and inconsistencies, leaving critical issues like data privacy and cybersecurity inadequately addressed. Additionally, the fragmented nature of policy across different jurisdictions further complicates matters, making it difficult to effectively regulate global platforms and technologies. That is, one country may decide that a certain policy is ethical and legal while another one may decide the very opposite. For instance, the GDPR is a regulation adopted in 2016 by the European Union (EU) and enforced in 2018. It is a legal framework that regulates how personal data is collected, used, and stored by organizations. Meta, just as an example, was fined $1.3 billion in 2023 for violating EU data privacy regulations while it acted in the way it acts in the United States, where Meta's data policies were legal (Topor, 2024; Satariano, 2023). Another recent regulatory example is the EU AI Act, which is dedicated to governing the use of AI systems within the EU (Hartmann et al., 2025). Bridging these policy gaps requires international cooperation and collaboration, an extremely difficult task to achieve in our power-driven realist world. Multilateral agreements on data privacy and security standards are crucial, as is the harmonization of national regulations. Governments need to be proactive in adapting existing frameworks and developing new ones to address emerging challenges. Furthermore, public participation in policymaking processes is essential to ensure that regulations reflect the needs and concerns of citizens (Rustad & Koenig, 2019; Bygrave, 2010). Some countries and companies protect user data, while others use or abuse it.

The third dilemma is privacy. The vast collection and analysis of personal data pose significant privacy risks. From targeted advertising to social engineering scams, individuals' data can be exploited for malicious purposes. The increasing sophistication of data collection techniques and the emergence of new technologies like generative AI and deepfakes further exacerbate these concerns. For instance, technology companies often use and sometimes abuse personal data in various ways that can breach privacy, often without users being fully aware of it. Apart from sharing information with third parties, they often collect information that is not necessary for their functionality in an overreach of permission. In other cases, they use collected data to create behavioral profiles and deliver highly targeted ads. This profiling can be invasive and manipulative. Of course, as was "leaked" by Snowden, governments often team up with private companies for optimal surveillance, known as the public-private partnership (PPP) (Macaskill & Dance, 2013; Chin & Lin, 2022).

Protecting privacy in the digital age requires a multi-layered approach. Strong data protection laws are essential, granting individuals control over their personal information and establishing clear rules for its collection, use, and disclosure. Additionally, technological solutions like anonymization and encryption can help mitigate privacy risks. Yet, many countries see encryption and anonymization as abusive tools and thus regulate against them. For instance, not just Russia and China oppose encryption and anonymization. The United Kingdom Online Safety Act, which became law in late October 2023, aims to make the internet a safer place for users, particularly children

(Guest, 2023). It censors some information while it also enables the British government to access private data (Macaskill & Dance, 2013; Chin & Lin, 2022).

The fourth dilemma is cybersecurity, obviously connected to the rest. Information systems are constantly under attack by cybercriminals or by adversarial state agents/state proxies that seek to steal data, disrupt operations, or extort money (Badman, 2023). The increasing sophistication of cyberattacks and the interconnected nature of systems make them increasingly vulnerable. The use of vulnerabilities in software and hardware, coupled with human error and/or manipulation, often provides the entry point for attackers (Casey, 2007). Strengthening cybersecurity requires a multifaceted approach. Investing in secure infrastructure and software development practices is crucial, as is regular security testing and vulnerability patching. Implementing strong access controls and user education programs can further reduce the risk of cyberattacks. Additionally, international cooperation is essential to combat cross-border cybercrime and share best practices in cybersecurity defense, an initiative that was strengthened with the 2001 Budapest Convention on Cybercrime (effective from July 2004; Wicki-Birchler, 2020).

The fifth dilemma is related to data authenticity and disinformation. Assuming a government or a company has addressed all of the other mentioned challenges, how can they be sure that actual data entries are real? Perhaps they were fabricated or manipulated? The rise of deepfakes and other forms of synthetic information or media poses a serious threat to the authenticity of information, mainly online. Malicious actors can use generative AI and deepfake technologies to create fake news, spread misinformation, and manipulate public opinion, input false readings, and so on. This has significant implications for any regime and any business (Guess & Lyons, 2020; Shuker & Topor, 2021; Blasius & Thiessen, 2015; Rossetti & Zaman, 2023). Even if espionage and global power struggles seem distant topics, even scientists and university professors can fake data. For instance, a prominent Harvard Business School professor has been accused of alleged data falsification in mid-2023. Sadly, there are many cases of scientific misconduct (Yang, 2023). Combating disinformation requires a multipronged approach, as in the other cases. Technology companies need to develop and deploy tools for detecting and flagging deepfakes and other forms of manipulated content. Media literacy campaigns can empower individuals to critically evaluate information online and identify potential biases or manipulations. Additionally, fact-checking organizations and social media platforms need to work collaboratively to debunk misinformation and promote trustworthy sources of information. Importantly, we all have to invest in information and online literacy.

It is important to understand that the dilemmas/challenges of information systems are complex, and addressing them effectively requires a holistic, systemic vision approach, taking ethics, policy, privacy, security, and data authenticity into account. In the next sections of this chapter, we discuss in detail each one of the information system dilemmas/challenges.

4.3.1 Ethical Challenges of Information Systems

The exponential rise of data and information systems, coupled with the ubiquitous presence of the internet, has ushered in an era of unprecedented technological advancement. Information is now everywhere. However, this progress has not been without its challenges, particularly regarding the ethical dilemmas posed by these technologies. The realm of ethical concerns surrounding data, information systems, and the internet is complex and multifaceted. Some challenges include policies of technology companies, algorithmic bias and discrimination, privacy, information ownership, the digital divide, and more. For instance, is it ethical to let a machine determine a person's future regarding employment, housing, and even imprisonment? In a more basic view, is it even ethical to collect a person's private information in the first place? Our private information is ours, and just as one would expect her/his bicycle not to be stolen, one should expect her/his private information not to be stolen and abused, especially in an AI-driven world (Gafni et al., 2024).

Why do ethical concerns emerge? Mainly because information systems are designed and developed by people who have biases. These biases could be cultural, educational, religious, or any other kind of preference. Some of the primary ethical concerns in the digital age pertain to data collection and privacy. With the exponential growth of data generation and collection through various online platforms, individuals' privacy rights are increasingly being jeopardized. The indiscriminate collection of personal data without explicit consent raises questions about autonomy, consent, and individual rights. Moreover, the commodification of personal data by tech giants for targeted advertising and profiling purposes raises concerns about the exploitation of individuals' information for commercial gains (Zuboff, 2023; Mann et al., 2003). This tension between the benefits of data-driven technologies and the protection of privacy underscores the need for robust regulatory frameworks and ethical guidelines to govern data collection practices.

The design and deployment of information systems give rise to ethical dilemmas, particularly concerning issues of fairness, bias, and discrimination. Algorithms and machine learning models used in various applications are designed by people with biases. The opacity of these systems further exacerbates the problem, as individuals may not be aware of the factors influencing decisions that affect their lives. This is particularly true for people with less orientation in technological systems. Moreover, the potential for unintended consequences, such as algorithmic manipulation and unintended outcomes, poses significant ethical challenges for designers and policymakers (Schwartz et al., 2022).

The internet, often heralded as a tool for democratization and empowerment, also presents ethical dilemmas concerning governance, censorship, and digital rights. The increasing centralization of online platforms and the concentration of power in the hands of a few tech giants raise concerns about monopolistic practices and the stifling of competition. At the same time, the rise of state surveillance and censorship efforts in the name of national security threatens fundamental rights to freedom of expression and privacy. The tension between security and privacy rights underscores the need for robust legal frameworks and international cooperation to safeguard digital rights and promote a free and open internet (Lyon, 2001). It is the authority of the state and the international society to decide on policies and ethical suggestions. However, companies have a significant say in these dilemmas as well (Topor, 2024).

Technology companies, either almost entirely free or under the tight regulation of a state, as the creators and custodians of these powerful technologies, and platforms, hold immense responsibility regarding the ethical implications of their practices. This responsibility encompasses aspects such as data collection and use, transparency around algorithms and decision-making processes, and mitigating potential harm. However, ensuring accountability in the digital landscape remains a significant challenge. The somewhat decentralized and global nature of the internet makes it difficult to establish and enforce clear guidelines around data practices and ethical conduct. Additionally, the opaqueness of algorithms and the lack of user control over their application further exacerbate accountability issues (Fishman, 2022). For instance, as explained later, Facebook admitted it had failed to protect user data and failed to prevent manipulation of its platform while around 87 million users were abused by Cambridge Analytica (Isaak & Hanna, 2018).

The increasing reliance on AI systems in decision-making processes across various sectors, from loan approvals to criminal justice, raises concerns about potential bias and discrimination. Algorithmic bias can arise from various factors, including the historical data used to train them, potentially perpetuating existing societal biases or inherent design flaws. For instance, in early 2023 in the United States, the tenant-screening service of SafeRent was accused of algorithmic bias. In a lawsuit filed against the service and the landlord who used it, some discriminated renters accused SafeRent of racism as the algorithms used by the service discriminate against Black and Hispanic renters, violating the 1968 Fair Housing Act, which prohibits discrimination based on race, disability, religion, or national origin (Johnson, 2023; Kirchner & Goldstein).

Additional ethical concerns can include issues related to price discrimination, predictive policing, and AI-based and biased decisions. From a privacy perspective, which will be addressed in detail later, in the digital age, personal data constitutes a valuable resource, often collected through the online domain. However, the pervasive collection and analysis of this data raise significant concerns about individual privacy—do we have a right to privacy? In this regard, people now worry about the state, but even non-state surveillance is made with data collection and pattern analysis, including biometric and facial recognition or location tracking, and more. While advocates argue that these technologies can enhance security and prevent crime, critics raise concerns about the erosion of civil liberties, the potential for misuse, and the creation of a "panoptic society" where individuals feel or are constantly watched and monitored. As Edward Snowden revealed in 2013, the United States is engaged in mass surveillance no less than China or Russia, raising concerns about the thin line between [national] security and individual privacy (Macaskill & Dance, 2013). In an example from both China and the United States, the Chinese application Temu was sued in February 2024 by more than a dozen plaintiffs all around the United States. Temu is accused of bypassing users' phone security and gaining access to private information, including private messages, biometric data, and usage information—something that might be legal elsewhere but not in the United States (Law, 2024).

The digital divide is another interesting dilemma. The term "digital divide" refers to the gap between those who have access to digital technologies and the internet and those who do not. It encompasses disparities in access to hardware (such as IoT sensors, computers, smartphones, and tablets), internet connectivity, digital literacy, and skills related to using technology effectively. The digital divide can exist within countries, between urban and rural areas, across socioeconomic groups, and even between different demographic categories such as age or ethnicity. The uneven distribution of access to information and communication technologies (ICTs) creates a digital divide, further marginalizing disadvantaged communities. Those who have access to information [systems] can have an unfair advantage over others. This is true for states but also for companies that mishandle data (Selwyn, 2004). For instance, as mentioned previously in this chapter, Meta was fined $1.3 billion in 2023 for the unlawful transfer of European users' data to the United States (Satariano, 2023). In another example, Google was fined $1.7 billion by the European Union in 2019 for unfair use and blocking of certain information, which violated the online advertising market (Satariano, 2019). This disparity can manifest in limited access to educational resources, job opportunities, healthcare services, and even basic communication channels. The digital divide exacerbates existing inequalities, hindering social mobility and perpetuating economic and social disparities.

While the digital divide regards the right to access services and information, mainly to follow global development, there is another concern regarding access. However, this concern deals not with access to but with access privileges. That is, who can legally and ethically access our data, how and what information can be used for. One particular case of ethical abuse of information systems is the Cambridge Analytica scandal. The scandal revolved around the unethical collection of private information from Facebook users by Cambridge Analytica, a now-defunct British political consulting firm, to influence public opinion and policy during the 2016 US presidential election. The incident highlighted the risks associated with the mass use of social networks like Facebook, where personal data can be exploited for malicious purposes. This includes some ethical concerns as the methods employed by Cambridge Analytica exploited vulnerabilities in Facebook's data-sharing policies, allowing them to access vast amounts of personal information without users' consent. Through sophisticated algorithms and psychographic profiling techniques, the firm manipulated individuals' beliefs, emotions, and voting intentions. By micro-targeting specific demographic groups with tailored messaging, they aimed to sway election outcomes in favor of their clients (Lapowsky, 2019; Wylie, 2019).

The ramifications of the Cambridge Analytica scandal were profound and far-reaching. It sparked widespread outrage over the misuse of personal data and raised concerns about the integrity of democratic processes. Facebook faced intense scrutiny and regulatory backlash for its lax data protection measures, resulting in congressional hearings, fines, and heightened public distrust. Responding to the scandal, the United States Federal Trade Commission fined Facebook $5 billion for privacy violations in July 2019, and the British Information Commissioner's Office (ICO) had earlier fined Facebook £500,000 on 25 October 2018. Cambridge Analytica itself was not fined, as it had declared bankruptcy by the time the fines were issued (Lapowsky, 2019; Wylie, 2019).

Yet, the Cambridge Analytica scandal is a stark example of the misuse of personal data and the potential for manipulation within the digital realm.

Cambridge Analytica, a political consulting firm, obtained the personal information of millions of Facebook users without their informed consent and used this data to build psychological profiles for targeted political advertising—a difficult situation to ethically argue for. Applying Immanuel Kant's categorical imperative, a core principle in moral philosophy, to the Cambridge Analytica scandal reveals that under the lens of the categorical imperative, Cambridge Analytica's actions fail the test (fail to be accepted as universal laws or norms). It would be impossible to universally wish for such practices (like manipulated data harvesting or manipulation of social media content) to become the norm without jeopardizing individual rights, democratic processes, and societal trust between people, businesses, and the government in general (Hu, 2020; Ward, 2018).

In a recent breach of privacy, and security, but more than anything else—ethics—OpenAI, the developer of ChatGPT, was pressured as it unfairly used a voice, generated by AI, which was similar to the actress Scarlett Johansson, even though she has previously declined OpenAI's offer to license her voice. Despite her refusals, OpenAI did use it up until several large newspapers voiced their concerns and criticism over this use. Although it is possible to find a legal loophole for such a usage, given the fact that Johansson is a renowned actress, it raises ethical concerns over information/data ownership related to biological features as well as security concerns as AI can now possibly bypass voice authentication (Mickle, 2024).

4.3.2 Policy Challenges of Information Systems

The ever-evolving landscape of information systems presents a complex array of policy challenges. These challenges stem from the need to balance the benefits of technological innovation with the protection of user privacy, security, and fundamental rights but also from orientation differences between countries (different ideologies may develop different information systems). The situation is further complicated by the global nature of the digital environment, where data often flows seamlessly across borders, and national regulations often struggle to keep pace. Interesting is the interplay between state and company policies, the difficulties of international compatibility, and the policy developments some countries are involved in.

In the current realm of the United Nations system, the state plays the role of sovereignty. Whether democratic or authoritarian, conservative or liberal, the state has sovereignty over its people and subsequently over organizations, businesses, and its acts. A policy of a country is set and determined by the governing entity or entities, developed by rules and regulations that altogether allow or forbid something. This could be an act, an establishment of some sort, or, in the context of this book, the control, or the lack, of information. There is, of course, a natural complexity and tension between personal desires for privacy, the bureaucratic or national security desires of countries, and those of private companies. This complexity is even more severe when different countries, different people, and different companies desire different things.

One such policy complexity is content moderation. One example is "unwanted" information, mainly in less democratic and less liberal countries where the regime seeks to gain full control of the content citizens consume. For instance, countries may pose legal- psychological barriers or legal- technological barriers to block content (Topor & Tabachnik, 2021). A representative case was in 2016, when Iran began developing the National Information Network (NIN) (Farsi: شبكهٔ ملی اطلاعات, Shabake- ye Melli- ye Ettelā'āt), which is aimed to creating a separate state-controlled network of information and communication—an air-gapped intranet. Thus, it was the Iranian policy that shaped information, related information systems and platforms, and the internet within Iran as a whole. Further, in 2021, Iran established the Supreme Council of Cyberspace (SCC) by decree of Supreme Leader Ayatollah Ali Khamenei, which serves as a powerful governmental body. It is the policy of the state to control information systems, and companies, both domestic and foreign, must comply. The SCC placed control of the internet in the hands of radical religious authorities. The SCC set the strategic direction of Iranian cyberspace. It places content moderation and information blocking and censored websites that are not aligned with the "Islamic values" of the Iranian regime (Freedom House, 2023; Topor, 2024).

In another example from Europe, the GDPR, Digital Markets Act (DMA), and Digital Services Act (DSA) have significant policy impacts in the European Union. The GDPR, enforced since 2018, focuses on protecting personal data by setting rules for its collection, use, and protection, giving individuals more control over their data. On the other hand, the DMA aims to prevent abuses of dominance by large tech companies like Google, Amazon, Meta (Facebook), Apple, and Microsoft by establishing a level playing field in the digital market. It targets platforms acting as "gatekeepers" to rebalance competition and combat oligopolistic situations. The DSA complements the DMA by regulating internet access, marketplaces, and service platforms to ensure transparency and accountability (Zaeem & Barber, 2020; Müller et al., 2019).

Challenges addressed by these regulations include ensuring fair competition, protecting user privacy, enhancing transparency in data usage, and preventing monopolistic or oligopolistic practices by tech giants. The GDPR addresses challenges related to data protection and privacy breaches, while the DMA and DSA tackle issues of market dominance and unfair practices in the digital market. These regulations aim to create a more transparent, fair, and competitive digital environment while safeguarding user rights and privacy. As was previously presented, the EU fines companies over non-compliance, and thus it demonstrates the implementation of a specific European policy to address the abovementioned issues (Eifert et al., 2021).

One contested topic related to regulation and policy is freedom of speech and content moderation, which is relevant both for countries and for social media platforms. As an example, it is the law and policy of the United States, under the First Amendment, to allow full freedom of speech, even hate speech, as long as there is no direct incitement for violence. In contrast, many other countries do not allow complete freedom of speech and censor unwanted information, disinformation, or hate speech (Beausoleil, 2019; Topor, 2024). In other examples concerning private companies, those companies—under restraints of local and international laws—do not always dictate a policy. Facebook, X (Twitter), TikTok, and many others have policies regarding privacy, content moderation, and use in general (Matamoros-Fernández & Farkas, 2021). Many countries limit social media platforms but also fine them. For instance, X has faced multimillion fines in Germany and France over violations of laws relating to hate speech (Rosemain, 2022; Scott & Goujard, 2023).

Yet, it appears as an intended policy to be fined. Based on the publicly available information, one can conclude that many companies prefer being fined yearly as they continue their services without addressing issues that may be too expensive to address. For instance, in 2023, Meta (Facebook) was fined \$1.3 billion by the European Data Protection Board (EDPB) for violating GDPR rules regarding the transfer of personal data to the US. That same year, Meta's revenue was \$134 billion, making the seemingly large fine of \$1.3 billion, just 0.97% of the company's revenue. Although estimating the cost of full GDPR compliance for a company like Meta is complex and multifaceted, it can be estimated more than the fine (with technological and system upgrades or changes, legal consultations, hiring more personnel, more data mapping, audits, and so on). It may be more economically feasible NOT to comply (Xynogalas & Leiser, 2024). In another example from 2023, TikTok was also fined by the EU \$370 million while having an overall revenue of \$14.3 billion, which is approximately 2.59% of its revenue (Satariano, 2023).

Another example of policy-related challenges is AI-related policies. Such challenges and complexities have become increasingly prominent as artificial intelligence technologies continue to advance and permeate various aspects of society. These challenges arise from the need to balance innovation and societal benefits with potential risks and ethical concerns, ranging from safety, security, and transparency to bias, fairness, and accountability. An example of an AI-related policy is the European AI Act, which was approved by the European Parliament on 13 March 2024. Under the act, AI systems are divided into risk categories and those of the highest risk are to be closely regulated. Some AI systems would be classified as "unacceptable" and might be banned altogether (Glichrist & Iordache, 2024).

To conclude, the challenges of regulation and policies relating to information systems are multifaceted, stemming from the rapid pace of technological evolution, the complexity of global digital ecosystems, and the diverse range of stakeholders involved. They include aspects of keeping pace with developments, data and privacy, cybersecurity and safety, ethical considerations, global governance issues, economic impact, socio-political impact, and more.

4.3.3 Privacy Challenges of Information Systems

In the digital age, information systems have become the backbone of business operations, government functions, and personal communications. However, as much as information systems have enhanced efficiency and connectivity, they have also introduced significant privacy challenges. Privacy in information systems refers to the right or opportunity of individuals (or other entities) to determine when, how, and to what extent their personal information is communicated to others and how others use it. With the proliferation of digital technologies, ensuring this privacy has become increasingly complex. Personal information can range from basic contact details to sensitive health records and financial transactions, each category requiring different levels of protection (Bélanger & Crossler, 2011).

Privacy is often addressed as a legal framework. At the heart of the privacy discussion are the legal and ethical frameworks that govern the collection, use, and disclosure of personal information. Laws such as the GDPR in the EU and the California Consumer Privacy Act (CCPA) in California, US, have set new benchmarks for privacy protection, emphasizing user consent, data minimization, and transparency. As with other challenges, legal frameworks are often struggling to keep pace with the rapid evolution of technology. Ethical considerations, therefore, play a critical role in filling these gaps, guiding organizations in their treatment of personal data beyond mere legal compliance (Mustafa et al., 2019; Barrett, 2019).

One of the most concerning aspects of information systems is the sheer volume of data they collect. Websites, applications, and online services, as well as governmental entities, gather information beyond what users explicitly provide or knowingly provide. Browsing history, location data, purchase patterns, social media activity, personal details, health and financial details, and more—these seemingly innocuous details can be combined to create a comprehensive profile of an individual. This can lead to manipulation of that person or a complete identity theft. The information collected by information systems is rarely confined to its original source. Data is frequently shared with third-party vendors or used for purposes beyond the initial intent, often without the user's knowledge or consent. In a more negative scenario, information is leaked or stolen altogether (Li et al. 2019).

As presented previously, one of the most emblematic cases of privacy challenges in information systems is the Facebook-Cambridge Analytica scandal. In 2018, it was revealed that Cambridge Analytica, a political consulting firm, had accessed the personal data of millions of Facebook users without their consent. This data was then used to influence voter behavior in the 2016 U.S. presidential election. Yet, it is by no means an exception. Privacy abuse occurs regularly.

In an example from mid-2017, Equifax, one of the largest credit reporting agencies in the U.S., experienced a massive data breach. Hackers accessed the personal information of approximately 147 million people, including Social Security Numbers (SSNs), birth dates, addresses, and, in some cases, driver's license numbers. This breach not only exposed individuals to the risk of identity theft but also raised questions about the security practices of companies holding vast amounts of sensitive data. Moreover, Equifax's delayed response and notification to the affected individuals compounded the breach's impact. The breach led to calls for stricter oversight of how personal data is secured and heightened scrutiny of the credit reporting industry. As it held information from around the world, a few regulatory bodies fined Equifax. The British Financial Conduct Authority (FCA) fined the company $13.4 million in 2023. Beforehand, in 2019, the US Federal Trade Commission (FTC), the Consumer Financial Protection Bureau (CFPB), and 50 US states and territories filed complaints, after which the company agreed to pay $575 million as part of a settlement agreement (Jones, 2023).

In another example from late 2023, one of many, the European Union, through the Irish Data Protection Commission (DPC), fined the Chinese company TikTok over child data breaches, following the fact that due to commercial incentives, TikTok did not protect the accounts of young people and made them public by default, meaning that they were exposed to all types of viewers, not their friends or followers alone (Fung, 2023). Companies do address privacy issues. For instance, in a significant move to enhance user privacy, Apple introduced the App Tracking Transparency (ATT) framework in April 2021. This initiative marked a significant shift in how applications on iOS devices can track user activity across other companies' applications and websites for advertising or data brokerage purposes. At its core, the ATT framework requires all applications to obtain explicit user permission before tracking their activities. This means that when an application wants to share the user's activity with other companies for advertising purposes, it must first present a prompt and receive consent. The ATT enhanced user privacy but some companies, especially those in the digital advertising sector, criticized the move, arguing it would disrupt the advertising ecosystem and harm small businesses. One such "small" business was Meta (Espósito, 2021).

The introduction of Apple's App Tracking Transparency framework, and the GDPR or the CCPA beforehand, alongside the cases of the Facebook-Cambridge Analytica scandal and the Equifax data breach (among many other data breaches), illustrates the multifaceted nature of privacy challenges in information systems. These examples highlight the need for a holistic approach that encompasses regulatory compliance, technological innovation, and ethical considerations to protect individual privacy while fostering an environment that supports digital progress and trust (Kollnig et al., 2022).

4.3.4 Security Challenges of Information Systems

"Security" is a broad term encompassing the measures taken to protect something from harm, loss, or unauthorized access. This can refer to physical security (protecting property or people), financial security (guarding assets), or even national security (defending a nation from threats). Security principles are applied in various contexts, and the specific measures employed will vary depending on the situation. As defined in the Cambridge Dictionary, and as common sense suggests, security is the "protection of a person, building, organization, or country against threats..." (Cambridge Dictionary, n.d.).

Cybersecurity is a critical practice aimed at protecting systems, networks, and programs from digital malicious attacks that seek to access, alter, or destroy sensitive information, extort money, or disrupt normal operations. It involves implementing measures to defend computers, servers, mobile devices, electronic systems, networks, and data from cyber threats. There are several aspects of cybersecurity, including network security, application security, information security, endpoint security, cloud, platform security, and more. Information systems, whether air-gapped or not, should remain secure. Defense is set against malicious actors like adversarial state agents and their proxies, terrorist organizations, and cybercriminals. In essence, it is commonly accepted by cybersecurity practitioners to address security as the CIA triad and ensure data Confidentiality, Integrity, and Availability (CIA).

To protect data and ensure CIA, in accordance with local or international law and compliance requirements, an information system needs to be protected from cyber-attacks, regardless of the question of who initiated them, cybercriminals or state agents. According to Kenneth Geers and NATO's Cooperative Cyber Defense Centre of Excellence (CCDCOE), cyber-attacks include five major tactics: espionage, propaganda, Denial of Service (DoS), data modification, and infrastructure manipulation/sabotage. Additionally, of course, information systems must be resilient to social engineering or insider threats or even zero-day attacks as much as possible (i.e., by network segmentation, the principle of least privilege—POLP; Geers, 2008).

There are countless examples of the abovementioned cyber-attacks. The infamous Stuxnet attack, discovered in 2010, stands as a watershed moment in the history of cybersecurity, marking the first instance of a digitally crafted weapon specifically designed to target and disrupt physical infrastructure. Stuxnet was a highly sophisticated computer worm developed to sabotage Iran's nuclear enrichment facilities. While the exact origins of Stuxnet remain officially unconfirmed, it is widely attributed to a joint effort by the United States and Israel as part of a covert operation to impede Iran's nuclear program. It is believed that the infection with Stuxnet occurred by somebody who injected the worm into the air-gapped system. The worm specifically targeted Siemens Step7 software, used to program industrial control systems (ICS) that operate machinery in manufacturing and utility facilities. The Stuxnet worm was unique in its complexity and the specificity of its target (Geers, 2008).

Stuxnet exploited multiple zero-day vulnerabilities, including four in Microsoft Windows to spread itself across networks. Once inside a system, it sought out Siemens PLCs (Programmable Logic Controllers) used in Iran's Natanz uranium enrichment facility. Stuxnet then altered the behavior of these PLCs to damage the centrifuges used for uranium enrichment while simultaneously reporting normal operating parameters to monitoring systems, thus remaining undetected for a considerable time. The impact of Stuxnet was profound. It successfully damaged approximately 1,000 centrifuges (about 20% of the total) at Natanz, setting back Iran's nuclear program by at least several months, if not years. Beyond its immediate physical damage, Stuxnet marked the first known instance of a cyberattack causing physical destruction of critical infrastructure, fundamentally changing the landscape of cyber warfare and international relations. Stuxnet changes the information of the centrifuges while presenting regular information. It is a prominent example of an abuse of information systems by data manipulation and sabotage (Topor, 2024).

Topor suggests that states and state proxies do the vast majority of attacks to control resources using infrastructure manipulation/sabotage and espionage. Information is indeed a resource, and examples of data breaches and privacy abuses were presented previously. In the specific case of security, the actual use of a resource or an information system needs to be protected (Topor, 2024). One example of such security challenges was demonstrated in the Kyivstar cyber-attack in late 2023.

On December 12, 2023, Kyivstar, the largest mobile network operator in Ukraine, fell victim to a significant cyberattack. The attack specifically targeted a company whose core business revolves around information systems. This attack crippled phone and internet services for over 24 million Ukrainians, disrupting communication and impacting critical infrastructure, including air raid alert systems in parts of Kyiv. As of March 2024, the exact details remained under investigation, but evidence suggests a compromised employee account was used as an initial entry point. Attackers likely leveraged this access to gain a foothold within Kyivstar's network and deploy further tools to disrupt operations. The attack not only disrupted millions of phone and internet users and air raid alerts but also harmed other connected things (IoT devices/systems) that had been operating with SIM cards like gates, ATMs, healthcare devices, and more. The Security Service of Ukraine (SBU) played a crucial role in investigating the attack and identifying potential methods used by hackers, such as phishing or trojan horse malware. They attributed the attack to Russia, highlighting the conflict between Russia and Ukraine (Ngendakumana, 2024; Ostiller, 2024).

Thus, one should not only design information systems to be private, against data breaches or information abuse, but one must design them to be robust enough against manipulation, sabotage, and other cyber-attacks. In this regard, denial of access to information systems is another key challenge to avoid or mitigate. What good is an information system if we cannot access it? For instance, from August to October 2023, a significant cybersecurity event unfolded as Amazon, Google, and Cloudflare detected what would become the largest distributed denial-of-service (DDoS) attacks on record (as of March 2024). This coordinated assault targeted major cloud infrastructure providers like Google Cloud, Cloudflare, and Amazon Web Services

(AWS). The perpetrators exploited a previously unknown vulnerability in the HTTP/2 protocol, dubbed "HTTP/2 Rapid Reset." This vulnerability allowed attackers to send massive amounts of malicious HTTP requests, overwhelming the targeted systems with useless traffic and hindering their ability to serve legitimate users. Google Cloud received 398 million requests per second (RPS), Cloudflare had 201 million RPS, and AWS had 155 million RPS (Greig, 2023).

The discovery of this vulnerability and the subsequent attacks highlighted the importance of having information available on demand, as these three platforms provide services to millions of people globally. These examples demonstrate the vitality of cybersecurity for the protection of devices, systems, and networks from malicious attacks that seek to disturb normal business operations and/or exploit corporate or personal information.

4.3.5 Data Authenticity Challenges of Information Systems

The lifeblood of information systems is, well, information—data. Information systems rely on the accuracy and authenticity of data to make decisions. It fuels decision-making, drives automation, and paints a picture of the world around us. But in our increasingly interconnected digital landscape, ensuring the authenticity of data presents a formidable challenge. Malicious actors can forge documents, manipulate information, and even create synthetic realities using generative AI and deepfakes. This undermines trust in information, potentially leading to flawed decisions, financial losses, and reputational damage, some of which could lead to actual physical harm. How can one be positive that the information presented is real, not forged or manipulated by a human, or, even worse, not forged or manipulated by a machine (AI)?

One example that comes to mind is the Stapel Affair. Diederik Stapel, a former professor of social psychology at Tilburg University in the Netherlands, was found to have fabricated data in at least 55 of his papers and several PhD theses he supervised. Stapel's fraudulent activities, discovered in 2011, involved the creation of non-existent data sets to support his hypotheses. This scandal had a significant impact on the field of psychology, leading to retractions of his papers and a broader discussion about research practices in the discipline (Enserink, 2012). Another such case is the case of Francesca Gino from the Harvard Business School (HBS). The accusations surfaced around 2021 after three researchers, Joe Simmons, Leif Nelson, and Uri Simonsohn, published blog posts on the blog Data Colada, pointing out signs of data manipulation in Gino's papers. They alleged that Gino tampered with data to enhance the results of her studies. The evidence included discrepancies in spreadsheets and alterations to data points to align better with her hypotheses. Gino herself denied the allegations. She claimed honest errors by research assistants or even potential tampering with her data by someone else, and the investigations were ongoing in 2023 (Yang, 2023).

Further, deepfake technology and artificial intelligence have introduced sophisticated methods for creating forged or manipulated data and information. These tools have been used in a variety of contexts, from creating fake videos and audio recordings to generating false narratives or misleading information. Politicians, celebrities, and even people in love were all abused by deepfakes and AI. For instance, during the 2024 US Presidential Election campaigns, some voters in the US received calls from an AI-generated machine telling them not to vote in their state's primary elections (Knibbs, 2024). In another case from 2024, a finance worker at a multinational company was tricked by fraudsters into paying out $25 million as they used deepfake technology and posed as the company's chief financial officer (CFO) in a video call (Chen & Magramo, 2024). This small set of cases exemplifies the urgent need for the assurance of information authenticity and subsequently raises the need for novel solutions for such challenges.

4.4 Conclusions

In the twenty-first century, information systems have become indispensable in shaping the fabric of our society, driving both advancements and presenting unprecedented challenges. It is crucial to acknowledge the multifaceted nature of these challenges, which span ethical dilemmas, policy hurdles, privacy concerns, security vulnerabilities, and the integrity of data authenticity. This chapter has illuminated the intricate dance between the immense potential of information systems and the shadows they cast, highlighting the need for a balanced systemic approach that nurtures innovation while safeguarding against abuses, and arguing that most complexities and challenges should be addressed holistically.

Ethical considerations lie at the heart of the IS domain, where the rapid pace of technological evolution often outstrips our collective ability to understand and mitigate potential harms. From the Cambridge Analytica scandal to the biases embedded within algorithms, these ethical quandaries require us to reevaluate our relationship with technology, ensuring it serves the greater good without compromising individual rights or societal values. Policy challenges underscore the tension between the borderless nature of the digital realm and the jurisdictional limitations of regulatory frameworks. The global internet landscape demands harmonized policies that respect individual freedoms while addressing the complexities of data protection, content moderation, and the equitable use of technology. Privacy, a cornerstone of digital rights, faces relentless threats in an era of pervasive surveillance and data commodification. Protecting individual privacy demands real legal protections, technological solutions, and a fundamental shift in the way we perceive and value personal data. Security challenges serve as a reminder of the perpetual arms race between defenders and adversaries in cyberspace. From state-sponsored cyberattacks to rampant cybercrime, securing the digital infrastructure requires relentless defense strategies and, of course, international cooperation. Lastly, the sanctity of data authenticity stands as a bulwark against the tide of disinformation and digital deception. In the age of deepfakes, synthetic media, and fraudulent data, maintaining the integrity of information is paramount for the functioning of human cooperation, the reliability of scientific research, and the trustworthiness of our digital interactions.

In conclusion, the future of information systems offers both promise and peril. While all the components of information systems are crucial and must be defended, addressing the many complexities and challenges of IS requires the engagement of all stakeholders—governments, industry, academia, civil society, and individuals. Architects of current and future IS will shape the legacy of tomorrow. The systemic, holistic approach to handling the complexities and challenges of information systems involves viewing systems as interconnected entities rather than isolated parts. This method emphasizes understanding the entire system and its interactions to address issues effectively. Hence, adopting a systemic perspective on IS will benefit our understanding of the upcoming era of information singularity and help mitigate the challenges and complexities of novel technologies (or their applications) like the use of AI and QIS.

References

Badman, A. (2023, September 1). *Types of cyberthreats*. IBM. https://www.ibm.com/blog/types-of-cyberthreats/

Barrett, L. (2019). Confiding in con men: U.S. privacy law, the GDPR, and information fiduciaries. *Seattle University Law Review, 42*(3), 1057–1113. https://digitalcommons.law.seattleu.edu/sulr/vol42/iss3/5/

Beausoleil, L. E. (2019). Free, hateful, and posted: Rethinking First Amendment protection of hate speech in a social media world. Boston College Law Review, 60(7), 2101–2144. https://bclawreview.bc.edu/articles/316

Bélanger, F., & Crossler, R. E. (2011). Privacy in the digital age: A review of information privacy research in information systems. *MIS Quarterly*, *35*(4), 1017–1041. https://doi.org/10.2307/41409971

Bellamy, F. D. (2023, January 12). *U.S. data privacy laws to enter new era in 2023.* Reuters. https://www.reuters.com/legal/legalindustry/us-data-privacy-laws-enter-new-era-2023-2023-01-12/

Blasius, J., & Thiessen, V. (2015). Should we trust survey data? Assessing response simplification and data fabrication. *Social Science Research*, *52*, 479–493. https://doi.org/10.1016/j.ssresearch.2014.09.008

Bygrave, L. A. (2010). Privacy and data protection in an international perspective. *Scandinavian Studies in Law*, *56*, 165–200.

Cambridge Dictionary. (n.d.). *Security*. https://dictionary.cambridge.org/dictionary/english/security

Casey, T. (2007, September). *Threat agent library helps identify information security risks* (White paper). Intel.

Chen, H., & Magramo, K. (2024, February 4). *Finance worker pays out $25 million after video call with deepfake "chief financial officer."* CNN. https://edition.cnn.com/2024/02/04/asia/deepfake-cfo-scam-hong-kong-intl-hnk/index.html

Chin, J., & Lin, L. (2022). *Surveillance state: Inside China's quest to launch a new era of social control.* St. Martin's Press.

Dobrovoljc, A., Trček, D., & Likar, B. (2017). Predicting exploitations of information systems vulnerabilities through attackers' characteristics. *IEEE Access*, *5*, 26063–26075. https://doi.org/10.1109/ACCESS.2017.2769063

Eifert, M., Metzger, A., Schweitzer, H., & Wagner, G. (2021). Taming the giants: The DMA/DSA package. *Common Market Law Review*, *58*(4). https://doi.org/10.54648/cola2021065

Enserink, M. (2012, November 28). *Final report: Stapel affair points to bigger problems in social psychology. Science.* https://www.science.org/content/article/final-report-stapel-affair-points-bigger-problems-social-psychology

Espósito, F. (2021, October 25). *Facebook again criticizes Apple's privacy policies, says they hurt "millions of small businesses."* 9to5Mac. https://9to5mac.com/2021/10/25/facebook-again-criticizes-apples-privacy-policies-says-they-hurt-millions-of-small-businesses/

Fishman, B. (2022, September 16). *What it really means to "hold Big Tech accountable."* Lawfare. https://www.lawfaremedia.org/article/what-it-really-means-hold-big-tech-accountable

Freedom House. (2023). *Freedom on the Net 2023: Iran.* https://freedomhouse.org/country/iran/freedom-net/2023

Fung, B. (2023, September 15). *TikTok fined $368 million in Europe for failing to protect children.* CNN. https://edition.cnn.com/2023/09/15/tech/tiktok-fine-europe-children

Gafni, R., Aviv, I., Kantsepolsky, B., Sherman, S., Rika, H., Itzkovich, Y., & Barger, A. (2024). Objectivity by design: The impact of AI-driven approach on employees' soft skills evaluation. *Information and Software Technology, 170*, Article 107430. https://doi.org/10.1016/j.infsof.2024.107430

Gafni, R., Kantsepolsky, B., & Sherman, S. (2025). Understanding and mitigating biases in AI systems. In I. Venezia & R. Calipha (Eds.), *Behavioral finance: Beyond the basics.* World Scientific.

Geers, K. (2008). *Cyberspace and the changing nature of warfare.* Cooperative Cyber Defence Centre of Excellence. https://ccdcoe.org/uploads/2018/10/Geers2008_CyberspaceAndTheChangingNatureOfWarfare.pdf

Gilchrist, K., & Iordache, R. (2024, March 13). *World's first major act to regulate AI passed by European lawmakers.* CNBC. https://www.cnbc.com/2024/03/13/european-lawmakers-endorse-worlds-first-major-act-to-regulate-ai.html

Greig, J. (2023, October 10). New technique leads to largest DDoS attacks ever, Google and Amazon say. The Record. https://therecord.media/largest-ddos-incidents-amazon-cloudflare-google

Guess, A. M., & Lyons, B. A. (2020). Misinformation, disinformation, and online propaganda. In N. Persily & J. A. Tucker (Eds.), *Social media and democracy: The state of the field, prospects for reform* (pp. 10–33). Cambridge University Press. https://doi.org/10.1017/9781108890960

Guest, P. (2023, October 26). *The UK's controversial Online Safety Act is now law. Wired.* https:// www.wired.com/ story/ the- uks- contro vers ial- onl ine- saf ety- act- is- now- law/

Hartmann, D., De Pereira, J. R. L., Streitbörger, C., & Berendt, B. (2025). Addressing the regulatory gap: Moving towards an EU AI audit ecosystem beyond the AI Act by including civil society. *AI and Ethics*, *5*(4), 3617–3638. https://doi.org/10.1007/s43681-024-00595-3

Hu, M. (2020). Cambridge Analytica's black box. *Big Data & Society*, *7*(2). 1–6. https://doi.org/10.1177/2053951720938091

Isaak, J., & Hanna, M. J. (2018). User data privacy: Facebook, Cambridge Analytica, and privacy protection. *Computer*, *51*(8), 56–59. https://doi.org/10.1109/MC.2018.3191268

Johnson, K. (2023, January 16). *Algorithms allegedly penalized Black renters. The US government is watching. Wired.* https://www.wired.com/story/algorithms-allegedly-penalized-black-renters-the-us-government-is-watching/

Jones, H. (2023, October 13). *UK watchdog fines Equifax $13.4 million for role in cyber breach.* Reuters. https://www.reuters.com/technology/uk-watchdog-fines-equifax-134-million-role-cyber-breach-2023-10-13/

Knibbs, K. (2024, January 26). *Researchers say the deepfake Biden robocall was likely made with tools from AI startup ElevenLabs. Wired.* https://www.wired.com/story/biden-robocall-deepfake-elevenlabs/

Kollnig, K., Shuba, A., Van Kleek, M., Binns, R., & Shadbolt, N. (2022, June). Goodbye tracking? Impact of iOS app tracking transparency and privacy labels. In *Proceedings of the 2022 ACM Conference on Fairness, Accountability, and Transparency* (pp. 508–520). Association for Computing Machinery. https://doi.org/10.1145/3531146.3533116

Lapowsky, I. (2019, March 17). *How Cambridge Analytica sparked the great privacy awakening. Wired.* https://www.wired.com/story/cambridge-analytica-facebook-privacy-awakening/

Law, J. (2024, February 27). *Class action lawsuit accuses Temu of spying, reading users' private messages.* Boston 25 News. https://www.boston25news.com/news/local/class-action-lawsuit-accuses-temu-spying-reading-users-private-messages/N7242XSV4ZCVPKG2IIRMCS3PI4/

Li, H., Yu, L., & He, W. (2019). The impact of GDPR on global technology development. *Journal of Global Information Technology Management, 22*(1), 1–6. https://doi.org/10.1080/1097198X.2019.1569186

Lyon, D. (2001). Facing the future: Seeking ethics for everyday surveillance. *Ethics and Information Technology, 3*(3), 171–180. https://doi.org/10.1023/A:1012227629496

Macaskill, E., & Dance, G. (2013, November 1). *NSA files: Decoded. The Guardian.* https://www.theguardian.com/world/interactive/2013/nov/01/snowden-nsa-files-surveillance-revelations-decoded#section/1

Mann, S., Nolan, J., & Wellman, B. (2003). Sousveillance: Inventing and using wearable computing devices for data collection in *surveillance environments. Surveillance & Society*, 1(3), 331–355. https://doi.org/10.24908/ss.v1i3.3344

Matamoros-Fernández, A., & Farkas, J. (2021). Racism, hate speech, and social media: A systematic review and critique. *Television & New Media, 22*(2), 205–224. https://doi.org/10.1177/1527476420982230

Michael, K., Abbas, R., Jayashree, P., Bandara, R. J., & Aloudat, A. (2022). Biometrics and AI bias. *IEEE Transactions on Technology and Society, 3*(1), 2–8. https://doi.org/10.1109/TTS.2022.3156405

Mickle, T. (2024, May 20). *Scarlett Johansson said no, but OpenAI's virtual assistant sounds just like her. The New York Times.* https://www.nytimes.com/2024/05/20/technology/scarlett-johannson-openai-voice.html

Moran, C. (2023, April 6). *ChatGPT is making up fake Guardian articles. Here's how we're responding. The Guardian.* https://www.theguardian.com/commentisfree/2023/apr/06/ai-chatgpt-guardian-technology-risks-fake-article

Müller, N. M., Kowatsch, D., Debus, P., Mirdita, D., & Böttinger, K. (2019). On GDPR compliance of companies' privacy policies. In *Text, Speech, and Dialogue: 22nd International Conference, TSD 2019* (pp. 151–159). Springer. https://doi.org/10.1007/978-3-030-27947-9_13

Mustafa, U., Pflugel, E., & Philip, N. (2019). A novel privacy framework for secure m-health applications: The case of the GDPR. In *2019 IEEE 12th International Conference on Global Security, Safety and Sustainability (ICGS3)* (pp. 1–9). IEEE. https://doi.org/10.1109/ICGS3.2019.8688019

Ngendakumana, P. E. (2024, January 4). *Ukraine says Russian hackers penetrated major telecoms network for months. Politico.* https://www.politico.eu/article/ukraines-cyber-spy-chief-vitiuk-says-russia-hackers-penetrated-kyvstarg-telecoms-system-for-months/

O'Connor, N. (2018, January 30). *Reforming the U.S. approach to data protection and privacy.* Council on Foreign Relations. https://www.cfr.org/report/reforming-us-approach-data-protection

Ostiller, N. (2024, January 4). *SBU cybersecurity chief: Hackers had access to Kyivstar months before December attack. The Kyiv Independent.* https://kyivindependent.com/reuters-sbu-cybersecurity-chief-says-russian-hackers-had-access-to-kyivstar-for-months-before-december-attack/

Rosemain, M. (2022, January 20). *Twitter loses online hate speech court battle in France.* Reuters. https://www.reuters.com/world/europe/twitter-loses-appeal-french-case-over-online-hate-speech-source-2022-01-20/

Rossetti, M., & Zaman, T. (2023). Bots, disinformation, and the first impeachment of U.S. President Donald Trump. *PLOS ONE, 18*(5), Article e0283971. https://doi.org/10.1371/journal.pone.0283971

Rustad, M. L., & Koenig, T. H. (2019). Towards a global data privacy standard. *Florida Law Review, 71*, 365.

Satariano, A. (2019, March 20). *Google fined $1.7 billion by EU for unfair advertising rules. The New York Times.* https://www.nytimes.com/2019/03/20/business/google-fine-advertising.html

Satariano, A. (2023, May 22). *Meta fined $1.3 billion for violating EU data privacy rules. The New York Times.* https://www.nytimes.com/2023/05/22/business/meta-facebook-eu-privacy-fine.html

Schmitt, M. N. (Ed.). (2017). *Tallinn Manual 2.0 on the international law applicable to cyber warfare.* Cambridge University Press.

Schwartz, R., Vassilev, A., Greene, K., Perine, L., Burt, A., & Hall, P. (2022, March). *Towards a standard for identifying and managing bias in artificial intelligence.* U.S. Department of Commerce, National Institute of Standards and Technology. https://doi.org/10.6028/NIST.SP.1270

Scott, M., & Goujard, C. (2023, December 18). *X vs. EU: Elon Musk hit with probe over spread of toxic content. Politico.* https://www.politico.eu/article/elon-musks-x-probed-by-eu-for-failing-to-curb-toxic-content/

Selwyn, N. (2004). Reconsidering political and popular understandings of the digital divide. *New Media & Society, 6*(3), 341–362. https://doi.org/10.1177/1461444804042519

Sham, A. H., Aktas, K., Rizhinashvili, D., Kuklianov, D., Alisinanoglu, F., Ofodile, I., Ozcinar, C., & Anbarjafari, G. (2023). Ethical AI in facial expression analysis: Racial bias. *Signal, Image and Video Processing, 17*(2), 399–406. https://doi.org/10.1007/s11760-022-02246-8

Shuker, P., & Topor, L. (2021). Russian influence campaigns against NATO in the Baltic region: Spread of chaos and *divide et impera*. In *The Russian Federation in global knowledge warfare: Influence operations in Europe and its neighbourhood* (pp. 295–314). Springer. https://doi.org/10.1007/978-3-030-73955-3_15

Stenzler-Koblentz, L., & Klempner, U. (2024, May). *From memes to mainstream: How far-right extremists weaponize AI to spread antisemitism and radicalization*. International Institute for Counter-Terrorism, Reichman University. https://ict.org.il/wp-content/uploads/2024/05/Koblentz-Stenzler_Klempner_From-Memes-to-Mainstream-How-Far-Right-Extremists-Weaponize-AI-to-Spread-Antisemitism-and-Radicalization_2024_01_05.pdf

Topor, L. (2024). *Cyber sovereignty: International security, mass communication, and the future of the Internet*. Springer Nature.

Topor, L. (2025). Memetic antisemitism: How memes teach age-old hatred. In *Imagery of hate online*. Open Book Publishers. https://doi.org/10.11647/obp.0447.03

Topor, L., & Tabachnik, A. (2021). Russian cyber information warfare: International distribution and domestic control. *Journal of Advanced Military Studies, 12*(1), 112–127. https://doi.org/10.21140/mcuj.20211201005

University of Minnesota. (n.d.). *Information and Decision Sciences PhD program*. Carlson School of Management. https://assets.csom.umn.edu/assets/124814.pdf

Ward, K. (2018). Social networks, the 2016 US presidential election, and Kantian ethics: Applying the categorical imperative to Cambridge Analytica's behavioral microtargeting. *Journal of Media Ethics, 33*(3), 133–148. https://doi.org/10.1080/23736992.2018.1477047

Wicki-Birchler, D. (2020). The Budapest Convention and the General Data Protection Regulation: Acting in concert to curb cybercrime? *International Cybersecurity Law Review, 1*(1), 63–72. https://doi.org/10.1365/s43439-020-00012-5

Wylie, C. (2019). *Mindf*ck: Cambridge Analytica and the plot to break America*. Random House.

Xynogalas, V., & Leiser, M. R. (2024). The metaverse: Searching for compliance with the General Data Protection Regulation. *International Data Privacy Law, 14*(2), 89–105. https://doi.org/10.1093/idpl/ipae004

Yang, M. (2023, June 25). *Harvard professor who studies honesty accused of falsifying data in studies. The Guardian*. https://www.theguardian.com/education/2023/jun/25/harvard-professor-data-fraud

Zaeem, R. N., & Barber, K. S. (2020). The effect of the GDPR on privacy policies: Recent progress and future promise. *ACM Transactions on Management Information Systems, 12*(1), 1–20. https://doi.org/10.1145/3389685

Zuboff, S. (2023). The age of surveillance capitalism. In C. Calhoun et al. (Eds.), *Social theory re-wired* (pp. 203–213). Routledge.

5

Legal and Regulatory Frameworks for Information Systems

5.1 Introduction

In the accelerating landscape of the information age, legal and regulatory frameworks form the often-invisible architecture that enables or constrains the evolution of information systems (IS). These frameworks underpin the trust, legitimacy, and operational feasibility of digital infrastructures across nations, sectors, and technologies. As data becomes a strategic asset, and systems powered by artificial intelligence (AI), quantum computing, and decentralized networks (i.e., Blockchain) redefine the boundaries of control and intelligence, the law must evolve as both a guardian and an enabler. Some aspects of modern technologies even touch on the realms of philosophy and ethics. This chapter investigates this dynamic interplay, offering a panoramic description and analysis of the laws, policies, and institutional responses shaping the governance of information systems worldwide. With these descriptions and analyses, one will better understand the debates in the later chapters.

While writing this chapter, we do not view IS regulation as static or siloed within national borders, even though this is the case in some countries where countries strive for full sovereignty. Instead, it explores law as a fluid, multiscalar system responding to disruptive technological shifts and transboundary challenges, from cross-border data flows and AI governance to cyber sovereignty and environmental accountability in digital infrastructure. This chapter critically examines how domestic law, international treaties, soft law instruments, and ethical frameworks interact to govern the design, deployment, and

B. Kantsepolsky, L. Topor, *Managing Information Singularity*,
https://doi.org/10.1007/978-3-032-26223-3_5

operation of IS technologies. These legal modalities not only reflect competing national priorities and value systems but also attempt to harmonize global digital operations in a fragmented legal environment.

The chapter begins by clarifying the conceptual distinctions and tensions between domestic and international law in IS governance. While domestic laws anchor national sovereignty and policy priorities, such as the U.S. CLOUD Act or China's data localization mandates, international law aspires toward cross-border cooperation and harmonization, exemplified by instruments like the Budapest Convention on Cybercrime and the OECD Privacy Guidelines. The interplay between these regimes is complex, often fraught with contradictions over jurisdiction, surveillance, privacy, and trade.

As a core contribution to the book, this chapter grounds the book's technological trajectory within the constraints and possibilities of global (or local) legal infrastructure. Earlier chapters may explore the exponential evolution of computation, intelligence, and systems complexity; this chapter explores the normative and institutional frameworks that determine whether these innovations can scale securely, ethically, and fairly. For example, the development of a "post-quantum" legal architecture is already being discussed, anticipating quantum decryption threats to today's encryption-based compliance systems. Likewise, AI laws such as the EU's AI Act offer a preview of how algorithmic accountability will be legally mandated in high-risk systems.

This chapter also speaks directly to one of the book's broader themes: the tension between singularity-driven technological acceleration and the slower-moving systems of social governance. Law, by design, emphasizes deliberation, transparency, and due process, qualities that often lag behind innovation. However, in the face of systemic risks like deepfake disinformation, cross-border ransomware campaigns, or algorithmic discrimination, the law must not only catch up, it must also become anticipatory. Legal regimes are now embedding principles of "ethics-by-design," "algorithmic auditability," and "preventative governance" into information system architectures themselves (Brey & Dainow, 2024).

Lastly, we engage with the geopolitical stakes of IS regulation. Legal conflicts over data sovereignty, surveillance, and platform accountability are now proxies for broader power struggles between liberal, less-liberal, and authoritarian digital orders. From the vision of a "Digital UNCLOS" governing cyberspace to the rise of Secure Cyber Domains (SCDs), as Topor has put it in his 2024 book, that restrict data flow in favor of strategic resilience, legal structures increasingly reflect the geopolitical divisions of the 21st century (Topor, 2024).

In sum, this chapter argues that law is not peripheral to IS, it is foundational. Whether the future of information systems leads toward hyperconnected pluralism or fragmented cyber blocs will depend as much on legal design and enforcement as on technological ingenuity. Legal frameworks will either enable the realization of the information singularity or constrain it.

5.2 Understanding Domestic and International Law

Understanding the respective frameworks, challenges, philosophies, and potential conflicts between domestic law and international law is crucial in comprehending their implications for information systems (IS). This section provides an extensive discussion of the needs, frameworks, and interactions of domestic and international legal systems, particularly focusing on their impact on information systems and digital governance.

Domestic law, often referred to as national law or municipal law, is established by a sovereign state and applies exclusively within its jurisdictional boundaries. These laws are created by legislative processes, upheld by courts, and enforced by local or national authorities. Domestic law embodies a state's sovereignty, reflecting its societal values, political ideologies, and economic interests. It is generally structured into constitutional law, statutory law, regulations, and common law. Domestic legal frameworks concerning information systems typically include privacy laws, cybersecurity statutes, data protection regulations, and intellectual property laws (Björgvinsson, 2015; Slaughter & Burke-White, 2006; Topor, 2024).

On the other hand, international law encompasses treaties, conventions, agreements, customary international norms, and general principles recognized by civilized nations. It primarily regulates relationships between states and international organizations, seeking to provide harmonized standards and mutual understanding across jurisdictions. International law derives from international conventions and treaties ratified by countries, customary practices, decisions of international courts, and scholarly writings such as the *Tallinn Manual on the International Law Applicable to Cyber Warfare* (Schmitt, 2017; Björgvinsson, 2015; Slaughter & Burke-White, 2006; Topor, 2024).

The philosophy underlying domestic law centers on national sovereignty and autonomy. Domestic legislation reflects the direct interests, culture, and priorities of a nation. Laws can adapt rapidly within this system, responding to emerging technological challenges, social issues, and economic dynamics. For instance, the European Union's General Data Protection Regulation

(GDPR) and the California Consumer Privacy Act (CCPA) reflect specific regional concerns about data privacy and consumer rights, emphasizing localized control over information flow and personal data protection (Celeste, 2021; Topor, 2024).

International law, conversely, is built upon principles of mutual cooperation, peace, global justice, and human rights. Its philosophy promotes harmonization, consensus, and collective responsibility. The goal is to provide a stable, predictable international legal environment enabling states to engage in cross-border activities, including commerce, technology transfer, data exchange, and cybersecurity collaboration. International frameworks such as the Budapest Convention on Cybercrime and the United Nations Convention on the Law of the Sea (UNCLOS) illustrate efforts to standardize regulations and foster collaboration in areas of transnational concern (Haber & Topor, 2023).

Despite these common objectives, challenges frequently arise due to differences in legal traditions, political ideologies, and economic priorities. One of the primary challenges is compliance and enforcement. While domestic law benefits from clear jurisdictional authority and robust enforcement mechanisms, international law often struggles with enforcement due to reliance on voluntary compliance, diplomatic channels, and consensus-building, which can be slow and contentious. This dynamic can pose significant challenges for multinational corporations and digital platforms operating across jurisdictions, as differing national regulations may conflict with international agreements (Bamberger, 2009).

A notable challenge arises in data protection and privacy regulations, where domestic laws frequently diverge significantly. For example, the United States and European Union have fundamentally different approaches to privacy, whereas the U.S. focuses on sector-specific, flexible frameworks with an emphasis on commercial interests, the EU's GDPR provides comprehensive, stringent, and rights-focused regulation. Such disparities can lead to international legal conflicts and complex compliance scenarios for companies operating transnationally, necessitating the development of sophisticated mechanisms for data management and cross-border transfers (Topor, 2024).

Collisions between domestic and international law can occur when nations prioritize sovereignty and domestic interests over international consensus. A prominent example is the issue of data localization, where countries such as Russia and China mandate data storage within national borders, conflicting with international trade agreements that advocate for free flow of data. Such collisions underscore the delicate balance between national interests and international obligations, creating legal ambiguities and operational difficulties for global information systems (Taylor, 2020).

Another critical area of conflict involves cybersecurity. While international law generally supports cooperative measures and collective responses to cyber threats, domestic priorities around national security and sovereignty often lead to unilateral cybersecurity measures and policies. These can conflict with international norms, potentially escalating international tensions. The lack of robust international agreements specifically addressing cyber conflicts and cyberwarfare exacerbates these issues, highlighting the need for clearer international frameworks and norms (Topor, 2024).

Efforts towards harmonization and resolution of these conflicts are ongoing, with international bodies such as the International Telecommunication Union (ITU) and the Organization for Economic Cooperation and Development (OECD) actively promoting standardization and collaboration. Initiatives such as the European AI Act demonstrate proactive attempts to harmonize emerging technological standards and regulations, anticipating and mitigating potential conflicts between domestic and international legal frameworks (Topor, 2024).

The future of domestic and international law interaction in information systems will likely involve increasingly sophisticated mechanisms for cooperation and compliance, mainly to preserve domestic sovereignty with global ease of use and trade. As technology evolves, so too must legal frameworks, both domestic and international, to maintain balance, fairness, and efficiency. Achieving this balance will require ongoing dialogue, negotiation, and innovation within and between nations (Björgvinsson, 2015; Topor, 2024).

In summary, domestic and international legal frameworks, while fundamentally distinct, must interact closely to effectively regulate and govern global information systems. Understanding the philosophical foundations, recognizing the challenges of enforcement, and acknowledging potential legal collisions are vital for effective legal compliance and international cooperation in the digital age. This complex interplay demands continuous evolution, foresight, and cooperation from both legal communities to ensure stability, security, and fairness in the governance of information systems worldwide.

5.3 Overview of Major Legal Frameworks Governing IS

In an era where data is a critical asset, information systems (IS) are regulated by a web of laws across different jurisdictions. The global legal landscape for IS is often described as a patchwork, with each country or region enacting laws tailored to its own challenges and values (Chaudhary et al., 2018). These frameworks aim to protect data privacy, ensure cybersecurity, and establish accountability for organizations that manage information systems. This section provides a global overview of major legal frameworks governing IS, including key international laws and standards such as the EU's General Data Protection Regulation (GDPR), the U.S. Health Insurance Portability and Accountability Act (HIPAA), Canada's Personal Information Protection and Electronic Documents Act (PIPEDA), and China's Cybersecurity Law, among others. It examines how these frameworks address core IS concerns, data protection, cybersecurity, access control, integrity, and accountability, and discusses examples of their impact across sectors like healthcare, finance, e-commerce, and government. One of the commonalities among most frameworks is that they focus on personal data and privacy, highlighting the importance of the latter in Information Systems. Finally, it addresses the challenges of harmonizing these diverse regulations and the need for greater global cooperation in IS governance.

5.3.1 Global Data Protection and Privacy Regulations

5.3.1.1 European Union: GDPR

The GDPR, implemented in 2018, is one of the most stringent and comprehensive data protection laws globally. It applies to any organization worldwide that processes personal data of individuals in the EU, setting a high standard for privacy and security compliance. The GDPR enshrines fundamental principles of data protection, including lawfulness, fairness, transparency, purpose limitation, data minimization, accuracy, integrity, confidentiality, and accountability. Organizations must implement technical and organizational measures to protect personal data (for example, encryption, access controls, and breach response plans) and are obliged to respect individuals' rights such as the right of access, rectification, erasure ("right to be forgotten"), and data portability. The regulation's integrity and confidentiality principle requires safeguarding data against unauthorized access or alteration, ensuring information integrity. The accountability principle further obliges data controllers to be responsible for compliance and to demonstrate it, for instance by appointing Data Protection Officers and conducting impact assessments. GDPR's enforcement is robust: supervisory authorities can issue severe penalties for non-compliance, up to the greater of €20 million or 4% of an organization's global annual turnover. These heavy fines and the regulation's broad scope underscore Europe's commitment to data protection and have effectively set a benchmark that many other countries have followed (Chaudhary et al., 2018; Goddard, 2017).

5.3.1.2 Council of Europe: Convention 108 and Modernized Convention 108+

The Council of Europe's Convention 108, formally known as the *Convention for the Protection of Individuals with regard to Automatic Processing of Personal Data* (opened in 1981 and entered into force in 1985), was the first legally binding international treaty dedicated to data protection. Its original purpose was to safeguard the privacy of individuals by ensuring that personal data was processed lawfully and fairly, while simultaneously enabling the free flow of information across borders among member states. Convention 108 established foundational principles, which have significantly influenced subsequent data protection legislation across Europe. These principles include fairness, purpose limitation, data minimization, accuracy, storage limitation, and security. By setting these minimum standards, Convention 108 required member states to adopt national laws that embed these principles, thus establishing a baseline of privacy and data protection across the continent (de Terwangne, 2021).

Recognizing the rapid evolution of digital technologies, the Council of Europe undertook a modernization initiative culminating in the Protocol amending Convention 108, commonly referred to as Convention 108+ , which opened for signature in 2018. Convention 108+ retains the original treaty's core principles but introduces significant enhancements designed to address contemporary challenges posed by advanced digital technologies and international data flows. Notable updates include stronger accountability measures, explicit obligations for transparency and data minimization, the incorporation of privacy by design and by default, and clearer provisions related to automated decision-making processes (de Terwangne, 2021).

Convention 108+ particularly emphasizes accountability by mandating data controllers to demonstrate active compliance through mechanisms like privacy impact assessments and breach notifications. The treaty also significantly strengthens the role and independence of national supervisory authorities, ensuring they have the necessary powers for enforcement and oversight. Furthermore, Convention 108+ provides individuals with enhanced rights, including the right to object to processing and the right to an explanation concerning decisions made via automated processes (de Terwangne, 2021).

Another crucial aspect of Convention 108+ is its refined approach to cross-border data flows. It explicitly facilitates data exchanges among Convention members by presuming an adequate level of protection among signatories. Transfers to countries outside the Convention require demonstrable safeguards such as legally binding contracts or corporate rules, aligning closely with the EU's General Data Protection Regulation (GDPR) framework (de Terwangne, 2021).

Convention 108 and its modernized version, Convention 108+, interact synergistically with EU data protection laws, especially the GDPR. While Convention 108 established foundational principles that shaped EU data protection directives and regulations, Convention 108+ explicitly aligns itself with GDPR standards, facilitating coherence and compatibility between European and international data protection regimes. The EU has formally recognized adherence to Convention 108/108+ as an important criterion when evaluating the adequacy of third-country data protection frameworks under the GDPR (de Terwangne, 2022).

National implementations across Council of Europe member states reflect Convention 108+'s growing influence. Member states updating their laws to comply with Convention 108+ standards have used it as an impetus for legislative reform, ensuring their domestic regulations are consistent with modern digital privacy expectations. For example, Serbia's Personal Data Protection Act (2018) and the UK's Data Protection Act (2018) explicitly align with Convention 108+, highlighting the treaty's role in shaping national legislation beyond mere compliance with EU law (de Terwangne, 2022).

Overall, Convention 108 and Convention 108+ represent essential components of Europe's regulatory framework for information systems, establishing foundational and evolving standards for data privacy and security. By providing a robust, coherent, and internationally recognized set of principles, these conventions facilitate not only enhanced data protection within Europe but also smoother international cooperation and data flows globally.

5.3.1.3 United States: Sectoral Privacy Laws

Unlike the EU, the United States lacks a single comprehensive federal data protection law, instead employing a *sectoral approach* where different laws govern different types of information. In healthcare, the Health Insurance Portability and Accountability Act (HIPAA) of 1996 and its subsequent rules (Privacy Rule and Security Rule) protect medical information. HIPAA's Security Rule establishes national standards for safeguarding electronic protected health information (e-PHI), requiring administrative, physical, and technical safeguards to ensure the confidentiality, integrity, and availability of health data. This includes access control mechanisms, encryption of data at rest and in transit, audit controls, and workforce training, all intended to prevent unauthorized access or breaches. HIPAA's very name highlights "Accountability," and it enforces accountability through mandatory breach notifications and penalties for violations. For instance, healthcare providers must notify affected patients and regulators of any significant data breach, and the Department of Health and Human Services (HHS) can impose fines for non-compliance (Levin & Nicholson, 2005).

In the financial sector, the Gramm-Leach-Bliley Act (GLBA) requires banks, insurers, and other financial institutions to explain their information-sharing practices to consumers and to safeguard sensitive customer data. GLBA's Safeguards Rule compels institutions to implement an information security program with appropriate administrative, technical, and physical protections (Cuaresma, 2002). Meanwhile, at the state level, the California Consumer Privacy Act (CCPA) (2018) gives consumers rights over personal data (access, deletion, and the ability to opt out of sale of their data), reflecting a growing trend in the U.S. toward comprehensive privacy protections at least on a state-by-state basis, similar to the European-styled GDPR (Pardau, 2018). Together, U.S. laws address data protection in a piecemeal fashion: health data via HIPAA, financial data via GLBA, children's data via COPPA (Children's Online Privacy Protection Act), and so on. This sector-specific regime results in uneven coverage, stringent in regulated sectors but leaving gaps elsewhere, which contrasts with the GDPR's all-encompassing approach (Levin & Nicholson, 2005).

5.3.1.4 Canada: PIPEDA

Canada's federal privacy law, the Personal Information Protection and Electronic Documents Act (PIPEDA), governs how private-sector organizations collect, use, and disclose personal information in the course of commercial activities. PIPEDA is built on ten Fair Information Principles, which include accountability, identifying purposes, consent, limiting collection, use and retention, accuracy, safeguards, openness, individual access, and the ability to challenge compliance. Notably, the accountability principle in PIPEDA requires organizations to appoint an individual (often a Privacy Officer) responsible for ensuring compliance with the law. Companies must protect personal information by security safeguards appropriate to the sensitivity of the information (for example, encrypting financial information or using access controls for customer data). PIPEDA also introduced a data breach notification requirement in 2018: organizations must report breaches to the federal Privacy Commissioner and notify affected individuals if there is a "real risk of significant harm" from the breach. They are additionally required to keep records of *all* data breaches, even those not reported, as part of demonstrating accountability. These measures align PIPEDA's approach with global norms on data protection, similar in spirit to GDPR's emphasis on transparency, security, and individual control, though PIPEDA is often considered slightly less prescriptive than the GDPR (Rosenstock, 2016).

5.3.1.5 China: Cybersecurity Law and Related Regulations

In the People's Republic of China, there is a framework of multiple laws addressing personal data and cybersecurity, and thus governing IS, from collection to processing and storage. The three main pillars are the Cybersecurity Law (CSL) of 2017, the Data Security Law (2021), and China's Personal Information Protection Law (PIPL), enacted in 2021. These all complement and follow the general projects of the Golden Shield Project (GSP) and the Great Firewall, which are aimed at protecting Chinese national interests. The Cybersecurity Law was China's first national law focusing on cybersecurity and personal data protection, enacted to ensure network security and protect citizens' information as a matter of national sovereignty. The CSL imposes obligations on "network operators" (broadly, owners or administrators of networks and providers of network services) to secure their networks and data. Key requirements include implementing security measures (such as data encryption and monitoring systems) and data localization mandates for critical information: certain personal and important data collected within China must be stored on servers in China (Topor, 2024; Calzada, 2022).

The CSL also empowers authorities to conduct spot checks of network security and requires critical infrastructure operators to undergo cybersecurity reviews. Complementing the CSL, China's Personal Information Protection Law (PIPL) (often compared to the GDPR) took effect in 2021, introducing detailed rules on consent, data minimization, and user rights for personal data, as well as cross-border data transfer restrictions. Violation of the PIPL can result in heavy fines (up to 5% of turnover) and even criminal penalties, reflecting China's increasing enforcement in the data protection arena. Finally, the Data Security Law establishes a framework for classifying data and protecting "important" and "core" data, emphasizing national security.

Together, China's legal regime for information systems heavily emphasizes state security interests (sometimes termed "cyber sovereignty") alongside personal data rights, and organizations operating in China must navigate strict requirements on cybersecurity practices, auditing, and government access to data (Topor, 2024; Calzada, 2022).

As for standards, China's TC260 (National Information Security Standardization Technical Committee) is the standards body that operationalizes the Cybersecurity Law (CSL), Data Security Law (DSL), and Personal Information Protection Law (PIPL) through national and industry specifications. Under TC260's jurisdiction, key standards such as GB/T 35273-2020 (Personal Information Security Specification) define granular personal information governance and security expectations that regulators and certification schemes routinely reference in practice, even when nominally "recommended." TC260 also issues practice guidelines and sectoral specs, and it has begun publishing AI governance/safety frameworks that anticipate binding rules for generative and high-risk AI (Kuczabski, 2020).

Regarding Chinese cybersecurity standards, a notable mention is the MLPS 2.0: Multi-Level Protection Scheme. It is the state's core cybersecurity baseline that operationalizes the CSL across all networked and information systems inside China, grading them from Level 1–5 and prescribing governance, technical, and testing obligations at each tier. The December 2019 overhaul ("MLPS 2.0") broadened the scope beyond traditional IT to cloud services, big data platforms, mobile apps, IoT, and industrial control systems, with baseline requirements codified in GB/T 22239-2019. In practice, network operators must file their systems with public security organs, implement graded controls like access management, encryption, monitoring, incident response, undergo inspections/assessments, and preferentially procure certified products while higher levels trigger tighter supervision and align with Critical Information Infrastructure duties. MLPS 2.0 thus acts as the bridge between statute (CSL/DSL/PIPL) and day-to-day architecture, complementing CAC's cross-border transfer mechanisms by mandating on-shore risk controls for data processing environments (Kuczabski, 2020).

5.3.1.6 Russia: Personal Data

Russia's data protection regime is centered on Federal Law No. 152-FZ "On Personal Data" which was implemented in July 2006. This law establishes fundamental principles for processing personal and organizational information, including that data must be collected for legitimate, specified purposes, processed fairly and lawfully, kept accurate and up-to-date, and stored only as long as necessary. Data controllers (termed "data operators" under Russian law) bear responsibility for safeguarding personal data, meaning they must implement appropriate organizational and technical measures to protect it and ensure compliance (for example, appointing a data protection officer and adopting internal policies) (Topor, 2024; Topor & Tabachnik, 2021).

Federal Law 152-FZ grants individuals rights over their personal data. Data subjects have the right to access their personal data and to obtain information about its processing, and they can request that inaccurate, outdated, or unnecessary personal data be corrected or deleted. Individuals may withdraw consent or object to certain processing (such as direct marketing or solely automated decisions), obligating the operator to cease that processing upon request. These rights align with global data protection norms and aim to give individuals control over their information (Topor, 2024; Topor & Tabachnik, 2021).

In September 2015, Russia introduced a data localization mandate. An amendment (Federal Law No. 242-FZ) to the Personal Data Law requires that personal data of Russian citizens be "recorded, systematized, accumulated, stored [and] updated" using databases located on Russian territory. In practice, this means any organization, even a foreign one, collecting personal data of Russian citizens must store and process that data on servers physically in Russia. The localization requirement was enacted to assert sovereignty over personal data and keep it under domestic jurisdiction, and Roskomnadzor was empowered to enforce this rule by blocking non-compliant services. A notable example came in 2016, when a Russian court upheld Roskomnadzor's blocking of LinkedIn for failing to store Russian user data on local servers (Topor, 2024; Topor & Tabachnik, 2021; Taylor, 2016).

Russian law also regulates cross-border data transfers. Article 12 of the Personal Data Law distinguishes between transfers to countries providing an "adequate" level of data protection (such as parties to Council of Europe Convention 108 or countries approved by Roskomnadzor) and transfers to other countries. Transfers to approved jurisdictions may proceed with fewer restrictions, whereas exporting data to non-approved countries is generally prohibited absent a specific legal basis such as the data subject's written consent, an international treaty obligation, contractual necessity, or protection of vital interests. Furthermore, authorities may forbid or suspend transfers to safeguard the constitutional order, public morality or health, or national security. Recent amendments require organizations to notify Roskomnadzor of intended transfers to non-approved destinations, and Roskomnadzor can delay or block such transfers if legal conditions are not met. Once Transfer

Impact Assessment (TIA), data could be transferred. Russia does accept data transfer in some cases without prior analysis of destination laws with countries like Israel, Japan, Canada, China, and others (Rumyantsev, 2023).

Roskomnadzor, Russia's data protection authority, oversees compliance and enforcement. The agency can conduct inspections, issue orders, and impose sanctions—including administrative fines or blocking access to service for violations of the Personal Data Law. The high-profile LinkedIn case in 2016 exemplified enforcement: LinkedIn was blocked after courts found it had violated the localization requirement. In recent years, Roskomnadzor has fined companies like Facebook and Twitter for localization breaches, and in 2019 lawmakers increased the penalties for such violations up to ₽18 million for repeat offenses. These actions underscore Russia's commitment to data sovereignty. Major companies like Apple, Samsung, Uber, Alibaba and more, complied (Muravyeva & Gurkov, 2021; Tilton, 2016).

5.3.1.7 Other International Frameworks

Many other countries have enacted laws mirroring or inspired by these major frameworks. For example, Japan's Act on the Protection of Personal Information (APPI) and Australia's Privacy Act regulate personal data in their jurisdictions, and Brazil's Lei Geral de Proteção de Dados (LGPD) is modeled after the GDPR. International bodies have also issued guidelines that influence national laws: the OECD's Privacy Guidelines and Security Guidelines (first issued in 1980 and 2002, respectively) introduced foundational principles like consent, transparency, and security that have been incorporated into modern regulations. Regional agreements such as the APEC (Asia-Pacific Economic Cooperation) Privacy Framework and the African Union Convention on Cyber Security and Personal Data Protection (Malabo Convention) likewise aim to set baseline standards across member economies. The result is a global trend toward stronger data protection: 137 out of 194 countries now have some form of data protection legislation in place, according to United Nations data. However, differences remain significant, and organizations engaged in international business must stay abreast of each jurisdiction's unique legal requirements (Apacible-Bernardo & Fisher, 2024).

In addition, the UN General Assembly's GGE (Group of Governmental Experts) and OEWG (Open-ended Working Group) have produced voluntary, non-binding norms for state behavior in cyberspace, affirming that international law applies online, discouraging attacks on critical infrastructure, and promoting CERT/CSIRT (Computer Emergency Response Teams/

Computer Security Incident Response Teams) cooperation, supply-chain security, vulnerability disclosure, and confidence-building. While not directly binding on companies, these norms shape national laws and procurement criteria, subtly steering organizational governance-by-design and cross-border incident response expectations (Henriksen, 2019).

5.3.2 Hardware Laws and Regulations in Information Systems

While much attention within legal frameworks for information systems (IS) is often given to software, data protection, and cybersecurity, hardware components form a crucial and sometimes overlooked aspect of IS governance. Hardware, encompassing physical devices such as servers, routers, personal computers, embedded processors, and critical telecommunications equipment, plays a foundational role in ensuring overall IS security, integrity, reliability, and compliance. Consequently, a variety of laws and regulations have emerged globally to address specific concerns regarding hardware manufacturing, security standards, supply chains, and environmental considerations.

5.3.2.1 Hardware Security and Supply Chain Regulations

A significant driver of hardware regulation relates to concerns around cybersecurity and national security vulnerabilities introduced through supply chains. Governments globally have become increasingly wary of potential risks posed by compromised or manipulated hardware sourced internationally. The U.S. has been particularly active in this domain through regulations such as the Secure and Trusted Communications Networks Act of 2019. This act targets hardware from companies identified as security threats, notably Chinese telecom equipment manufacturers like Huawei and ZTE, banning their use in critical telecommunications infrastructure funded by federal subsidies. The law mandates that telecommunications providers remove such equipment, supported financially by federal reimbursement programs. Furthermore, through the Federal Acquisition Regulation (FAR) amendments, the U.S. government prohibits procurement from entities linked to adversarial nations or posing supply-chain risks (Shepardson & Freifeld, 2019; Ryan & Burman, 2024).

Similarly, the European Union has addressed hardware security through regulatory measures, prominently exemplified by the EU Cybersecurity Act (2019). This framework established a comprehensive certification scheme overseen by the European Union Agency for Cybersecurity (ENISA). It includes requirements for hardware security certification, particularly affecting Internet of Things (IoT) devices, telecommunications infrastructure, and industrial control systems. Hardware manufacturers seeking to market products in the EU should demonstrate compliance with defined security standards covering aspects such as secure boot, firmware integrity, and resistance to hardware-level tampering (Khurshid et al., 2022).

China's regulatory approach to hardware security is exemplified by its updated Multi-Level Protection Scheme (MLPS 2.0). MLPS 2.0 imposes mandatory cybersecurity measures for hardware used across various sectors classified as critical infrastructure. While it does not regulate hardware explicitly, it addresses hardware as part of the backbone of infrastructure. The scheme mandates security certification of hardware and software products used in sensitive areas, aiming to ensure that devices employed in financial services, energy, transportation, and telecommunications adhere to stringent national security guidelines. Hardware providers must achieve government certification to sell into these regulated sectors, reflecting China's policy emphasis on national sovereignty over information technology infrastructure (KPMG China, 2019; Kuczabski, 2020).

5.3.2.2 Export Controls and Trade Restrictions

Hardware components are also subject to stringent international export controls. Notable among these are the U.S. Export Administration Regulations (EAR) administered by the Bureau of Industry and Security (BIS). The EAR regulates the export of hardware items identified on the Commerce Control List (CCL), including advanced computing equipment, semiconductors, telecommunications hardware, and encryption-capable devices. These controls limit exports to specific countries or entities deemed security threats or involved in proliferation activities. Similar export restrictions are enforced through the EU's Dual-Use Regulation, designed to prevent advanced technologies from reaching actors who could use them maliciously or for military purposes. Violations of such export controls result in severe penalties, illustrating their seriousness in international trade (Eichler, 2019; Phillips et al., 2024).

5.3.2.3 Environmental and Safety Regulations

Environmental and safety considerations have also driven substantial regulatory activity surrounding hardware. The EU's environmental directives notably include the Restriction of Hazardous Substances (RoHS) Directive, limiting the use of specific hazardous substances such as lead, mercury, and cadmium in electronic hardware. Complementary to this, the EU's Waste Electrical and Electronic Equipment (WEEE) Directive mandates producers to take responsibility for electronic waste generated by hardware devices at the end of their lifecycle, emphasizing recycling and safe disposal practices (Deubzer, 2019). Comparable environmental laws exist globally, such as California's Electronic Waste Recycling Act, which enforces guidelines on handling and recycling e-waste and managing toxic substances in consumer electronics. Compliance with these regulations significantly affects hardware manufacturers by influencing material selection, manufacturing processes, product design, and disposal procedures (Bergner, 2004).

5.3.2.4 Emerging Regulatory Trends and Consumer Safety

Emerging regulatory trends highlight the increasing importance placed on consumer safety and security within hardware manufacturing, particularly for IoT and smart devices. California's IoT Security Law (SB-327) mandates basic security features, such as unique default passwords, in connected devices sold within the state; it opts for "reasonable security". This law exemplifies broader global efforts to mitigate risks from insecure hardware at the consumer level, driving manufacturers to integrate security into hardware design from inception rather than as an afterthought (Nelson, 2022).

A particularly significant development in this context is the European Union's Artificial Intelligence Act (AI Act), adopted in 2024. While framed as a comprehensive regulation for AI systems, the AI Act also carries direct implications for smart hardware and embedded AI technologies. Devices such as AI-powered home assistants, biometric authentication systems, wearable health monitors, and even autonomous drones often embed AI models in their physical architecture. If these devices are classified as "high-risk AI systems", they fall under strict regulatory obligations under the Act. The AI Act requires that such high-risk systems undergo conformity assessments, include robust human oversight mechanisms, and ensure transparency and traceability in AI decision-making processes. For hardware manufacturers, this means AI-capable devices must now be evaluated not just for physical safety or cybersecurity, but also for algorithmic bias, explainability, and data governance. Manufacturers will also need to maintain detailed technical documentation and logs of AI behavior, a regulatory expectation that directly affects device architecture, chip design, and data processing capabilities. Furthermore, certain AI-enabled consumer products that influence behavior, such as toys or voice assistants, may be subject to prohibited or limited uses if they exploit the vulnerabilities of specific groups (e.g., children or the elderly). This reinforces the idea that consumer safety is no longer purely physical, it now includes psychological, informational, and algorithmic dimensions (Cancela-Outeda, 2024; Novelli et al., 2024).

In summary, hardware regulation encompasses a broad spectrum of legal concerns, ranging from cybersecurity and national security threats, export controls, and trade restrictions, to environmental standards and consumer safety. Compliance with these regulations is integral to responsible hardware manufacturing and deployment, shaping the foundation upon which secure, reliable, and sustainable information systems are built. As technology advances and global digital interdependencies increase, regulatory frameworks surrounding hardware will continue evolving to meet emerging challenges, reinforcing hardware's pivotal role within comprehensive IS governance.

5.3.3 Cybersecurity and Information Systems Regulations

Beyond personal data protection, many legal frameworks focus on the broader security of information systems, especially those supporting critical services or official/Federal services. Cybersecurity laws typically mandate measures for protecting systems against unauthorized access, disruptions, and attacks, thereby addressing concerns of system integrity, availability, and confidentiality beyond just personal data.

5.3.3.1 EU Network and Information Security (NIS) Directive

The European Union's NIS Directive (2016) was the first EU-wide cybersecurity law, aimed at achieving a high common level of security for network and information systems across member states. It requires that operators of *essential services* (OES) in sectors like energy, transportation, banking, healthcare, water supply, and digital infrastructure, as well as key digital service providers (like cloud services, online marketplaces, and search engines), implement appropriate cybersecurity risk management measures and report significant incidents to authorities. For example, a healthcare provider in the EU must not only protect patient data under GDPR but also ensure the continuity and security of its hospital information system under NIS obligations. The NIS Directive led EU countries to establish Computer Security Incident Response Teams (CSIRTs) and national authorities to oversee compliance and foster cross-border cooperation in incident handling (Markopoulou et al., 2019; Schmitz-Berndt, 2023).

In 2023, the EU updated this regime with NIS2 (EU, 2022), expanding the scope to more sectors (including finance and public administration) and tightening security requirements and penalties. Under NIS/NIS2, organizations in scope must conduct risk assessments, use measures like access controls, encryption, and network monitoring, and have incident response plans. By focusing on critical infrastructure and essential digital services, these laws address IS concerns of cybersecurity and integrity, ensuring that systems are robust against attacks and that incidents are managed transparently (Schmitz-Berndt, 2023).

5.3.3.2 United States: FISMA and Critical Infrastructure

The U.S. federal government and critical industries are subject to cybersecurity mandates as well. The Federal Information Security Management Act (FISMA) (originally 2002, updated 2014) requires each federal agency to develop, document, and implement an agency-wide program to secure its information systems and data. Under FISMA, agencies must follow risk management frameworks (largely based on NIST standards) which include categorizing system risk levels, implementing baseline security controls (per NIST SP 800-53), continuously monitoring systems, and annually reporting on compliance. This ensures that government IS maintain confidentiality, integrity, and availability appropriate to the sensitivity of federal data. In the private sector, U.S. cybersecurity requirements are often industry-specific: for example, electric utilities follow standards set by the North American Electric Reliability Corporation (NERC) for grid security, and the financial sector follows guidance from regulators and the NIST Cybersecurity Framework on protecting financial systems (Rosset al., 2005; Philott & Gantz, 2012).

Additionally, many U.S. states have passed laws requiring companies to implement "reasonable" cybersecurity practices and to notify individuals of data breaches. While the U.S. approach to cybersecurity has been somewhat fragmented, there is increasing recognition of certain baseline expectations across industries, such as encryption of sensitive data, authentication requirements, and prompt breach disclosure (all 50 U.S. states have breach notification laws). These requirements map to core IS concerns: protecting data integrity (preventing tampering), ensuring only authorized access control, and maintaining availability of critical services (DLA PIPER, 2025).

5.3.3.3 Global Cybercrime Treaty and Cooperation

It is also worth noting international efforts to harmonize laws against cybercrime, which indirectly bolster information system security. The Budapest Convention on Cybercrime (2001) is a treaty joined by over 65 countries that requires signatories to criminalize offenses like hacking, malware distribution, and data interference, and to cooperate on cross-border investigations. It seeks to harmonize national laws and enhance cross-border collaboration for cybercrime cases. For instance, it obliges each country to empower law enforcement to secure electronic evidence and assist other nations' investigations, which helps hold attackers accountable across jurisdictions. Such cooperative frameworks complement domestic cybersecurity regulations by addressing the accountability of malicious actors and creating a legal environment where cyber threats are more likely to be prosecuted. New challenges like ransomware have prompted calls for even greater international coordination in cybersecurity law enforcement and the development of norms for state behavior in cyberspace (e.g., through the UN's cybercrime treaty negotiations and norms proposed in the UN Group of Governmental Experts reports) (Chang, 2020; Topor, 2024).

5.3.4 Sectoral Impact and Implementation Examples

Legal frameworks for IS have concrete impacts in different industry sectors, often shaping how organizations design and operate their information systems.

5.3.4.1 Healthcare

In the healthcare sector, patient privacy and data security are paramount, and organizations must navigate multiple laws. A hospital in the United States, for example, must comply with HIPAA, ensuring access controls so that only authorized medical staff can view electronic health records, using audit logs to maintain accountability for who accessed data, and encrypting patient information to maintain confidentiality. Hospitals also perform regular risk assessments and training to fulfill HIPAA's security rule requirements. In the EU, a hospital must comply with GDPR: since "data concerning health" is classified as sensitive personal data, it can only be processed under strict conditions (such as with explicit patient consent or for the provision of care) and with heightened security safeguards (Article 9 GDPR).

Healthcare providers in Europe thus implement strong pseudonymization or anonymization techniques when using patient data for research, and they must be prepared to notify regulators and patients within 72 hours in the event of a data breach (per GDPR's breach notification rules). Additionally, if the hospital is large, it may be considered an essential service under the NIS Directive, meaning it needs robust continuity plans for its IS (e.g., backup systems to keep critical care running during a cyber incident). Real-world consequences underscore these duties: breaches of health data can lead to substantial fines and reputational damage, Anthem Inc., a U.S. health insurer, paid record penalties for a 2015 breach, and several EU hospitals have faced GDPR fines for failing to secure patient data. These examples show that healthcare entities have to embed legal compliance into their IT governance, from patient record systems to medical IoT device networks, to protect both privacy and safety (Tovino, 2016; Pierson, 2017).

5.3.4.2 Finance

The financial services sector handles highly sensitive personal and transactional data, and is thus heavily regulated for information security. Banks and investment firms in the U.S. abide by GLBA's Privacy Rule (issuing annual privacy notices to customers and allowing them to opt out of certain data sharing) and the Safeguards Rule, which might involve measures like multi-factor authentication for online banking, network intrusion detection systems, and strict employee access controls to financial databases ftc.gov. Financial regulators (such as the U.S. Federal Reserve or the SEC) also enforce cybersecurity guidelines; for instance, the New York State Department of Financial Services *Cybersecurity Regulation* (NYDFS 23 NYCRR 500) requires banks and insurers in New York to implement written cybersecurity policies, encrypt nonpublic information, and report cyber incidents within 72 hours (Chabinsky et al., 2017).

In the EU, banks must comply with GDPR for customer data and also adhere to payment security mandates under the Payment Services Directive 2 (PSD2), which introduced requirements like strong customer authentication for online payments, thereby improving access control and reducing fraud. Many banks are also considered critical infrastructure; thus, under laws like the NIS2 Directive (EU, 2022), they must regularly audit their information systems' security and report significant cyber incidents (Romanova at al., 2018). An example of sector impact is the swift evolution of payment card industry standards: while the PCI-DSS is an industry standard (not law) for any business handling credit card data, it is often effectively mandated by contractual obligations and backed by data breach laws (Morse & Raval, 2008). Non-compliance in finance can have cascading effects, data breaches undermine consumer trust and can trigger legal liabilities, as seen in cases like the 2017 Equifax breach, which led to lawsuits and regulatory scrutiny. Therefore, financial institutions have developed advanced cybersecurity operations centers, employ encryption for data in transit and at rest, and follow strict integrity checks to detect any unauthorized alteration of financial records, all in line with legal expectations for safeguarding information systems in this sector (Cowley, 2019; Gaglione, 2019).

5.3.4.3 E-Commerce and Tech Companies

Online retailers and tech platforms handle vast volumes of user data, ranging from personal details and purchase history to behavioral preferences. As such, they are subject to a multifaceted and evolving landscape of data protection, digital services, and competition regulations. The General Data Protection Regulation (GDPR) in the EU and the California Consumer Privacy Act (CCPA) in the U.S. exemplify foundational data protection laws. Compliance with GDPR might require companies to integrate "privacy by design" into their systems, such as limiting data collection at registration and offering robust user controls (e.g., "download your data" or "delete your account" features). Similarly, the CCPA, and its 2023 enhancement under the California Privacy Rights Act (CPRA), demands that California consumers have the right to opt-out of data sales, prompting firms to restructure their advertising and analytics systems accordingly (Goddard, 2017; Pardau, 2018).

In parallel, platform regulation in the EU has been significantly expanded through two landmark acts: the Digital Services Act (DSA) and the Digital Markets Act (DMA), both of which came into effect in 2023. The DSA imposes new transparency, safety, and content moderation obligations on online platforms, especially Very Large Online Platforms (VLOPs), to ensure the protection of fundamental rights online and mitigate systemic risks like disinformation. It requires clear terms of service, user reporting mechanisms, algorithmic accountability, and independent audits. Complementing the DSA, the DMA focuses on curbing anti-competitive behavior by major digital "gatekeepers", platforms that control access to essential digital markets. Obligations under the DMA include preventing self-preferencing (e.g., ranking their own products higher in search results), ensuring data portability, and prohibiting certain exclusivity arrangements that limit competition. Tech giants who fail to comply can face fines of up to 10% of their global turnover. Compliance with these frameworks increasingly requires companies to adopt advanced access control, authentication, and cybersecurity measures, including fraud detection systems and secure user verification, to prevent unauthorized transactions and account takeovers.

These measures not only align with good security practices but also fulfill legal obligations to protect consumer data. Furthermore, e-commerce firms must be prepared for regulatory consequences in the event of data breaches (Chiarella, 2023). The 2018 Marriott/Starwood breach, which affected EU residents, led to enforcement action under the GDPR, demonstrating that non-EU firms may still be liable if they process EU citizens' data without adequate safeguards (Page, 2020). To mitigate these risks and demonstrate legal compliance, many tech firms certify under international standards such as ISO/IEC 27001 for information security management. This standard, along with regular penetration testing, encryption, and network security protocols, helps organizations align their information practices with both regulatory expectations and cybersecurity best practices. In this way, the legal environment for e-commerce and tech companies is shaped not only by data protection laws like the GDPR and CCPA but also increasingly by platform-specific regulations like the DSA and DMA, which together set the tone for responsible digital conduct, user rights, and fair competition in the digital age.

5.3.4.4 Government and Public Sector

Government agencies themselves must comply with legal frameworks for their information systems, as they manage citizens' data and critical public services. In the U.S., federal agencies follow FISMA and related policies (OMB Circular A-130), which mandate strict information security programs. This means an agency like the IRS or Social Security Administration will categorize its IT systems by sensitivity and impact (e.g., citizen tax data is highly confidential), implement baseline controls, and be audited annually on its security posture. Government systems often carry some of the strongest access controls and encryption standards, given the sensitivity of data like social security numbers or intelligence information.

Similarly, in Europe, government departments must comply with GDPR when handling personal data of citizens (for instance, a city government must secure the data in its citizen registries and respond to subject access requests just like a private company would). Additionally, governments designate certain agencies as operators of essential services under the NIS framework (for example, an agency running a national ID database or election infrastructure would be subject to cybersecurity requirements). One challenge in the public sector is balancing openness with security: governments are expected to be transparent and provide information (freedom of information laws), yet they must also guard against cyber threats (e.g., ransomware attacks on municipal systems). A high-profile example of this impact is the wave of ransomware attacks on city governments and public hospitals worldwide; these incidents tested legal requirements for preparedness and incident response. They prompted some jurisdictions to pass specific laws enhancing public-sector cybersecurity or banning ransom payments.

The government sector also plays a role in leading by example—for instance, when a country enacts a national cybersecurity strategy or sets standards for critical infrastructure, it often first ensures its own house is in order via compliance with frameworks like FISMA, the Cybersecurity Maturity Model Certification (CMMC) for defense contractors, or equivalent guidelines. In sum, government information systems are not exempt from the global push for better security and privacy; rather, they are on the front lines, implementing the same principles of data protection, integrity, access control, and accountability that laws demand of the private sector.

5.3.5 Harmonization Challenges and the Need for Global Cooperation

While numerous laws now govern information systems, they often differ in scope and requirements, leading to significant harmonization challenges. Globally, we see "a web of national and regional regulations" that can become complicated, costly, and sometimes conflicting. For example, what constitutes personal data, how long logs must be retained, or when a breach must be reported can vary between the GDPR, HIPAA, and China's laws. An action permitted in one jurisdiction (e.g., using certain analytics cookies by implied consent in the U.S.) might be illegal in another (without explicit consent under EU rules), creating compliance dilemmas for multinational companies. Cross-border data transfers exemplify this challenge: EU law forbids personal data from flowing to countries without "adequate" protection, which has led to legal tussles (such as the invalidation of the EU–US Privacy Shield framework in the Schrems II case) and uncertainty for businesses moving data internationally. Similarly, data localization requirements in countries like China or Russia conflict with the global cloud computing model that many companies use. This fragmented landscape has been likened to an orchestra "with each section playing in a different key," resulting in discordant and confusing regulations that burden companies and consumers alike. Organizations must navigate a maze of rules: for instance, a single cybersecurity incident might trigger obligations under EU law (GDPR breach notice within 72 hours), U.S. state laws (notify affected individuals within, e.g., 30 days), and APAC laws, all with different thresholds and definitions of what an incident is. Complying with one set of regulations does not guarantee compliance with another, leading to duplicated effort and higher costs (Bolatbekkyzy, 2024).

These challenges have prompted calls for greater global cooperation and convergence in IS regulation. There is broad agreement that cyber threats and data flows do not respect national borders, so purely national solutions are insufficient. International organizations and forums are working to bridge differences: the Organisation for Economic Co-operation and Development (OECD) has updated guidelines to encourage interoperability of privacy regimes; the G7 and G20 have discussed common principles for data-free flow with trust; and trade agreements increasingly include data protection and cybersecurity provisions to align standards. Industry leaders have also advocated for harmonization—in 2022, a coalition of corporate Chief Information Security Officers (CISOs) urged governments to synchronize cybersecurity regulations to reduce complexity and improve security outcomes. Benefits of harmonization would include easier compliance (one global standard or a few interoperable standards instead of dozens of different rules), enhanced innovation (since developers could build to one set of security requirements), and improved security and privacy for users (as gaps between laws close). We have seen some practical steps toward this: for example, the EU and U.S. recently cooperated on the Trans-Atlantic Data Privacy Framework to facilitate lawful data exchange, and a number of countries in the Asia-Pacific participate in the APEC Cross-Border Privacy Rules system, which maps to common principles. Additionally, international standards organizations (ISO/IEC) provide certifiable standards (like ISO 27701 for privacy information management) that help as a common reference across jurisdictions (Aaronson et al., 2021).

However, full global unification of IS laws remains difficult. National laws reflect local priorities. Europe's laws are rooted in privacy as a fundamental human right, the U.S. emphasizes a blend of consumer protection and free enterprise, and China centers on state control and security. Bridging these differences requires trust and negotiation. In the meantime, what is emerging is a de facto convergence on certain core concepts: data protection (transparency, consent, individual rights), cybersecurity best practices (risk assessments, encryption, incident response), access control (least privilege principles, authentication), integrity (anti-tampering measures, data validation), and accountability (appointing responsible officers, audits, and penalties for non-compliance) are recognized in most major frameworks, even if the exact implementations vary. Global cooperation is crucial not only to ease compliance but also to effectively tackle threats like cybercrime and to enable the free flow of information that underpins the digital economy. As cyberattacks grow in sophistication and data-driven innovation continues, countries are increasingly realizing that a *fragmented approach is ineffective*, and efforts to establish international norms and agreements for information system security and privacy will likely intensify. In conclusion, while companies today must navigate a maze of IS regulations, the trajectory is toward greater alignment and collaborative governance, making information systems more secure and trustworthy on a global scale (Alter & Vardigan, 2015; Topor, 2024).

The regulation of information systems is now a fundamental part of the digital world's legal order. From personal data protection regimes like the GDPR and PIPEDA, to sectoral rules like HIPAA and GLBA, to cybersecurity laws such as China's Cybersecurity Law and the EU's NIS Directive, a wide array of legal frameworks seeks to safeguard data and ensure the proper functioning of information systems. These frameworks uniformly stress core concerns: protecting data privacy, securing systems against breaches, controlling access to sensitive information, preserving the integrity of data, and holding organizations accountable for compliance. Through examples in healthcare, finance, e-commerce, and government, we see that these laws are not abstract obligations but drivers of concrete practices—encrypting a database, training staff in cybersecurity hygiene, or conducting audits—that ultimately benefit consumers and society by reducing the risks associated with modern information systems. Yet, the diversity of laws across jurisdictions also presents challenges, as businesses and governments must reconcile sometimes divergent requirements. The push for global cooperation and harmonization is a response to the reality that cyber threats and data flows cross borders faster than laws can. While achieving a single global legal framework for IS may be unlikely in the near term, ongoing dialogue and treaties are gradually knitting together a more coherent global approach. In the meantime, understanding the major legal frameworks and their principles is essential for any organization or stakeholder in the digital ecosystem. By complying with these laws and advocating for smart alignment among them, we move toward a safer, more privacy-respecting, and resilient global information infrastructure—one where innovation can thrive alongside robust legal protections for information systems and the data they hold.

5.4 Regulatory Compliance, Standards, and Risk Management

As organizations grow increasingly reliant on IS to manage operations, store sensitive data, and enable innovation, the imperatives of regulatory compliance, adherence to industry standards, and effective risk management have become foundational to both legal legitimacy and strategic resilience. These three pillars, compliance, standards, and risk, operate in dynamic interaction, shaping the governance architecture that protects digital assets, assures trust, and mitigates harm across jurisdictions and sectors (Taylor et al., 2021; Trim & Lee, 2016).

Regulatory compliance refers to the mandatory adherence of organizations to laws, policies, and regulations that govern how data and information systems are handled. These obligations vary widely by jurisdiction and sector, but they share core goals: to protect privacy, ensure data security, and hold organizations accountable for failures. As mentioned earlier, examples include the GDPR, HIPAA, PIPL, and so on. Compliance regimes typically require organizations to be certified with standards like the ISO/IEC27001 and others (explained below) and to maintain formal data governance policies, to conduct Data Protection Impact Assessments (DPIAs), to implement breach notification procedures, to designate responsible personnel (e.g., Data Protection Officers, a DPO), and to undergo regular regulatory or third-party audits. Importantly, regulatory compliance is mandatory and jurisdiction-specific, often enforced through audits, penalties, and litigation. Non-compliance can result in significant legal and financial consequences, reputational damage, and operational disruption, it can even halt business altogether (Taylor eat al., 2021; Trim & Lee, 2016).

While legal compliance is compulsory, many organizations also adhere to voluntary information security standards, non-regulatory but widely recognized frameworks that define best practices for securing information systems. These standards serve as global benchmarks for building trust, demonstrating due diligence, and aligning with contractual or industry expectations (Marotta & Madnick, 2021; Stallings, 2018).

A widely known and used standard is the ISO/IEC 27001, published by the International Organization for Standardization (ISO) and the International Electrotechnical Commission (IEC). It is a globally recognized standard for Information Security Management Systems (ISMS). It provides a systematic approach to managing sensitive company information, encompassing risk assessment and treatment, asset management, access control, audits, business continuity, and more. Organizations that implement ISO/IEC 27001 can obtain certification, which serves as independent assurance of a mature security posture. While not legally required, ISO 27001 certification is often a prerequisite for business partnerships, especially in regulated industries such as finance or defense (Stallings, 2018). The NIST Cybersecurity Framework (2.0) complements these by organizing controls into functions like Govern, Identify, Protect, Detect, Respond, and Recover, which map naturally to enterprise processes and technical architectures. Together, they provide a common grammar for reconciling multi-jurisdictional requirements, including GDPR accountability, NIS2 risk management, breach-notification timelines, and sectoral mandates (Möller, 2023). Earlier work proposed an information-security maturity model for measuring NIST CSF implementation progress (Almuhammadi & Alsaleh, 2017).

There are many more standards and compliance, some like ISO/IEC 27701 address privacy, while others like PCI-DSS (Payment Card Industry Data Security Standard) address the security of financial transactions, as this one was developed by major credit card companies to ensure the secure handling of cardholder data. It applies to any organization that processes, stores, or transmits payment information (Lachaud, 2020; Stallings, 2018). Another example is COBIT (Control Objectives for Information and Related Technologies), which was published by the Information Systems Audit and Control Association (ISACA). COBIT is a governance and management framework that aims to help enterprises align IT with business goals while ensuring compliance, control, and risk management (De Haes et al., 2013).

Effective IS governance requires organizations to look beyond compliance and proactively manage risks that threaten their assets, operations, and reputation. Information risk refers to the probability and impact of adverse events—whether from cyberattacks, system failures, human error, or natural disasters—that compromise the confidentiality, integrity, or availability (CIA) of information systems. Frameworks like ISO/IEC 27005 and NIST SP 800-30 provide structured methodologies for conducting risk assessments, while standards like ISO/IEC 31000 offer high-level principles for risk management across organizational contexts (Barafort et al., 2019).

AI-enabled systems introduce distinctive hazards that warrant specialized, yet integrated, treatment. The NIST AI Risk Management Framework (AI RMF 1.0) supplies a lifecycle scaffold that aligns with established compliance systems while addressing AI-specific risks such as bias and discrimination, explainability limits, adversarial manipulation, privacy leakage, model drift, and misuse. Organized around the functions of Govern, Map, Measure, and Manage, the framework embeds AI oversight within corporate governance, sets expectations for role clarity, documentation, and risk appetite, and requires contextual mapping of use cases, stakeholders, socio-technical impacts, and data provenance (NIST, 2023).

The convergence of compliance, standards, and risk is thus inevitable. While regulatory compliance addresses what *must* be done by law, and risk management addresses what *should* be done to reduce harm, standards provide structured tools to bridge the two. Organizations increasingly adopt Governance, Risk, and Compliance (GRC) platforms to unify these domains, enabling holistic oversight and continuous improvement. Moreover, regulatory authorities are increasingly recognizing international standards as evidence of due diligence. For instance, GDPR Article 42 explicitly endorses certification mechanisms (e.g., ISO 27701) as one way to demonstrate compliance (Papazafeiropoulou & Spanaki, 2016).

In the contemporary IS landscape, regulatory compliance, adherence to global standards, and risk management are interdependent domains that together form the foundation of responsible digital governance. Compliance ensures legality. Standards ensure consistency and interoperability, and risk management ensures resilience. Organizations that integrate all three not only protect themselves against legal liabilities and cyber threats but also gain a competitive advantage through trust, transparency, and operational excellence (Papazafeiropoulou & Spanaki, 2016).

5.5 Ethical and Social Considerations in IS Law

As information systems increasingly permeate nearly every aspect of public and private life, informing decisions, shaping behaviors, and mediating power relations, legal and regulatory frameworks are compelled to engage with ethical and social questions that extend far beyond compliance and liability. These frameworks must address normative imperatives such as fairness, transparency, autonomy, and human dignity in a digital context. The ethical dimension of IS law is not ancillary but central to its legitimacy and effectiveness in governing technology's growing influence over individuals and societies.

At a foundational level, law reflects societal values, and this is evident in how IS regulations are crafted and justified. Instruments such as the European Union's General Data Protection Regulation (GDPR) and the Council of Europe's Convention 108+ explicitly frame data protection not merely as a technical safeguard, but as a matter of fundamental rights. They seek to preserve individual autonomy and dignity by embedding concepts like informed consent, purpose limitation, and data minimization into enforceable legal standards. These regulatory commitments affirm ethical values in tangible legal form: for instance, Article 7 of the GDPR emphasizes meaningful, informed consent, supporting the notion of individual autonomy; Article 25 requires privacy by design and by default, which operationalizes the principle of proactive, rather than reactive, ethical engineering (Kurtz et al., 2018).

Nonetheless, the integration of ethics into IS law is fraught with tensions. Legal systems often face difficult trade-offs between competing values such as national security and personal privacy, or corporate confidentiality and public transparency. Surveillance regimes illustrate this challenge: governments and corporations justify mass data collection for purposes ranging from crime prevention to service optimization, yet such practices raise profound concerns about state overreach, the chilling of speech, and the erosion of trust. Legal responses to surveillance vary significantly across jurisdictions, while the European Court of Justice has struck down indiscriminate data retention measures, other states prioritize national security even at the expense of individual rights. Similarly, legal requirements for transparency in automated decision-making systems, such as those in Article 22 of the GDPR, are often counterbalanced by competing interests in trade secrets and intellectual property, leading to regulatory ambiguity and implementation difficulties (Topor, 2024).

Another significant tension lies in the intersection of innovation and harm prevention. Emerging technologies such as artificial intelligence, predictive analytics, and algorithmic systems promise efficiency and new capabilities, yet they also pose novel ethical hazards, such as biased outcomes, opaque logic, and disproportionate impacts on marginalized groups. Legal frameworks often struggle to keep pace with these developments, resulting in ethical gray zones where vulnerable populations may lack adequate protection. The evolving regulatory efforts, including the European AI Act, reflect growing recognition of these concerns by classifying high-risk systems and requiring ex ante assessments, human oversight, and fairness-enhancing measures (Lucivero, 2016).

Social justice is also becoming a central axis of legal discussions surrounding information systems. The question is no longer only about whether technologies comply with procedural rules but also whether they foster equitable and inclusive outcomes. Legal efforts increasingly promote digital inclusion by ensuring access for underrepresented communities, such as individuals with disabilities or those in rural areas. Algorithmic fairness has become a focal point in regulating systems used for high-stakes decisions in finance, employment, and law enforcement. Furthermore, regulations like the U.S. Children's Online Privacy Protection Act (COPPA) and Article 8 of the GDPR provide special protections for minors, acknowledging their vulnerability in digital environments prone to exploitation, misinformation, and behavioral manipulation (Pessach & Shmueli, 2023).

The concept of embedding ethics into the architecture of IS is gaining prominence. Rather than merely responding to harms after they occur, regulations are starting to institutionalize proactive design principles. The GDPR mandates privacy by design and default, pushing organizations to internalize ethical considerations from the inception of a system. Regulatory instruments increasingly require data protection officers, impact assessments, and internal auditing mechanisms that aim to create accountability infrastructures within organizations. These shifts signal a move toward preventative governance, where legal norms are embedded into both the code and the culture of digital systems (Mingers & Walsham, 2010).

Real-world controversies underscore the stakes and complexities of ethical governance. The Cambridge Analytica scandal revealed how massive data aggregation and behavioral targeting can distort democratic processes, exposing failures in consent, transparency, and accountability. Similarly, facial recognition technologies used by police and private firms have triggered debates over mass surveillance, racial bias, and the absence of informed consent, prompting some jurisdictions to impose outright bans while others adopt regulatory controls. Predictive policing systems also highlight systemic risks, as they often replicate existing biases and are shielded from public scrutiny due to proprietary algorithms, undermining transparency and fairness (Hu, 2020).

In addition to formal legislation, soft law instruments and ethical guidelines issued by international bodies are playing an increasingly influential role. Initiatives such as the OECD's AI Principles and UNESCO's Recommendation on the Ethics of Artificial Intelligence emphasize human-centered design, transparency, sustainability, and protections against algorithmic abuse. Similarly, the IEEE's "Ethically Aligned Design" offers practical frameworks for embedding values into autonomous and intelligent systems. While these are non-binding, they shape the ethical discourse and often inform national legislation and corporate governance strategies (IEEE, 2019).

Ultimately, ethical and social considerations are not peripheral to IS law; they constitute its evolving foundation. As digital technologies continue to shape governance, markets, and social life, legal systems must address the normative challenges they pose. A robust legal framework for IS must not only protect rights and manage risks but also actively promote inclusion, justice, and dignity. This calls for a multilayered governance approach, anchored in enforceable regulations, supported by institutional accountability, and guided by cultural values that prioritize ethical responsibility. IS law, therefore, must not only regulate digital systems but also embody the kind of digital society we aspire to build.

5.6 International and Cross-Border Regulatory Issues

As the global economy becomes increasingly dependent on transnational data flows, cloud computing, and cross-border digital services, international and cross-border regulatory issues have emerged as some of the most complex and contentious challenges in the governance of information systems (IS). While information systems inherently transcend national boundaries, legal and regulatory regimes remain largely territorial. This creates tensions, conflicts, and gaps that both regulators and organizations must navigate. This section examines the major international legal challenges, conflicts between jurisdictions, and emerging solutions to foster legal interoperability, data protection, and cybersecurity across borders (Topor, 2024).

5.6.1 Jurisdictional Fragmentation and Legal Incompatibility

One of the most pressing issues is regulatory fragmentation- different countries and regions impose divergent, and sometimes contradictory, rules on privacy, cybersecurity, and digital trade. For example:

- The EU General Data Protection Regulation (GDPR) imposes strict controls on personal data processing and requires that personal data not be transferred to countries without "adequate" protection.
- The U.S. legal regime relies on sector-specific and state-level laws, leading to less comprehensive protection from an EU perspective.
- China and Russia require data localization, compelling companies to store personal data of their citizens within national borders, raising barriers to global data flow and compliance difficulties for multinationals.

Such divergence results in legal uncertainty and high compliance costs. A multinational corporation may have to redesign systems, segregate databases, or obtain additional consent mechanisms depending on the jurisdiction, potentially making a single service model legally unviable globally (Topor, 2024).

5.6.2 Cross-border Data Transfers and Restrictions

Cross-border data transfer mechanisms are among the most heavily regulated and contested areas. Transfers of personal or sensitive data from one country to another require legal safeguards to ensure equivalent protection. One example, previously mentioned, is the GDPR, but another interesting example is the U.S. CLOUD Act. Enacted in March 2018, the Clarifying Lawful Overseas Use of Data (CLOUD) Act modernizes the legal framework for U.S. law enforcement agencies to access electronic data stored abroad by U.S.-based technology companies. Specifically, it amends the Stored Communications Act to affirm that service providers must comply with court orders to disclose data within their "possession, custody, or control," regardless of the data's physical location (Perault & Salgado, 2024; Topor, 2024).

Some mechanisms include adequacy decisions (e.g., by the European Commission), Standard Contractual Clauses (SCCs), Binding Corporate Rules (BCRs) for multinational groups, and Data Transfer Impact Assessments (TIAs) for high-risk jurisdictions. However, these mechanisms are vulnerable to legal challenges. The Schrems II decision by the European Court of Justice (July 2020) invalidated the EU-US Privacy Shield framework, citing insufficient protection from U.S. surveillance, leading to significant compliance uncertainty. The new Trans-Atlantic Data Privacy Framework was intended as a replacement; it was developed and published in March 2022, but faces scrutiny (Tracol, 2020; Rojszczak, 2020; Cochrane, 2021).

5.6.3 Data Localization and Digital Sovereignty

Many governments now assert digital sovereignty by demanding that data generated within their borders be stored and processed domestically. This is framed as necessary for national security, economic control, and privacy enforcement, but it raises issues for global interoperability and innovation. For instance, Russia's Personal Data Law requires the data of Russian citizens to be stored on Russian soil. Similarly, China's Cybersecurity Law and PIPL mandate data localization for critical infrastructure operators and sensitive personal information. In India, the government drafted the Digital Personal Data Protection Bill, which initially included strict localization requirements, but has since moderated its stance. These requirements complicate cloud services, global analytics, and redundancy planning, and may be used as tools of digital protectionism (Topor, 2024).

5.6.4 Cybersecurity and Global Cooperation

Cybersecurity threats are inherently cross-border, yet national responses are often siloed and unilateral. While domestic laws (e.g., FISMA in the U.S., NIS2 in the EU) mandate security controls, cyber incidents do not respect borders, necessitating international cooperation.

International efforts include the Budapest Convention on Cybercrime (Council of Europe), the first and only binding international treaty on cybercrime, the UN efforts toward a global cybercrime convention; the regional cooperation through APEC, G7, and G20 digital economy groups; or the CERT (Computer Emergency Response Team) collaborations for incident response, to name a few. However, legal and political disagreements, especially regarding surveillance, law enforcement access to data, and encryption standards, hinder consensus (Topor, 2024).

For instance, the NIS2 Directive (EU, 2022) serves as a good example of cross-border issues. Adopted in 2022, the NIS2 Directive (Directive (EU) 2022/2555) is the successor to the EU's original NIS Directive of 2016, which was the first piece of EU-wide legislation focused specifically on cybersecurity and the protection of critical infrastructure. NIS2 significantly broadens the scope, depth, and enforcement mechanisms of its predecessor and represents a major legal development in European and cross-border information systems security governance (Schmitz-Berndt, 2023).

The directive applies to a wide range of "essential" and "important" entities in sectors such as energy, healthcare, digital infrastructure, banking, public administration, and manufacturing. It mandates that these entities implement robust cybersecurity risk management practices, including vulnerability and risk assessments, technical and organizational security controls, supply chain security oversight, mandatory breach notification within 24 hours, and governance structures involving management-level accountability (Bamberger, 2009; Phillips et al., 2024).

One of NIS2's central features is its cross-border coordination mechanism. It establishes stronger cooperation among EU member states through the European Cyber Crisis Liaison Organisation Network (EU-CyCLONe) and reinforces the mandate of national Computer Security Incident Response Teams (CSIRTs). It also introduces harmonized sanctions across member states for non-compliance, creating a more unified regulatory landscape.

NIS2 is directly relevant to multinational corporations and service providers that operate pan-European IS infrastructure, use cross-border data hosting, or serve critical sectors. It reinforces the EU's position on cybersecurity as a matter of public interest, while promoting international alignment with frameworks like ISO/IEC 27001 and the NIST CSF. Importantly, its extraterritorial reach applies to non-EU firms that serve EU markets, further internationalizing IS obligations.

5.6.5 Conflicts Between National Security and Privacy Norms

One of the thorniest international issues is the conflict between national surveillance laws (for intelligence or counterterrorism) and international data protection norms. The U.S. CLOUD Act, for instance, allows American authorities to compel access to data stored abroad by U.S.-based companies. This has triggered resistance from privacy-focused jurisdictions such as the EU.

Efforts such as Mutual Legal Assistance Treaties (MLATs) are often slow and underdeveloped in digital contexts. Tensions also arise when one jurisdiction's secrecy or data retention laws violate another's privacy expectations. Legal battles, such as those involving Microsoft and Irish data, demonstrate how sovereignty claims over data lead to litigation and geopolitical disputes (Barton, 2018).

5.6.6 The Push for Harmonization and Interoperability

Recognizing these challenges, various efforts aim to harmonize or interconnect privacy and cybersecurity regimes such as the OECD Guidelines on Privacy and Security, which promote global principles of transparency, accountability, and purpose limitation. The APEC Cross-Border Privacy Rules (CBPR) create a multilateral certification system to enable trusted flows of personal data. In addition, the ISO/IEC 27701 and ISO/IEC 27001 are international standards used as interoperability frameworks between legal systems and corporate practices (Gribakov, 2019; Wright et al., 2011).

At the same time, bilateral and multilateral trade agreements now increasingly include digital chapters to regulate data flows, intellectual property, and cybersecurity. For instance, the EU–Japan Economic Partnership Agreement includes a mutual adequacy recognition, while CPTPP and USMCA include commitments on cross-border data flows and non-discrimination of digital services (Gribakov, 2019; Wright et al., 2011).

5.6.7 The UNCLOS Analogy and Digital Commons

Some legal scholars have drawn parallels between the need for international IS governance and the United Nations Convention on the Law of the Sea (UNCLOS). Just as UNCLOS governs global commons like the oceans, a future "Digital UNCLOS" might define global rules for cyberspace, jurisdictional limits, and rights to data resources. However, achieving this level of consensus in cyberspace, characterized by rapid innovation, commercial interests, and state competition, remains speculative (Stahl, 2011; Topor, 2024).

International and cross-border regulatory issues in information systems represent one of the most complex frontiers of digital governance. National laws are insufficient in isolation, yet global harmonization remains elusive. Regulatory fragmentation, data localization, legal conflicts, and divergent values over surveillance and privacy all contribute to an unstable and high-risk legal environment for cross-border IS operations (Stahl, 2011; Topor, 2024).

Nevertheless, significant progress has been made in building interoperability mechanisms, fostering bilateral agreements, and developing global standards. Going forward, greater trust, transparency, and institutional innovation will be essential to balancing digital sovereignty with international cooperation, ensuring that information systems can function securely, lawfully, and fairly across borders (Stahl, 2011; Topor, 2024).

5.7 Conclusions

This chapter has shown that IS governance is no longer a matter of isolated statutes or sectoral rules; it is an evolving architecture that must reconcile domestic sovereignty, cross-border interdependence, and rapid technical change. By surveying leading privacy and cybersecurity regimes alongside treaties and soft-law instruments, we demonstrated how legal commitments shape cloud, platform, and enterprise design in practice, translating principles into controls through standards and risk frameworks.

Yet the center of gravity is shifting and jurisdictional frictions over data localization, surveillance, and platform accountability now double as proxies for wider geopolitical alignment, forcing organizations to engineer for legal plurality rather than uniformity. Whether the networked world tends toward interoperable pluralism or fragmented cyber blocs will depend as much on enforceable legal design as on technical ingenuity. Against this backdrop, two imperatives emerge. First, operationalization: rights, duties, and security expectations must be embedded by default through governance-by-design, privacy impact assessments, continuous risk management, auditability, and certifiable controls that travel across borders. Legal norms only scale when they are coupled to widely adopted reference models and verifiable processes. The growing use of ISO/IEC and NIST, or even China's TC260 families, as common baselines points to a pragmatic path toward *de facto* alignment even where statutes diverge.

Second, anticipation: AI and quantum advances compress regulatory reaction time and test core concepts like agency, explainability, liability, and confidentiality. The policy response must therefore move from retrospective compliance to lifecycle oversight, which often includes algorithmic impact assessments, independent auditing capacity, provenance and authenticity mechanisms for content, and coordinated transitions to post-quantum cryptography in sectors where cryptographic failure is systemic risk. These are not optional enhancements but preconditions for legitimacy as systems grow more autonomous and adversaries more capable.

Bridging sovereignty with interdependence will require legal interoperability of frameworks that differ in philosophy yet converge on portable duties. These duties might include transparency, data minimization, breach notification, encryption, access control, and accountability. Ongoing efforts (e.g., transatlantic data arrangements, APEC CBPR, ISO/IEC certification pathways) show how shared practices can knit together disparate legal orders and reduce friction without erasing local values.

In sum, law and regulation are foundational to the future of IS. If we embed verifiable safeguards and adopt anticipatory, standards-anchored governance, legal systems can serve not as brakes on innovation but as its trust infrastructure, supporting resilient, rights-respecting, and globally interoperable information systems in an era defined by intelligent automation and quantum-scale computation.

References

Aaronson, S. A., Kimura, F., Lee-Makiyama, H., & Stephenson, S. M. (2021). *Actions to make "data free flow with trust" operational in practice.* T20 Italy. https://www.global-solutions-initiative.org/publication/actions-to-make-datafree-flow-with-trust-operational-in-practice/

Almuhammadi, S., & Alsaleh, M. (2017). Information security maturity model for NIST cyber security framework. *Computer Science & Information Technology, 7*(3), 51–62. https://doi.org/10.5121/csit.2017.70305

Alter, G. C., & Vardigan, M. (2015). Addressing global data sharing challenges. *Journal of Empirical Research on Human Research Ethics, 10*(3), 317–323. https://doi.org/10.1177/1556264615591561

Apacible-Bernardo, A., & Fisher, L. (2024, March 19). *Identifying global privacy laws, relevant DPAs.* IAPP. https://iapp.org/news/a/identifying-global-privacy-laws-relevant-dpas

Bamberger, K. A. (2009). Technologies of compliance: Risk and regulation in a digital age. *Texas Law Review, 88,* 669.

Barafort, B., Mesquida, A. L., & Mas, A. (2019). ISO 31000-based integrated risk management process assessment model for IT organizations. *Journal of Software: Evolution and Process, 31*(1), Article e1984. https://doi.org/10.1002/smr.1984

Barton, J. (2018). Reforming the mutual legal assistance treaty framework to protect the future of the Internet. *Ohio State Law Journal Furthermore, 79,* 91.

Bergner, D. M. (2004). The Electronic Waste Recycling Act of 2003: California's response to the electronic waste crisis. *Marquette Law Review, 88,* 377. https://scholarship.law.marquette.edu/mulr/vol88/iss2/5

Björgvinsson, D. T. (2015). *The intersection of international law and domestic law: A theoretical and practical analysis.* Edward Elgar Publishing.

Bolatbekkyzy, G. (2024). Legal issues of cross-border data transfer in the era of digital government. *Journal of Digital Technologies and Law, 2*(2), 286–307. https://doi.org/10.21202/jdtl.2024.15

Brey, P., & Dainow, B. (2024). Ethics by design for artificial intelligence. *AI and Ethics, 4*(4), 1265–1277. https://doi.org/10.1007/s43681-023-00330-4

Calzada, I. (2022). Citizens' data privacy in China: The state of the art of the Personal Information Protection Law (PIPL). *Smart Cities, 5*(3), 1129–1150. https://doi.org/10.3390/smartcities5030057

Cancela-Outeda, C. (2024). The EU's AI Act: A framework for collaborative governance. *Internet of Things, 27,* Article 101291. https://doi.org/10.1016/j.iot.2024.101291

Celeste, E. (2021). Digital sovereignty in the EU: Challenges and future perspectives. In *Data protection beyond borders: Transatlantic perspectives on extraterritoriality and sovereignty* (pp. 211–228). Hart Publishing. https://doi.org/10.5040/9781509940691.ch-013.

Chabinsky, S. R., Petrasic, K. L., & Lee, H. Y. (2017). NYDFS cybersecurity regulations compliance guide: Applicability, exemptions, and penalties. *Banking Law Journal, 134,* 263.

Chang, L. Y. C. (2020). Legislative frameworks against cybercrime: The Budapest Convention and Asia. In T. J. Holt & A. M. Bossler (Eds.), The Palgrave handbook of international cybercrime and cyberdeviance (pp. 327–343). Palgrave Macmillan. https://doi.org/10.1007/978-3-319-78440-3_6

Chaudhary, T., Jordan, J., Salomone, M., & Baxter, P. (2018). Patchwork of confusion: The cybersecurity coordination problem. *Journal of Cybersecurity, 4*(1), Article tyy005. https://doi.org/10.1093/cybsec/tyy005

Chiarella, M. L. (2023). Digital Markets Act (DMA) and Digital Services Act (DSA): New rules for the EU digital environment. *Athens Journal of Law, 9*, 33.

Cochrane, T. (2021). Hiding in the eye of the storm cloud: How CLOUD Act agreements expand U.S. extraterritorial investigatory powers. *Duke Journal of Comparative & International Law, 32*, 153.

Cowley, S. (2019, July 22). *Equifax to pay at least $650 million in largest-ever data breach settlement. The New York Times.* https://www.nytimes.com/2019/07/22/business/equifax-settlement.html

Cuaresma, J. C. (2002). The Gramm-Leach-Bliley Act. *Berkeley Technology Law Journal, 17*, 497.

De Haes, S., Van Grembergen, W., & Debreceny, R. S. (2013). COBIT 5 and enterprise governance of information technology: Building blocks and research opportunities. *Journal of Information Systems, 27*(1), 307–324. https://doi.org/10.2308/isys-50422

De Terwangne, C. (2021). Council of Europe Convention 108+: A modernised international treaty for the protection of personal data. *Computer Law & Security Review, 40*, Article 105497. https://doi.org/10.1016/j.clsr.2020.105497

De Terwangne, C. (2022). Privacy and data protection in Europe: Council of Europe's Convention 108 and the European Union's GDPR. In *Research handbook on privacy and data protection law* (pp. 10–35). Edward Elgar Publishing. https://doi.org/10.4337/9781786438515

Deubzer, O. (2019). Reduction of hazardous materials in electrical and electronic equipment. In *Waste Electrical and Electronic Equipment (WEEE) handbook* (pp. 207–230). Woodhead Publishing. https://doi.org/10.1016/B978-0-08-102158-3.00007-0

DLA Piper. (2025). *Data protection laws in the United States.* https://www.dlapiperdataprotection.com/index.html?t=law&c=US

Eichler, R. R. (2019). Cybersecurity, encryption, and defense industry compliance with United States export regulations. *Texas A&M Journal of Property Law, 5*, 5.

European Parliament, & Council of the European Union. (2022, December 14). *NIS2 Directive.* https://www.nis-2-directive.com/NIS_2_Directive_Articles.html

Gaglione, G. S., Jr. (2019). The Equifax data breach: An opportunity to improve consumer protection and cybersecurity efforts in America. *Buffalo Law Review, 67*, 1133.

Goddard, M. (2017). The EU General Data Protection Regulation (GDPR): European regulation that has a global impact. *International Journal of Market Research, 59*(6), 703–705. https://doi.org/10.2501/IJMR-2017-050

Gribakov, A. (2019, January 3). *Cross-border privacy rules in Asia: An overview.* Lawfare. https://www.lawfaremedia.org/article/cross-border-privacy-rules-asia-overview

Haber, E., & Topor, L. (2023). Sovereignty, cyberspace, and the emergence of internet bubbles. *Journal of Advanced Military Studies, 14*(1), 144–165. https://doi.org/10.21140/mcuj.20231401006

Henriksen, A. (2019). The end of the road for the UN GGE process: The future regulation of cyberspace. *Journal of Cybersecurity, 5*(1), Article tyy009. https://doi.org/10.1093/cybsec/tyy009

Hu, M. (2020). Cambridge Analytica's black box. *Big Data & Society*, 7(2), 1–6. https://doi.org/10.1177/2053951720938091

IEEE. (2019). *Ethically aligned design.* https://standards.ieee.org/wp-content/uploads/import/documents/other/ead_v2.pdf

Khurshid, A., Alsaaidi, R., Aslam, M., & Raza, S. (2022). EU Cybersecurity Act and IoT certification: Landscape, perspective and a proposed template scheme. *IEEE Access, 10*, 129932–129948. https://doi.org/10.1109/ACCESS.2022.3225973

KPMG China. (2019, May). *MLPS 2.0: Insights and strategies.* https://web.archive.org/web/20211125185807/https://assets.kpmg.com/content/dam/kpmg/cn/pdf/en/2019/05/mlpsinsights-strategies.pdf

Kuczabski, M. J. (2020). Asian cyber security standards. *Safety & Defense*, 6(2), 21–32. https://doi.org/10.37105/sd.75

Kurtz, C., Semmann, M., & Böhmann, T. (2018). Privacy by design to comply with GDPR: A review on third-party data processors. In Proceedings of the 24th Americas Conference on Information Systems (AMCIS 2018) (Paper 36). Association for Information Systems. https://aisel.aisnet.org/amcis2018/Security/Presentations/36/

Lachaud, E. (2020). ISO/IEC 27701 standard: Threats and opportunities for GDPR certification. *European Data Protection Law Review, 6*, 194.

Levin, A., & Nicholson, M. J. (2005). Privacy law in the United States, the EU and Canada: The allure of the middle ground. *University of Ottawa Law & Technology Journal, 2*, 357.

Lucivero, F. (2016). *Ethical assessments of emerging technologies.* Springer.

Markopoulou, D., Papakonstantinou, V., & De Hert, P. (2019). The new EU cybersecurity framework: The NIS Directive, ENISA's role and the General Data Protection Regulation. *Computer Law & Security Review, 35*(6), Article 105336. https://doi.org/10.1016/j.clsr.2019.06.007

Marotta, A., & Madnick, S. (2021). Convergence and divergence of regulatory compliance and cybersecurity. *Issues in Information Systems, 22*(1), 10–50 https://doi.org/10.48009/1_iis_2021_10-50

Mingers, J., & Walsham, G. (2010). Toward ethical information systems: The contribution of discourse ethics. *MIS Quarterly, 34*(4), 833–854. https://doi.org/10.2307/25750707

Möller, D. P. (2023). NIST cybersecurity framework and MITRE cybersecurity criteria. In *Guide to cybersecurity in digital transformation: Trends, methods, technologies, applications and best practices* (pp. 231–271). Springer Nature Switzerland. https://doi.org/10.1007/978-3-031-26845-8_5

Morse, E. A., & Raval, V. (2008). PCI DSS: Payment card industry data security standards in context. *Computer Law & Security Review, 24*(6), 540–554. https://doi.org/10.1016/j.clsr.2008.07.001

Muravyeva, M., & Gurkov, A. (2021). Law and digitization in Russia. In D. Gritsenko, M. Wijermars, & M. Kopotev (Eds.), *The Palgrave handbook of digital Russia studies* (pp. 77–93). Palgrave Macmillan. https://doi.org/10.1007/978-3-030-42855-6_5

Nelson, C. (2022). Local data privacy for an IoT world: The Internet of Things and state-level IoT device security laws. *Kansas Journal of Law & Public Policy, 32*, 143.

National Institute of Standards and Technology. (2023, January). *Artificial Intelligence Risk Management Framework (AI RMF 1.0)*. https://doi.org/10.6028/NIST.AI.100-1

Novelli, C., Casolari, F., Rotolo, A., Taddeo, M., & Floridi, L. (2024). Taking AI risks seriously: A new assessment model for the AI Act. *AI & Society, 39*(5), 2493–2497. https://doi.org/10.1007/s00146-023-01723-z

Page, C. (2020, October 30). *Marriott hit with £18.4 million GDPR fine over massive 2018 data breach. Forbes*. https://www.forbes.com/sites/carlypage/2020/10/30/marriott-hit-with-184-million-gdpr-fine-over-massive-2018-data-breach/

Papazafeiropoulou, A., & Spanaki, K. (2016). Understanding governance, risk and compliance information systems (GRC IS): The experts' view. *Information Systems Frontiers, 18*, 1251–1263. https://doi.org/10.1007/s10796-015-9572-3

Pardau, S. L. (2018). The California Consumer Privacy Act: Towards a European-style privacy regime in the United States. *Journal of Technology Law & Policy, 23*, 68.

Perault, M., & Salgado, R. (2024). *Untapping the full potential of CLOUD Act agreements*. Center for Strategic and International Studies. https://www.csis.org/analysis/untapping-full-potential-cloud-act-agreements

Pessach, D., & Shmueli, E. (2023). Algorithmic fairness. In *Machine learning for data science handbook: Data mining and knowledge discovery handbook* (pp. 867–886). Springer International Publishing. https://doi.org/10.1007/978-3-031-24628-9_37

Phillips, J., Lis, S., & Lamy, A. (2024, May 24). *Cyber transparency, risk & sanctions: How cyber incidents give rise to export control issues*. Connect on Tech. https://connectontech.bakermckenzie.com/cyber-transparency-risk-sanctions-how-cyber-incidents-give-rise-to-export-control-issues/

Philpott, D. R., & Gantz, S. D. (2012). *FISMA and the risk management framework: The new practice of federal cyber security*. Syngress.

Pierson, B. (2017, June 24). *Anthem to pay record $115 million to settle U.S. lawsuits over data breach*. Reuters. https://www.reuters.com/article/business/anthem-to-pay-record-115-million-to-settle-us-lawsuits-over-data-breach-idUSKBN19E2MK/

Rojszczak, M. (2020). CLOUD Act agreements from an EU perspective. *Computer Law & Security Review, 38*, Article 105442. https://doi.org/10.1016/j.clsr.2020.105442

Romanova, I., Grima, S., Spiteri, J., & Kudinska, M. (2018). The Payment Services Directive II and competitiveness: The perspective of European fintech companies. *European Research Studies Journal, 21*(2), 3–22.

Rosenstock, M. (2016). Is there a "right to be forgotten" in Canada's Personal Information Protection and Electronic Documents Act (PIPEDA)? *Canadian Journal of Law and Technology, 14*(1), 6.

Ross, R., Katzke, S., & Toth, P. (2005, October). The new FISMA standards and guidelines changing the dynamic of information security for the federal government. In *MILCOM 2005 IEEE Military Communications Conference* (pp. 864–870). IEEE. https://doi.org/10.1109/MILCOM.2005.1605789

Rumyantsev, S. (2023, March 17). *Russia adopts new rules on cross-border data transfer.* Gorodissky. https://www.gorodissky.com/publications/articles/russia-adopts-new-rules-on-cross-border-data-transfers/

Ryan, M., & Burman, S. (2024). The United States–China "tech war": Decoupling and the case of Huawei. *Global Policy, 15*(2), 355–367. https://doi.org/10.1111/1758-5899.13352

Schmitt, M. N. (Ed.). (2017). *Tallinn manual 2.0 on the international law applicable to cyber operations.* Cambridge University Press.

Schmitz-Berndt, S. (2023). Defining the reporting threshold for a cybersecurity incident under the NIS Directive and the NIS 2 Directive. *Journal of Cybersecurity, 9*(1), 1–11. https://doi.org/10.1093/cybsec/tyad009

Shepardson, D., & Freifeld, K. (2019, May 16). *China's Huawei, 70 affiliates placed on U.S. trade blacklist.* Reuters. https://www.reuters.com/article/business/chinas-huawei-70-affiliates-placed-on-us-trade-blacklist-idUSKCN1SL2W4/

Slaughter, A. M., & Burke-White, W. (2006). The future of international law is domestic (or, the European way of law). *Harvard International Law Journal, 47*, 327.

Stahl, W. M. (2011). The uncharted waters of cyberspace: Applying the principles of international maritime law to the problem of cybersecurity. *Georgia Journal of International & Comparative Law, 40*, 247.

Stallings, W. (2018). *Effective cybersecurity: A guide to using best practices and standards.* Addison-Wesley Professional.

Taylor, A. (2016, November 17). *Russia moves to block professional networking site LinkedIn. The Washington Post.* https://www.washingtonpost.com/news/worldviews/wp/2016/11/17/russia-moves-to-block-professional-networking-site-linkedin/

Taylor, R. D. (2020). "Data localization": The Internet in the balance. *Telecommunications Policy, 44*(8), Article 102003. https://doi.org/10.1016/j.telpol.2020.102003

Taylor, S., Surridge, M., & Pickering, B. (2021, May). Regulatory compliance modelling using risk management techniques. In *2021 IEEE World AI IoT Congress (AIIoT)* (pp. 474–481). IEEE. https://doi.org/10.1109/AIIoT52608.2021.9454188

Tilton, A. (2016, November 17). *LinkedIn vs. Russia*. DW. https://www.dw.com/en/linkedin-vs-russia-moscow-blocks-networking-site/a-36430648
Topor, L. (2024). *Cyber sovereignty: International security, mass communication, and the future of the Internet*. Springer Nature. https://doi.org/10.1007/978-3-031-58199-1
Topor, L., & Tabachnik, A. (2021). Russian cyber information warfare: International distribution and domestic control. *Journal of Advanced Military Studies, 12*(1), 112–127. https://doi.org/10.21140/mcuj.20211201005
Tovino, S. A. (2016). The HIPAA Privacy Rule and the EU GDPR: Illustrative comparisons. *Seton Hall Law Review, 47*, 973.
Tracol, X. (2020). Schrems II: The return of the Privacy Shield. *Computer Law & Security Review, 39*, Article 105484. https://doi.org/10.1016/j.clsr.2020.105484
Trim, P., & Lee, Y. I. (2016). *Cyber security management: A governance, risk and compliance framework*. Routledge. https://doi.org/10.1007/978-3-031-58199-1
Wright, D., De Hert, P., & Gutwirth, S. (2011). Are the OECD guidelines at 30 showing their age? *Communications of the ACM, 54*(2), 119–127. https://doi.org/10.1145/1897816.1897848

6

Implications of Artificial Intelligence for Information Systems

6.1 Introduction

Information systems are entering a phase transition commonly described here as information singularity: the point (or inflection point) at which the production, circulation, and operationalization of information become predominantly machine-generated, machine-validated, and machine-acted. Rather than a single moment, this is a regime change, driven by the coupling of large-scale models, ubiquitous data exhaust, inexpensive compute, and real-time integration, where informational velocity and autonomy exceed human supervisory bandwidth. In this regime, the value and risk of information are no longer confined to analytics; they propagate through entire workflows and institutions.

Artificial intelligence accelerates this transition in two distinct ways. Traditional model-centric AI improved discrete tasks (classification, prediction, anomaly detection) and thereby increased informational throughput. Agentic AI goes further: it plans, calls tools, retrieves from and writes to knowledge bases, and executes multi-step work across TPS, MIS, DSS/ESS, ERP/CRM/SCM, and BI. The result is not just more information but operative information, decisions, and actions taken at machine cadence. This moves organizations toward a practical singularity in which information is

B. Kantsepolsky, L. Topor, *Managing Information Singularity*,
https://doi.org/10.1007/978-3-032-26223-3_6

both the substrate and the actuator of systems, shrinking the gap between "knowing" and "doing."

The implications are double-edged. On the opportunity side, agentic architectures enable end-to-end optimization, shorter cycle times, fewer escalations, higher data quality, and decisions delivered closer to real time, while compounding institutional learning as agents write back explanations, plans, and artifacts. On the risk side, autonomy relocates failure from model accuracy to system-level safety: mis-specified objectives, over-permissioned tools, prompt-/retrieval-injection that steers behavior, cascading errors across platforms, and automation bias amplified by seemingly complete machine-executed tasks. Thus, governance should evolve from static controls to life-cycle and provenance discipline with dataset lineage, versioned pipelines and evaluation gates, least-privilege tool scopes, human-in-the-loop approvals for irreversible actions, immutable logs of goals/plans/tool calls/outcomes, and continuous adversarial testing, translated into living artifacts (system/model cards, audit trails, rollback playbooks) that bind compliance to day-to-day operations.

This chapter proceeds accordingly. First, we distinguish classical agents from agentic AI and explain why autonomy is the pivotal driver of singularity-like dynamics. Then, we detail enhancements across core IS types. We also conceptually operationalize integration and lifecycle (MLOps) under provenance and auditability. Afterward, we examine challenges and legal-regulatory duties in cross-border, high-velocity settings. Lastly, we address over-reliance and automation bias in agentic environments.

As this technology evolves, it is redefining how IS are designed, deployed, and maintained, as well as the fundamental principles by which organizations operate. Within IS, AI helps automate routine decision-making to enable predictive analytics and adaptive learning. No longer an optional enhancement, it has quickly become a staple of current technology and an integral component of modern IS across the public, private, and academic sectors.

Ultimately, this chapter aims to offer a holistic view of the AI–IS relationship, one that recognizes the technological, organizational, and societal dimensions of this evolving landscape. When the IS cycle of collecting, storing, processing, and disseminating information is all completed automatically by AI, how do we know what is correct and true? By addressing both the opportunities and vulnerabilities of AI, this chapter seeks to prepare readers to critically engage with the future of IS in an AI-driven world.

6.2 Artificial Intelligence: Evolution, Types, Functions, and Approaches

AI refers to a computer system's ability to perform tasks that normally require human intelligence, such as visual perception, understanding speech, decision-making, language translation, and (somewhat) creative writing. AI has become an integral component of modern IS, enhancing how organizations manage data, make decisions, and interact with users. From smartphone assistants to fraud detection algorithms, AI now reaches into every aspect of our lives, transforming consumer experiences and business operations alike. Conceptually, there are three main types of AI, as well as several functional types, that this chapter will go on to explore, although other typologies exist. However, before diving into the types, categories, and functions, we will begin with a brief overview of the evolution of AI over the past several decades.

AI has evolved significantly since its conceptual origins, driven by theoretical advancements, technological breakthroughs, and the rapid expansion of computational capabilities. Although its roots can be traced back to myths of automated beings in classical antiquity, the modern conception of AI began formally in the mid-20th century (Mucci, 2024; Haenlein & Kaplan, 2019; Ein-Dor, 1999).

In 1950, Alan Turing published a seminal paper proposing the "Turing Test," a method to determine whether a machine exhibited intelligent behavior indistinguishable from humans. This idea paved the way for forays into computational intelligence. The term "artificial intelligence" itself was coined in 1956 during the Dartmouth Conference, where pioneers like John McCarthy, Marvin Minsky, Allen Newell, and Herbert Simon gathered to discuss machine intelligence, envisioning a future where computers could emulate human thought processes (Mucci, 2024; Haenlein & Kaplan, 2019; Ein-Dor, 1999).

In the early optimism of AI research in the 1950s and 1960s, advances were made, such as the Logic Theorist (Newell & Simon, 1956), the first AI program capable of proving mathematical theorems, and ELIZA (Weizenbaum, 1966), a rudimentary natural language processing (NLP) program developed by Joseph Weizenbaum at MIT. However, by the 1970s, progress had slowed dramatically due to technological constraints, insufficient computational resources, and overly ambitious expectations. This period, referred to as the "AI winter," persisted through the late 1980s and early 1990s and was characterized by skepticism and limited funding (Mucci, 2024; Haenlein & Kaplan, 2019; Ein-Dor, 1999).

In the late 1980s and 1990s, improvements in computer processing power drove an AI revival marked by the emergence of machine learning (ML) methods and the successful application of expert systems. In 1997, IBM's Deep Blue famously defeated world chess champion Garry Kasparov, highlighting AI's growing capability in complex reasoning tasks (Mucci, 2024; Haenlein & Kaplan, 2019; Ein-Dor, 1999).

Progress accelerated in the 2000s, with increased data availability and computing power and the continuing rise of ML, especially neural networks and deep learning. In 2011, IBM's Watson defeated human champions in the game show "Jeopardy!," demonstrating powerful NLP and question-answering abilities. This achievement drove home AI's potential to handle nuanced human language. In 2012, Geoffrey Hinton and his students, Alex Krizhevsky and Ilya Sutskever, developed AlexNet, a deep neural network that achieved a major breakthrough in image recognition. Its performance far surpassed previous methods, revolutionizing computer vision (CV) and catalyzing the global rise of deep learning (Mucci, 2024; Haenlein & Kaplan, 2019; Ein-Dor, 1999; Krizhevsky et al., 2012).

The era from the mid-2010s onward has been dominated by advancements in deep learning and neural networks, particularly by companies like Google, Microsoft, OpenAI, and Facebook. In 2016, Google's DeepMind achieved a milestone with AlphaGo, an AI that defeated world champions at the game of Go, showcasing a level of strategic complexity previously thought impossible for machines (Mucci, 2024; Haenlein & Kaplan, 2019; Ein-Dor, 1999).

Recent breakthroughs have centered on large language models (LLMs) such as OpenAI's GPT series, culminating in GPT-3 in 2020 and GPT-4 in 2023, which exhibit remarkable capabilities in generating human-like text, answering complex questions, and engaging in coherent conversations. Concurrently, AI's role in vision tasks, robotics, autonomous vehicles, healthcare, and personalized services expanded significantly (Mucci, 2024; Haenlein & Kaplan, 2019; Ein-Dor, 1999).

Today, AI continues to rapidly evolve, raising significant questions about ethical implications, job displacement, transparency, accountability, and data privacy. Researchers and policymakers worldwide are actively addressing these challenges, with the aim of aligning AI development with human values and societal benefits. The challenges are discussed in more detail later in this chapter.

6.2.1 Artificial Intelligence: Types

Artificial Narrow Intelligence (ANI), also known as *weak AI*, describes AI systems that specialize in a single task or a limited domain. Narrow AI is the only form of AI that has been realized so far. These systems excel at specific tasks, *far* beyond human speed or accuracy, yet they **cannot generalize** their intelligence to unrelated areas. Examples of narrow AI abound: voice assistants like Siri or Alexa that can answer questions or control smart devices, image recognition algorithms that categorize photos, recommendation engines that suggest movies or products, and even advanced chatbots like ChatGPT, which (despite their versatile language abilities) still perform the narrow task of generating text-based responses. Narrow AI systems aim to **assist rather than replace** human workers in their domain, for instance, by filtering spam emails, detecting credit card fraud, or sorting information, and they operate under *predefined constraints* without true understanding beyond their training (IBM Data and AI Team, 2023; Martinez, 2018).

Artificial General Intelligence (AGI), sometimes called *strong AI*, refers to a hypothetical AI that possesses broad cognitive abilities comparable to those of a human. An AGI system would be able to **understand, learn, and apply knowledge** flexibly across *any* task or context, rather than being limited to specific problems. In essence, AGI would be capable of the diverse learning and reasoning that humans demonstrate, from solving novel problems to daily commonsense reasoning. As of today, AGI remains purely theoretical; it **has not been achieved**. Researchers consider AGI a distant goal, and they have proposed thought experiments to test for it. For example, Nils Nilsson suggested that an AGI should be able to learn any job a human can perform, whether intellectual or manual. Achieving AGI would likely require breakthroughs enabling machines to autonomously acquire new skills and adapt to unfamiliar challenges as freely as humans do. Until such breakthroughs occur, AGI lives in the realm of science fiction and speculative research (IBM Data and AI Team, 2023; Martinez, 2018).

Artificial Superintelligence (ASI) is a term for intelligence that *vastly exceeds* human cognitive capabilities. Like AGI, superintelligent AI is **entirely theoretical** at this stage. If realized, ASI could outperform humans at virtually every task. It would not only master logical and analytical thinking faster than any person, but might also form its own goals, emotional understanding, and creative insights beyond human levels. In other words, ASI would **surpass human intelligence** to an extreme degree, perhaps developing its own needs, desires, or self-awareness.

This concept, popularized in futurist discussions, raises profound questions about control and ethics: a superintelligent AI might be capable of innovations or decisions that are inscrutable to humans. Nevertheless, although it certainly captivates the imagination, ASI is not a current reality in IS. It serves mainly as a thought experiment about the upper limits of AI, reminding us that as AI capabilities advance, it will be crucial to ensure they remain aligned with human values. Today, organizations and researchers are focused on narrow AI applications, with AGI and ASI as future possibilities rather than present tools (IBM Data and AI Team, 2023; Martinez, 2018).

6.2.2 Artificial Intelligence: Functional Types

Within AI, we can distinguish several functional types based on their capabilities: reactive, limited memory, theory of mind, and self-aware. Of these, only reactive machine AI and limited memory AI are available today. Reactive machines are AI systems that are designed exclusively for specific tasks and operate without memory. Rather than learning from or utilizing past outcomes or experiences, they rely solely on current data inputs. Their functionality arises from statistical mathematics, allowing them to process extensive data to generate seemingly intelligent responses. Examples include IBM's Deep Blue chess-playing computer and spam filtering mechanisms (Raj & Kos, 2023; IBM Data and AI Team, 2023).

Limited memory AI systems differ from reactive machines in that they retain information from past events for short periods. They utilize this short-term memory to enhance decision-making, though they lack the capability for long-term retention of historical data. Such AI systems can improve their performance progressively with increased data exposure. Examples include ChatGPT, DeepSeek, Gemini, and similar models (Raj & Kos, 2023; IBM Data and AI Team, 2023).

A theory-of-mind AI falls under AGI and currently remains theoretical. This AI type aims to recognize and interpret thoughts and emotions, enabling more human-like interactions and allowing AI to adjust its behavior and communication according to individual emotional states and intentions (Raj & Kos, 2023; IBM Data and AI Team, 2023). A notable ongoing development is emotion AI, which aims to analyze voices, facial expressions, and other data to understand and simulate emotional responses. Currently, emotion AI is in the developmental stage and lacks any true capability to interpret and respond authentically to human emotions (Raj & Kos, 2023; IBM Data and AI Team, 2023).

Lastly, self-aware AI, a hypothetical class associated with ASI, extends beyond theory of mind capabilities by possessing self-awareness and consciousness. Such an AI would have the capacity to understand its own internal state, emotions, and beliefs, and potentially have independent emotional needs and motivations. Self-aware AI remains strictly theoretical, with significant philosophical and practical barriers to its realization (Raj & Kos, 2023; Qu et al., 2024; IBM Data and AI Team, 2023).

6.2.3 Technological Approaches

6.2.3.1 Rule-Based Systems and Expert Systems (Symbolic AI)

One early approach to AI that was dominant in the mid-20th century was the **rule-based system**, often termed *symbolic AI* or *an expert system* in its advanced form. Rule-based AI relies on **explicitly encoded human knowledge**: developers hand-craft a set of logical rules and facts, and the system uses these to infer conclusions or actions. In essence, such a system follows *if-then* rules: *if* certain conditions are met in the input, *then* apply a specific action or conclusion. For example, an early bank loan application program might grant a loan if an applicant's financial metrics satisfy all the predefined criteria (income above X, credit score above Y, etc.). Similarly, a medical system could diagnose a disease by checking off symptoms against a knowledge base of *if* symptom combinations *then* possible diagnoses (Bhuyan et al., 2024; Lourdusamy & Gnanaprakasam, 2023).

Later, expert systems became especially popular in the 1970s and 1980s as a way to capture specialist knowledge. Pioneering examples include DENDRAL, developed in 1965 to help chemists identify molecular structures, and MYCIN, developed in the early 1970s to diagnose blood infections. These systems demonstrated that computers could emulate human expertise by following a chain of logical rules. Organizations adopted expert systems for tasks like credit approval, troubleshooting equipment failures, and scheduling, seeing them as intelligent assistants that could improve consistency and efficiency (Bhuyan et al., 2024; Lourdusamy & Gnanaprakasam, 2023).

Rule-based systems offer the advantages of **transparency and accuracy within their domain**, as every decision can be traced to a clear rule, and when given the same input, they will always produce the same output, ensuring predictability. Using relatively small amounts of data (just the rules and a few facts), they can produce immediate outputs without lengthy training. However, they have notable limitations. Because they cannot learn or adapt on their own, their **scope is fixed** to the original rule set. If a situation falls outside the rules, the system cannot handle it. Maintaining and updating a large rule base can become *labor-intensive*, and such systems can become brittle as rules proliferate. In short, rule-based AI is **only as good as the human knowledge encoded in it**; it cannot discover new patterns or improve its performance beyond its initial programming (Bhuyan et al., 2024; Lourdusamy & Gnanaprakasam, 2023).

In the context of IS, rule-based AI was an early way to embed intelligence into software. It set the stage for later AI by demonstrating that automated decision-making was possible. Many of today's business rule engines still operate on this principle, for example, fraud detection systems with hard-coded thresholds and IT systems that trigger alerts based on set conditions. Yet, as data volumes grew and problems became more complex, a new approach rose to prominence: letting the *machine* learn the rules on its own from the data. This shift led to the era of machine learning (del Mar Roldán-García et al., 2017).

6.2.3.2 Machine Learning: Learning from Data

Machine learning (ML) is a branch of AI in which systems **learn from data examples** rather than relying on explicit rules. In an ML approach, developers provide a large dataset and choose an algorithm to **discover patterns** in that data, enabling the system to adjust its parameters to improve performance. The system thus essentially "programs itself," creating a model that can make predictions or decisions without being explicitly told the step-by-step logic by humans. In short, ML algorithms are *trained* on data and can then recognize patterns, make predictions, and continuously improve their performance over time (Zhou, 2021).

The key advantage of ML is **adaptability**. Because it learns its logic from examples, an ML system can handle a level of complexity and nuance that would be impractical to capture with manual rules. For instance, consider email spam filtering: rather than writing tens of thousands of rules to catch every spam phrase or sender (an impossible task), an ML model can be trained on a large set of emails labeled "spam" or "not spam." It will statistically infer which features (words, sender attributes, etc.) differentiate spam from legitimate mail. Over time, as spammers change tactics, the model can be retrained or even continue learning, thus *adapting* to new spam patterns (Zhou, 2021).

Various ML techniques have been developed, including **supervised learning** (learning from labeled examples), **unsupervised learning** (finding hidden structures in unlabeled data), and **reinforcement learning** (RL; learning via trial-and-error feedback). Each technique is best suited to specific types of problems. Supervised learning is widely used for classification tasks (e.g., recognizing handwritten digits or classifying loan applicants as low/high risk) and regression (predicting numeric values, such as sales forecasts). Unsupervised learning is useful for clustering (e.g., customer segmentation) and anomaly detection (spotting unusual network activity). RL shines in sequential decision problems, famously in game-playing AIs and resource optimization (Zhou, 2021).

ML underpins many familiar **IS use cases** today. Recommendation engines are a prime example: streaming services and online retailers use ML models to analyze a customer's past behavior and predict what they might want next. In the banking sector, fraud detection also relies heavily on ML: models learn to flag suspicious transactions by training on historical transaction data, detecting subtle patterns of fraudulent behavior that humans might miss. In healthcare, ML models can learn from vast datasets of patient records or images to identify disease risk factors or assist in diagnoses. The power of ML in IS lies in its ability to turn large, complex datasets into *actionable insights or decisions* and to improve over time as more data becomes available (Zhou, 2021; Varmedja et al., 2019).

While ML has opened the door to far more sophisticated AI capabilities, it has also introduced challenges. Models act as "black boxes," meaning their decision logic is often not as transparent as a set of rules. It is critical to ensure data quality and avoid biased or spurious correlations in training data; otherwise, the ML system may learn the "wrong" patterns. Despite these challenges, ML represents a monumental shift from static IS to **adaptive systems** that can evolve with data. A significant subtype of ML known as deep learning has driven many of the most remarkable AI achievements in the past decade.

6.2.3.3 Deep Learning and Neural Networks

Deep learning is a specialized subfield of ML that uses *multilayered neural networks*, inspired by the structure of the human brain, to learn from data. The term "deep" refers to the many layers in these networks. Whereas a traditional ML model might examine input data in one or two stages of computation, a deep neural network may have dozens or even hundreds of layers of simulated neurons, each layer transforming the data and passing it to the next. This layered approach allows deep learning systems to learn *hierarchical representations*, as the model can first capture low-level features (edges in an image, or phonetic sounds in audio), then combine them into higher-level concepts (shapes, objects, or words), and so on, culminating in a rich understanding of the input (LeCun et al., 2015; Shinde & Shah, 2018; Janiesch et al., 2021).

The **neural networks** at the heart of deep learning consist of interconnected nodes (analogous to neurons) with weighted connections. During training, the network adjusts these weights by comparing its predictions to the correct answers and propagating the errors backward in a process known as *backpropagation*. Over many iterations on large datasets, a deep network progressively improves at its task, whether this involves classifying images, recognizing speech, or predicting trends. Crucially, a deep learning system can often learn directly from **raw, unstructured data** (like pixels or audio waveforms) without the need for manual feature engineering. This ability to automatically extract relevant features has led to breakthrough performance on problems once thought extremely hard for machines to solve (Gurney, 2018).

Deep learning's impact on AI has been revolutionary, triggering what some call the "deep learning resurgence" of the 2010s. As mentioned above, AlexNet, created by Geoffrey Hinton, along with his students Alex Krizhevsky and Ilya Sutskever, was a groundbreaking deep neural network that dramatically outperformed earlier approaches in image recognition, revolutionizing CV and sparking widespread adoption of deep learning techniques (Krizhevsky et al., 2012). Suddenly, AI systems began to match or exceed human accuracy in areas like image recognition and voice recognition, tasks that had stubbornly resisted prior AI methods. By 2016, deep learning models were defeating human champions at complex games (the victory of Google DeepMind's AlphaGo in a game of Go being a famous example), and within a few years of that, they were powering everything from autonomous driving perception to real-time language translation (Stanko, 2020).

Many of the AI capabilities we take for granted today are driven by deep learning. When an email service accurately filters spam, a deep neural network is likely parsing the text (building on traditional ML, as mentioned previously). When a banking application flags a suspicious transaction, a deep model might weigh dozens of variables in the blink of an eye. Credit card fraud detection, for instance, is significantly bolstered by deep learning models that sift through large volumes of transaction data to catch anomalies. Personal digital assistants (like Google Assistant or Alexa) use deep learning both for voice recognition (to understand spoken words) and for natural language understanding (to interpret what you mean). In CV, **convolutional neural networks (CNNs)**, a class of deep networks, have become the standard for tasks like identifying objects in photos, detecting faces in camera feeds, or inspecting products on an assembly line for defects. The success of deep learning in these domains stems from its ability to handle enormous complexity and volume of data: more data usually makes deep models perform better, whereas older methods would saturate in performance or require manual tweaking (Alzubaidi et al., 2021; Purwono et al., 2022).

It is worth noting that deep learning models typically demand **extensive computing resources** (powerful GPUs or even specialized AI chips) and vast training datasets. This makes them resource-intensive to develop, and their complexity can make them hard to interpret. Nonetheless, deep learning's versatility and high accuracy have made it a cornerstone of modern AI in IS, driving innovations in automation, predictive analytics, and intelligent user interfaces (Alzubaidi et al., 2021).

6.2.3.4 Natural Language Processing and Conversational AI

One particularly important domain of AI in IS is **natural language processing (NLP),** the branch of AI focused on enabling computers to understand, interpret, and generate human language. Language is at the heart of many ISs (think search engines, customer service chatbots, document analysis tools, virtual assistants, and so on). NLP techniques allow software to deal with text and speech data in intelligent ways, making human-computer interaction much more natural (Chowdhary, 2020).

Understanding language involves multiple challenging tasks: a system must parse the raw text or audio (speech-to-text transcription), interpret the meaning (natural language understanding, which may involve grammar, context, and semantics), possibly generate a useful response or action (natural language generation), and sometimes even produce spoken output (text-to-speech synthesis). As noted above, early NLP systems from the 1960s, such as the famous ELIZA chatbot, were rule-based. ELIZA used pattern matching and scripts to mimic a psychotherapist, fooling some users into thinking they were chatting with a real human. This was a breakthrough at the time because it demonstrated that even simple language rules could create an illusion of understanding. However, ELIZA did not truly "understand" the conversation; it merely followed a script (Kumar et al., 2021; Lo et al., 2023).

Modern NLP has leapt far beyond those beginnings, largely thanks to ML and deep learning. Today's NLP models learn from **vast text datasets**. They can translate between languages, summarize documents, answer questions about a passage, or carry on an open-ended dialogue. A major breakthrough in NLP came with the introduction of **transformer-based models** in 2017, which allowed models to handle language with unprecedented context and nuance. Transformer architecture led to the development of LLMs such as

BERT (introduced by Google in 2018) and OpenAI's **GPT** series. Trained on billions of words from the internet and other sources, such models are able to learn statistical patterns of language at a massive scale (Gillioz et al., 2020; Singla et al., 2024).

A direct outcome of these advances is the new generation of **conversational AI** systems. These LLM-based systems, such as OpenAI's ChatGPT, can generate remarkably human-like text and engage in dialogue on a wide range of topics, thanks to their training on diverse internet text and fine-tuning for conversational ability. These AI chatbots can assist users with tasks like answering questions, writing emails or reports, tutoring students, and providing customer support. Virtual assistants such as Siri, Google Assistant, and Alexa also rely on NLP to interpret voice commands and respond meaningfully, combining this facility with voice recognition and synthesis to hold spoken conversations (Bansal et al., 2024).

Beyond chatbots, NLP permeates many IS applications. **Text analytics** tools use NLP to extract insights from documents, analyzing customer reviews to determine sentiment or scanning legal contracts to find key clauses, for example. **Search engines** use NLP techniques (including understanding synonyms and intent) to parse user queries and match them with relevant documents. **Machine translation services** like Google Translate rely on advanced language models to convert text from one language to another. In business, NLP-driven systems can automate the processing of emails and support tickets, routing them to the correct departments or even drafting initial replies. By enabling machines to handle the nuances of human language, NLP greatly expands the scope of tasks that IS can automate or augment, making technology more accessible and useful in everyday scenarios (Guo et al., 2024).

6.2.3.5 Computer Vision and Perception

Another major domain of AI is CV, the use of machines to interpret and understand visual information, such as images or videos. Just as human vision is a primary sense that enables us to navigate the world, CV allows IS to bridge the gap between the digital and physical worlds by analyzing visual data. Narrow AI applications with CV can be trained to analyze the visual world, identifying and classifying objects within images or video streams. This capability underlies a wide array of intelligent systems today (Laad et al., 2024).

Key tasks in CV include image recognition (classifying an image as, say, a photo of a cat or a dog), **object detection** (finding and labeling multiple objects within an image, such as detecting all the cars and pedestrians in a street scene), **facial recognition** (identifying or verifying individuals' faces), **object tracking** (following a moving object across video frames), and content-based image retrieval (finding images in a database that are similar to a query image). The success of these tasks has surged with the advent of deep learning, particularly the use of CNNs designed for image data. For example, modern photo apps can categorize pictures by the scenery or people they contain, surveillance systems can automatically spot intruders or identify faces, and quality inspection cameras in manufacturing can pick out defective products, all using CV algorithms trained on relevant image data (Laad et al., 2024).

CV is particularly critical for autonomous systems that need to perceive their surroundings. Self-driving cars are a prime example: vision (from cameras) is crucial for them to recognize lane markings, traffic signs, other vehicles, and pedestrians in real time. Indeed, an autonomous vehicle is essentially an IS on wheels, fusing CV with other AI components to make driving decisions. In warehouses and factories, AI-powered robots and drones use vision to navigate aisles, identify inventory, and monitor equipment. Even consumer devices like the iRobot Roomba vacuum use CV to map home layouts and avoid obstacles as they clean (Laad et al., 2024).

In the field of medicine, CV algorithms assist doctors by analyzing medical images, including radiology scans, MRIs, X-rays, and microscopic cell images, to detect anomalies such as tumors or fractures. These AI systems act as a diagnostic aid, flagging areas of concern for further review. In narrow tasks, the **accuracy of CV systems can approach or exceed human levels**. For instance, some AI models have matched dermatologists at spotting certain skin cancers in photos. In the security and defense sectors, vision algorithms monitor CCTV feeds for unusual activity and can help autonomous drones identify targets or disaster survivors (Eswaran & Khang, 2024).

It is important to note that, like all AI, CV systems perform best in narrow contexts with well-defined objectives. They might be "superhuman" at detecting defects in metal casting from high-resolution images, yet they lack the general understanding of a human viewer, and they cannot *interpret* a scene beyond the patterns they were trained to recognize (Gafni et al., 2024a). Nonetheless, as part of an IS, CV modules serve as powerful eyes, converting raw pixels into meaningful insights. Combined with other AI components (for example, combined with NLP to caption images or with robotics to take action), CV greatly extends the reach of IS into real-world environments.

6.2.3.6 Generative AI and Creative Systems

A rapidly advancing frontier in AI is **generative AI**, which refers to systems capable of **creating new content** (text, images, music, code, etc.) rather than merely analyzing existing data. Generative AI leverages sophisticated ML models (usually deep learning) to produce original outputs in response to prompts or questions. In essence, these models learn the patterns of a training dataset so well that they can generate *novel* data with similar characteristics. For example, a generative image model can create a realistic photograph of a face that never existed, and a language model can write a coherent paragraph on a given topic that reads as if a human authored it (Feuerriegel et al., 2024).

One popular class of generative models is that of **generative adversarial networks (GANs),** introduced by Ian Goodfellow and colleagues in 2014. GANs pit two neural networks against each other—one generating candidates, another evaluating them—to produce outputs such as believable fake images, ranging from photorealistic human faces (so-called *deepfakes*) to stylistic art transformations. More recently, a newer type of generative model, the **diffusion model,** has gained attention for its high-quality image generation, as seen in tools like DALL-E 2 and Stable Diffusion (Alqahtani et al., 2021).

However, the generative AI revolution truly caught the public eye with LLMs and AI chatbots. As mentioned earlier, OpenAI's GPT-3 and ChatGPT are generative models that produce text, answers to questions, essays, and even poetry, based on patterns learned from enormous corpora of human writing. These models exemplify how generative AI can capture knowledge across domains and *generate* useful responses or content on demand. Beyond text and images, generative models are also being applied in the areas of music composition, video generation, and even software code generation (for instance, GitHub's Copilot tool helps programmers by generating code snippets) (Fui-Hoon Nah et al., 2023). Generative AI opens up exciting possibilities for ISs, such as content creation, design and media creation, data augmentation, and conversational agents.

Generative AI does come with certain challenges, notably the risk of it producing incorrect information (in text) or realistic-looking fake media. It can have hallucinations, as well as issues of bias in generated content reflecting biases in training data. Nonetheless, its rise marks a shift in AI use from a tool for analysis to a *creative collaborator*. In IS, generative AI components can produce content or solutions dynamically, making systems more interactive and capable of tackling open-ended tasks. The surge of interest and investment in generative AI since 2022 (the watershed moment when the global spotlight fell on ChatGPT) suggests that these capabilities will increasingly be embedded in enterprise software and consumer applications, fundamentally changing how we produce and consume information (Janéafik & Dusek, 2024).

6.3 AI Agents and Agentic AI in Information Systems

In classical IS, software agents, even while called an AI agent, traditionally mean a software entity that perceives inputs from its environment and executes actions according to a predefined policy. The policy may be rules-based (e.g., if-then logic, business rules) or learned (e.g., a trained classifier that routes tickets), but its behavior is bounded by what designers enumerate in advance, whether by triggers, permissible actions, or escalation paths. Classic service-desk triage bots, rules-driven RPA (Robotic Process Automation) scripts, and FAQ (Frequently Asked Questions) chatbots are paradigmatic examples. They are typically stateless or lightly stateful, operate within a single application surface. They are optimized for reliability, predictability, and auditability (Murugesan, 2025; Hosseini & Seilani, 2025).

Contemporary *agentic AI* differs from a traditional AI agent by shifting from reactive, rule-bound execution to goal-directed autonomy. Instead of mapping a fixed input to a predefined action within one workflow, agentic systems couple foundation models with planning, tool use (function calls/APIs – an Application Programming Interface), retrieval-based memory, and iterative self-evaluation to decompose objectives and adapt across steps. This enables cross-system orchestration of querying knowledge bases, invoking enterprise services, validating intermediate results, and revising plans, while structured outputs and policy-aware controllers make actions inspectable before commit. In short, the move is architectural and behavioral: from brittle scripts to adaptive, instrumented problem-solving over time (Murugesan, 2025; Hosseini & Seilani, 2025).

The difference is not merely semantic but operational. First, the difference is in the scope of action as AI agents usually act within one application or a tightly scoped workflow, while agentic AI orchestrates actions across systems (ERP, CRM, ticketing, CI/CD pipelines). A second difference is in decision formation, where agents follow enumerated rules or narrow learned policies. Agentic systems synthesize plans at runtime and can invent novel action sequences within a permitted toolset. Third, there is a difference in memory and context as agents rely primarily on the current input. Agentic systems accumulate and retrieve context from prior steps, knowledge bases, and vector stores, allowing long-horizon tasks. Fourth, evaluation loops are different. Agents often terminate once an action begins (or ends), but agentic systems observe consequences and iterate until a goal or guard condition is reached. These properties make agentic AI more adaptable and valuable in complex environments, but they also reshape the locus of risk (Murugesan, 2025; Hosseini & Seilani, 2025).

In IS practice, agentic systems can reconcile financial exceptions by retrieving supporting documents, drafting justifications, and initiating approvals. They can also monitor supply-chain signals, propose rerouting within cost-risk constraints, and place provisional holds; they can act as MLOps co-pilots that watch drift metrics, propose retraining, and prepare rollback pull-requests for sign-off. In customer operations, they can summarize multi-channel histories, propose next-best actions, check compliance flags, and schedule follow-ups while updating the CRM. These tasks exceed the brittle coverage of classic agents because the system can plan, choose tools, and adapt when intermediate steps do not match any prewritten script (Murugesan, 2025; Hosseini & Seilani, 2025).

However, the same affordances introduce new failure modes. Because plans are synthesized at runtime, mis-specified objectives or mis-scoped permissions can yield harmful but procedurally "reasonable" behavior. A model that would be harmless in a read-only chat surface becomes consequential when it can send emails, modify records, or invoke infrastructure tools. Long-horizon memory creates accountability challenges: who decided what, on what basis, and when? Meanwhile, tool use broadens the attack surface for prompt or retrieval-injection (malicious content that steers the agent via instructions embedded in tickets, documents, or knowledge bases). Traditional agents fail predictably when a rule is missing, but agentic systems can fail creatively in ways that elude rule-based test suites (Murugesan, 2025; Hosseini & Seilani, 2025; Raheem & Hossain, 2025).

Of course, the assurance problem therefore shifts from verifying a model's accuracy to verifying system safety under autonomy. Static post-hoc explanation techniques remain useful for local decisions, but agentic behavior distributes causality across planning modules, retrieval layers, and tool executors. This motivates stronger instrumentation, such as a) durable provenance over data sources; b) logging of goals, intermediate plans, tool calls, inputs, and outputs; and c) cryptographic timestamps that support audit, replay, and appeal. In addition explanation quality should be measured for stability across model and policy updates, not merely for plausibility at a single point in time (Murugesan, 2025; Hosseini & Seilani, 2025; Raheem & Hossain, 2025).

One should also consider governance and control of humans or other mediated means. Effective governance treats autonomy as a permission that must be earned, bounded, and revocable. Least-privilege design constrains the tool surface by granting capabilities per request with short-lived credentials and explicit allowlists. High-impact actions (funds movement, data deletion, configuration changes) require human approval, ideally with a "dry-run" or diff for inspection before commit. Execution should occur in sandboxes with time and step budgets, heartbeats, and kill-switches that terminate on anomaly or policy violation. Continuous adversarial evaluation, simulating jailbreaks, prompt-injection, and tool-overreach, moves from a one-off launch exercise to an operational routine, tracked with metrics such as unsafe-action rate, time-to-detect, and time-to-contain. Finally, governance frameworks should bind these controls to lifecycle management, such as dataset lineage, model versioning, pre-deployment evaluation gates, runtime monitoring for drift and outliers, incident post-mortems, and documented rollback procedures (Murugesan, 2025; Hosseini & Seilani, 2025; Raheem & Hossain, 2025).

In the organizational scope, organizations should evaluate agentic deployments with paired outcome and safety metrics. Outcome metrics include task-success rate, throughput gains, SLA/SLO deltas, and human-intervention frequency. Safety metrics include policy-violation incidence, near-miss counts, explanation stability, and the rate of successful red-team prompts. Where systems mediate user experience or public information, fairness and exposure-diversity metrics complement efficiency to prevent goal-seeking from collapsing into narrow or biased content corridors. Organizations must also consider adoption paths. A staged adoption model mitigates risk while demonstrating value. At the lowest autonomy level, the system proposes plans and drafts actions but can execute them only after human review and approval. With evidence of reliability and containment, organizations can graduate to mixed autonomy in low-impact domains, while retaining human-in-the-loop gates for irreversible steps. Higher autonomy tiers remain conditional on mature instrumentation, incident learning, and governance capabilities. The point is not to maximize autonomy, but to calibrate it, the right autonomy for the right task under the right controls (Murugesan, 2025; Hosseini & Seilani, 2025).

Thus, AI agents and agentic AI are related but distinct constructs. The former are bounded executors of predefined policies. The latter are goal-directed systems that plan, use tools, remember, and adapt over time. Agentic AI therefore holds greater promise for complex, cross-system work in modern enterprises, precisely because it does more than react, but it also requires a corresponding elevation in design discipline, principled scoping, supervision at decision points, comprehensive provenance, and continuous adversarial scrutiny. With these constraints, information systems can harness agentic capabilities while preserving predictability, accountability, and public or organizational trust (Raheem & Hossain, 2025).

6.4 AI Use Cases and Applications in Information Systems

AI technologies, across their various types, have been deployed in virtually every industry to address a wide range of problems. Below, we outline several **general use cases** of AI that illustrate its role in modern IS. These examples are sector-agnostic, highlighting how AI's functional and technical capabilities translate into practical applications. One example is **intelligent assistants and chatbots.** Many organizations use AI-driven virtual assistants to handle routine inquiries and provide services. Voice-activated agents like Siri, Google Assistant, and Alexa use speech recognition and NLP to understand user requests and respond helpfully (e.g., by setting reminders or answering questions). Text-based chatbots on websites and messaging apps can engage customers in dialogue, answer FAQs, and even complete transactions. These systems leverage narrow AI in language processing to deliver 24/7 assistance. For instance, banking apps may use chatbots to help users check their account balance or make payments conversationally, and IT helpdesks may employ AI bots to guide employees through troubleshooting steps. Such assistants augment customer service and user experience through their ability to efficiently handle high volumes of simple queries, allowing human staff to focus on more complex issues (Shawn & Hissain, 2024).

Another example is recommendation systems. Whenever one sees "You might also like…" on an e-commerce website, social media, or receives movie suggestions on a streaming platform, an AI recommendation engine is at work. These systems analyze past behavior (purchases, ratings, views) and compare it with patterns from millions of other users to predict what you might be interested in next. Using ML (often collaborative filtering or deep learning models), recommendation systems personalize content in media, retail, news, and beyond. Netflix's recommendation engine, for example, processes viewing history data to present each user with content they are likely to enjoy. In IS terms, this is AI-driven personalization, it increases user engagement and can significantly drive sales or viewership by promoting the most relevant options for each individual (Chang & Park, 2024).

An important example in risk management is **fraud detection and anomaly detection.** AI can be used to detect irregular patterns that may indicate fraud or security breaches. In finance, banks deploy AI models to monitor transactions in real time and flag suspicious activities, such as unusual credit card purchases or unauthorized account access attempts. These models often mix rules for known fraud patterns with ML that adapts to new fraud tactics. Similarly, telecom companies use AI to identify network intrusions or abnormal usage that might signal hacking. The advantages of AI in these contexts lie in its speed and pattern recognition, it can sift through enormous logs of data and catch subtle correlations that a human might overlook, reducing the time it takes to respond to potential threats. As fraudsters change strategies, ML models can be retrained on the latest data, making the system resilient in protecting assets and keeping it up to date (Varmedja et al., 2019).

As explained earlier in this chapter, AI can also "see" and analyse video and image, and "hear" for that matter as well. Use cases for AI-powered image analysis range from healthcare to public safety. As noted above, in medicine, **diagnostic image analysis** tools help radiologists by examining various medical imaging outputs, highlighting signs of disease that might otherwise be easily missed. In retail and manufacturing, CV checks product images for quality control, detecting defects or mismatches. Security systems employ AI to analyze CCTV feeds, automatically detecting if someone falls on a train platform and alerting staff or recognizing faces at secure entrances, for instance. Even in agriculture, drones with AI vision can survey crops to identify pest infestations or nutrient deficiencies from aerial images. These applications showcase AI's ability to **extract actionable information from visual data**, enabling faster and often more accurate interpretations than manual inspection (Eswaran & Khang, 2024).

An interesting case is autonomous systems and robotics. AI forms the "brains" of **autonomous machines** that perform tasks in the physical world. Self-driving cars are the best-known example, they integrate CV (to perceive roads and obstacles), planning algorithms, and decision-making AI to drive safely. In warehouses, AI guides autonomous robots to move inventory along optimal routes by processing sensor inputs to avoid collisions and ensure efficient operations. Similarly, drones use AI to stabilize their flight and follow targets or predefined delivery paths. Even consumer robotics (like robotic vacuum cleaners) use simple AI to navigate homes and remember room layouts. Autonomous systems can operate *continuously and consistently* and are well-suited to labor-intensive or hazardous tasks. IS that manage logistics, for instance, increasingly include AI components to orchestrate fleets of autonomous vehicles or robots, improving efficiency and safety in supply chains and fulfillment centers (Rajasekaran et al., 2024).

Of course, in the business context, AI also provides predictive analytics and decision support. A classic use case of AI is predicting future trends or outcomes to support decision-making. This spans many scenarios. For instance, **predictive maintenance** models analyze sensor data from equipment to predict failures before they happen, allowing proactive servicing (important in manufacturing, utilities, aviation, etc.). **Demand forecasting** models help retailers and suppliers anticipate product demand based on historical sales data, economic indicators, and even weather patterns, enabling them to optimize inventory and staffing. In HR, AI tools can predict employee attrition or identify high-potential candidates by learning from past employee data (Gafni et al., 2024a). What ties these examples together is the use of ML to uncover patterns in historical and real-time data and **forecast what might happen next**. Expert systems and modern ML models alike have been used to simulate the decision-making of experienced managers or analysts in complex domains, providing recommendations or early warnings. By infusing predictive insights into IS (e.g., an AI-driven dashboard highlighting which factory machine is likely to fail soon), organizations can move from reactive to proactive strategies (Badmus et al., 2024; Bhuyan et al., 2024; Lourdusamy & Gnanaprakasam, 2023).

These use cases demonstrate that the technological approaches to AI we defined above: rule-based, learning-based, vision-oriented, language-centric, and generative, are not abstract concepts but working tools within IS. AI components enhance traditional IS by introducing capabilities like learning from data, natural language interaction, perception of the physical world, and autonomous action. Often, these are combined for optimal effect. For instance, a modern ERP system might include an AI module for demand forecasting (predictive ML), a chatbot interface for queries (NLP), and an anomaly detector for financial transactions (rules and ML). The result is an IS that is more intelligent, adaptive, and useful to its users.

6.5 How AI Enhances Information Systems

Traditional IS, as outlined in Chapters 2 and 3, have long been categorized based on their organizational function and complexity. TPS handles routine transactions, MIS generates structured reports for mid-level management,

DSS supports analytical decision-making, and ESS presents executives with summarized, strategic insights. Over time, enterprise-wide systems like ERP, customer relationship management (CRM), and supply chain management (SCM) systems emerged to break down functional silos, while business intelligence (BI) tools enabled data-driven decision-making. As these systems matured, a new challenge arose over how to make them smarter, faster, and more adaptive to rapidly changing data environments. In the 2020s, with capabilities such as ML, NLP, CV, and intelligent automation, AI has injected dynamism and efficiency into IS, turning static data systems into interactive and predictive ecosystems. For that reason, it is important to uncover how AI enhances each IS type.

Furthermore, as outlined in the section about AI agents and agentic AI, AI can orchestrate multi-step workflows across IS surfaces. Here, we focus on how that orchestration is visible in practice within TPS, MIS, DSS, ERP/CRM/SCM, and BI, using concrete, system-specific patterns and controls. For instance, in a workflow, instead of returning a single answer or triggering a fixed rule, an agentic system decomposes a business objective (e.g., reduce order-to-cash delays) into sequenced actions: querying operational databases, drafting and validating remediation steps, invoking sanctioned APIs, verifying intermediate outcomes against policy, and persisting until a success or guard condition is reached. This shifts "enhancement" from isolated model outputs to end-to-end workflow gains, shorter cycle times, fewer escalations, and higher data quality, while keeping human oversight for irreversible steps (Huang, 2025).

An important point is that AI can enhance not only human productivity and IS but also itself. One of the most profound and speculative implications of AI for IS lies in the concept of recursive self-improvement (RSI). This idea envisions AI systems capable of modifying and enhancing their own architecture, learning processes, and performance without human intervention. In effect, once an AI reaches a certain threshold of generality and capability, it may be able to design better versions of itself, initiating a feedback loop of increasingly powerful systems evolving at exponential speeds (Qu et al., 2024; Majot & Yampolskiy, 2017).

In the IS context, the possibility of RSI has dual significance. First, it presents a radical shift in the development lifecycle of IS itself, from static, human-designed artifacts to dynamic, self-evolving agents. Second, it raises unprecedented challenges for governance, auditability, and control. If traditional IS are shaped by known specifications and human oversight, RSI-capable systems challenge these foundations. For instance, how can we validate the output, security, or ethics of a system that has rewritten its own code base multiple times, perhaps in ways that are opaque or not understandable by humans? (Qu et al., 2024; Majot & Yampolskiy, 2017).

MIS, for instance, which generates regular management reports by processing data from TPS and other sources, has evolved into a more dynamic systems through AI augmentation. First, automated trend analysis enables the identification of latent patterns in structured datasets. Tools like Microsoft Dynamics 365 leverage embedded AI to offer adaptive dashboards that adjust based on user roles, previous queries, and emergent data patterns. Second, natural language interfaces allow users to interact with systems conversationally. NLP engines can translate human questions into system queries, for example, "What were our top-selling products in Q1 across all regions?," making data exploration more accessible for non-technical users. Moreover, AI supports personalized report generation, summarizing key performance indicators (KPIs) relevant to specific managers and alerting them to unusual trends. This shifts MIS from a passive repository to a proactive decision-support companion (Shawn & Hissain, 2024).

Another example, now integrated into MIS, is TPS. These foundational systems handle routine and high-volume transactions such as payroll processing, point-of-sale operations, and banking transactions. Historically designed for speed and reliability, TPS have seen considerable enhancement through AI integration. One major advancement is real-time fraud detection. AI models trained on large transaction datasets can identify anomalies indicative of fraud. For instance, platforms like PayPal and Stripe deploy AI algorithms that flag suspicious activities instantaneously, far beyond the capabilities of rule-based systems. AI also introduces predictive error detection in data entry processes. For example, Oracle Autonomous Transaction Processing uses ML to monitor performance, self-optimize queries, and predict transaction anomalies before they affect performance or accuracy. These enhancements ensure greater reliability, faster issue resolution, and reduced need for human intervention (Varmedja et al., 2019).

In the case of DSS, these systems were built to assist with non-routine, data-intensive decisions. These systems traditionally required human-defined rules and statistical modeling, while AI has significantly deepened their analytical capabilities. ML models now power predictive analytics in DSS, forecasting outcomes such as sales demand, market risks, and customer churn. For example, Tableau has integrated Einstein Discovery (from Salesforce) to enable non-technical users to access predictive models without code. Another enhancement is in the area of prescriptive analytics, where AI can not only predict what is likely to happen but also suggest optimal responses. IBM's Watson Decision Platform exemplifies this; it uses AI to model various business scenarios, simulate outcomes, and recommend the most beneficial options. Additionally, in complex DSS, such as in logistics and energy management, RL enables the system to continuously improve its decision-making strategy based on feedback from previous actions (Waqar, 2024; Guidi et al., 2016).

For ESS, which aggregates and summarizes internal and external data for high-level strategic decision-making, AI-driven features have enhanced their traditional function by improving clarity, relevance, and foresight. Here, AI provides real-time strategic alerts based on sentiment analysis, risk assessment, and competitor tracking. For instance, Oracle EPM Cloud uses AI to highlight potential financial risks by summarizing external market movements that could affect corporate strategy. In addition, AI-powered executive dashboards now use predictive analytics to offer tailored insights. Systems like IBM Cognos Analytics can generate executive summaries, forecast business performance, and answer "what-if" questions via natural language queries. These AI enhancements ensure that ESS can not only present an overview of past and current performance but also illuminate possible future trajectories, supporting more informed and agile leadership decisions (Henriksen & Blond, 2023).

AI also enhances ERP systems as it helps integrate key business processes—finance, HR, procurement, and manufacturing—into a unified system. AI enhances ERP by making these processes predictive, responsive, and self-optimizing. For example, SAP S/4HANA utilizes AI to automate procurement matching, forecast inventory needs, and suggest preventive maintenance schedules in manufacturing. AI also supports intelligent financial closing by detecting anomalies in transactions and speeding up audits. Oracle Fusion Cloud ERP uses AI to detect fraud in employee expenses and predict cash flow based on real-time revenue and expense trends. This proactive visibility enables businesses to make more timely and strategic financial decisions (Nyathani et al., 2024).

CRM systems manage interactions with current and potential customers. AI has also transformed CRM from a passive record-keeping tool to an active engagement engine. Salesforce Einstein, for instance, provides predictive lead scoring, helping sales teams focus on those prospects most likely to convert. It also suggests next-best actions and provides automated insights based on behavioral data. Similarly, Zoho CRM's AI assistant, Zia, can detect anomalies in sales trends, provide performance forecasts, and even identify emotional sentiment in customer communications. These AI tools significantly improve customer segmentation, personalization, and retention strategies, allowing businesses to build more nuanced and lasting relationships (Roba & Malic, 2023).

With SCM systems that coordinate the flow of goods, information, and finances across the supply chain, AI can improve the efficiency, transparency, and agility of SCM operations. Blue Yonder (formerly JDA Software) is a leading example, it uses AI to conduct demand sensing, anticipating customer needs using real-time market signals. Its ML models optimize replenishment, logistics routing, and warehouse operations. In another example, SAP Integrated Business Planning (IBP) uses AI to simulate supply chain disruptions and recommend contingency strategies. AI also enables real-time supplier risk monitoring, factoring in political events, environmental factors, and social sentiment. These enhancements allow SCM systems to shift from reactive fulfillment to proactive orchestration, minimizing costs and improving service levels even in volatile conditions (Singh et al., 2022).

In pure business analytics where BI systems enable organizations to make informed decisions based on data analytics and visualization, AI amplifies the power of BI by providing cognitive capabilities and automated insights. Microsoft Power BI, now equipped with Copilot, allows users to ask natural language questions and instantly receive visualizations or summaries. It also highlights unexpected trends and forecasts future KPIs. Tableau, in integration with Einstein Discovery, offers automated pattern detection, correlation insights, and predictive modeling embedded within dashboards. Additionally, Qlik AutoML enables low-code deployment of ML models directly within BI workflows, enhancing strategic planning through rigorous forecasting. These advancements democratize data access and analytical capability, empowering business users to uncover hidden opportunities without needing deep technical expertise (Bulusu & Abellera, 2020).

The examples above illustrate that AI's influence on IS is not limited to enhancing discrete system types; it also manifests through systemic capabilities that cut across all categories of IS. At the foundation of these enhancements lie the core technologies of NLP, ML, CV, and RL. Collectively, these capabilities enable systems to interact more naturally with users, detect patterns in vast datasets, interpret visual information, and optimize actions in dynamic environments. For instance, through NLP, executive dashboards and CRM platforms can support conversational interfaces, while ML enhances TPS with real-time fraud detection and improves BI systems by enabling predictive analytics. CV adds intelligence to supply chain monitoring and product quality control, and RL optimizes scheduling, pricing, and logistics in ERP and DSS environments (Gruetzemacher & Whittlestone, 2022).

Emerging technologies such as generative AI, federated learning, and explainable AI (XAI) further deepen the systemic functions of AI. Generative models can create summaries, generate reports, or simulate alternative strategies, making IS more responsive and communicative. Federated learning and edge AI enable secure, decentralized model training, crucial in industries with strict data privacy concerns. Meanwhile, XAI ensures transparency and trust by allowing users to understand how AI-based decisions are made, particularly important in regulatory or ethically sensitive environments. Together, these systemic capabilities transform traditional IS into adaptive, intelligent ecosystems that not only automate and optimize processes but also interpret, learn, and co-create with human users (Dwivedi et al., 2023).

It is important to mention here that modern AI, especially agentic systems, both consumes and generates the data that later conditions its own behavior, creating feedback loops that can amplify errors or biases (positive loops) or dampen them (negative loops). In IS this shows up when model outputs (rankings, flags, summaries) change user behavior, which then shifts the data distribution the model "learns" from or grounds on and, over time, narrow signals get overrepresented, confidence becomes inflated, and edge cases disappear. Designing for "healthy" loops means adding diversity/novelty injection, counterfactual evaluation, hold-out telemetry not exposed to the model, and policy "dampers" (caps, cooldowns, exposure quotas) so performance improves without collapsing into self-reinforcement (Stray, 2023).

6.6 Challenges and Negative Implications

AI has emerged as a disruptive force that has considerably enhanced the entire spectrum of IS. However, its advancements are not without cost. The integration of AI into IS has introduced new technical vulnerabilities, ethical dilemmas, and governance challenges, adding to traditionally present vulnerabilities. This technology also consumes a lot of power and raises some sustainability concerns. For every algorithm that streamlines a supply chain, another may inadvertently discriminate against a vulnerable group. For every AI-powered chatbot that improves customer service, another may be harvesting sensitive data without adequate transparency or consent. This duality demands a cautious, systematic, and critical examination of AI's role within IS (Tredinnick & Laybats, 2023).

One particular concern is agentic models, as agentic AI introduces risks that differ in kind from traditional model errors because plans and actions are synthesized at run-time across multiple systems. Mis-specified objectives or proxy metrics can drive "reasonable" but harmful behavior; over-permissioned tools expand the blast radius from bad text to consequential actions (data deletion, fund movement, configuration change). Long-horizon memory and multi-step planning complicate accountability and auditability, obscuring who decided what and why. Exposure to untrusted inputs creates new attack surfaces—such as prompt-injection and retrieval poisoning in tickets, documents, or knowledge bases—that can steer the agent under the guise of grounding. Autonomy also raises persistence hazards, where scheduled jobs or cached plans re-activate after nominal revocation, and increases the risk of cascading failures as an agent coordinates TPS/MIS/ERP components. These dynamics shift assurance from static accuracy checks to continuous, system-level safety, provenance, and containment (Murugesan, 2025).

Generally, some of the challenges and complexities of AI use include issues with data authenticity, bias, accountability, security and privacy issues, legal and regulatory concerns, and ethical considerations. Further complexities include integration and interpretability concerns, scalability, maintenance, cost, environmental concerns, human adaptation (and training), and, last but not least, over-reliance on AI.

6.6.1 Data Integrity and Authenticity in the Age of AI

Data integrity is a foundational element of any IS. In the pre-AI era, this primarily involved ensuring that data was accurate and remained uncorrupted during entry, transmission, and storage. Today, AI systems do not just consume data, they also generate it. Generative models such as GPT, StyleGAN, and DALL-E are creating text, images, and audio that are often indistinguishable from human-created content. While this opens new opportunities, it also introduces unprecedented risks to information authenticity (Tredinnick & Laybats, 2023). A prominent example is a 2019 case where criminals used deepfake audio to impersonate the voice of a German CEO, successfully tricking the CEO of a UK-based subsidiary into wiring €220,000 to a fraudulent account. The attacker used AI-generated voice mimicking to simulate the German executive's accent, tone, and urgency. This incident was among the first high-profile deepfake-enabled frauds, revealing how AI-generated content can undermine traditional identity verification mechanisms in enterprises' ISs (Strupp, 2019).

Similarly, AI-generated fake news articles, photos, and videos have been used to manipulate public opinion. A particularly chilling example was a deepfake video, which was debunked, of Ukrainian President Volodymyr Zelenskyy from 2022 which showed him appearing to surrender to Russia, a video quickly debunked but not before being shared widely. In both corporate and geopolitical contexts, IS that cannot verify the provenance and authenticity of digital content are at risk of being manipulated, misled, or exploited (Miller, 2022). In response, some companies are adopting technologies such as cryptographic watermarking or content provenance chains (like those developed by the Coalition for Content Provenance and Authenticity, C2PA) to track and validate digital content. Nevertheless, widespread implementation is still limited, and the arms race between detection and deception continues to escalate (Hatchimonji, 2025).

6.6.2 Accountability and Explainability

As AI becomes increasingly central to decision-making in IS, questions surrounding accountability and explainability have become critical. Traditional IS models were designed with traceable logic; decisions could be audited and verified against established rules and workflows. However, AI, especially the deep learning manifestations thereof, operates on non-transparent processes that are difficult to explain even to their developers. This "black box" nature complicates oversight, regulatory compliance, and trust (Coeckelbergh, 2020).

An interesting example of this problem, although about statistical algorithms and not AI *per se*, occurred in 2020 when the UK's Office of Qualifications and Examinations Regulation (Ofqual) used a statistical algorithm to assign A-level scores during the COVID-19 pandemic. Due to the cancellation of standardized exams, the algorithm was used to moderate teacher assessments. It transpired that students from historically underperforming schools were systematically downgraded, whereas those from traditionally high-achieving institutions were disproportionately favored. The resulting backlash was swift and severe, with widespread protests and a government-mandated rollback. The lack of transparency in how the algorithm operated, compounded by the inability of students, teachers, and even policymakers to understand its basis for grading, exemplified the perils of opaque AI systems (Hao, 2020).

In response, the field of XAI is developing methods to open the AI "black box" and make outputs more interpretable. For instance, LIME (local interpretable model-agnostic explanations) and SHAP (shapley additive explanations) are gaining traction in enterprise settings where model accountability is vital (Dwivedi et al., 2023; Salih et al., 2025). However, challenges persist. For many neural network applications, explainability methods provide approximations rather than true insights into decision logic. This becomes particularly problematic in high-stakes environments such as healthcare, where AI diagnostics must be explainable to practitioners, or finance, where risk models are subject to auditing. In such contexts, a lack of clarity can lead to regulatory non-compliance or an erosion of stakeholder trust.

Explainability in AI hinges not only on model architecture and interpretability tools but also on the integrity and dynamics of the data that flows into these systems. A foundational principle in computing, *Garbage In, Garbage Out (GIGO)*, remains highly relevant in the age of AI-driven IS. GIGO highlights the reality that flawed, biased, or low-quality input data will inevitably result in flawed, biased, or misleading outputs, regardless of the sophistication of the underlying algorithm. In the context of AI-enhanced IS, this is particularly dangerous, decisions made on such outputs can affect credit scores, hiring outcomes, medical diagnoses, or criminal justice assessments (Vidgen & Derczynski, 2020; Stray, 2023).

When machine learning models learn from historical data that reflects systemic biases, such as discriminatory policing or inequitable hiring practices, the model may encode and perpetuate those injustices. The feedback loop emerges when these biased outputs are reintegrated into the system as new inputs. For example, a predictive policing algorithm that over-patrols certain neighborhoods due to biased historical data may generate new arrest records that further reinforce its initial assumptions. This self-reinforcing cycle not only damages explainability but also undermines the legitimacy of AI-enhanced decision-making. These feedback loops can be either positive, amplifying existing patterns, or negative, suppressing anomalies, but both pose risks if left unmonitored. In opaque systems, they may remain undetected until they cause significant harm. Therefore, explainability must go beyond post hoc tools like SHAP or LIME. It must also encompass transparent data provenance, robust input auditing, and systemic checks that identify and break harmful feedback cycles (Vidgen & Derczynski, 2020; Stray, 2023). A truly explainable AI system is one that not only makes its reasoning accessible but also ensures that its reasoning is grounded in valid, well-curated, and continually evaluated data.

6.6.3 Bias, Fairness, and Algorithmic Discrimination

AI systems learn from data, and data is a reflection of the society that produces it. This means that historical injustices and societal inequities may be present in the datasets used to train ML models and subsequently encoded into the outputs of IS that employ these models. In many cases, this results in biased systems that reinforce discrimination rather than mitigating it (Gafni et al., 2024b; Hanna et al., 2025). In 2018, for instance, Amazon discontinued an AI-based recruitment tool after discovering that it penalized resumes containing the word "women's," as in "women's chess club captain." The model had been trained on ten years of hiring data that included predominantly male candidates. As a result, it began to downgrade resumes that deviated from this norm, showing how historical biases can shape algorithmic judgments in employment (Winick, 2018).

Similarly, the COMPAS (Correctional Offender Management Profiling for Alternative Sanctions) system used by U.S. courts to assess recidivism risk has been shown to be racially biased. A ProPublica investigation in 2016 found that Black defendants were more likely to be falsely labeled as high risk compared to white defendants. This finding raises serious concerns about the use of AI in judicial IS, where fairness and impartiality are legally and ethically mandated (Larson et al., 2016).

Bias can also appear in consumer-facing IS. For example, facial recognition technologies used in retail security and smart surveillance systems have significantly higher error rates for individuals with darker skin tones. A 2019 study by the National Institute of Standards and Technology (NIST) found that many commercial facial recognition systems exhibited demographic differentials in their false positive rates. These disparities not only affect the usability of IS but can also result in reputational damage and legal liability for organizations (Singer & Metz, 2019; NIST, 2019).

6.6.4 Security and Privacy Risks

Digital systems face many security and privacy risks, of which the "traditional" risks have previously been reviewed. Here, we present some specific risks in the context of AI, IS, and information intake. While AI strengthens IS by improving anomaly detection and response automation, it also introduces novel risks to security and privacy. Breaches of AI-enabled IS can expose large datasets, making them lucrative targets for cybercriminals. Moreover, AI models themselves can be vulnerable; adversarial attacks can manipulate input data to trick AI systems into making faulty decisions, for instance, jeopardizing the integrity and reliability of critical systems such as fraud detection or automated decision-making, or even self-driving cars (Li & Zhang, 2017).

Privacy risks are amplified by AI's capacity for inference. Advanced algorithms can deduce sensitive attributes about individuals, even from anonymized datasets, undermining traditional data protection safeguards. For example, combining disparate data sources can enable re-identification of individuals, violating privacy expectations and regulatory requirements such as the GDPR. Furthermore, AI-driven profiling and automated decisions can erode individuals' control over their personal information and raise ethical questions about surveillance, discrimination, and bias (Ye et al., 2022).

One major concern is the susceptibility of AI models to adversarial attacks, where subtle, carefully crafted manipulations to input data lead to incorrect outputs; these are also, in their various forms, known as poisoning attacks. For instance, even physical-world interruptions can cause AI systems to behave differently than intended. A good example is a study done on autonomous cars and stop signs, where researchers strategically placed a few stickers on a stop sign, causing it to be misidentified by a self-driving car. Such vulnerabilities are not merely academic; they have serious implications for autonomous IS, including those used in transportation, surveillance, and smart cities (Li & Zhang, 2017; Yerlikaya & Bahtiyar, 2022).

Another example of a similar threat is where attackers insert malicious data into training datasets to compromise a model's integrity. In the context of IS, this could mean corrupting inventory forecasting models, financial fraud detectors, or cybersecurity systems to misclassify threats. An interesting example is a study from the University of Chicago that introduced "Nightshade," a tool that subtly corrupts training data scraped from the internet to poison generative AI models. The tool's purpose was to protect artists' works; however, it exemplifies the disruptive potential of such attacks by malicious actors. As AI training increasingly relies on publicly available data, IS face elevated exposure to this risk (Shan et al., 2024).

From a privacy standpoint, AI systems can also leak sensitive information. For example, OpenAI's ChatGPT models were found to occasionally reproduce snippets of their training data verbatim, including email addresses, phone numbers, and other personal identifiers. In another example, a zero-click AI vulnerability (CVE-2025-32711) in Microsoft's Copilot allowed malicious actors to exfiltrate sensitive data from Microsoft 365. Particularly in IS handling health, legal, or financial data, such lapses could result in severe regulatory penalties (Pearson, 2023; Lakshamanan, 2025). Although privacy-preserving machine learning (PPML) techniques, such as fully homomorphic encryption (FHE) for deep neural networks, are emerging to address these concerns, these technologies are still in their early stages (Parikh et al., 2024).

6.6.5 Legal and Regulatory Complexities

The legal environment for AI in IS is fragmented across jurisdictions and conceptually strained by technologies that do not fit legacy categories of products and services. In the US, constitutional speech protections and platform immunities have left most algorithmic amplification beyond the reach of liability, even where recommender systems plausibly contribute to the spread of harmful content like in the case of the Supreme Court's handling of Gonzalez v. Google, where it preserved the core of Section 230, maintaining substantial shields for platforms despite their algorithmic curation roles in promoting radicalization for terrorism (Chowdhury, 2023). By contrast, the European Union's Digital Services Act (DSA) and the AI Act establish risk-based obligations and systemic-risk duties for very large platforms, including transparency for recommender systems and labeling of deepfakes. Still, enforcement capacity, cross-border evasion, and migration to encrypted or extra-EU services limit the practical reach of these provisions. In parallel, policy in the U.S. has emphasized innovation capacity, for example, the National Artificial Intelligence Initiative Act of 2020 (2021) and the January 23, 2025 executive order "Removing Barriers to American Leadership in AI," which strengthens standards work and commercialization while further complicating any uniform rules set for enterprise deployments (White House, 2025).

A further development in this trajectory is the White House's Project Genesis, launched in late 2025 as a national AI 'moonshot' mission to build secure, aligned, and publicly accountable frontier AI infrastructure. Unlike traditional regulatory instruments, Genesis combines innovation funding, safety-by-design requirements, national evaluation testbeds, and cross-sector governance mechanisms into a single mission-driven framework. For IS, the initiative illustrates how modern states increasingly govern AI not only through statutes but also through strategic programs that embed oversight, provenance, and risk-management directly into national AI capabilities. Project Genesis, therefore, represents an emerging model of state-led AI governance that blends regulatory intent with infrastructural power, shaping how AI-driven IS will be developed and deployed in the coming decade (White House, 2025a).

These divergences reveal a deeper structural problem where the law lags behind technologies that generate novel risks (i.e., deepfakes, autonomous agents, coordinated botnets), render older assumptions obsolete (human authorship, local publication), and resist precise targeting under existing doctrines. This is a regulatory gap—characterized by uncertainty, targeting mismatches, obsolescence, and novelty—which helps explain why extremists (and, more broadly, malicious actors) can exploit borderless networks to evade territorially bounded rules. Given this reality, organizational compliance for AI in IS must go beyond box-checking to include provenance, auditability, as well as continuous risk evaluations that anticipate rather than react to cross-system misuse, so legal accountability can attach to processes, not only to static model artifacts (Habbal et al., 2024).

In this context, one notable example of regulation by framework recommendations is NIST's AI Risk Management Framework (AI RMF 1.0), mentioned in Chapter 5 as well, that operationalizes responsible AI as a lifecycle discipline of Map, Measure, Manage, and Govern, linking context definition and risk identification to concrete controls, monitoring, and oversight. For IS that now includes agentic behaviors, the RMF is especially useful because it translates abstract principles into deployable artifacts: system/model cards, dataset lineage records, risk registers, evaluation gates, red-team playbooks, least-privilege tool scopes with human-in-the-loop approvals, and immutable audit logs of goals, plans, tool calls, and outcomes. The framework emphasizes continuous measurement (drift, bias, robustness, security) and incident learning, so governance is not a one-off compliance task but an ongoing operational loop. Practically, adopting the RMF helps IS leaders demonstrate due diligence while keeping autonomy bounded, auditable, and recoverable (NIST, 2023).

6.6.5.1 Can AI (or Agentic AI) be a Legal "Person"?

A parallel debate asks whether advanced AI systems should be granted some form of legal personhood. The analogy to corporate personhood and to non-human legal subjects (such as protected natural entities) is conceptually familiar. Advocates claim that vesting autonomous systems with rights and duties could simplify attribution and allow assets/insurance to sit with the AI entity itself. Yet, this move is premature and potentially hazardous. Even if some autonomy is real, personhood risks producing unaccountable actors in precisely those spaces where accountability is most needed (e.g., synthetic disinformation, discriminatory decision-support), enabling creators to launder responsibility through artificial "proxies." As Kurki's (2019) analysis underscores, tools remain instruments of human agency; relocating liability to the tool obscures human control without supplying meaningful sanctions or remediation against a non-sentient "person."

From an IS governance standpoint, treating agentic AI as a legal person would complicate, not clarify, enterprise risk, as it would blur corporate accountability lines, weaken deterrence for negligent design or deployment, and collide with sectoral regimes that already allocate duties to developers, deployers, and controllers. Current regulatory trajectories instead favor transparency, duty-of-care, and risk-based controls (e.g., deepfake labeling, systemic-risk mitigation), which keep obligations with human and corporate principals rather than fictional AI entities. In short, before any personhood experiments, law and policy should be able to strengthen enforceable duties on the humans and organizations that build, integrate, and operate agentic systems (Doomen, 2023; Möslein, 2025).

6.6.5.2 Cross-Border Data and Model Flows

Modern IS rarely operate within a single jurisdiction. Data moves not only as rows in databases but also as embeddings, prompts, logs, and fine-tuning corpora, models themselves can be "data in derivative form." This creates transfer risk in three layers: (1) data at rest (storage and backups across cloud regions), (2) data in use (RAG retrievals, tool calls, telemetry sent to vendors), and (3) model artifacts (weights, vector stores, and cached plans that may encode PII or sensitive information). Because agentic systems orchestrate multi-step actions across services, they can silently traverse borders (e.g., ticket content in the EU, log parsing in the US, email via APAC), triggering conflicting laws on privacy, surveillance, and sectoral secrecy (Koppel & Parkhomchuk, 2025).

Legally, most regimes permit international transfers only with adequate safeguards (lawful basis, proportionality, security). In practice this means scoping roles (controller/processor), using data minimization and pseudonymization, and binding vendors with DPAs, transfer impact assessments, and contractual clauses that address government access. But AI adds two issues. First, "grounding" and log data can re-identify through linkage and, second, model portability (moving weights across regions) can re-create the original risk even when raw data stays local. Risk therefore attaches to where inference, planning, and tool execution happen, not only where databases reside (Koppel & Parkhomchuk, 2025; Bolatbekkyzy, 2024).

6.6.6 Ethical Considerations and Social Harms

Aside from technical and legal challenges, the integration of AI into IS also raises profound ethical concerns. As IS become increasingly autonomous and capable of making decisions about individuals' lives, the risks of their infringing upon people's fundamental rights and social values intensify (Završnik & Simončič, 2023).

One major ethical issue is surveillance. AI-enhanced IS, particularly in the public sector, are often used for predictive policing, border control, and behavioral monitoring. In China, the use of facial recognition AI combined with mass surveillance IS in Xinjiang has drawn international condemnation. Reports indicate that AI-enabled IS are being used to track ethnic minorities, flag behavior deemed suspicious by authorities, and enforce social conformity through predictive risk scoring. These practices challenge global norms on privacy, due process, and freedom of expression (Byler, 2019).

In democratic societies, the use of AI for surveillance, though less overt, is still troubling. The UK's Metropolitan Police, for example, faced criticism after deploying facial recognition in public spaces without clear legal or ethical oversight. The system was found to have a high false positive rate, particularly among people from minority ethnic backgrounds. This example underscores the ethical dilemma of balancing public safety with individual rights, particularly when algorithmic decisions are opaque and difficult to challenge (Dearden, 2019).

Another ethical concern involves the use of AI in content moderation. Social media platforms like Facebook and YouTube use AI-based IS to identify and remove harmful content. However, these systems are not always accurate and often struggle with context, leading both to wrongful censorship and a failure to act against genuinely harmful material. For instance, during the COVID-19 pandemic, automated moderation systems frequently removed posts discussing legitimate vaccine side effects while failing to curb widespread misinformation (Balendra, 2025).

Additionally, the rise of generative AI has introduced new ethical dilemmas around authorship, originality, and intellectual property. Tools like ChatGPT, Midjourney, and DALL·E are increasingly being used to generate content for business, academia, and entertainment. Yet, who owns AI-generated outputs? And are the creators of training data being fairly credited or compensated? Courts and legislatures have only begun to grapple with these questions, and IS developers may find themselves operating in legal and ethical gray zones (Hanna et al., 2025).

Fairness and inclusion are also central ethical concerns. AI models may inadvertently marginalize users who are underrepresented in their training data. For instance, voice assistants like Amazon's Alexa and Apple's Siri have historically struggled to understand non-native English speakers or those with regional accents (Larkin, 2018). In financial IS, credit scoring algorithms have been found to disadvantage minority borrowers, even when explicitly excluding race as a variable (Garcia et al., 2024). These examples illustrate the limitations of purely technical fixes and highlight the need for continuous ethical evaluation throughout the AI development lifecycle.

In response, ethical frameworks such as "ethics-by-design" and "value-sensitive design" are gaining traction. These approaches embed ethical considerations into the early stages of IS design, rather than treating them as post hoc add-ons. For example, companies have begun to institute "ethics boards" that include ethicists, legal experts, and engineers to review and guide the ethical development of AI systems. Similarly, the Montreal Declaration for a Responsible Development of Artificial Intelligence provides a voluntary code of principles that institutions can adopt to align their AI design with public values (Brey & Dainow, 2024; Université de Montréal, 2018).

Despite these efforts, the ethical use of AI remains, for the most part, voluntary and unenforced. There is growing consensus that ethical oversight must be institutionalized via ethics committees, public consultations, algorithmic impact assessments, and legal mandates, to ensure that AI-enhanced IS do not compromise democratic values or human dignity.

6.6.7 Sustainability Concerns

The integration of AI into IS is often lauded for its potential to address global challenges, including climate change and resource optimization. AI can indeed support sustainability goals through applications such as optimizing energy grids, reducing waste, and enhancing environmental monitoring. However, this optimistic narrative frequently obscures the environmental footprint of AI itself, raising urgent questions about its long-term sustainability.

The environmental impact of AI spans multiple layers: from the energy-intensive training of large models, to the constant operation of data centers, and the mining, manufacturing, and disposal of the hardware that powers intelligent systems. The term "digital pollution" has emerged to describe these costs. Despite the metaphor of the "cloud," data is stored and processed in very tangible, resource-consuming infrastructures. These facilities, often powered by fossil fuels, consume vast amounts of electricity and water for cooling, and emit significant levels of greenhouse gases. As an example, one study by Strubell et al. (2020) found that training a single large AI model like GPT-2 generated emissions equivalent to the lifetime carbon footprint of five cars (Lucivero, 2024; Dhiman et al., 2024).

Even more elusive are the indirect or systemic effects, such as the "rebound effect," where increased efficiency leads to greater overall consumption. For instance, more efficient natural language processing (NLP) models might reduce costs, prompting researchers to run more experiments, inadvertently increasing energy use. Similarly, the societal shift toward AI-integrated services in everyday life, with virtual assistants, automated content moderation, and smart recommendations—raises baseline consumption levels of computational resources (Lucivero, 2024; Dhiman et al., 2024).

Current regulatory frameworks rarely account for this complexity. Environmental sustainability is often framed as a voluntary principle, not a binding requirement. While some tech corporations have announced commitments to carbon neutrality or "net-zero" emissions, these pledges are inconsistently defined and often criticized as greenwashing. Moreover, there is a stark imbalance in how the environmental burdens and benefits of AI are distributed: the Global North often reaps the gains, while electronic waste, resource extraction, and climate risks are disproportionately borne by the Global South (Lucivero, 2024; Dhiman et al., 2024).

Critically, these challenges cannot be resolved by technical efficiency alone. In addition, traditional cost-benefit analyses are inadequate in a domain where both costs and benefits are often uncertain, non-monetizable, or unequally distributed. Instead, sustainability governance for AI must embrace value-based and political approaches, ones that include environmental justice, intergenerational equity, and the full life-cycle assessment of AI systems (Lucivero, 2024; Dhiman et al., 2024).

This is a concerning topic, as the industry often paces for profit and not for the common good; policymakers should move beyond self-regulation and establish binding monitoring, accountability, and mitigation frameworks, potentially including sustainability audits for large-scale AI systems, standards for green data centers, and enforceable emissions caps. Without such global, enforceable governance, AI risks becoming a driver of unsustainable digital expansion rather than a tool for ecological resilience.

6.6.8 Operational and Organizational Challenges

While the theoretical potential of AI to enhance IS is often highlighted in research and media, the reality of implementation is considerably more complex. Organizations face a host of operational and institutional challenges that can stall or distort the integration of AI into IS. First, many institutions rely on legacy IS that are incompatible with modern AI architectures. These systems may lack the data infrastructure, processing capabilities, or modularity needed to support ML algorithms or real-time decision engines. For instance, the U.S. Internal Revenue Service (IRS) still depends on systems written in COBOL, a language from the 1960s, which makes it nearly impossible to integrate AI-driven fraud detection or taxpayer assistance modules without a complete overhaul. Such integration challenges are not limited to the public sector. Banks, hospitals, and supply chain firms often run mission-critical systems on outdated platforms that resist integration with AI services. The cost, complexity, and risk of migrating data or rewriting backend code deter many organizations, forcing them to deploy AI in fragmented or peripheral ways and limiting its overall strategic impact (GAO, 2023; Melo et al., 2025).

Second, even when technical integration is achieved, organizations must grapple with how intelligible and controllable their AI systems are. This is particularly pressing in sectors like healthcare, law, and finance, where decisions must be explainable to users, regulators, and clients (Dwivedi et al., 2023). In such contexts, "black box" models are not just a technical concern; they represent a governance liability. Increasingly, companies are adopting interpretable models or employing tools like SHAP to generate explanations post hoc (Dwivedi et al., 2023; Salih et al., 2025). However, because these tools often require specialized knowledge to interpret, they create barriers for non-technical decision-makers within IS workflows.

Third, AI is not a "set-and-forget" technology. Models require regular retraining, calibration, and monitoring to remain accurate and relevant. This operational burden is frequently underestimated. Moreover, maintenance costs extend beyond technical upkeep. AI models must comply with evolving regulatory standards, privacy mandates, and ethical expectations. These layers of oversight require a dedicated cross-functional team, composed of data scientists, lawyers, ethicists, and business analysts, to ensure that AI functions within the bounds of the organization's goals and societal norms (Law, 2024; Shivashankar et al., 2025).

Lastly, one of the most significant bottlenecks to effective AI integration is a lack of talent. Many organizations struggle to recruit and retain personnel with the necessary expertise in AI development, data governance, and ethical assessment. This skills gap often leads to poor implementation or underutilization of AI tools, or reliance on third-party vendors whose systems may not align with internal policies or compliance standards. Even when skilled workers are available, there can be institutional resistance to change. Employees may be skeptical of AI's role, fearing job displacement or loss of autonomy. Without deliberate change management strategies, such as transparent communication, retraining programs, and participatory design, AI initiatives may encounter organizational inertia (Tambe et al., 2019; Dima et al., 2024).

6.6.9 Over-Reliance on AI and the Risk of Automation Bias

As AI becomes increasingly central to IS, organizations face the risk of over-reliance on algorithmic decision-making. This dependence can erode critical human oversight, leading to what is known as "automation bias," the tendency for users to trust machine-generated outcomes even when they are incorrect or misleading. Further, agentic AI amplifies automation bias because the system does not merely recommend but also acts, planning steps, calling tools, and presenting "completed" outcomes that carry a strong presumption of correctness. The resulting closure illusion, a sense that a task is finished because the agent has produced a plausible plan, or ticket, can suppress critical scrutiny, especially when outputs are syntactically precise and polished. In multi-step workflows, each apparently successful sub-action (i.e., query run, API call logged, PR opened) further reinforces user trust while masking upstream mis-specification, retrieval contamination, or policy mismatches (Habbal et al., 2024; Zhai et al., 2024; Raees et al., 2025).

Over time, people can adapt to the agent's cadence, allowing tacit knowledge to atrophy and degrading the very human checks needed when the agent encounters out-of-distribution cases. Yet, the risk is systemic as automation bias migrates from decision points to entire processes, where a single mis-goal or injected instruction can propagate across, for instance, TPS/MIS/ERP, and re-surface under the cover of "autonomous completion."

One notable example is in aviation, where over-reliance on automated systems has contributed to several major incidents. The Boeing 737 MAX crashes in 2018 and 2019 were partly attributed to the flight control software (MCAS – Maneuvering Characteristics Augmentation System) acting autonomously, with pilots either unaware of its behavior or ill-equipped to override it. These tragedies demonstrate how even well-trained professionals may defer to automation under pressure, sometimes with catastrophic results (Chary, 2024).

In the healthcare domain, AI diagnostic tools have been praised for their accuracy; however, studies have shown that physicians may rely too heavily on algorithmic suggestions, especially under time constraints. In business contexts, customer service systems that use AI chatbots sometimes escalate issues to humans too late, frustrating users and damaging brand reputation. Similarly, algorithmic trading systems in financial markets have triggered flash crashes when automated decision-making has spiraled out of control without timely human intervention (Habbal et al., 2024; Zhai et al., 2024; Raees et al., 2025).

In addition, hallucinations, the generation of outputs that are convincingly fluent yet factually incorrect, misleading, or entirely fabricated, are one of the most pressing and underappreciated risks of deploying AI. Hallucinations are especially prevalent in LLMs like the GPT-series models and other generative systems that lack a grounding in verified, real-time knowledge. Unlike traditional rule-based or statistical systems, LLMs generate text based on probabilistic associations learned from massive training corpora. While this enables impressive creativity and human-like responses, it also means the models can "invent" citations, names, or details that do not exist (Janéafik & Dusek, 2024).

Further, hallucinations pose unique challenges for information authenticity, system reliability, and accountability. In critical domains such as finance, healthcare, and compliance reporting, AI-generated inaccuracies can propagate errors downstream, amplifying misinformation and undermining stakeholder trust. Moreover, because these outputs are often presented with high confidence and natural language fluency, human users may fail to detect them, a phenomenon that exacerbates the risk of over-reliance (Janéafik & Dusek, 2024).

The danger of over-reliance is further compounded by a lack of transparency in how many AI systems arrive at their conclusions. If users cannot understand or audit AI outputs, they are more likely to defer to them without questioning, especially in high-volume or high-pressure environments.

To mitigate these risks, organizations must cultivate a culture of critical engagement with AI. Ultimately, AI should be seen as a tool that supports, rather than replaces, human decision-making. A practical solution to the risk of overreliance on AI is to foster strong digital literacy, equipping people with the skills to question sources, cross-check facts, understand how algorithms shape outputs, and recognize bias or manipulation in automated solutions (Baskara, 2025). This would empower individuals to critically evaluate AI-generated information instead of accepting it at face value.

6.6.10 Cognitive and Lifecycle Sources of Bias in AI Systems

Concluding the discussion on risks, challenges, and biases, a critical approach is the cognitive biases of people working with AI systems. These biases are not solely a consequence of flawed or incomplete datasets, but rather emerge from the continuous interaction between human cognitive tendencies, algorithmic design choices, and contextual misalignment across the AI lifecycle. As Gafni et al. (2024b) emphasize, biases must be understood as socio-technical phenomena that originate both in human reasoning and in system architecture, reinforcing each other unless explicitly mitigated. Human actors involved in an AI system's conception, design, training, and use are susceptible to cognitive heuristics that can silently distort system behavior.

For example, confirmation bias leads developers to preferentially interpret model behavior in ways that validate their prior assumptions, potentially overlooking contradictory evidence during data selection, annotation, or evaluation. Similarly, anchoring bias causes users to overweight the first, last, latest, or middle answer, classification, or suggestion produced by a model, even when later information indicates that the initial output was arbitrary or unstable. In knowledge-management environments, this can freeze organizational knowledge structures around a single AI-generated interpretation, creating an illusory sense of certainty (Gafni et al., 2026).

Beyond human cognition, AI systems develop structural biases that arise from their internal mechanics or from mismatches between training and deployment environments. For instance, presentation bias occurs in ranking and recommendation systems where items shown first receive disproportionate engagement. This reinforces the model's belief that top-ranked items are inherently superior, creating a feedback loop that marginalizes alternative or minority knowledge. In organizational contexts, this can shape how institutional knowledge is retrieved, reproduced, or how non-top-ranked information is ignored. Another example is the appropriate-use (deployment) or misuse bias that emerges when a model optimized for one domain or demographic is deployed elsewhere without recalibration. A diagnostic system trained on adult clinical data, for example, may perform poorly in pediatric settings, not because the algorithm is "wrong," but because its intended scope was exceeded (Gafni et al., 2026).

These biases accumulate across stages of the AI lifecycle: design, development, training, evaluation, and deployment, highlighting the need for governance mechanisms that operate before, during, and after model creation (Schwartz et al., 2022; Gafni et al., 2024b). Mitigating these biases requires intervention at the earliest stages of system planning. Hadar et al. (2025) argue that Responsible AI (RAI) principles must be embedded into Requirements Engineering (RE) processes rather than addressed retroactively. Because traditional RE techniques were developed for deterministic software systems, they are ill-suited for probabilistic and data-driven AI environments.

A fairness-by-design approach, aligned with principles such as transparency, non-maleficence, accountability, and explainability, requires organizations to articulate ethical constraints as explicit system requirements. This shifts bias mitigation from a late-stage auditing exercise to a foundational design priority. Embedding these principles early also helps counteract the cognitive biases of developers, shapes organizational decision-making climates, and reduces the systemic biases that emerge from model architecture and deployment (Gafni et al., 2024b).

6.7 Conclusions

Artificial intelligence no longer functions only as an analytical add-on to IS. With the emergence of agentic architectures, it now plans, calls tools, and executes multi-step work across TPS, MIS, DSS/ESS, ERP/CRM/SCM, and BI surfaces. This shift from reactive prediction to goal-directed autonomy reframes enhancement as end-to-end process optimization, shorter cycle times, fewer escalations, and higher data quality, while simultaneously relocating the locus of risk from individual models to the composite system that perceives, decides, and acts over time. The central question for IS leaders is therefore not whether AI is useful, but how to make autonomous usefulness safe, auditable, and governable.

Answering that question requires an operational governance stance. Risk management must bind model development to enterprise controls: provenance and dataset lineage; versioned pipelines and pre-deployment evaluation; least-privilege tool scopes and human-in-the-loop gates for irreversible actions; immutable, queryable logs of goals, plans, tool calls, and outcomes; and continuous adversarial testing for prompt-/retrieval-injection, jailbreaks, and tool overreach. Regulatory frameworks (e.g., the EU's risk-based duties and practice-oriented standards like the NIST AI RMF) are most effective when translated into living artifacts: system/model cards, audit trails, incident post-mortems, and rollback playbooks that tie compliance to day-to-day operations. Measurement should prioritize "safe usefulness": task success and SLA deltas paired with policy-violation rates, explanation stability, and time-to-detect/contain.

Finally, adoption should be staged and scoped with a calibrated autonomy ladder, from assistive drafting to bounded execution, letting organizations accumulate evidence, retain human expertise, and prevent automation bias from propagating across processes. Cross-border data flows, model hosting choices (cloud, on-prem, edge), and content provenance mechanisms deserve explicit design treatment, because they determine not just performance but also accountability and jurisdiction. With these constraints in place, agentic

AI becomes a disciplined extension of information systems, amplifying institutional capability without surrendering control. Table 6.1 presents a summary of the key aspects and concerns of AI on and for ISs.

As this chapter has shown, AI is revolutionizing how IS operate, learn, and make decisions. However, as these systems grow in complexity and scale, they increasingly push the boundaries of what classical computing can support. This sets the stage for the next major paradigm shift, Quantum Information Science (QIS). While AI focuses on intelligent behavior and data-driven insights, QIS fundamentally redefines how information is stored, transmitted, and processed at the most basic level. The next chapter explores this emerging field, examining how quantum computing, quantum communication, and quantum sensing promise to transform the IS infrastructure, offering capabilities that classical systems, even the most advanced AI, cannot achieve alone. Together, AI and QIS may not just enhance but entirely reimagine the landscape of digital intelligence.

As we move deeper into the era of information singularity, the intersection of AI and IS will become the axis upon which digital society rotates. Navigating this frontier will require interdisciplinary thinking, collaborative governance, and a renewed commitment to aligning technological advancement with societal well-being. This chapter has aimed to provide the conceptual and practical tools necessary to understand and shape that future.

Table 6.1 AI in Information Systems

Aspect	Key Themes	Elements	Outcomes / Implications
Enhancements Brought by AI	Integration of AI into core IS types	• Automation of TPS and ERP • AI-enhanced DSS, BI, and ESS/EIS • Predictive analytics in CRM and SCM • Personalization and recommendation engines • NLP, vision, reinforcement learning	• Increased efficiency • Faster, smarter decisions • Customization • System-level intelligence

Table 6.1 (continued)

Aspect	Key Themes	Elements	Outcomes / Implications
Challenges and Risks	Risks arising from AI-IS convergence	• Bias and algorithmic discrimination • Privacy and data breaches • Explainability and black-box systems • Integration difficulties with legacy systems • High development and maintenance costs • Over-reliance and critical thinking erosion • Environmental degradation	• Erosion of trust • Legal and compliance uncertainty • Unequal access and impact • Sustainability risks
Environmental Sustainability (AI Lifecycle)	Digital pollution and ecological footprint	• Model training energy use • Data storage and data center cooling • Rebound effects and efficiency paradox • Hardware waste and e-waste export • Lifecycle emissions (cradle-to-grave) • Rare mineral extraction and toxic waste	• High carbon footprint • Global environmental justice issues • Need for lifecycle accountability • Tension between AI-for-sustainability and AI-as-polluter
Governance and Future Directions	Regulating AI use in IS	• Ethics-by-design and algorithmic audits • AI impact assessments • Transparent explainability frameworks • Environmental monitoring tools • AI-specific sustainability standards • International cooperation (e.g., EU AI Act)	• Accountability in AI deployment • Risk mitigation • Sustainability targets • Global governance over self-regulation

References

Alqahtani, H., Kavakli-Thorne, M., & Kumar, G. (2021). Applications of generative adversarial networks (GANs): An updated review. *Archives of Computational Methods in Engineering, 28*, 525–552. https://doi.org/10.1007/s11831-019-09388-y

Alzubaidi, L., Zhang, J., Humaidi, A. J., Al-Dujaili, A., Duan, Y., Al-Shamma, O., ... Farhan, L. (2021). Review of deep learning: Concepts, CNN architectures, challenges, applications, future directions. *Journal of Big Data, 8*, Article 53. https://doi.org/10.1186/s40537-021-00444-8

Badmus, O., Rajput, S. A., Arogundade, J. B., & Williams, M. (2024). AI-driven business analytics and decision making. *World Journal of Advanced Research and Reviews, 24*(1), 616–633. https://doi.org/10.30574/wjarr.2024.24.1.3093

Balendra, S. (2025). Meta's AI moderation and free speech: Ongoing challenges in the Global South. *Cambridge Forum on AI: Law and Governance, 1*, e21. https://doi.org/10.1017/cfl.2025.5

Bansal, G., Chamola, V., Hussain, A., Guizani, M., & Niyato, D. (2024). Transforming conversations with AI: A comprehensive study of ChatGPT. *Cognitive Computation, 16*(5), 2487–2510. https://doi.org/10.1007/s12559-023-10236-2

Baskara, F. (2025). Conceptualizing digital literacy for the AI era: A framework for preparing students in an AI-driven world. *Data and Metadata, 4*, Article e530. https://doi.org/10.56294/dm2025530

Bhuyan, B. P., Ramdane-Cherif, A., Singh, T. P., & Tomar, R. (2024). Rule-based systems and expert systems. In *Neuro-symbolic artificial intelligence: Bridging logic and learning* (pp. 63–85). Springer Nature. https://doi.org/10.1007/978-981-97-8171-3_5

Bolatbekkyzy, G. (2024). Legal issues of cross-border data transfer in the era of digital government. *Journal of Digital Technologies and Law, 2*(2), 286–307. https://doi.org/10.21202/jdtl.2024.15

Brey, P., & Dainow, B. (2024). Ethics by design for artificial intelligence. *AI and Ethics, 4*(4), 1265–1277. https://doi.org/10.1007/s43681-023-00330-4

Bulusu, L., & Abellera, R. (2020). *AI meets BI: Artificial intelligence and business intelligence*. Auerbach Publications.

Byler, D. (2019, April 11). China's hi-tech war on its Muslim minority. *The Guardian*. https://www.theguardian.com/news/2019/apr/11/china-hi-tech-war-on-muslim-minority-xinjiang-uighurs-surveillance-face-recognition

Chang, W., & Park, J. (2024). A comparative study on the effect of ChatGPT recommendation and AI recommender systems on the formation of a consideration set. *Journal of Retailing and Consumer Services, 78*, 103743. https://doi.org/10.1016/j.jretconser.2024.103743

Chary, S. (2024). Employee grievance redressal and corporate ethics: Lessons from the Boeing 737-MAX crashes. *Science and Engineering Ethics, 30*(2), Article 14. https://doi.org/10.1007/s11948-024-00475-3

Chowdhary, K. R. (2020). Natural language processing. In *Fundamentals of artificial intelligence* (pp. 603–649). Springer. https://doi.org/10.1007/978-81-322-3972-7_19

Chowdhury, O. (2023). Gonzalez v. Google: Testing the boundaries of Section 230. *Hastings Communications and Entertainment Law Journal, 45*(2), 135–160. https://repository.uclawsf.edu/hastings_comm_ent_law_journal/vol45/iss2/3/

Coeckelbergh, M. (2020). Artificial intelligence, responsibility attribution, and a relational justification of explainability. *Science and Engineering Ethics, 26*(4), 2051–2068. https://doi.org/10.1007/s11948-019-00146-8

Dearden, L. (2019, May 7). Facial recognition wrongly identifies public as potential criminals 96% of time, figures reveal. *The Independent.* https://www.independent.co.uk/news/uk/home-news/facial-recognition-london-inaccurate-met-police-trials-a8898946.html

del Mar Roldán-García, M., García-Nieto, J., & Aldana-Montes, J. F. (2017). Enhancing semantic consistency in anti-fraud rule-based expert systems. *Expert Systems with Applications, 90*, 332–343. https://doi.org/10.1016/j.eswa.2017.08.036

Dhiman, R., Miteff, S., Wang, Y., Ma, S.-C., Amirikas, R., & Fabian, B. (2024). Artificial intelligence and sustainability: A review. *Analytics, 3*(1), 140–164. https://doi.org/10.3390/analytics3010008

Dima, J., Gilbert, M. H., Dextras-Gauthier, J., & Giraud, L. (2024). The effects of artificial intelligence on human resource activities and the roles of the human resource triad: Opportunities and challenges. *Frontiers in Psychology, 15*, Article 1360401. https://doi.org/10.3389/fpsyg.2024.1360401

Doomen, J. (2023). The artificial intelligence entity as a legal person. *Information & Communications Technology Law, 32*(3), 277–287. https://doi.org/10.1080/13600834.2023.2196827

Dwivedi, R., Dave, D., Naik, H., Singhal, S., Omer, R., Patel, P., ... Ranjan, R. (2023). Explainable AI (XAI): Core ideas, techniques, and solutions. *ACM Computing Surveys, 55*(9), 1–33. https://doi.org/10.1145/3561048

Ein-Dor, P. (1999). Artificial intelligence: A short history and the next 40 years. In *Emerging information technologies: Improving decisions, cooperation, and infrastructure* (pp. 117–140). SAGE Publications. https://doi.org/10.4135/9781483345505.n6

Eswaran, U., & Khang, A. (2024). Artificial intelligence (AI)-aided computer vision (CV) in healthcare systems. In *Computer vision and AI-integrated IoT technologies in the medical ecosystem* (pp. 125–137). CRC Press.

Feuerriegel, S., Hartmann, J., Janiesch, C., & Zschech, P. (2024). Generative AI. *Business & Information Systems Engineering, 66*(1), 111–126. https://doi.org/10.1007/s12599-023-00834-7

Fui-Hoon Nah, F., Zheng, R., Cai, J., Siau, K., & Chen, L. (2023). Generative AI and ChatGPT: Applications, challenges, and AI-human collaboration. *Journal of*

Information Technology Case and Application Research, 25(3), 277–304. https://doi.org/10.1080/15228053.2023.2233814
Gafni, R., Aviv, I., Kantsepolsky, B., Sherman, S., Rika, H., Itzkovich, Y., & Barger, A. (2024a). Objectivity by design: The impact of AI-driven approach on employees' soft skills evaluation. *Information and Software Technology, 170*, 107430. https://doi.org/10.1016/j.infsof.2024.107430
Gafni, R., Kantsepolsky, B., & Sherman, S. (2024b). Understanding and mitigating biases in AI systems: Insights and recommendations. In I. Venezia & R. Calipha (Eds.), *Behavioral finance: Beyond the basics* (pp. 299–333). World Scientific. https://doi.org/10.1142/9789811290633_0013
Gafni, R., Kantsepolsky, B., & Sherman, S. (2026). Biases and ethical considerations in AI-driven knowledge management. In M. Russ & M. D. Lytras (Eds.), *AI-driven knowledge management processes: Strategies for the modern business landscape* (Vol. 1, pp. 319–337). Emerald Publishing Limited. https://doi.org/10.1108/978-1-80592-391-620261013
Government Accountability Office. (2023, February 15). *Outdated and old IT systems slow government and put taxpayers at risk*. https://www.gao.gov/blog/outdated-and-old-it-systems-slow-government-and-put-taxpayers-risk
Garcia, A. C. B., Garcia, M. G. P., & Rigobon, R. (2024). Algorithmic discrimination in the credit domain: What do we know about it? *AI & Society, 39*(4), 2059–2098. https://doi.org/10.1007/s00146-023-01676-3
Gillioz, A., Casas, J., Mugellini, E., & Abou Khaled, O. (2020, September). Overview of the transformer-based models for NLP tasks. In *Proceedings of the 15th Conference on Computer Science and Information Systems (FedCSIS)* (pp. 179–183). IEEE. https://doi.org/10.15439/2020F20
Gruetzemacher, R., & Whittlestone, J. (2022). The transformative potential of artificial intelligence. *Futures, 135*, 102884. https://doi.org/10.1016/j.futures.2021.102884
Guidi, G., Miniati, R., Mazzola, M., & Iadanza, E. (2016). Case study: IBM Watson Analytics cloud platform as analytics-as-a-service system for heart failure early detection. *Future Internet, 8*(3), Article 32. https://doi.org/10.3390/fi8030032
Guo, F., Gallagher, C. M., Sun, T., Tavoosi, S., & Min, H. (2024). Smarter people analytics with organizational text data: Demonstrations using classic and advanced NLP models. *Human Resource Management Journal, 34*(1), 39–54. https://doi.org/10.1111/1748-8583.12426
Gurney, K. (2018). *An introduction to neural networks*. CRC Press.
Habbal, A., Ali, M. K., & Abuzaraida, M. A. (2024). Artificial intelligence trust, risk and security management (AI TRiSM): Frameworks, applications, challenges and future research directions. *Expert Systems with Applications, 240*, 122442. https://doi.org/10.1016/j.eswa.2023.122442
Hadar, I., Kantsepolsky, B., Sadovski, E., & Sherman, S. (2025). Requirements engineering for accountable and conscious human-centered AI: Preface. In *2025 IEEE*

33rd International Requirements Engineering Conference Workshops (REW) (pp. 402–404). IEEE. https://doi.org/10.1109/REW66121.2025.00058
Haenlein, M., & Kaplan, A. (2019). A brief history of artificial intelligence: On the past, present, and future of artificial intelligence. *California Management Review, 61*(4), 5–14. https://doi.org/10.1177/0008125619864925
Hanna, M. G., Pantanowitz, L., Jackson, B., Palmer, O., Visweswaran, S., Pantanowitz, J., ... Rashidi, H. H. (2025). Ethical and bias considerations in artificial intelligence/machine learning. *Modern Pathology, 38*(3), 100686. https://doi.org/10.1016/j.modpat.2024.100686
Hao, K. (2020, August 20). The UK exam debacle reminds us that algorithms can't fix broken systems. *MIT Technology Review*. https://www.technologyreview.com/2020/08/20/1007502/uk-exam-algorithm-cant-fix-broken-system/
Hatchimonji, G. (2025, January 14). What is the Coalition for Content Provenance and Authenticity (C2PA)? *TechTarget*. https://www.techtarget.com/whatis/definition/Coalition-for-Content-Provenance-and-Authenticity-C2PA
Henriksen, A., & Blond, L. (2023). Executive-centered AI? Designing predictive systems for the public sector. *Social Studies of Science, 53*(5), 738–760. https://doi.org/10.1177/03063127231163756
Hosseini, S., & Seilani, H. (2025). The role of agentic AI in shaping a smart future: A systematic review. *Array*, 26, Article 100399. https://doi.org/10.1016/j.array.2025.100399
Huang, K. (2025). AI agents and business workflow. In *Agentic AI: Theories and practices* (pp. 135–166). Springer Nature. https://doi.org/10.1007/978-3-031-90026-6_5
IBM Data and AI Team. (2023, October). *Understanding the different types of artificial intelligence*. https://www.ibm.com/think/topics/artificial-intelligence-types
Janéafik, A., & Dusek, O. (2024, October). The problem of AI hallucination and how to solve it. In *Proceedings of the European Conference on e-Learning* (pp. 122–128). Academic Conferences International.
Janiesch, C., Zschech, P., & Heinrich, K. (2021). Machine learning and deep learning. *Electronic Markets, 31*(3), 685–695. https://doi.org/10.1007/s12525-021-00475-2
Koppel, O., & Parkhomchuk, O. (2025). Cross-border relations in the context of artificial intelligence development: Challenges and prospects. *Actual Problems of International Relations*, 1(163), 41–48. https://doi.org/10.17721/apmv.2025.163.1.41-48
Krizhevsky, A., Sutskever, I., & Hinton, G. E. (2012). ImageNet classification with deep convolutional neural networks. In F. Pereira, C. J. Burges, L. Bottou, & K. Q. Weinberger (Eds.), *Advances in neural information processing systems* (Vol. 25, pp. 1097–1105). Curran Associates. https://proceedings.neurips.cc/paper_files/paper/2012/file/c399862d3b9d6b76c8436e924a68c45b-Paper.pdf
Kumar, R., Gupta, M., & Sapra, S. R. (2021). Speech to text community application using natural language processing. In *2021 5th International Conference on*

Information Systems and Computer Networks (ISCON) (pp. 1–6). IEEE. https://doi.org/10.1109/ISCON52037.2021.9702428

Kurki, V. A. (2019). *A theory of legal personhood.* Oxford University Press.

Laad, M., Maurya, R., & Saiyed, N. (2024, April). Unveiling the vision: A comprehensive review of computer vision in AI and ML. In *2024 International Conference on Advances in Data Engineering and Intelligent Computing Systems (ADICS)* (pp. 1–6). IEEE. https://doi.org/10.1109/ADICS58448.2024.10533631

Lakshamanan, R. (2025, June 12). Zero-click AI vulnerability exposes Microsoft 365 Copilot data without user interaction. *The Hacker News.* https://thehackernews.com/2025/06/zero-click-ai-vulnerability-exposes.html

Larkin, X. N. (2018, August 10). "Okay Google, play 'Dura.'": Voice assistants still can't understand bilingual users. *New York Magazine.* https://nymag.com/intelligencer/2018/08/why-are-google-siri-and-alexa-so-bad-at-understanding-bilingual-accents-voice-assistants.html

Larson, J., Mattu, S., Kirchner, L., & Angwin, J. (2016, May 23). *How we analyzed the COMPAS recidivism algorithm.* ProPublica. https://www.propublica.org/article/how-we-analyzed-the-compas-recidivism-algorithm

Law, M. (2024, August 22). Deloitte: Enterprises face GenAI scaling challenges. *Technology Magazine.* https://technologymagazine.com/articles/deloitte-enterprises-face-gen-ai-scaling-challenges

LeCun, Y., Bengio, Y., & Hinton, G. (2015). Deep learning. *Nature, 521*(7553), 436–444. https://doi.org/10.1038/nature14539

Li, X., & Zhang, T. (2017, April). An exploration of artificial intelligence application: From security, privacy and ethics perspectives. In *2017 IEEE 2nd International Conference on Cloud Computing and Big Data Analysis (ICCCBDA)* (pp. 416–420). IEEE. https://doi.org/10.1109/ICCCBDA.2017.7951949

Lo, A. W., & Singh, M. (2023). From ELIZA to ChatGPT: The evolution of natural language processing and financial applications. *The Journal of Portfolio Management, 49*(7), 201–235. https://doi.org/10.3905/jpm.2023.1.512

Lourdusamy, R., & Gnanaprakasam, J. (2023). Expert systems in AI: Components, applications, and characteristics focusing on chatbot. In A. Patel & N. C. Debnath (Eds.), *Data science with semantic technologies: Deployment and exploration* (Vol. 2, pp. 217–231). CRC Press. https://doi.org/10.1201/9781003310792-13

Lucivero, F. (2024). AI and environmental sustainability. In *Handbook on public policy and artificial intelligence* (pp. 158–169). Edward Elgar Publishing. https://doi.org/10.4337/9781803922171.00019

Majot, A., & Yampolskiy, R. V. (2017). Diminishing returns and recursive self-improving artificial intelligence. In V. Callaghan, J. Miller, R. V. Yampolskiy, & S. Armstrong (Eds.), *The technological singularity* (pp. 111–129). Springer. https://doi.org/10.1007/978-3-662-54033-6_7

Martinez, R. (2018). Artificial intelligence: Distinguishing between types and definitions. *Nevada Law Journal, 19*, 1015–1042.

Melo, I., Polónia, D., & Teixeira, L. (2025). Human–AI collaboration in the modernization of COBOL-based legacy systems: The case of the Department of Government Efficiency (DOGE). *Computers, 14*(7), 244. https://doi.org/10.3390/computers14070244

Miller, J. M. (2022, March 17). Deepfake video of Zelensky telling Ukrainians to surrender removed from social platforms. *New York Post.* https://nypost.com/2022/03/17/deepfake-video-shows-volodymyr-zelensky-telling-ukrainians-to-surrender/

Möslein, F. (2025). Robots in the boardroom: Artificial intelligence and corporate law. In *Research handbook on the law of artificial intelligence* (pp. 614–635). Edward Elgar Publishing. https://doi.org/10.4337/9781035316496.00036

Mucci, T. (2024, October 12). *The history of AI.* IBM. https://www.ibm.com/think/topics/history-of-artificial-intelligence

Murugesan, S. (2025). The rise of agentic AI: Implications, concerns, and the path forward. *IEEE Intelligent Systems, 40*(2), 8–14. https://doi.org/10.1109/MIS.2025.3544940

National Artificial Intelligence Initiative Act of 2020, Pub. L. No. 116-283, div. E, 134 Stat. 4523 (2021). https://www.congress.gov/116/plaws/publ283/PLAW-116publ283.pdf

National Institute of Standards and Technology. (2023, January). *Artificial intelligence risk management framework (AI RMF 1.0).* https://doi.org/10.6028/NIST.AI.100-1

National Institute of Standards and Technology. (2019, December 19). *NIST study evaluates effects of race, age, sex on face recognition software.* https://www.nist.gov/news-events/news/2019/12/nist-study-evaluates-effects-race-age-sex-face-recognition-software

Newell, A., & Simon, H. (1956). The logic theory machine—A complex information processing system. IRE Transactions on Information Theory, 2(3), 61–79. https://doi.org/10.1109/TIT.1956.1056797

Nyathani, R., Allam, K., Engineer, B. I., Joseph, S., Daniel, S., & Godwin, G. O. (2024). Synergizing AI, cloud computing, and big data for enhanced enterprise resource planning (ERP) systems. *International Journal of Computer Technology, 11*, 1–6.

Parikh, D., Radadia, S., & Eranna, R. K. (2024). Privacy-preserving machine learning techniques: Challenges and research directions. *International Research Journal of Engineering and Technology, 11*(3), 499–503.

Pearson, J. (2023, November 29). ChatGPT can reveal personal information from real people, Google researchers show. *VICE.* https://www.vice.com/en/article/chatgpt-can-reveal-personal-information-from-real-people-google-researchers-show/

Purwono, P., Ma'arif, A., Rahmaniar, W., Fathurrahman, H. I. K., Frisky, A. Z. K., & ul Haq, Q. M. (2022). Understanding convolutional neural networks (CNN): A review. *International Journal of Robotics and Control Systems, 2*(4), 739–748. https://doi.org/10.31763/ijrcs.v2i4.888

Qu, Y., Zhang, T., Garg, N., & Kumar, A. (2024). Recursive introspection: Teaching language model agents how to self-improve. *Advances in Neural Information Processing Systems, 37*, 55249–55285.

Raees, M., Khan, V. J., & Papangelis, K. (2025). Exploring persuasive engagement to reduce over-reliance on AI assistance in a customer classification case. In *Proceedings of the 33rd ACM Conference on User Modeling, Adaptation and Personalization* (pp. 295–300). https://doi.org/10.1145/3699682.3728320

Raheem, T., & Hossain, G. (2025, May). Agentic AI systems: Opportunities, challenges, and trustworthiness. In *2025 IEEE International Conference on Electro Information Technology (eIT)* (pp. 618–624). IEEE. https://doi.org/10.1109/eIT64391.2025.11103638

Raj, R., & Kos, A. (2023). Artificial intelligence: Evolution, developments, applications, and future scope. *Przegląd Elektrotechniczny, 99*(2), 1–13. https://doi.org/10.15199/48.2023.02.01

Rajasekaran, U., Malini, A., & Murugan, M. (2024). Artificial intelligence in autonomous vehicles: A survey of trends and challenges. In *Artificial intelligence for autonomous vehicles* (pp. 1–24). Wiley. https://doi.org/10.1002/9781119847656.ch1

Roba, G. B., & Maric, P. (2023). AI in customer relationship management. In *Developments in information and knowledge management systems for business applications* (Vol. 7, pp. 469–487). Springer Nature Switzerland. https://doi.org/10.1007/978-3-031-25695-0_21

Salih, A. M., Raisi-Estabragh, Z., Galazzo, I. B., Radeva, P., Petersen, S. E., Lekadir, K., & Menegaz, G. (2025). A perspective on explainable artificial intelligence methods: SHAP and LIME. *Advanced Intelligent Systems, 7*(1), 2400304. https://doi.org/10.1002/aisy.202400304

Schwartz, R., Vassilev, A., Greene, K., Perine, L., Burt, A., & Hall, P. (2022). T*owards a standard for identifying and managing bias in artificial intelligence* (NIST Special Publication 1270). National Institute of Standards and Technology. https://doi.org/10.6028/NIST.SP.1270

Shan, S., Ding, W., Passananti, J., Wu, S., Zheng, H., & Zhao, B. Y. (2024, May). Nightshade: Prompt-specific poisoning attacks on text-to-image generative models. In *2024 IEEE Symposium on Security and Privacy (SP)* (pp. 807–825). IEEE.

Shawn, A. A., & Hossain, M. Z. (2024). Integrating artificial intelligence into MIS: Transforming business processes and predictive analytics. *Pacific Journal of Business Innovation and Strategy, 1*(1), 19–27. https://doi.org/10.70818/pjbis.2024.v01i01.012

Shinde, P. P., & Shah, S. (2018, August). A review of machine learning and deep learning applications. In *2018 Fourth International Conference on Computing, Communication, Control and Automation (ICCUBEA)* (pp. 1–6). IEEE. https://doi.org/10.1109/ICCUBEA.2018.8697857

Shivashankar, K., Al Hajj, G., & Martini, A. (2025). Maintainability and scalability in machine learning: Challenges and solutions. *ACM Computing Surveys, 57*(12), Article 318. https://doi.org/10.1145/3736751

Singer, N., & Metz, C. (2019, December 19). Many facial-recognition systems are biased, says U.S. study. *The New York Times*. https://www.nytimes.com/2019/12/19/technology/facial-recognition-bias.html

Singh, S. P., Rawat, J., Mittal, M., Kumar, I., & Bhatt, C. (2022). Application of AI in SCM or Supply Chain 4.0. In S. L. Fernandes & T. K. Sharma (Eds.), *Artificial intelligence in industrial applications* (Vol. 25). Springer. https://doi.org/10.1007/978-3-030-85383-9_4

Singla, S., Thakur, A., Swami, A., Sawarn, U., & Singla, P. (2024). Advancements in natural language processing: BERT and transformer-based models for text understanding. In *2024 Second International Conference on Advanced Computing & Communication Technologies (ICACCTech)* (pp. 372–379). IEEE. https://doi.org/10.1109/ICACCTech65084.2024.00068

Stanko, I. (2020). The architectures of Geoffrey Hinton. In *Guide to deep learning basics: Logical, historical and philosophical perspectives* (pp. 79–92). Springer. https://doi.org/10.1007/978-3-030-37591-1_8

Stray, J. (2023). The AI learns to lie to please you: Preventing biased feedback loops in machine-assisted intelligence analysis. *Analytics, 2*(2), 350–358. https://doi.org/10.3390/analytics2020020

Strubell, E., Ganesh, A., & McCallum, A. (2020, April). Energy and policy considerations for modern deep learning research. In *Proceedings of the AAAI Conference on Artificial Intelligence, 34*(9), 13693–13696. https://doi.org/10.1609/aaai.v34i09.7123

Strupp, C. (2019, August 30). Fraudsters used AI to mimic CEO's voice in unusual cybercrime case. *The Wall Street Journal*. https://www.wsj.com/articles/fraudsters-use-ai-to-mimic-ceos-voice-in-unusual-cybercrime-case-11567157402

Tambe, P., Cappelli, P., & Yakubovich, V. (2019). Artificial intelligence in human resources management: Challenges and a path forward. *California Management Review, 61*(4), 15–42. https://doi.org/10.1177/0008125619867910

Tredinnick, L., & Laybats, C. (2023). The dangers of generative artificial intelligence. *Business Information Review, 40*(2), 46–48. https://doi.org/10.1177/02663821231183756

Université de Montréal. (2018). *Montréal declaration for responsible development of artificial intelligence*. https://declarationmontreal-iaresponsable.com/wp-content/uploads/2023/04/UdeM_Decl-IA-Resp_LA-Declaration-ENG_WEB_09-07-19.pdf

Varmedja, D., Karanovic, M., Sladojevic, S., Arsenovic, M., & Anderla, A. (2019, March). Credit card fraud detection using machine learning methods. In *2019 18th International Symposium INFOTEH-JAHORINA (INFOTEH)* (pp. 1–5). IEEE. https://doi.org/10.1109/INFOTEH.2019.8717766

Vidgen, B., & Derczynski, L. (2020). Directions in abusive language training data: A systematic review: Garbage in, garbage out. *PLOS ONE, 15*(12), e0243300. https://doi.org/10.1371/journal.pone.0243300

Waqar, A. (2024). Intelligent decision support systems in construction engineering: Artificial intelligence and machine learning approaches. *Expert Systems with Applications, 249*, 123503. https://doi.org/10.1016/j.eswa.2024.123503

Weizenbaum, J. (1966). ELIZA—A computer program for the study of natural language communication between man and machine. *Communications of the ACM, 9*(1), 36–45. https://doi.org/10.1145/365153.365168

The White House. (2025, January 23). *Removing barriers to American leadership in artificial intelligence.* https://www.whitehouse.gov/presidential-actions/2025/01/removing-barriers-to-american-leadership-in-artificial-intelligence/

Winick, E. (2018, October 10). Amazon ditched AI recruitment software because it was biased against women. *MIT Technology Review.* https://www.technologyreview.com/2018/10/10/139858/amazon-ditched-ai-recruitment-software-because-it-was-biased-against-women/

Ye, M., Shen, J., Lin, G., Xiang, T., Shao, L., & Hoi, S. C. H. (2022). Deep learning for person re-identification: A survey and outlook. *IEEE Transactions on Pattern Analysis and Machine Intelligence, 44*(6), 2872–2893. https://doi.org/10.1109/TPAMI.2021.3054775

Yerlikaya, F. A., & Bahtiyar, Ş. (2022). Data poisoning attacks against machine learning algorithms. *Expert Systems with Applications, 208*, 118101. https://doi.org/10.1016/j.eswa.2022.118101

Završnik, A., & Simončič, K. (Eds.). (2023). *Artificial intelligence, social harms and human rights*. Springer Nature.

Zhai, C., Wibowo, S., & Li, L. D. (2024). The effects of over-reliance on AI dialogue systems on students' cognitive abilities: A systematic review. *Smart Learning Environments, 11*(1), Article 28. https://doi.org/10.1186/s40561-024-00316-7

Zhou, Z.-H. (2021). *Machine learning.* Springer Nature.

7

Introduction to Quantum Information Science

7.1 Introduction

Quantum Information Science (QIS) is an interdisciplinary field that bridges the domains of physics, mathematics, engineering, and computer science to explore how the principles of quantum mechanics can be used *as resources to gather, process,* and *transmit* information in *fundamentally new ways* (Aspect, 2023). As a scientific field, QIS emerged in the eightieth of the twentieth century, and over the past two decades, has matured from theoretical proposals to working prototypes and experimental testbeds. At a time when modern information technologies and networks are reaching their limits, early prototypes of quantum technologies already demonstrate the unprecedented potential for revolutionary applications in sensing, computation, simulation, and communication, generating *a paradigm shift* in how we think about *managing, utilizing, and securing information* (Kantsepolsky, 2025).

To increase public awareness of the importance of quantum science and applications, on June 7, 2024, the United Nations (UN) proclaimed 2025 as the International Year of Quantum Science and Technology (UNESCO, 2024; United Nations, 2024). In addition to marking 100 years since the birth of quantum mechanics, following an exponential rise in patent filings, governmental and private investments, and startup activity, the UN stressed the importance of QIS *as a key cross-cutting scientific field* in the twenty-first century, with potentially *groundbreaking applications* for digital economies and society (OECD, 2025).

B. Kantsepolsky, L. Topor, *Managing Information Singularity*,
https://doi.org/10.1007/978-3-032-26223-3_7

According to the literature, quantum technologies are expected *to impact every field of human activities* at least as dramatically as the birth of quantum mechanics and, following it, the first quantum revolution that led to the invention of transistors, semiconductors, integrated circuits, lasers, and more that serve as the basis of modern electronics and telecommunications (Aspect, 2023; Purohit et al., 2024). Through this chapter, we provide a comprehensive overview of QIS, including a historical overview, the foundational concepts of QIS, and its key subfields, leaving the discussion on socio-technical challenges in adopting quantum technologies and future research directions to Chapter 8.

7.2 Introduction to Quantum Theory

7.2.1 From Energy Quanta to Quantum Mechanics

The era of quantum science began in the early twentieth century, as a result of discovering a serious discrepancy between the predictions of classical physics and experimental measurements of black-body radiation. In 1900, Max Planck derived his famous relation $E = h\nu$ to explain why a black body, as an idealized radiator, emits light unevenly across different frequencies. Instead of the belief that energy exchanged between matter and light could vary continuously, Planck quantized the allowed energies of microscopic resonators, introducing *energy elements* $\varepsilon = \mathrm{h}\nu$. To describe these elements mathematically, Planck applied Boltzmann's ideas of statistical mechanics and concluded that the only formula consistent with the experimental results was $E_n = nh\nu$, for n = 1, 2, 3, . . ., so that a single step corresponds to $E = h\nu$. Planck referred to these energy elements as *energy quanta,* adopting the Latin word *quantum*—*"how much"* (Planck, 1900; Klein, 1961). This revolutionary discovery for the first time established the quantitative link between frequency and discrete energy elements.

While the Greek letter "nu" (ν) was used to *denote* the *frequency* of the oscillator, Planck introduced h as *a new fundamental constant* of nature that sets the scale for these *energy elements* and has dimensions of *action (energy × time)*. By matching his formula to empirical data, Planck initially determined a numerical value of $\mathrm{h} \approx 6.55\times10^{-27}$ erg·s (Mehra & Rechenberg, 2001). This initial value of h presented *the units of action* or *the measured energy* (in ergs) multiplied by time (in seconds), where *erg* is the work done by a force of one dyne acting through a distance of one centimeter (Taylor & Thompson,

2008). Later measurements further refined this value and, according to the International System of Units (SI), it is now fixed as $6.62607015 \times 10^{-34}$ J·s (joule second). Planck's constant became a fundamental quantum-mechanical constant associated with the quantization of light and matter, setting the scale of quantum effects by linking classical and quantum physics. It is used, among other things, for the definitions of ohm, volt, and even the 2019 SI definition of kilogram (Nauenberg, 2016; Stock et al., 2022; Newell & Tiesinga, 2019).

7.2.1.1 The Wave–Particle Duality Concept

While Planck's radiation formula was accepted as describing the experimental facts simply and adequately, its breakthrough idea that energy exchange is not continuous but occurs in discrete chunks proportional to frequency did not draw special attention until 1905. That year, Albert Einstein reinterpreted and extended Planck's black-body model to understand the nature of light. In his famous work, explaining the photoelectric effect, Einstein introduced the concept of *light quanta* and hypothesized that light itself consists of *discrete packets of energy* (Einstein, 1905), later called *photons*, with an energy of $h\nu$.

Einstein's work on the photoelectric effect was recognized with the Nobel Prize in Physics in 1921 for its revolutionary approach. Since 1905 and over the next two decades, Niels Bohr, Louis de Broglie, Werner Heisenberg, Erwin Schrödinger, and Paul Dirac formalized quantum mechanics. First, Bohr's model of the hydrogen atom quantized electron orbits to explain atomic spectra (Bohr, 1913). Then, de Broglie (1924) proposed that matter has wave-like properties, paving the way to the *wave particle duality* concept. Finally, Bohr's (1928) principle of complementarity framed wave-like and particle-like descriptions as mutually necessary yet non-simultaneous, providing a unifying interpretive lens for quantum phenomena, which became a cornerstone of quantum mechanics (Huang et al., 2020).

7.2.1.2 The Uncertainty Principle and Matrix Mechanics

In 1925, Werner Heisenberg fundamentally altered the understanding of particle behavior at the quantum level. While working on understanding atomic spectra behavior, rather than trying to visualize atomic motion, which classical physics struggled to describe accurately, Heisenberg focused on *position (q)* and *momentum (p)* as the fundamental physical quantities that describe the state of a particle on spectral lines. Heisenberg's paper became revolutionary in several respects.

First, it replaced the classical mechanics' continuous variables of position *q(t)* and momentum *p(t)* with *arrays of numbers* q_{mn} and p_{mn}, whose elements correspond to transitions between quantized energy states. Second, Heisenberg suggested that in matrix mechanics, physical quantities are represented by matrices that do not commute, which means pq ≠ qp. These features enabled the establishment of *a mathematical framework where reality is described by a probabilistic, non-commutative algebraic framework*. Finally, Heisenberg also showed that, when quantum numbers are large, his equations reproduce classical results, ensuring continuity with Newtonian mechanics (Poojary, 2015).

Born and Jordan (1925), followed by Born et al. (1926), further codified this new algebraic framework, whose non-commuting structure dictates the fundamental limits of simultaneous measurements. These works, Heisenberg's introduction of observable transition arrays together with Born and Jordan's matrix formalism, crystallized into what is now known as *matrix mechanics*, the first complete formulation of *quantum theory*, and established non-commutativity and uncertainty as intrinsic features of the microscopic world.

In his follow-up publication, Heisenberg (1927) introduced the famous *γ-ray microscope* thought experiment to illustrate the theoretical impossibility of arbitrarily precise simultaneous measurements of q and p. Thus, Heisenberg showed that *any attempt to localize an electron's position disrupts its momentum*, cementing the shift from deterministic trajectories to probabilistic descriptions, which underscores the radical conceptual shift. By his famous statement, "the path [of an electron] is no longer an objective attribute of the system but rather the result of an experimental arrangement" (Heisenberg, 1927, p. 173), Heisenberg concluded that classical pictures of particle trajectories must be abandoned entirely.

Moreover, since the relevant operators do not commute, as formalized by Born and Jordan's (1925) canonical commutation relation $[q, p] = i\hbar$, the order of multiplication or *non-commutativity* matters, which later led him to the definition of the *uncertainty principle*—one cannot simultaneously know both a particle's position and momentum with arbitrary precision. Likewise, the more accurately one property is known, the less accurately the other can be determined (Heisenberg, 1927; Poojary, 2015). The precise uncertainty bound $\Delta x \Delta p \geq \hbar/2$ was proved by Kennard (1927) and later generalized by Robertson (1929). Heisenberg's (1925, 1927) studies highlight the probabilistic nature of quantum mechanics and provide a mathematical framework that accurately describes the behavior of quantum systems. This body of work was recognized by the 1932 Nobel Prize in Physics and established the era of the first quantum revolution.

7.2.1.3 The Wave Mechanics and Quantum Theory

Approximately at the same time that Werner Heisenberg introduced *matrix mechanics*, leading to the birth of a non-commutative algebraic formulation of quantum theory, Erwin Schrödinger began publishing his series on *wave mechanics*. In his first paper, Schrödinger (1926a) framed quantum behavior in terms of continuous wavefunctions. According to Schrödinger, the *time-independent wave equation* could replace discrete transition arrays to calculate energy eigenvalues for simple systems. So, while in classical mechanics, the position is well-defined and has a precise coordinate, according to Schrödinger, position is described probabilistically, using a wave function ψ(q), which gives the probability density of finding a particle at a particular location. Schrödinger's (1926a) wave equation provided a tool to calculate the allowed states and energies of quantum systems.

A few months later, Schrödinger generalized his approach by addressing boundary conditions and multi-dimensional systems (Schrödinger, 1926b), and by the end of 1926, he demonstrated that *matrix mechanics* and *wave mechanics* are *formally equivalent,* yielding identical eigenvalue spectra and dynamical descriptions (Schrödinger, 1926c). Dirac's (1930) work, The principles of quantum mechanics expanded on these dual formulations by unifying *both concepts as distinct representations (or bases) of the same underlying operator algebra.* To show that one may *transform* between the matrix and wave representations without altering the theory's physical content, Dirac proposed the idea of abstract state vectors and operators operating on them (Mehra & Rechenberg, 2001; Nauenberg, 2016).

7.2.2 The Fundamental Concepts of Quantum Mechanics

Quantum mechanics uncovered several phenomena that had no classical analogs. *Superposition* is one of these fundamental concepts. According to quantum theory, a quantum system can exist in multiple states simultaneously until it is measured, at which point it collapses into a definite state (Nielsen & Chuang, 2010). For example, unlike a conventional bit that can have a strict multi-exclusive value of 0 or 1, a quantum bit (qubit) can be a combination of both 0 and 1, as defined by a wave function ψ(q), which assigns probability to each result (Nielsen & Chuang, 2010). To understand this phenomenon using conventional logic, consider a spinning coin that, rather than landing heads or tails, continues to spin endlessly, effectively displaying both options at once. Thanks to superposition, quantum systems may encode and process a lot more information at the same time, so that a quantum computer with n qubits may represent 2^n states simultaneously, resulting in exponential processing capacity for specialized workloads compared to classical computers (Di Meglio et al., 2021; Kop et al., 2024).

Quantum *entanglement* is another counterintuitive and even more striking concept. Entanglement was described by Einstein et al. (1935) as the phenomenon wherein two or more quantum particles become interconnected so that measuring the quantum state of one particle instantaneously influences (defines) the state of the other, regardless of the distance separating them. For example, if two particles are entangled, measuring the spin of one particle instantly determines the spin of the other. To describe the phenomenon of entanglement in conventional terms, imagine that two coins are flipped simultaneously in distant locations, and they will always land identically. Entanglement defies classical logic and understanding of space and time, so that even Einstein famously expressed his skepticism about the phenomenon, describing it as *spooky action at a distance* (Born, 1971). Because of Einstein's skepticism, entanglement became one of the most tested and, decades later, experimentally validated features of quantum theory (Aspect et al., 1982; Horodecki et al., 2009).

Another distinctive feature of quantum theory is *tunneling*, which allows particles to pass through barriers that, according to classical physics, should be impenetrable due to insufficient particle energy (Grifoni & Hänggi, 1998). Quantum tunneling constitutes yet another quantum phenomenon that has no classical equivalent, and human intuition also fails here—a ball should not roll over a hill if it lacks the energy to climb. Quantum tunneling is explained by the wave-like behavior of quantum particles governed by the Schrödinger equation (Razavy, 2014). Because a particle's wave function has finite amplitude inside the barrier, there is a non-zero probability that the particle emerges on the other side (Grifoni & Hänggi, 1998). Based on the prior example, imagine a ball rolling up a hill and magically appearing on the other side without having climbed it. Tunneling is essential to modern semiconductor devices and also explains alpha decay in radioactive materials, in which alpha particles escape atomic nuclei despite insufficient classical energy to surmount nuclear binding forces. This is a critical mechanism enabling radioactive decay processes underlying nuclear chain reactions (Phillips, 2013).

Finally, quantum *coherence*, described as the ability of a quantum system to maintain its state over time despite external perturbations, underlies the stability of superposition and entanglement. Coherence is achieved thanks to the wave properties of preserving phase relations among its superposed states (Streltsov et al., 2017). Since decoherence induces computational errors, extended coherence times are crucial for quantum computation, so that the longer the coherence is maintained, the more computations a quantum computer can perform (Nielsen & Chuang, 2010). In sensing applications, long-lived coherence allows quantum sensors to provide unprecedentedly reliable measurements even in environments with high noise and interference levels, such as construction, transportation, and more (Kantsepolsky & Aviv, 2024a). At the beginning of the twentieth century, superposition, entanglement, tunneling, and coherence were treated as purely theoretical concepts. Nevertheless, they laid the groundwork for the later exploitation of quantum effects in technology and nowadays form the basis of cutting-edge quantum technologies, as discussed in the next sections.

7.2.3 The First Quantum Revolution

By explaining particles' behavior at atomic and subatomic scales, quantum mechanics supplied the theoretical basis for a host of twentieth-century technologies. Understanding of discrete atomic energy levels, electron transport in solids, and the role of impurities enabled the invention of the *transistor* in 1947. This invention was the first crucial step toward *semiconductors, integrated circuits*, and *microprocessors*, serving as the basis of modern electronics and computing (Riordan & Hoddeson, 1997).

The theory of *stimulated emission* (Einstein, 1917) introduced the concept of light amplification by stimulated emission of radiation, or what is known as a *laser*. Following the first demonstration by Maiman in 1960, nowadays lasers are broadly used in telecommunications, medicine, manufacturing, and more (Svelto, 2010). Likewise, a phenomenon of *nuclear magnetic resonance* that was predicted by quantum mechanics evolved into Magnetic Resonance Imaging (MRI) in the 1970s, enabling the revolution in medical diagnostics (Damadian, 1971; Lauterbur, 1973; Ai et al., 2012). Furthermore, exploiting *quantum transitions* in cesium and other atoms to achieve *accuracy for precision timing* makes the global positioning system (GPS) possible (Schmittberger & Scherer, 2020).

These and additional related developments collectively constitute *the first quantum revolution* or *"Quantum 1.0,"* in which scientists and engineers, even without directly manipulating individual quantum states, leveraged quantum-mechanical principles embedded in materials to create the above-mentioned transistors, semiconductors, lasers, nuclear power, MRI, and atomic clocks. These inventions established the technological foundations of modern industrial and information societies, driving massive productivity gains from the

1960s onward (Hossain, 2023; Aspect, 2023). Although quantum effects remained hidden in large ensembles of atoms, these advances set the stage for Quantum 2.0, in which researchers gained the ability to isolate, control, and entangle single quantum systems.

7.3 Quantum Information Science

Since the middle of the twentieth century, engineers and scientists have relied on Claude E. *Shannon's mathematical theory of computation*, also known as *classical information theory*, to understand how to compress data, send it reliably over noisy channels, and store it efficiently. Shannon's (1948) theory treats information as a probability distribution over symbols, introduces *entropy as the average information content*, and proves that error-free communication is possible up to a channel capacity determined by mutual information. In his landmark paper, to define a quantitative measure of information, Shannon chose a logarithmic measure with base 2, so that *one unit of information* corresponds to a choice between two equally likely alternatives, like yes and no. "If the base 2 is used, the resulting units may be called *binary digits,* or more briefly *bits*" (Shannon, 1948, p. 380). This way, Shannon established the term *"bit"* as a *unit for measuring information.* Shannon's bits, being distinguishable and cloneable, yield compression and reliable coding theorems that underpin all modern digital technology.

QIS emerged from the *understanding that quantum mechanics' unique features, particularly superposition and entanglement, could be used as resources for storing, processing, and transmitting information.* Already in 1929, Leo Szilard explicitly connected information with entropy (a measure of disorder) and energy, inaugurating the thermodynamics of information—the study of how information's gain or loss has physical consequences. According to Szilard (1929), information works like fuel—you can use it to get work done, but every measurement adds unavoidable waste heat you cannot recover (Szilard, 1929).

Decades later, Landauer (1961) and Bennett (1982) clarified that information erasure has a fundamental thermodynamic cost, thus *re-entangling* information theory with physical law. In turn, Helstrom (1969) and Holevo (1973) showed the limits on classical information that can be extracted from quantum states, giving rise to the concept of quantum channel capacities. Hence, *QIS origins belong to the reevaluation of the relationship between physics and information*, while its foundations were laid by combining Shannon's foundational work on information entropy with the operator formalism of quantum mechanics.

7.3.1 From Classical to Quantum Bits and Vice Versa

During the 1980s and 1990s of the twentieth century, laboratory techniques had advanced to the point where scientists could trap single atoms and ions, manipulate single photons, and observe entanglement in the lab. Based on these developments, researchers realized that information could be encoded in quantum states. This understanding gave rise to the evolving concept of using quantum mechanics for computation, and consequently, the need for defining the unit of quantum information. In 1980, Paul Benioff proposed a *quantum mechanical model of a Turing machine*, arguing that quantum processes could perform computations. However, Benioff's proposal remained largely theoretical as it did not yet provide a practical design. Soon after, Richard Feynman (1982) claimed that quantum systems could exponentially outperform classical ones for certain tasks, notably simulating physics.

The need to formally define quantum information units became evident following the no-cloning theorem of Wootters and Zurek (1982), who proved that an unknown quantum state cannot be copied and thus emphasized that *quantum information units* behave *differently* from classical bits. It is worth mentioning that at this period, the notion of a two-state or two-level quantum system was already well known, for example, a spin-½ particle with two possible spin orientations or a photon with two orthogonal polarization states. In the literature, these notations were widely used, although it was not yet named as a qubit.

Around the same period of time, Charles Bennett and Gilles Brassard developed a quantum cryptography protocol, which became known as BB84, using two-state quantum systems to encode bits securely, leveraging quantum uncertainty to detect eavesdropping (Bennett & Brassard, 1984). Although they did not use the term "qubits" yet, the practical use of quantum two-level systems for information was underway. Meanwhile, David Deutsch (1985) formulated the first quantum Turing machine model, effectively treating two-state quantum systems as carriers of information in algorithms, although again without the name "qubit." Deutsch's model provided the first detailed conceptual blueprint of how a computing machine governed by quantum mechanics could, in principle, realize any computable algorithm. Together, these developments established a new paradigm of computation grounded in the principles of quantum mechanics. Key ideas of that time, such as reversible operations, quantum logic gates, and quantum parallelism, would shape all subsequent advances in the field.

By the early 90s, interest in quantum computation surged along with the need for a theoretical framework to quantify quantum information analogously to Shannon's classic bits. In 1995, Schumacher introduced the notion of the *quantum bit* (or *qubit*) and formulated the quantum analog of Shannon's source coding theorem. "For our elementary coding system, we choose *the two-level spin system, which we will call a 'quantum bit' or qubit. The qubit will be our fundamental unit of quantum information,* and all signals will be encoded into sequences of qubits" (Schumacher, 1995, p. 2744). According to Schumacher's acknowledgments, the term qubit was coined during the author's conversations with W. K. Wootters, a fellow physicist and colleague. One cannot overestimate this pivotal understanding—researchers had a name and a theory for the *fundamental unit of quantum information.*

Analogous to how Shannon entropy gives the number of bits for classical data, Schumacher (1995) proved that the quantum entropy of an ensemble of quantum states quantifies the number of quantum bits needed to encode them. When a qubit is measured, its superposition collapses, and the outcome becomes one of the two classical states (0 or 1), yielding one classical bit of information. In fact, according to *quantum information theory* (Holevo, 1973), n qubits cannot convey more than n classical bits of information to a measuring observer. Thus, the *bit* remains the basic unit for quantified information even in quantum contexts. Shannon's bit is the unit in which classical information gain or communication capacity is measured. Hence, *quantum information theory* uses the qubit as the carrier of information in a quantum system, while upholding the bit as the unit of *classical information.*

7.3.2 The Rise of Quantum Information Science

The mid-90s saw rapid progress in leveraging qubits for computation. The concept of the qubit as the basic unit in quantum information devices had moved from theory to experiment and became central to an entirely new field of quantum information science. In 1995, Shor and, independently, Andrew Steane developed quantum error-correcting codes to protect qubits from decoherence and errors. Shor's nine-qubit code (Shor, 1995) and Steane's seven-qubit code (Steane, 1996) showed that by entangling a logical qubit with extra physical qubits, one could detect and correct both bit flips and phase flips, arbitrary single-qubit errors, without directly measuring, and thereby collapsing, the logical qubit's state. These works and the idea of using entangled extra qubits to detect and correct errors in other qubits established that, in principle, large-scale quantum computation could be made fault-tolerant despite fragile coherence.

Also in 1995, Ignacio Cirac and Peter Zoller proposed a concrete scheme for a trapped-ion quantum computer, showing how to use the collective vibrational modes of ions in a linear trap as a *data bus* to mediate two-qubit entangling operations (Cirac & Zoller, 1995). In this protocol, each ion's internal electronic two-level system serves as a qubit, and laser pulses tuned to the motional sidebands enact entangling *Cirac–Zoller gates* by coupling electronic and motional degrees of freedom. Within months, David Wineland's group at NIST implemented the first experimental demonstration of a two-qubit *quantum logic gate* using a trapped-ion platform (Monroe et al., 1995; Rowe et al., 2001). This milestone proved that one could coherently manipulate individual qubits and generate entanglement in the laboratory, thereby placing the qubit concept at the heart of experimental quantum information science.

With error-correcting codes and ion-trap gates in hand, the qubit's role crystallized as both a theoretical unit of quantum information and an experimentally realizable physical system, enabling quantum information theory to mature. Central to this evolution was the recognition of entanglement as a quantifiable resource.

In 1998, William K. Wootters introduced quantitative measures of entanglement, such as *concurrence*, which rendered entanglement a computable quantity and established its role as a measurable resource in two-qubit systems (Wootters, 1998). Building on earlier work by Bennett and Brassard (1984) in quantum cryptography, Bennett et al. (1993) introduced quantum teleportation, a protocol that uses shared entanglement together with two bits of classical communication to transfer an unknown qubit state from one location to another. This breakthrough demonstrated the power of entanglement-assisted communication, marking one of the first concrete applications of entanglement in QIS.

Beyond computation and communication, the qubit concept was also deployed for measurements. While traditional measurements are often limited by the standard quantum limit, scaling as $1/\sqrt{N}$ for N unentangled probes, by preparing measurement probes in entangled or squeezed quantum states, quantum metrology can approach the Heisenberg limit, scaling as $1/N$ for the same number of resources, thereby achieving superior precision. Already in 1981, Caves showed that squeezed states of light could improve interferometric phase sensing (Caves, 1981). Giovannetti et al. (2004, 2006,

2011) generalized these ideas, showing that by linking many particles through quantum entanglement, one could measure things like time and phase with far greater accuracy than classical physics allows. These proposals spurred experiments in atomic clocks, magnetometry, and gravitational wave detectors, illustrating how qubits are transforming the very foundations of measurement science. We further discuss measurements in the dedicated section on quantum sensing and metrology.

> Supported by fundamental texts and experiments, qubits became the bedrock of quantum information theory. Nowadays, QIS stands as the unifying framework describing how qubits and quantum channels can carry out information-related tasks in communication, computation, and measurement, with efficiencies and functionalities impossible in a purely classical world (Nielsen & Chuang, 2010).

In the next section, we discuss the currently ongoing second quantum revolution, which is being driven by the principles and applications of QIS.

7.4 The Second Quantum Revolution

Over the last two decades, research in QIS has accelerated worldwide, moving from laboratory curiosity to a vibrant, cross-disciplinary endeavor (Acín et al., 2018). According to Nobel Laureate Alain Aspect, it became possible only once researchers learned how to isolate and manipulate single quanta. By actively engineering quantum phenomena as resources for technology, advances in QIS are being marshaled to build technologies beyond anything possible in the classical realm. Hence, by standing at the intersection of quantum physics and information technology, QIS has initiated and constitutes the driving force of the second quantum revolution.

Nowadays, one can witness the initial results of the second revolution. National governments have launched major programs aimed at advancing quantum R&D and building a quantum-trained workforce. Ambitious quantum technology initiatives exist in the USA, the United Kingdom, the European Union, China, and more. At the same time, industry participation has exploded from giants like IBM, Google, Microsoft, etc., to defense contractors and startups—all racing to develop quantum devices and applications while fiercely competing for QIS talent on a global scale. The following subsections provide an overview of the second quantum revolution, including its foundations, technologies, and potential applications.

7.4.1 Foundations, Enabling Technologies and Applications

Unlike the first revolution, when quantum mechanics was used to understand natural systems, the second revolution involves controlling individual quantum systems, such as atoms, electrons, and photons, while exploiting their properties, including superposition and entanglement, for entirely new capabilities and practical applications (Aspect, 2023; Purohit et al., 2024). Hence, the defining feature of the second quantum revolution is the ability to control quantum coherence by sustaining superposition and entanglement rather than just passively observing or averaging it (Hossain, 2023).

While quantum theory allows us to understand why electrons in atoms have stable orbits or how semiconductors work, now, in the second revolution, we are learning to design quantum systems almost from the ground up by assembling tailored quantum circuits, quantum materials, and entangled networks. Modern laboratories can trap single ions or atoms in electromagnetic traps, emit single photons on demand, and manipulate single electrons in quantum dots or superconducting circuits. Advances in experimental techniques, such as laser cooling, optical trapping, and quantum state manipulation, have allowed scientists to manipulate individual quanta with precision. For example, cooling them to eliminate thermal noise, using lasers and microwave fields to control their states, etc. By leveraging precise control over quantum coherence to achieve capabilities impossible with classical technologies, the second quantum revolution represents not merely evolutionary progress but a radical technological transformation (Deutsch, 2020; Kantsepolsky, 2025).

French physicist Alain Aspect is renowned for his pioneering experimental tests of quantum entanglement and Bell's inequalities. Aspect's work at the beginning of 80s provided the conceptual green light for the second quantum revolution. It demonstrated the extraordinary character of entanglement experimentally, shifting it from a quantum curiosity to a resource that could be used in technology. The Bell test experiments and many advances since were enabled by new techniques to isolate, observe, and control individual quantum objects. Together with John F. Clauser and Anton Zeilinger, Alain Aspect received in 2022 the Nobel Prize in Physics award "for experiments with entangled photons, establishing the violation of Bell inequalities and pioneering quantum information science" (The Nobel Prize in Physics 2022; Aspect, 2023).

A basic taxonomy of QIS identifies three key domains of the second quantum revolution. These domains are *Quantum Computation, Quantum Communication* (or networking), *and Quantum Sensing* (and metrology).

While the three domains are stable and acknowledged across all classification schemes, variation exists in how supporting or adjacent areas are organized. The two main points of variance concern the status of quantum *simulation* and the treatment of *transversal/enabling layers*.

Regarding quantum simulation, the key question is whether it should be treated as an independent pillar or as a subcategory within quantum computing. For example, Acín et al. (2018) presented simulation as its own distinct domain. Similarly, some policy discussions, such as those in the U.S. Congressional Research Service report (Figliola, 2020), adopt a four-category structure that lists computing, simulation, communications, and sensing or metrology as separate elements. In contrast, more recent roadmaps, such as the U.S. (DOE) *Quantum Information Science Applications Roadmap* (DOE, 2024), merge simulation into the broader quantum computing category, treating it as one of many use cases performed by a quantum computer. In this view, computing serves as the overarching umbrella under which simulation naturally falls. In practice, the distinction depends on context. While foundational/research taxonomies often separate simulation as a discrete domain to highlight its unique physical and algorithmic challenges, application-driven and funding roadmaps simplify the structure by embedding simulation within the computing pillar (De Luca, 2024; DOE, n.d.; Håkegård & Rauniyar, 2025; PNNL, 2023).

As for transversal or enabling layers, those layers consist of foundational concerns that underpin all domains, such as quantum theory, software, control, and materials. According to the European quantum technologies roadmap, quantum theory, software, and control constitute transversal areas that "cut across" all domains (Acín et al., 2018). Subsequent European strategic documents, including the Strategic Research and Industry Agenda for Quantum Technologies in the European Union (Quantum Flagship, 2023), further developed this approach by classifying materials, control, and theory or software as foundational supports for all quantum technologies. By contrast, U.S. institutional documents, such as those from the DOE (2024) and the U.S. National Science Foundation (NSF, 2023), position fundamental science, instrumentation, and enabling tools as underlying elements that support all QIS domains without separating them into distinct categories. Therefore, one can conclude that while European frameworks tend to make the transversal layers explicit and visible, the U.S. approach generally embeds them within domain-specific programs.

Despite these variations, reflecting a difference in structural emphasis rather than conceptual disagreement, the consensus remains that QIS encompasses *quantum computing*, *quantum communication/networking*, and *quantum sensing/metrology*, sometimes extended by simulation, cryptography, or foundational science (Figliola, 2020; De Luca, 2024; DOE, n.d.; PNNL, 2023). Collectively, these domains represent how quantum principles enable fundamental information functions of *measurement, processing,* and *transmission.* The advances in one domain often feed the others, making these domains highly interrelated. Together, these domains form the core of "Quantum 2.0," the term coined to describe the emerging wave of *quantum technologies* enabling entirely new capabilities (Rapp, 2021).

The second quantum revolution is still in its early stages, with many of its practical impacts yet to be realized. Analysts predict Quantum 2.0 supertechnologies will *massively change our lives and work, shaping a new era* across fields from computing and communications to cybersecurity, precision measurement, ultra-sensitive quantum sensors, quantum simulators, and more (Rapp, 2021). In the next subsections, we explain the main enabling technologies of Quantum 2.0.

7.4.2 Quantum Computation

Quantum computing is perhaps the most well-known facet of the second quantum revolution and Quantum 2.0 technologies, often drawing headlines for its transformative potential. Quantum computers utilize superposition and entanglement of qubits to process information in ways classical computers cannot, enabling them to perform specific algorithms more efficiently than a classical computer. Being the most publicized subfield of QIS (over 433,000 items in Google Scholar as of June 2025), it holds the promise of solving certain computational problems much faster than classical computers (Rieffel & Polak, 2000; Kantsepolsky, 2025).

7.4.2.1 A History and Basics of Quantum Computing

As presented in Section 3, a key insight driving the field occurred in 1982, when Richard Feynman proposed that classical computers would be inefficient at simulating quantum mechanics and that only quantum systems could efficiently simulate other quantum systems, thus laying the conceptual foundation for quantum computation (Feynman, 1982). However, at that time, no one was sure how to practically utilize the quantum effects to speed up computation. In 1984, Bennett and Brassard showed how quantum mechanics could enable secure communication impossible under classical physics, thus demonstrating the first practical use of quantum information principles

(Bennett & Brassard, 1984). Finally, in 1985, David Deutsch generalized the classical Turing machine to the quantum domain, showing that any classically computable function could be implemented using reversible quantum gates (Deutsch, 1985). This formulation of the universal quantum Turing machine provided the first rigorous theoretical foundation for quantum computation, uniting quantum physics with computational theory. Though at the time, there was no clear method to harness quantum effects for computational advantage.

In 1994, Peter Shor surprised the world by describing a polynomial-time quantum algorithm for factoring integers. Shor's algorithm (1994) showed that a quantum computer could factor large numbers in polynomial time, providing a dramatic speedup over the best-known classical algorithms. Shor's work implicitly relied on manipulating qubits, though in the original paper, they were described as quantum two-state particles and provided a concrete reason to build quantum computers.

Subsequent works of Shor (1995) and Steane (1996) on error-correcting codes for quantum information showed that coherent control of single quantum systems could, in principle, be made fault-tolerant. Finally, Grover (1996) demonstrated quadratic speedup for unstructured search. Together, these breakthroughs established quantum computation as a viable and mathematically grounded branch of QIS, demonstrating that quantum mechanics could deliver computational advantages unattainable by classical means. Since then, experimentalists have been trying to build quantum computers, and theoreticians are trying to find other quantum algorithms (Rieffel & Polak, 2000).

It is worth emphasizing that not all computations benefit from quantum algorithms, but for those that do, the gains can be revolutionary. The advantages of quantum computers stem from their ability to represent and process information in superposed and entangled states. While n classical bits define *only one of* 2^n possible configurations at a time, n qubits function as a system that can represent *all* 2^n *possible states at once*, allowing quantum operations to act on multiple possibilities simultaneously (Rieffel & Polak, 2000).

By encoding the structure of a problem into these quantum states, quantum algorithms use interference as a computational filtering mechanism. Each potential solution carries a certain probability weight that evolves during the computation. The quantum operations are designed so that the weights of incorrect solutions cancel out, while those of the correct solutions reinforce each other. This process increases the likelihood of obtaining the right answer, enabling certain problems to be solved in dramatically fewer steps than would be possible on a classical computer. However, the final output of these algorithms is still a classical bit string, such as the factors of the number or the index of the found item. Hence, it is important to understand that quantum computing is not a panacea that will replace classical computers. Rather, it is expected to function as a powerful co-processor for specialized tasks.

7.4.2.2 The Current State of Quantum Computing

Harnessing the potential of quantum computing is challenging because quantum states are extremely fragile. Interactions with the environment can cause decoherence and introduce errors in computations, and simply reading the qubit state collapses its state, yielding only a random outcome (Hossain, 2023). A challenge is that quantum error correction requires encoding qubits into entangled groups that can be frequently checked and corrected for errors. This, in turn, demands many physical qubits to represent a single logical or error-corrected qubit, pushing the total required qubit count to very high levels.

Moreover, a functional quantum computer requires not only stable qubits and high-fidelity gates, but also supporting components for qubit initialization, readout, and error correction. Implementing these functions requires complex hardware systems such as cryogenic refrigeration to reduce decoherence, classical electronic controllers to generate and synchronize gate pulses, and specialized interconnects to couple qubits.

Although quantum processors have improved dramatically in scale and coherence, they still lack the fault tolerance required for deep, long-duration algorithms (Deutsch, 2020). As a result, the current state of quantum hardware is defined as the *Noisy Intermediate-Scale Quantum (NISQ) era*, where devices with a few hundred qubits are prone to errors and cannot yet perform sustainable error correction for extended algorithmic runs (Preskill, 2018).

Beyond hardware limitations, obtaining a useful computational result also requires clever algorithmic strategies. One must devise algorithms and interference schemes that bias the quantum state toward the desired answer before measurement. This necessitates *nontraditional programming techniques* and fundamentally different algorithmic thinking than in classical computing. Hence, while the raw computational potential of quantum mechanics is extraordinary, unlocking it demands overcoming both profound scientific and engineering challenges. From the perspective of market presence, superconducting qubit systems are pioneered by IBM and Google, while ion-trapped systems are led by IonQ and Honeywell, and according to a composite performance metric, quantum volume, which captures both qubit count and operational fidelity, shows approximately doubling each year (IBM Quantum, 2024).

Despite their imperfections, NISQ devices have already achieved important proof-of-concept milestones. Here are some examples. In 2023, IBM announced its Condor processor, featuring 1,121 superconducting qubits and an average two-qubit gate fidelity of 99.1%, and projects reaching >4,000 qubits by (IBM Quantum, 2023, 2024). Google's superconducting-qubit program has gone beyond isolated demonstrations of quantum advantage to achieve below-threshold quantum error correction on its latest generations of processors. On its 105-qubit Willow processor, Google realized fully below-threshold operation using combinations of data and measurement qubits for demonstrating stable below-threshold performance over millions of cycles (Google Quantum AI, 2025). These results mark Google's transition from NISQ-era algorithms toward truly fault-tolerant operation, which is already being forged in the laboratory.

IonQ's Forte system, available since 2022, operates 36 ions in a cryogenic trap, achieving single- and two-qubit gate fidelities of 99.9% and 99.5%, respectively, with coherence times over 60 s (IonQ, 2024). In turn, Quantinuum, formed in 2021 by the merger of Honeywell Quantum Solutions and Cambridge Quantum, has outlined an ambitious trapped ion roadmap aiming for universal, fault-tolerant quantum computing by the end of the 2020s (Buhrman & Langer, 2024). In the near term, Quantinuum plans to deploy Helios—a 100-qubit system with a novel CMOS-fabricated quantum charge-coupled device architecture featuring on-chip junction routing for scalable 2D qubit arrays. Their Sol processor is expected to scale to several hundred qubits, laying the groundwork for Apollo in the late 2020s—a multi-thousand-qubit machine targeting logical qubit lifetimes and error rates sufficient for practical fault-tolerant algorithms. These milestones position Quantinuum as one of the leaders to transit from the NISQ era to large-scale, error-corrected quantum computation. As one can see, the landscape of NISQ-era quantum devices is rich and rapidly evolving. While each technology has its unique strengths, no matter the quantum processor's hardware, a critical figure of merit is the qubit count and quality.

According to Stanford Emerging Technology Review (2025), although qubit counts now exceed 1,000 on leading superconducting and trapped-ion platforms and basic quantum logic, small-molecule simulations, and random-circuit sampling have all been demonstrated, today's quantum hardware remains too noisy and insufficiently scaled for broad-based fault-tolerant quantum computing. The field, therefore, focuses on improving coherence, developing error-mitigation and error-correction techniques, and exploring hybrid classical-quantum algorithms within the NISQ paradigm, while laying the groundwork for a future transition to fully fault-tolerant architectures. Similarly, Quantum Computing Report (2024) analysis confirms that NISQ devices will predominate through at least 2029, noting that *quantum advantage* has been demonstrated only for contrived tasks, while general-purpose, large-scale utility remains out of reach.

It is an exciting time. We are witnessing the crossover point where quantum hardware performs tasks that cannot be emulated classically, even if those tasks are somewhat contrived. Over the next 5+ years, we expect to see a progression from improved NISQ devices to early fault-tolerant quantum computing (FTQC) machines. One example is the IBM announcement from June 10, 2025, where IBM promises to deliver Starling, a large-scale fault-tolerant quantum computer capable of running quantum circuits comprising 100 million quantum gates on 200 logical qubits by 2029, which will broaden the range of quantum algorithms that can run on it. According to IBM, they are already building this system in Poughkeepsie, New York (IBM Quantum, 2025).

7.4.3 Quantum Communication and Cryptography

Quantum communication is the second-largest category of QIS with over 159,000 items in Google Scholar as of June 2025. By the transmission of information using individual or entangled particles, quantum communication aims to achieve security guaranteed by the laws of physics or functionality beyond classical analogs (Acín et al., 2018). While the typical carriers of quantum information through fibers or free-space links are photons, the toolset of quantum communications includes single-photon sources and detectors, entangled photon pair sources, and devices like beam splitters and phase modulators (Gisin & Thew, 2007; Hadfield, 2009; Pan et al., 2012).

7.4.3.1 Quantum Key Distribution

Quantum Key Distribution (QKD) is the most mature application, which allows two parties, commonly named in the literature as Alice and Bob, to establish a shared, secret cryptographic key with security guaranteed by the laws of quantum physics (Bennett & Brassard, 1984; Ekert, 1991). The security of QKD arises from the fact that measuring a quantum system disturbs it, and any eavesdropper intercepting the photons will unavoidably introduce anomalies that alert the legitimate parties to the presence of surveillance. In the seminal BB84 protocol (Bennett & Brassard, 1984), Alice encodes random bit values onto the polarization of single photons in one of two non-orthogonal bases. Bob measures each arriving photon on a randomly chosen basis, and by later comparing subsets of their basis choices over a classical authenticated channel, can estimate the error rate. Any eavesdropper (Eve) attempting to intercept or measure the qubits unavoidably disturbs their states, introducing detectable errors.

QKD contrasts with classical key exchange, such as Diffie & Hellman (1976), which relies on computational assumptions, for example, the difficulty of factoring. This is why, theoretically, they may be broken by quantum computers running Shor's algorithm (Shor, 1994). Since QKD offers information-theoretic security, even an adversary with unbounded computing power cannot learn the key without detection (Scarani et al., 2009; Lo et al., 2014). This makes QKD especially attractive. QKD has been successfully demonstrated over fiber optics and satellite links in real-world conditions. Over standard telecommunications fibers, QKD has reached ranges exceeding 400 km using decoy-state and measurement-device-independent protocols (Yin et al., 2016; Boaron et al., 2018). In China, the Micius satellite successfully performed QKD between ground stations separated by over 1,200 km, demonstrating quantum-secured video calls (Liao et al., 2017). Major cities have seen the deployment of quantum-secured fiber networks for banking and government communication, albeit still on a limited scale. For example, field trials were performed in Vienna, Tokyo, and other cities, demonstrating continuous key services for banking and government (Peev et al., 2009; Sasaki et al., 2011). Some recent examples include a 46-node quantum metropolitan area network over existing fiber in Hefei (Chen et al., 2021) and a multi-node QKD link across Padova's city center (Kržič et al., 2023). Also, commercial QKD systems through fiber optics or ground-to-satellite links are already available. Companies, such as ID Quantique and Toshiba, offer turnkey QKD systems for enterprise and research use (ID Quantique, 2024; Toshiba Corporation, 2020). Therefore, quantum-secure cryptographic solutions such as QKD are expected to proliferate in tandem with the threat quantum computers pose to traditional encryption (How & Cheah, 2023).

7.4.3.2 Post-Quantum Cryptography

The basis of modern digital security, starting from HTTPS web traffic and up to banking transactions, relies on cryptographic algorithms such as RSA and ECC that could be broken by a sufficiently powerful quantum computer (Mosca, 2018). Unsurprisingly, the urgent need to transition to quantum-resistant cryptographic methods has spurred efforts in two complementary directions: a) deploying QKD for high-security links and b) developing post-quantum cryptography (PQC)—new encryption algorithms that are believed to be resistant to quantum attacks but can run on classical computers (Chen et al., 2016; How & Cheah, 2023).

Governments and standards bodies are actively vetting PQC schemes to future-proof communications against the threat of quantum codebreaking. NIST's standardization process has selected lattice-, code-, and hash-based schemes, which are now recommended for long-term security. In the interim, a *quantum-safe* strategy might combine PQC with QKD for extra security. QKD integration with existing telecom infrastructure, often called *QKD overlay* (van Deventer et al., 2022). The European Quantum Flagship and similar programs are prioritizing quantum network development as a long-term strategic goal (Acín et al., 2018). Thus, quantum communication technologies play a dual role: an *offensive* one, by enabling fundamentally new secure communication channels, and a *defensive* one, by mitigating the cybersecurity threats that quantum computing poses to classical encryption systems.

7.4.3.3 A Quantum Internet

Beyond QKD, quantum communication encompasses the broader vision of a quantum internet—a global network capable of distributing entanglement and transmitting qubits between distant nodes (Kimble, 2008). Such a network, which has no analog in classical communication, would enable, via quantum repeaters, long-distance entanglement distribution along with quantum teleportation of unknown quantum states (Bennett et al., 1993; Briegel et al., 1998).

How would it work? Achieving a large-scale quantum network requires quantum repeaters, which use entanglement swapping and quantum memories to extend entanglement over long distances, while overcoming fiber loss and preventing decoherence. Instead of transmitting fragile quantum particles directly over long distances, quantum repeaters divide the channel into shorter segments and link them through *entanglement swapping,* forming a chain of entangled connections between intermediate nodes (Briegel et al., 1998). Using this entanglement, a process known as *quantum teleportation* can transfer the quantum state of a particle from one node to another without moving the physical particle itself. The transfer is achieved by performing a joint measurement and sending two classical bits of information that allow the receiver to reconstruct the original state (Bennett et al., 1993). In this way, quantum information can be transmitted safely across great distances, as envisioned in the architecture of the emerging *quantum internet* (Kimble, 2008; Wehner et al., 2018).

This approach could eventually enable secure *distributed quantum computing* or *quantum computing in the cloud*, where clients send encrypted quantum data to a remote quantum processor for computation without revealing information, and results are teleported back—all with the user's data protected by quantum laws (Broadbent et al., 2009). Another possible application for quantum internet could be distributed quantum sensing, where multiple sensors are connected by entanglement and thus improve baseline sensitivity. On a longer horizon, fully quantum networks may merge with classical networks to support hybrid communication systems, where both classical bits and qubits flow between nodes. However, this approach requires rethinking network architectures along with interfacing quantum devices with classical Internet infrastructure, which by itself presents a substantial interdisciplinary engineering challenge (Proctor et al., 2018).

7.4.4 Quantum Simulation

According to Google Scholar, the next category of quantum technologies is quantum simulation, with over 75,000 items as of June 2025. The basic idea of quantum simulation, first articulated by Feynman in the 1980s, is that "nature isn't classical... and if you want to make a simulation of nature, you'd better make it quantum mechanical" (Feynman, 1982, p. 486). Whereas quantum computers aim for arbitrary algorithmic tasks such as integer factorization or database search, quantum simulators focus on specific Hamiltonians or dynamical processes by trading a quantum computer's universality for resource efficiency (Georgescu et al., 2014). Hence, instead of trying to solve complex foundational problems in chemistry, materials science, and condensed-matter physics on conventional computers, quantum simulators leverage controllable quantum systems to mimic target quantum models (Acín et al., 2018).

7.4.4.1 Analog Versus Digital Quantum Simulation

In *analog simulators*, the actual hardware, for example, a grid of ultracold atoms in laser light, or an array of trapped ions is engineered so it directly emulates the model of interest—those natural interactions that are chosen or tuned so that they match the mathematical description (the Hamiltonian) of the problem you want to study (MacDonell et al., 2021; Shaffer et al., 2021). So, in an analog quantum simulator, you build or adjust the device so that its own physics is the physics you want to understand. You then prepare and measure that device, and its behavior tells you about the target model. According to Acín et al. (2018), analog simulators excel at large-scale, long-timescale experiments without full fault-tolerance, effectively serving as "quantum analog computers" for targeted tasks.

In turn, *digital quantum simulation* programs a gate-based quantum processor to approximate time evolution via techniques like Trotter–Suzuki decomposition or variational algorithms (Lloyd, 1996). Digital simulators offer universality. They can, in principle, reproduce any local Hamiltonian. However, they are currently limited by gate errors, decoherence, and circuit depth as discussed in Section 4.2. To leverage both paradigms' strengths, researchers have developed hybrid *digital-analog* simulators. One example is the work of Andersen et al. (2024), which demonstrated a 69-qubit superconducting device that interleaves native Hamiltonian evolution with digital gate sequences within the same experiment, achieving high-precision studies of thermalization and critical dynamics. Looking ahead, it is probable that *hybrid workflows* combining conventional computing with analog and digital quantum simulators will become widely deployed in research, accelerating breakthroughs in materials, chemistry, and fundamental physics (McClean et al., 2016), truly fulfilling Feynman's vision of a *quantum-mechanical* simulation of nature.

7.4.4.2 Key Applications

Among the most prominent applications of quantum simulation are *Condensed Matter Physics, Quantum Chemistry, High-Energy Physics, Materials Discovery, and Industrial R&D.* Condensed matter physics deals, among others, with the exploration of high superconductivity models, quantum phase transitions, and non-equilibrium dynamics (Brown et al., 2017; Zhang et al., 2017). Quantum chemistry is focused on Variational Quantum Eigensolver calculations for small molecules (Kandala et al., 2017; Nam et al., 2020) and analog photochemistry on single ions (MacDonell et al., 2021).

In turn, high-energy physics deals with the simulation of lattice gauge theories (Martinez et al., 2016; Yang et al., 2020) and variational studies of non-trivial topologies to explore quantum phases and confinement phenomena, thereby extending quantum simulation to regimes relevant for strongly interacting systems (Kokail et al., 2019). Finally, industrial R&D targets hybrid quantum-classical pipelines for catalyst discovery and drug design (McClean et al., 2016). These few examples illustrate how quantum simulators as *scientific tools* complement classical supercomputers, extending our ability to calculate and predict natural behavior in previously inaccessible regimes.

7.4.4.3 Quantum Sensing and Metrology

Quantum sensing and metrology exploit quantum phenomena to measure physical quantities with ultra-high precision and accuracy, often beyond the limits of classical sensors (Degen et al., 2017; Giovannetti et al., 2011; Kantsepolsky et al., 2023). By utilizing quantum control to interrogate the world around us, quantum sensing possesses the potential to generate entirely new commercial products or industries (Bongs et al., 2023; Kantsepolsky & Aviv, 2024a; 2024b). A key advantage of quantum sensors is that quantum states can transduce weak perturbations into measurable signals. Hence, this *fragility, as a resource*, while often considered an obstacle in quantum computing, improves sensitivity and therefore constitutes a virtue for quantum sensing. Table 7.1, adapted from Kantsepolsky & Aviv (2024a), presents a comparative analysis of the most common types of quantum sensors. It is worth mentioning that the values in the table are illustrative, not universal. Each modality is summarized with a single, standard figure of merit, for example, fT/√Hz for magnetometers. Moreover, reported numbers depend on bandwidth, averaging time, shielding, environmental noise, size, weight, and power. Consult the cited sources for exact experimental contexts.

Table 7.1 Common quantum sensing types: representative performance

Sensing technology	Conventional performance	Quantum performance
Magnetometers	Sensitivity: $\approx 10^{-12}$T Noise ≈ pT/√Hz	Sensitivity < 10^{-15}T Noise < fT/√Hz
Gravimeters	Sensitivity: 1 cm/s^2 Drift: 0.01 μm/s^2/h	Sensitivity: 50 nm/s^2 Drift: 1 nm/s^2/h
Accelerometers	Precision: 10 nm/s² Noise: 100 nm/s²	Precision: 1 nm/s² Noise: 10 nm/s²
Gyroscopes	Accuracy: up to 0.01°/h Drift: up to 0.001°/h	Accuracy: <$1x10^{-6}$°/h Drift: <$1x10^{-6}$°/h
Acoustics Imaging	Resolution: 10 cm Resolution: ≈1 cm@10 m	Resolution: 1 mm Resolution: <1 mm@10 m

According to Google Scholar, quantum sensing currently has the lowest number of publications, with about 35,800 results for June 2025. One reason is that, according to the recent OECD (2025) report, most mature applications of quantum technologies are already found in the sensing branch. Quantum magnetometers and atomic clocks are already among the most sensitive and accurate devices that exist. While cesium atomic clocks are highly mature technologies, widely used and integrated into numerous critical systems, optical atomic clocks are in the advanced prototype and demonstration stages. Fieldable systems of optically pumped magnetometers already exist, though deployment requires shielding and careful calibration (Tierney et al., 2019; Cheng et al., 2024).

Cold-atom gravimetry/gradient sensors have progressed from lab to outdoor field trials, including tunnel detection. However, these systems remain comparatively bulky, and ruggedization/miniaturization are active engineering goals (Stray et al., 2022). Vendors and labs prototypes report about early products utilizing Rydberg-atom RF electrometry and atom-interferometric inertial devices, although many of them are still pre-commercial or application-specific. (Schlossberger et al., 2024; OECD, 2025). In the field of photonics, photon detectors, counters, and other types of detectors are already commercially available, and more advanced quantum imaging approaches are in development (Barzanjeh et al., 2020; OECD, 2025). In the next subsections, we discuss the main application domains of quantum sensors.

7.4.4.4 Key Applications

According to Acín et al. (2018), quantum sensing promises to revolutionize numerous industries, including navigation, astronomy, microscopy, and more. The most well-known example of a quantum sensor is the atomic clock. Atomic clocks exploit hyperfine microwave or electronic optical transitions in atoms as reference oscillators for extremely stable timekeeping, even used for the SI time definition. For example, microwave cesium Cs-133 clocks define the SI second with 10^–16 stability over one second (Ludlow et al., 2015). In turn, optical clocks trap neutral strontium in an optical lattice or use single aluminum ions to count the frequency of absorbed/emitted light. Optical clocks achieve 10^–18 stability, implying a loss of less than one second over tens of billions of years (Ludlow et al., 2015; Bothwell et al., 2019; Brewer et al., 2019; Nicholson et al., 2015).

Ultra-precise timekeeping and synchronization across data centers and 5G/6G nodes are required for telecom backhaul (Bothwell et al., 2019), smart grid phasor measurement, and high-frequency trading timestamping (McGrew et al., 2018). Because atomic clocks are incomparably better than any classical quartz oscillator, they are also used as the time standard, in navigation satellite systems, relativistic geodesy, detecting drifts in fundamental physical constants, and many more. In addition to stationary devices, experiments on transportable atomic clocks show future field deployment without sacrificing performance (McGrew et al., 2018). These achievements make *Time-Based Operations and Synchronization* the most mature domain of quantum sensors utilization.

The next domain is *GPS-Free Positioning and Navigation* in environments where GPS is unavailable or jammed (Kantsepolsky et al., 2023). Quantum inertial sensors such as accelerometers and gyroscopes promise autonomous, GPS-independent navigation for autonomous vehicles, submarines, and spacecraft (Cartlidge, 2019). Because quantum gravimeters and magnetometers enable differential gravimetry and magnetic anomaly mapping, they can serve as *quantum compasses*, aiding subterranean or underwater navigation by referencing local gravity and geomagnetic signatures (Kantsepolsky et al., 2023).

In the fields of *topological visibility*, *subsurface and structural imaging*, quantum gravimetry and magnetometry enable to the unveiling of hidden structures below or within large objects, revolutionizing surveying and structural health monitoring. For example, quantum gravimeters can be used for detecting cavities or voids, mapping buried utilities, reinforcing bars, or archaeological artifacts without excavation (Kantsepolsky et al., 2023).

The combination of gravimetry, magnetometry, and advanced photonic ranging or spectroscopy allows the production of high-resolution 3D maps of underground features for *civil infrastructure and construction*, *mining*, and *environmental remediation* (Stray et al., 2022). Other potential applications are detecting stress-induced magnetic anomalies in infrastructure and volcanic monitoring (Cartlidge, 2019; Kantsepolsky & Aviv, 2024b). In turn, high-resolution quantum imaging and spectroscopy offer new capabilities in *environmental monitoring, pollution tracking, and climate science*. For example, quantum spectroscopy enables the detection of greenhouse gases, volatile organic compounds, and water contaminants, vastly improving pollution source attribution and leak detection in pipelines (Coddington et al., 2016). Moreover, single-photon and entangled-photon schemes overcome classical shot-noise limits, enabling *seeing through fog* and beyond conventional range for atmospheric LIDAR and remote sensing (Barzanjeh et al., 2020). These and additional domains represent the leading edges of applied quantum sensing. As prototypes mature toward commercial readiness, although timelines vary by modality, it is expected that over the next 5–10 years, one can expect significant advances in autonomous navigation, time distribution, subsurface surveying, and environmental stewardship, realizing the first pragmatic triumphs of the second quantum revolution.

Since quantum sensing can provide higher-fidelity data, it extends the reach of information systems into regimes of precision and accuracy that were previously inaccessible. Future smart city infrastructures will likely incorporate networks of quantum sensors for environmental monitoring, resource management, and hazard detection (Kantsepolsky & Aviv, 2024a, 2024b). However, tackling challenges such as device cost and integration into conventional IT systems will first need to be solved. As quantum sensing matures, standardization of performance benchmarks and interface protocols will be needed, along with the specialists who can maintain these sophisticated instruments (Kantsepolsky, 2025). Despite these barriers, the consensus is that quantum sensing will become an enabler of future high-performance information systems, opening new frontiers in data acquisition and accuracy (OECD, 2025).

7.5 Conclusions

Through this chapter, we provided an overview of QIS, including its historical overview, foundational concepts, and key subfields. Tracing back to how QIS emerged from the fusion of quantum physics with Shannon's information theory, and to how the principles of quantum mechanics can be used to gather, process, and transmit information in fundamentally new ways, we outlined four core domains of quantum computing, quantum communication and cryptography, quantum simulation, and quantum sensing. Together, these technologies constitute a driving force of the second quantum revolution, generating a paradigm shift in how we think about managing, utilizing, and securing information.

While quantum computers promise dramatic speedups for specific tasks, quantum communication and QKD introduce security rooted in physical law. In turn, quantum sensors and simulators expand the frontiers of data acquisition and modeling. Today's devices are already powerful enough to show quantum advantage, but still too complicated, expensive, and error-prone for broad, fault-tolerant use.

In the foreseeable future, quantum technologies create opportunities and risks as they open new design spaces for hybrid classical-quantum workflows, quantum-secured networks, and quantum-enhanced analytics, while also raising challenges around skills, standards, governance, and long-term uncertainty. In the next section, we discuss the broader societal-technical implications of these developments, how the convergence of quantum technologies with AI, cybersecurity, digital sovereignty, and geopolitical competition will affect societies, economies, and industries at the time of the emerging information singularity.

References

Acín, A., Bloch, I., Buhrman, H., Calarco, T., Eichler, C., Eisert, J., ... Wilhelm, F. K. (2018). The quantum technologies roadmap: A European community view. *New Journal of Physics, 20*(8), 080201. https://doi.org/10.1088/1367-2630/aad1ea

Ai, T., Morelli, J. N., Hu, X., Hao, D., Goerner, F. L., Ager, B., & Runge, V. M. (2012). A historical overview of magnetic resonance imaging, focusing on technological innovations. *Investigative Radiology, 47*(12), 725–741. https://doi.org/10.1097/RLI.0b013e318272d29f

Andersen, T. I., Astrakhantsev, N., Karamlou, A. H., Berndtsson, J., Motruk, J., Szasz, A., ... Neven, H. (2024). *Thermalization and criticality on an analogue–digital quantum simulator* (arXiv:2405.17385). arXiv. https://arxiv.org/abs/2405.17385

Aspect, A. (2023). The second quantum revolution: From basic concepts to quantum technologies. In M. Genovese & I. Ruo Berchera (Eds.), *Photonic quantum technologies: Science and applications* (pp. 7–30). Wiley-VCH. https://doi.org/10.1002/9783527837427.ch2

Aspect, A., Grangier, P., & Roger, G. (1982). Experimental realization of Einstein-Podolsky-Rosen-Bohm gedankenexperiment: A new violation of Bell's inequalities. *Physical Review Letters, 49*(2), 91–94. https://doi.org/10.1103/PhysRevLett.49.91

Barzanjeh, S., Pirandola, S., Vitali, D., & Fink, J. M. (2020). Microwave quantum illumination using a digital receiver. *Science Advances, 6*(26), eabb0451. https://doi.org/10.1126/sciadv.abb0451

Benioff, P. (1980). The computer as a physical system: A microscopic quantum mechanical Hamiltonian model of computers as represented by Turing machines. *Journal of Statistical Physics, 22*, 563–591. https://doi.org/10.1007/BF01011339

Bennett, C. H. (1982). The thermodynamics of computation: A review. *International Journal of Theoretical Physics, 21*, 905–940. https://doi.org/10.1007/BF02084158

Bennett, C. H., & Brassard, G. (1984). Quantum cryptography: Public key distribution and coin tossing. In *Proceedings of the IEEE International Conference on Computers, Systems & Signal Processing* (pp. 175–179). IEEE.

Bennett, C. H., Brassard, G., Crépeau, C., Jozsa, R., Peres, A., & Wootters, W. K. (1993). Teleporting an unknown quantum state via dual classical and

Einstein-Podolsky-Rosen channels. *Physical Review Letters, 70*(13), 1895–1899. https://doi.org/10.1103/PhysRevLett.70.1895

Boaron, A., Korzh, B., Boso, G., Rusca, D., Vulliez, C., Autebert, C., ... Gisin, N. (2018). Secure quantum key distribution over 421 km of optical fiber. *Physical Review Letters, 121*(19), 190502. https://doi.org/10.1103/PhysRevLett.121.190502

Bohr, N. (1913). I. On the constitution of atoms and molecules. *The London, Edinburgh, and Dublin Philosophical Magazine and Journal of Science, 26*(151), 1–25. https://doi.org/10.1080/14786441308634955

Bohr, N. (1928). The quantum postulate and the recent development of atomic theory. *Nature, 121*, 580–590. https://doi.org/10.1038/121580a0

Bongs, K., Bennett, S., & Lohmann, A. (2023). Quantum sensors will start a revolution—if we deploy them right. *Nature, 617*(7962), 672–675. https://doi.org/10.1038/d41586-023-01663-0

Born, M. (Ed.). (1971). *The Born–Einstein letters: Correspondence between Albert Einstein and Max and Hedwig Born from 1916 to 1955* (I. Born, Trans.). Macmillan.

Born, M., & Jordan, P. (1925). Zur Quantenmechanik. In J. Mehra & H. Rechenberg (Eds.), *The historical development of quantum theory* (Vol. 2, *The discovery of quantum mechanics 1925–1926*, pp. 64–101). Springer.

Born, M., Heisenberg, W., & Jordan, P. (1926). Zur Quantenmechanik II. *Zeitschrift für Physik, 35*, 557–615. https://doi.org/10.1007/BF01379806

Bothwell, T., Kedar, D., Oelker, E., Robinson, J. M., Bromley, S. L., Tew, W. L., Ye, J., & Kennedy, C. J. (2019). JILA SrI optical lattice clock with uncertainty of 2.0 × 10^−18. *Metrologia, 56*(6), 065004. https://doi.org/10.1088/1681-7575/ab4089

Brewer, S. M., et al. (2019). ^27Al^+ quantum-logic clock with a systematic uncertainty below 10^−18. *Physical Review Letters, 123*(3), 033201. https://doi.org/10.1103/PhysRevLett.123.033201

Briegel, H.-J., Dür, W., Cirac, J. I., & Zoller, P. (1998). Quantum repeaters: The role of imperfect local operations in quantum communication. *Physical Review Letters, 81*(26), 5932–5935. https://doi.org/10.1103/PhysRevLett.81.5932

Broadbent, A., Fitzsimons, J., & Kashefi, E. (2009). Universal blind quantum computation. In *2009 50th Annual IEEE Symposium on Foundations of Computer Science* (pp. 517–526). IEEE. https://doi.org/10.1109/FOCS.2009.36

Brown, P. T., Mitra, D., Guardado-Sanchez, E., Schauß, P., Kondov, S. S., Khatami, E., Paiva, T., Trivedi, N., Huse, D. A., & Bakr, W. S. (2017). Spin-imbalance in a 2D Fermi-Hubbard system. *Science, 357*(6358), 1385–1388. https://doi.org/10.1126/science.aam7838

Buhrman, H., & Langer, C. (2024, September 17). *Technical perspective: By the end of the decade, we will deliver universal, fully fault-tolerant quantum computing*. Quantinuum Blog. https://www.quantinuum.com/blog/technical-perspective-by-the-end-of-the-decade-we-will-deliver-universal-fault-tolerant-quantum-computing

Cartlidge, E. (2019). Quantum sensors: A revolution in the offing? *Optics & Photonics News, 30*(9), 24. https://doi.org/10.1364/OPN.30.9.000024

Caves, C. M. (1981). Quantum-mechanical noise in an interferometer. *Physical Review D, 23*(8), 1693–1708. https://doi.org/10.1103/PhysRevD.23.1693

Chen, L. K., Jordan, S., Liu, Y. K., Moody, D., Peralta, R., Perlner, R., ... Smith-Tone, D. (2016). *Report on post-quantum cryptography* (NIST IR 8105). National Institute of Standards and Technology. https://doi.org/10.6028/NIST.IR.8105

Chen, T.-Y., Jiang, X., Tang, S.-B., Zhou, L., Yuan, X., Zhou, H., Wang, J., Liu, Y., Chen, L.-K., Liu, W.-Y., Zhang, H.-F., Cui, K., Liang, H., Li, X.-G., Mao, Y., Wang, L.-J., Feng, S.-B., Chen, Q., Zhang, Q., Li, L., Liu, N.-L., Peng, C.-Z., Ma, X., & Pan, J.-W. (2021). Implementation of a 46-node quantum metropolitan area network. *npj Quantum Information, 7*(1), Article 134. https://doi.org/10.1038/s41534-021-00474-3

Cheng, H., He, K., Li, C., Ma, X., Zheng, F., Xu, W., Liao, P., Yang, R., Li, D., Qin, L., Na, S., Lyu, B., & Gao, J.-H. (2024). Wireless optically pumped magnetometer MEG. *NeuroImage, 300*, 120864. https://doi.org/10.1016/j.neuroimage.2024.120864

Cirac, J. I., & Zoller, P. (1995). Quantum computations with cold trapped ions. *Physical Review Letters, 74*(20), 4091–4094. https://doi.org/10.1103/PhysRevLett.74.4091

Coddington, I., Newbury, N., & Swann, W. (2016). Dual-comb spectroscopy. *Optica, 3*(4), 414–426. https://doi.org/10.1364/OPTICA.3.000414

Damadian, R. (1971). Tumor detection by nuclear magnetic resonance. *Science, 171*(3976), 1151–1153. https://doi.org/10.1126/science.171.3976.1151

de Broglie, L. (2004). *On the theory of quanta* (A. F. Kracklauer, Trans.; original work published 1924). Fondation Louis de Broglie. https://fondationlouisdebroglie.org/LDB-oeuvres/De_Broglie_Kracklauer.pdf

De Luca, S. (2024, April 10). *Quantum: What is it and where does the EU stand?* European Parliamentary Research Service. https://epthinktank.eu/2024/04/10/quantum-what-is-it-and-where-does-the-eu-stand/

Degen, C. L., Reinhard, F., & Cappellaro, P. (2017). Quantum sensing. *Reviews of Modern Physics, 89*(3), 035002. https://doi.org/10.1103/RevModPhys.89.035002

Deutsch, D. (1985). Quantum theory, the Church–Turing principle and the universal quantum computer. *Proceedings of the Royal Society A: Mathematical and Physical Sciences, 400*(1818), 97–117. https://doi.org/10.1098/rspa.1985.0070

Deutsch, I. H. (2020). Harnessing the power of the second quantum revolution. *PRX Quantum, 1*(2), 020101. https://doi.org/10.1103/PRXQuantum.1.020101

Di Meglio, A., Doser, M., Frisch, B., Grabowska, D. M., Pierini, M., & Vallecorsa, S. (2021). *CERN quantum technology initiative: Strategy and roadmap* (Version 1.0 Rev. 2) [Report]. Zenodo. https://doi.org/10.5281/zenodo.5571809

Diffie, W., & Hellman, M. (1976). New directions in cryptography. *IEEE Transactions on Information Theory*, *22*(6), 644–654. https://doi.org/10.1109/TIT.1976.1055638

Dirac, P. A. M. (1930). *The principles of quantum mechanics*. Clarendon Press.

Einstein, A. (1905). On a heuristic viewpoint concerning the production and transformation of light. *Annalen der Physik*, *322*(6), 132–148. https://doi.org/10.1002/andp.19053220607

Einstein, A. (1917). On the quantum theory of radiation (English translation of *Zur Quantentheorie der Strahlung*). In A. J. Kox, M. J. Klein, & R. Schulmann (Eds.), *The collected papers of Albert Einstein* (Vol. 6, *The Berlin years: Writings, 1914–1917*, Doc. 38). Princeton University Press. https://einsteinpapers.press.princeton.edu/vol6-doc/

Einstein, A., Podolsky, B., & Rosen, N. (1935). Can quantum-mechanical description of physical reality be considered complete? *Physical Review*, *47*(10), 777–780. https://doi.org/10.1103/PhysRev.47.777

Ekert, A. K. (1991). Quantum cryptography based on Bell's theorem. *Physical Review Letters*, *67*(6), 661–663. https://doi.org/10.1103/PhysRevLett.67.661

Feynman, R. P. (1982). Simulating physics with computers. *International Journal of Theoretical Physics*, *21*(6), 467–488. https://doi.org/10.1007/BF02650179

Figliola, P. M. (2020, April 28). *Quantum information science: Congressional activity and federal policy recommendations* (CRS In Focus No. IF11524). Congressional Research Service. https://crsreports.congress.gov/product/pdf/IF/IF11524

Georgescu, I. M., Ashhab, S., & Nori, F. (2014). Quantum simulation. *Reviews of Modern Physics*, *86*(1), 153–185. https://doi.org/10.1103/RevModPhys.86.153

Giovannetti, V., Lloyd, S., & Maccone, L. (2004). Quantum-enhanced measurements: Beating the standard quantum limit. *Science*, *306*(5700), 1330–1336. https://doi.org/10.1126/science.1104149

Giovannetti, V., Lloyd, S., & Maccone, L. (2006). Quantum metrology. *Physical Review Letters*, *96*(1), 010401. https://doi.org/10.1103/PhysRevLett.96.010401

Giovannetti, V., Lloyd, S., & Maccone, L. (2011). Advances in quantum metrology. *Nature Photonics*, *5*(4), 222–229. https://doi.org/10.1038/nphoton.2011.35

Gisin, N., & Thew, R. (2007). Quantum communication. *Nature Photonics*, *1*(3), 165–171. https://doi.org/10.1038/nphoton.2007.22

Google Quantum AI. (2025). Quantum error correction below the surface code threshold. *Nature*, *638*, 920–926. https://doi.org/10.1038/s41586-024-08449-y

Grifoni, M., & Hänggi, P. (1998). Driven quantum tunnelling. *Physics Reports*, *304*(5–6), 229–354. https://doi.org/10.1016/S0370-1573(98)00022-2

Grover, L. K. (1996). A fast quantum mechanical algorithm for database search. In *Proceedings of the twenty-eighth annual ACM symposium on Theory of computing* (pp. 212–219). Association for Computing Machinery. https://doi.org/10.1145/237814.237866

Hadfield, R. H. (2009). Single-photon detectors for optical quantum information applications. *Nature Photonics*, *3*(12), 696–705. https://doi.org/10.1038/nphoton.2009.230

Håkegård, J. E., & Rauniyar, A. (2025, May 23). *Quantum communication: What it is and why it matters now*. SINTEF Digital Blog. https://blog.sintef.com/digital-en/quantum-communication/

Heisenberg, W. (1925). Quantum-theoretical re-interpretation of kinematic and mechanical relations. *Zeitschrift für Physik, 33*, 879–893. https://doi.org/10.1007/BF01328377

Heisenberg, W. (1927). On the perceptual content of quantum-theoretical kinematics and mechanics. *Zeitschrift für Physik, 43*, 172–198. https://doi.org/10.1007/BF01397280

Helstrom, C. W. (1969). Quantum detection and estimation theory. *Journal of Statistical Physics, 1*, 231–252. https://doi.org/10.1007/BF01007479

Holevo, A. S. (1973). Bounds for the quantity of information transmitted by a quantum communication channel. *Problems of Information Transmission, 9*(3), 177–183.

Horodecki, R., Horodecki, P., Horodecki, M., & Horodecki, K. (2009). Quantum entanglement. *Reviews of Modern Physics, 81*(2), 865–942. https://doi.org/10.1103/RevModPhys.81.865

Hossain, K. A. (2023). The potential and challenges of quantum technology in the modern era. *Scientific Research Journal, 11*(6), 41–49.

How, M.-L., & Cheah, S.-M. (2023). Business renaissance: Opportunities and challenges at the dawn of the quantum computing era. *Businesses, 3*(4), 585–605. https://doi.org/10.3390/businesses3040036

Huang, J., Wu, D., Cai, Y., Xu, Y., Li, C., Gao, Q., Zhao, L., Liu, G., Xu, Z., & Zhou, X. J. (2020). High precision determination of the Planck constant by modern photoemission spectroscopy. *Review of Scientific Instruments, 91*(4), Article 045116. https://doi.org/10.1063/1.5129140

IBM Quantum. (2023). *Quantum roadmap to 2033*. IBM Quantum Blog. Retrieved June 9, 2025, from https://www.ibm.com/quantum/blog/quantum-roadmap-2033

IBM Quantum. (2024). *Development & innovation roadmap: 2024 update* [PDF]. IBM Corporation. Retrieved June 9, 2025, from https://www.ibm.com/quantum/technology#roadmap

IBM Quantum. (2025). *Large-scale FTQC*. IBM Quantum Blog. Retrieved June 10, 2025, from https://www.ibm.com/quantum/blog/large-scale-ftqc

ID Quantique. (2024). *ID Quantique QKD systems*. https://www.idquantique.com/quantum-safety/quantum-key-distribution/

IonQ. (2024). *Forte: High-performance trapped-ion quantum system*. Retrieved June 9, 2025, from https://ionq.com/quantum-systems/forte

Kandala, A., Mezzacapo, A., Temme, K., et al. (2017). Hardware-efficient variational quantum eigensolver for small molecules and quantum magnets. *Nature, 549*(7671), 242–246. https://doi.org/10.1038/nature23879

Kantsepolsky, B. (2025). Quantum transformation of electrical systems: The potential for decentralization of infrastructures, governance, and organizational structures. In S. Sareen, T. H. Jackson Inderberg, & P. O. Eikeland (Eds.), *Are low-carbon futures decentralized? Visions and praxis in governing collective electric systems* (pp. 38–49). Edward Elgar Publishing. https://doi.org/10.4337/9781035355198.00009

Kantsepolsky, B., & Aviv, I. (2024a). Sensors in civil engineering: From existing gaps to quantum opportunities. *Smart Cities, 7*(1), 277–301. https://doi.org/10.3390/smartcities7010012

Kantsepolsky, B., & Aviv, I. (2024b). Quantum sensing for the cities of the future. In *The International Archives of the Photogrammetry, Remote Sensing and Spatial Information Sciences, XLVIII-4/W10-2024* (pp. 93–100). https://doi.org/10.5194/isprs-archives-XLVIII-4-W10-2024-93-2024

Kantsepolsky, B., Aviv, I., Weitzfeld, R., & Bordo, E. (2023). Exploring quantum sensing potential for systems applications. *IEEE Access, 11*, 31569–31582. https://doi.org/10.1109/ACCESS.2023.3262506

Kennard, E. H. (1927). Zur Quantenmechanik einfacher Bewegungstypen. *Zeitschrift für Physik, 44*, 326–352. https://doi.org/10.1007/BF01391200

Kimble, H. J. (2008). The quantum internet. *Nature, 453*(7198), 1023–1030. https://doi.org/10.1038/nature07127

Klein, M. J. (1961). Max Planck and the beginnings of the quantum theory. *Archive for History of Exact Sciences, 1*, 459–479. https://doi.org/10.1007/BF00327765

Kokail, C., Maier, C., van Bijnen, R. M. W., Brydges, T., Joshi, M. K., Jurcevic, P., Muschik, C. A., Silvi, P., Blatt, R., Roos, C. F., & Zoller, P. (2019). Self-verifying variational quantum simulation of lattice models. *Nature, 569*(7756), 355–360. https://doi.org/10.1038/s41586-019-1177-4

Kop, M., Aboy, M., de Jong, E., Gasser, U., Minssen, T., Cohen, I. G., Brongersma, M., Quintel, T., Floridi, L., & Laflamme, R. (2024). Ten principles for responsible quantum innovation. *Quantum Science and Technology, 9*(3), 035013. https://doi.org/10.1088/2058-9565/ad3776

Kržič, A., Sharma, S., Spiess, C., Chandrashekara, U., Töpfer, S., Sauer, G., González-Martín del Campo, L. J., Kopf, T., Petscharnig, S., Grafenauer, T., Lieger, R., Ömer, B., Pacher, C., Berlich, R., Peschel, T., Damm, C., Risse, S., Goy, M., Rieländer, D., Tünnermann, A., & Steinlechner, F. (2023). Towards metropolitan free-space quantum networks. *npj Quantum Information, 9*, Article 95. https://doi.org/10.1038/s41534-023-00754-0

Landauer, R. (1961). Irreversibility and heat generation in the computing process. *IBM Journal of Research and Development, 5*(3), 183–191. https://doi.org/10.1147/rd.53.0183

Lauterbur, P. C. (1973). Image formation by induced local interactions: Examples employing nuclear magnetic resonance. *Nature, 242*(5394), 190–191. https://doi.org/10.1038/242190a0

Liao, S.-K., Cai, W.-Q., Liu, W.-Y., Zhang, L., Li, Y., Ren, J.-G., ... Pan, J.-W. (2017). Satellite-to-ground quantum key distribution. *Nature, 549*(7670), 43–47. https://doi.org/10.1038/nature23655

Lloyd, S. (1996). Universal quantum simulators. *Science, 273*(5278), 1073–1078. https://doi.org/10.1126/science.273.5278.1073

Lo, H.-K., Curty, M., & Tamaki, K. (2014). Secure quantum key distribution. *Nature Photonics, 8*(8), 595–604. https://doi.org/10.1038/nphoton.2014.149

Ludlow, A. D., Boyd, M. M., Ye, J., Peik, E., & Schmidt, P. O. (2015). Optical atomic clocks. *Reviews of Modern Physics, 87*(2), 637–701. https://doi.org/10.1103/RevModPhys.87.637

MacDonell, R. J., Dickerson, C. E., Birch, C. J. T., Kumar, A., Edmunds, C. L., Biercuk, M. J., Hempel, C., & Kassal, I. (2021). Analog quantum simulation of chemical dynamics. *Chemical Science, 12*(37), 9794–9805. https://doi.org/10.1039/D1SC02142G

Maiman, T. H. (1960). Stimulated optical radiation in ruby. *Nature, 187*(4736), 493–494. https://doi.org/10.1038/187493a0

Martinez, E. A., Muschik, C., et al. (2016). Real-time dynamics of lattice gauge theories with a few-qubit quantum computer. *Nature, 534*(7608), 516–519. https://doi.org/10.1038/nature18318

McClean, J. R., Romero, J., Babbush, R., & Aspuru-Guzik, A. (2016). The theory of variational hybrid quantum-classical algorithms. *New Journal of Physics, 18*(2), 023023. https://doi.org/10.1088/1367-2630/18/2/023023

McGrew, W. F., Zhang, X., Fasano, R. J., Schäffer, S. A., Beloy, K., Nicolodi, D., Brown, R. C., Hinkley, N., Milani, G., Schioppo, M., Yoon, T. H., & Ludlow, A. D. (2018). Atomic clock performance enabling geodesy below the centimetre level. *Nature, 564*(7734), 87–90. https://doi.org/10.1038/s41586-018-0738-2

Mehra, J., & Rechenberg, H. (2001). *The historical development of quantum theory* (Vol. 6, Parts 1–2). Springer.

Monroe, C., Meekhof, D. M., King, B. E., Itano, W. M., & Wineland, D. J. (1995). Demonstration of a fundamental quantum logic gate. *Physical Review Letters, 75*(25), 4714–4717. https://doi.org/10.1103/PhysRevLett.75.4714

Mosca, M. (2018). Cybersecurity in an era with quantum computers: Will we be ready? *IEEE Security & Privacy, 16*(5), 38–41. https://doi.org/10.1109/MSP.2018.3761723

Nam, Y., Chen, J.-S., Pisenti, N. C., Wright, K., Delaney, C., Maslov, D., Brown, K. R., Allen, S., Amini, J. M., Apisdorf, J., Beck, K. M., Blinov, A., Chaplin, V., Chmielewski, M., Collins, C., Debnath, S., ... Kim, J. (2020). Ground-state energy estimation of the water molecule on a trapped-ion quantum computer. *npj Quantum Information, 6*(1), Article 33. https://doi.org/10.1038/s41534-020-0259-3

Nauenberg, M. (2016). Max Planck and the birth of the quantum hypothesis. *American Journal of Physics, 84*(9), 709–720. https://doi.org/10.1119/1.4955146

Newell, D. B., & Tiesinga, E. (2019). *The International System of Units (SI)* (NIST Special Publication 330). National Institute of Standards and Technology. https://doi.org/10.6028/NIST.SP.330-2019

Nicholson, T. L., et al. (2015). Systematic evaluation of an atomic clock at 2 × 10^−18 total uncertainty. *Nature Communications, 6*, Article 6896. https://doi.org/10.1038/ncomms7896

Nielsen, M. A., & Chuang, I. L. (2010). *Quantum computation and quantum information* (10th anniversary ed.). Cambridge University Press.

Organisation for Economic Co-operation and Development. (2025). *A quantum technologies policy primer* (OECD Digital Economy Papers No. 371). OECD Publishing. https://doi.org/10.1787/fd1153c3-en

Pacific Northwest National Laboratory. (2023). *What is quantum information science?* U.S. Department of Energy. https://www.pnnl.gov/quantum-information-science

Pan, J.-W., Chen, Z.-B., Lu, C.-Y., Weinfurter, H., Zeilinger, A., & Żukowski, M. (2012). Multiphoton entanglement and interferometry. *Reviews of Modern Physics, 84*(2), 777–838. https://doi.org/10.1103/RevModPhys.84.777

Peev, M., Pacher, C., Alléaume, R., Barreiro, C., Bouda, J., Boxleitner, W., Debuisschert, T., Diamanti, E., Dianati, M., Dynes, J. F., Fülling, J., Gobby, C., Grangier, P., Hentschel, M., Hölzl, M., Hübel, H., Pivoluska, M., Poppe, A., Querasser, E., ... Zeilinger, A. (2009). The SECOQC quantum key distribution network in Vienna. *New Journal of Physics, 11*(7), 075001. https://doi.org/10.1088/1367-2630/11/7/075001

Phillips, A. C. (2013). *Introduction to quantum mechanics.* John Wiley & Sons.

Planck, M. (1900). Zur Theorie des Gesetzes der Energieverteilung im Normalspectrum. *Verhandlungen der Deutschen Physikalischen Gesellschaft, 2*, 237–245.

Poojary, B. (2015). Origin of Heisenberg's uncertainty principle. *American Journal of Modern Physics, 4*(4), 203–211. https://doi.org/10.11648/j.ajmp.20150404.17

Preskill, J. (2018). Quantum computing in the NISQ era and beyond. *Quantum, 2*, Article 79. https://doi.org/10.22331/q-2018-08-06-79

Proctor, T. J., Knott, P. A., & Dunningham, J. A. (2018). Multiparameter estimation in networked quantum sensors. *Physical Review Letters, 120*(8), 080501. https://doi.org/10.1103/PhysRevLett.120.080501

Purohit, A., Kaur, M., Seskir, Z. C., Posner, M. T., & Venegas-Gomez, A. (2024). Building a quantum-ready ecosystem. *IET Quantum Communication, 5*(1), 1–18. https://doi.org/10.1049/qtc2.12072

Quantum Computing Report. (2024). *NISQ versus FTQC in the 2025–2029 timeframe.* Retrieved June 9, 2025, from https://quantumcomputingreport.com/nisq-versus-ftqc-in-the-2025-2029-timeframe/

Quantum Flagship. (2023). *Strategic research and industry agenda 2030.* European Commission. https://qt.eu/media/pdf/Strategic-Reseach-and-Industry-Agenda-2030.pdf

Rapp, H. P. (2021). *Economic-technological revolution through Quantum 2.0: New super technologies are within reach* (Germany Monitor Report). Deutsche Bank Research.

Razavy, M. (2014). *Quantum theory of tunneling* (2nd ed.). World Scientific. https://doi.org/10.1142/8901

Rieffel, E. G., & Polak, W. (2000). An introduction to quantum computing for non-physicists. *ACM Computing Surveys, 32*(3), 300–335. https://doi.org/10.1145/367701.367709

Riordan, M., & Hoddeson, L. (1997). *Crystal fire: The birth of the information age.* W. W. Norton & Company.

Robertson, H. P. (1929). The uncertainty principle. *Physical Review, 34*(1), 163–164. https://doi.org/10.1103/PhysRev.34.163

Rowe, M. A., Kielpinski, D., Meyer, V., Sackett, C. A., Itano, W. M., Monroe, C., & Wineland, D. J. (2001). Experimental violation of a Bell's inequality with efficient detection. *Nature, 409*(6822), 791–794. https://doi.org/10.1038/35057215

Sasaki, M., Fujiwara, M., Ishizuka, H., Klaus, W., Wakui, K., Takeoka, M., Tokura, Y., & Tanaka, A. (2011). Field test of quantum key distribution in the Tokyo QKD Network. *Optics Express, 19*(11), 10387–10409. https://doi.org/10.1364/OE.19.010387

Scarani, V., Bechmann-Pasquinucci, H., Cerf, N. J., Dušek, M., Lütkenhaus, N., & Peev, M. (2009). The security of practical quantum key distribution. *Reviews of Modern Physics, 81*(3), 1301–1350. https://doi.org/10.1103/RevModPhys.81.1301

Schlossberger, N., Hati, A., Nelson, C., & Holloway, C. L. (2024). *Rydberg states of alkali atoms in atomic vapour as SI-traceable E-field sensors* (NIST Technical Note). National Institute of Standards and Technology.

Schmittberger, B. L., & Scherer, D. R. (2020). *A review of contemporary atomic frequency standards.* arXiv. https://arxiv.org/abs/2004.09987

Schrödinger, E. (1926a–c/1983). Quantization as an eigenvalue problem (First, Second, and Third communications; English translations). In J. A. Wheeler & W. H. Zurek (Eds.), *Quantum theory and measurement* (pp. 46–124). Princeton University Press.

Schumacher, B. (1995). Quantum coding. *Physical Review A, 51*(4), 2738–2747. https://doi.org/10.1103/PhysRevA.51.2738

Shaffer, R., Megidish, E., Broz, J., Chen, W., & Häffner, H. (2021). Practical verification protocols for analog quantum simulators. *npj Quantum Information, 7*(1), Article 50. https://doi.org/10.1038/s41534-021-00380-8

Shannon, C. E. (1948). A mathematical theory of communication. *Bell System Technical Journal, 27*(3), 379–423. https://doi.org/10.1002/j.1538-7305.1948.tb01338.x

Shor, P. W. (1994, November). Algorithms for quantum computation: Discrete logarithms and factoring. In *Proceedings of the 35th Annual Symposium on Foundations of Computer Science* (pp. 124–134). IEEE. https://doi.org/10.1109/SFCS.1994.365700

Shor, P. W. (1995). Scheme for reducing decoherence in quantum computer memory. *Physical Review A, 52*(4), R2493–R2496. https://doi.org/10.1103/PhysRevA.52.R2493

Stanford Emerging Technology Review. (2025). *Quantum tech remains a long-term bet*. Retrieved June 9, 2025, from https://thequantuminsider.com/2025/05/03/quantum-tech-remains-a-long-term-bet-stanford-report-says/

Steane, A. M. (1996). Error correcting codes in quantum theory. *Physical Review Letters, 77*(5), 793–797. https://doi.org/10.1103/PhysRevLett.77.793

Stock, M., Davidson, S., & Fang, H. (2022). Dissemination of the kilogram following its redefinition. In *Proceedings of the IMEKO 24th TC3, 14th TC5, 6th TC16, and 5th TC22 International Conference* (pp. 1–6). International Measurement Confederation. https://doi.org/10.21014/tc3-2022.011

Stray, B., et al. (2022). Quantum sensing for gravity cartography. *Nature, 602*(7897), 590–594. https://doi.org/10.1038/s41586-021-04315-3

Streltsov, A., Adesso, G., & Plenio, M. B. (2017). Colloquium: Quantum coherence as a resource. *Reviews of Modern Physics, 89*(4), 041003. https://doi.org/10.1103/RevModPhys.89.041003

Svelto, O. (2010). *Principles of lasers* (5th ed.). Springer. https://doi.org/10.1007/978-1-4419-1302-9

Szilard, L. (1929). Über die Entropieverminderung in einem thermodynamischen System bei Eingriffen intelligenter Wesen [On the decrease of entropy in a thermodynamic system by the intervention of intelligent beings]. *Zeitschrift für Physik, 53*(11–12), 840–856. https://doi.org/10.1007/BF01341281

Taylor, B. N., & Thompson, A. (2008). *Guide for the use of the International System of Units (SI)* (NIST Special Publication 811, 2008 ed.). National Institute of Standards and Technology. https://doi.org/10.6028/NIST.SP.811e2008

The Nobel Foundation. (2022). *The Nobel Prize in Physics 2022*. Retrieved from https://www.nobelprize.org/prizes/physics/2022/summary/

Tierney, T. M., Mellor, S. J., Holmes, N., Boto, E., Leggett, J., Bowtell, R., & Brookes, M. J. (2019). Optically pumped magnetometers: From quantum origins to MEG. *NeuroImage, 199*, 598–608. https://doi.org/10.1016/j.neuroimage.2019.05.063

Toshiba Corporation. (2020, October 19). *Toshiba launches systems aimed at $20 billion quantum key distribution market* [Press release]. https://thequantuminsider.com/2020/10/19/toshiba-launches-systems-aimed-at-20-billion-quantum-key-distribution market/

UNESCO. (2024). About IYQ. https://quantum2025.org/about/

U.S. Department of Energy, Office of Science. (n.d.). *Quantum information science (QIS)*. https://science.osti.gov/Initiatives/QIS

U.S. Department of Energy. (2024). *Quantum information science applications roadmap*. Office of Science. https://www.quantum.gov/wp-content/uploads/2024/12/DOE_QIS_Roadmap_Final.pdf

U.S. National Science Foundation. (2023). *Quantum information science (QIS): FY 2023 budget focus area*. https://www.nsf.gov/focus-areas/quantum

United Nations. (2024). *Resolution adopted by the General Assembly on 7 June 2024: 78/287. International Year of Quantum Science and Technology, 2025*. United Nations Digital Library. https://digitallibrary.un.org/record/4052700/files/A_RES_78_287-EN.pdf

van Deventer, O., Spethmann, N., Loeffler, M., Amoretti, M., van den Brink, R., Bruno, N., Comi, P., Farrugia, N., Gramegna, M., Jenet, A., Kassenberg, B., Kozlowski, W., Länger, T., Lindstrom, T., Martin, V., Neumann, N., Papadopoulos, H., Pascazio, S., Peev, M., ... Wilhelm-Mauch, F. K. (2022). Towards European standards for quantum technologies. *EPJ Quantum Technology, 9*, Article 33. https://doi.org/10.1140/epjqt/s40507-022-00150-1

Wehner, S., Elkouss, D., & Hanson, R. (2018). Quantum internet: A vision for the road ahead. *Science, 362*(6412), eaam9288. https://doi.org/10.1126/science.aam9288

Wootters, W. K. (1998). Entanglement of formation of an arbitrary state of two qubits. *Physical Review Letters, 80*(10), 2245–2248. https://doi.org/10.1103/PhysRevLett.80.2245

Wootters, W. K., & Zurek, W. H. (1982). A single quantum cannot be cloned. *Nature, 299*(5886), 802–803. https://doi.org/10.1038/299802a0

Yang, B., Sun, H., Ott, R., Wang, H.-Y., Zache, T. V., Halimeh, J. C., Yuan, Z.-S., Hauke, P., Pan, J.-W., Bloch, I., & Lukin, M. D. (2020). Observation of gauge invariance in a 71-site Bose–Hubbard quantum simulator. *Nature, 587*(7834), 392–396. https://doi.org/10.1038/s41586-020-2910-8

Yin, J., Cao, Y., Li, Y.-H., Liao, S.-K., Zhang, L., Ren, J.-G., ... Pan, J.-W. (2016). Measurement-device-independent quantum key distribution over a 404 km optical fiber. *Physical Review Letters, 117*(19), 190501. https://doi.org/10.1103/PhysRevLett.117.190501

Zhang, J., Pagano, G., et al. (2017). Observation of a many-body dynamical phase transition with a 53-qubit quantum simulator. *Nature, 551*(7682), 601–604. https://doi.org/10.1038/nature24654

8

Toward Information Singularity

8.1 Introduction

As discussed in previous chapters, Information Systems (IS) are more than just hardware and software. IS encompasses the human and organizational elements through the interplay of "what" (technology), the "who" (people), and the "how" (processes) of information management (Pearlson et al., 2024). Contemporary IS constitutes the coordinated networks of people, processes, and technology that collect, process, store, and share information to support decision-making and control in an organization (Ali, 2023).

Fueled by digital technologies, humanity's ability to generate and disseminate information has now been accelerated further by artificial intelligence (AI). In parallel, advances in quantum information science (QIS) demonstrate unprecedented computational and simulation power, new modes of sensing, and communication. These trends have prompted scholars and futurists to warn of approaching *singularities*—transformative points beyond which the future becomes fundamentally unpredictable. Two related concepts that are often discussed are the *technological singularity*, referring to runaway progress in technology, and the *information singularity*, referring to an overwhelming explosion of information beyond human ability to comprehend or manage.

In this chapter, we analyze the definitions and implications of technological and information singularities, discussing both concepts, assessing how AI and QIS intersect with these phenomena, and examining whether next-generation IS that leverage these technologies could avert chaos or instead struggle to cope

B. Kantsepolsky, L. Topor, *Managing Information Singularity*,
https://doi.org/10.1007/978-3-032-26223-3_8

with the deluge of data. Finally, we connect these trajectories to governance, ethics, security, and sustainability, arguing that the coming decades will test not only our technical ingenuity but also our societal readiness and institutional resilience to cope with their disruptive potential. To operationalize this readiness, the chapter also introduces a conceptual Information Singularity Readiness Maturity Model that frames staged organizational capabilities for governing AI-enabled autonomy in the era of QIS. In doing so, we position information singularity as a critical lens presented in this book through which we view the future of IS.

8.2 Defining Singularity

Over the past decades, humanity's capacity to generate and disseminate information has been fueled by digital technologies and is now accelerated further by AI. In parallel, advances in QIS promise unprecedented computational and simulation power, new modes of sensing, and communication. These trends have prompted scholars and futurists to warn of approaching "singularities"—transformative points beyond which the future becomes fundamentally unpredictable. One can find two related concepts that are often discussed—the *technological singularity*, referring to runaway progress in AI and technology, and the *information singularity*, referring to an overwhelming explosion of information beyond human ability to comprehend or manage.

8.2.1 Technological Singularity

The technological singularity is a theoretical future point at which technological progress, particularly in AI, accelerates beyond human control or understanding. At its core, the term denotes a tipping point where machines become smarter than humans and begin improving themselves in a positive feedback loop, triggering an intelligence explosion. According to Shanahan (2015), regardless of whether the singularity presents an existential threat or an opportunity for humanity to transcend its limitations, we should imagine both possibilities if we want to bring it to a better outcome.

The concept of technological singularity traces back to the middle of the 20th century. As described by Ulam (1958), one of the 20th century's most influential mathematicians and physicists, John von Neumann is often cited as one who introduced the term. According to Ulam, in one conversation focused on the ever-accelerating progress of technology and causing the change of human life, Neumann hinted that it may lead to "some essential singularity in the history of the race beyond which human affairs, as we know them, could not continue" (p. 6). A few years later, I. J. Good (1966), one of the early researchers of AI, envisioned the creation of an *ultraintelligent machine* that can design ever better machines, leading to an *intelligence explosion* that would leave human intellect far behind. This prescient remark encapsulates both the promise and peril of the technological singularity—a superintelligent AI could solve every problem or, if misaligned, render human invention and perhaps humans themselves obsolete.

In his seminal essay, Vinge (1993) popularized the term *technological singularity*. Vinge argued that within 30 years, we would likely create superhuman AI, whose effects of surpassing human intelligence are comparable to the physics of a black hole singularity—a point beyond which our current models break down. Once machines surpass our cognitive abilities and begin recursive self-improvement, technological progress would become "uncontrollable and irreversible, resulting in significant and unpredictable transformations to human civilization" (Katkov et al., 2025, p. 997). In other words, all our extrapolations and understanding might cease at this singular point, since superintelligence could advance in ways we cannot foresee.

In 2005, based on extrapolating exponential growth in computing power and AI capabilities, futurist Ray Kurzweil forecasted a singularity by 2045 (Kurzweil, 2005). While estimates vary and range from around 2030 to 2100 or beyond (Müller & Bostrom, 2016), the crux of the hypothesis is consistent: a future Artificial Superintelligence (ASI) could improve itself in rapid cycles, surpassing all human intelligence and rendering the future after this point fundamentally unknowable to human minds.

It is important to note that the technological singularity remains a hypothetical, debated scenario. Many scientists are skeptical of the strong version of this hypothesis, arguing that there may be natural limits or diminishing returns that prevent infinite acceleration. For example, Russell and Norvig (2021) point out that technological improvement often follows an S-curve, with rapid growth at first, then plateauing, rather than endless exponential growth. Nonetheless, the concept of technological singularity as a moment when AI's capability and rate of improvement outstrip human intelligence so completely that, from the human perspective, technology's trajectory becomes opaque and uncontrollable has become deeply influential in discussions of AI futures. Since a misaligned superintelligence could pose extreme dangers to humanity, the discussions on technological singularity highlight the existential risk and the need for AI safety and ethics, as discussed in Chapter 6.

8.2.2 Information Singularity

Whereas technological singularity focuses on runaway intelligence, information singularity focuses on runaway information—a critical point in the growth of information where the volume and velocity of data generation exceed IS's capacity to manage or make sense of it. In an information singularity, traditional IS and institutions become perpetually information-overloaded, unable to keep up with the torrent of knowledge being produced. One of the definitions frames information singularity as "the state of the information system, when the rate of new digital data appearance per unit of time exceeds the rate of their processing and interpretation" (Solovyev, 2023, p. 101). In other words, new information is accumulating faster than any system can analyze or even store.

It is quite an intriguing fact that since the seminal work of Vinge (1993), and by 2022, when generative AI became available to the masses, there was almost no discussion on the information singularity. Among a few exceptions from the beginning of the 21st century, one notable paper is by Francis Heylighen, describing how the feedback between social and technological advances drives hyperbolic (which is faster than exponential) growth in information flows and presenting an information singularity as the point at which those flows become infinitely rapid (Heylighen, 2007). Starting in 2022, the term came to the surface again. Kostikov (2022) argued that "In the state of information singularity, it becomes impossible to search for and receive third-party (not prepared for you in advance) information . . . the information singularity is not progress and development, but simply the absence of a choice" (para. 4). According to Kostikov, while the technological singularity is "a kind of consumer infantilism raised to the absolute," the information singularity is something less pleasant and more dangerous. It means that the user's inability to discover unsolicited information amid the overload.

Daniel Schmachtenberger, Director of R&D at Neurohacker Collective, discussed humanity's current existential risks and identified them. Throughout the conversation, Schmachtenberger illustrates how the information singularity—an overwhelming flood of data beyond human processing capacity—is already reshaping political discourse, institutional trust, and decision-making at every level. Along with pandemics, climate change, and political breakdown, Schmachtenberger listed multiple singularities, including information overload & sense-making breakdown leading to nonstop data streams that are fracturing our shared reality, undermining traditional sense-making and trust in institutions. Individuals increasingly inhabit *reality tunnels*, trusting only curated or algorithm-filtered information. Liberal democracy and market systems have been strained by technological acceleration, such as deepfakes and automation, which have uncovered the need for reimagining governance and economic models to internalize true social costs. Schmachtenberger emphasizes the importance of existential hope and cultivating shared purpose and creative solutions, while acknowledging that once humanity reaches the stage when so much information is published that no human could process all the relevant information about anything, human cognition alone would not be able to keep pace with the velocity of technological and social change (Schmachtenberger, 2022).

Another angle is to consider not just raw data, but human knowledge. Prolific expansion of scientific and technical knowledge might itself follow an exponential or even super-exponential curve. In a hyperbolic scenario, the *doubling time* of knowledge keeps shortening—for example, from decades to years to months, potentially reaching a point where breakthroughs occur so rapidly that it is as if infinite knowledge is generated in finite time. While true infinity is impossible, the implication is a phase transition in the nature of knowledge itself. In 2010, IBM estimated that human knowledge was doubling every ~12 months by the early 2010s and could be doubling every 12 hours in the near future (IBM, 2010). Regardless of the exact numbers, experts agree that the growth of published information is extraordinary. One example: in 2020, an estimated 90% of all data in existence had been created in just the prior 10 years (Kostikov, 2022). The International Data Corporation forecasts the global digital data volume will reach 163–175 zettabytes by 2025, up from only 16 ZB in 2016—a tenfold increase in under a decade (Reinsel et al., 2017). Such explosive growth is unprecedented in history.

Considering knowledge management in organizations, the singularity of accounting and analytical systems is a state where such systems, based on AI technology, will develop so quickly that the principles and algorithms of their operation will be inaccessible to the understanding by management for whom these systems are organized (Katkov et al., 2025; Gafni et al., 2026). According to Katkov, it is obvious that we are already witnessing information singularly concerning humans. People are no longer able to process endless arrays of new information, and this is a global problem for humanity, which can get out of people's control and understanding, bringing technological singularity closer. Similarly, Simmons (2025) claims that we already "have entered the event horizon of the Information Singularity" (para. 1). According to Simmons, the information singularity is reached when no individual or group can update their mental models fast enough to incorporate all relevant new information, leading to chronic overwhelm, erosion of expertise, and decision paralysis. Hence, in essence, *information singularity* is defined as a tipping point where information dynamics escape our control, much as the technological singularity describes uncontrolled AI. Simmons lists a range of observable signs, including even AI experts being overwhelmed despite unprecedented access to AI research and real-time updates, and defines it as a chronic symptom of FOMO—Fear of Missing Out.

There are different opinions on what needs to be done to overcome the information singularity. One possibility to overcome the potential threats is solutions like selective long-term archival, e.g., only keeping data with assessed value and intelligent compression (Solovyev, 2023). These approaches accept that not all data is equal and that curating what we keep accessible may stave off paralysis. Other mitigation strategies include AI-powered curation, human-machine augmentation, and further broadening these concepts into societal and ethical domains. There are also some futuristic approaches, such as scanning and transforming the human mind into an information cluster, the introduction of synthetic genes into human DNA to enhance brain function, and even integration of the human brain and nano-neurobots for broad interaction of humans with external information and computing systems (Katkov et al., 2025).

According to Katkov et al. (2025), the most important way out of this problem is that once a computer with intelligence like that of a human, or superior to it, becomes available, people will begin to understand the nature of their intelligence much better, and this is where a solution can be found. In other words, even to learn about themselves, a person needs to actively use the opportunities that AI provides. Simmons (2025) also argues that thriving in the era of information singularity requires an integrated human–AI cognitive partnership underpinned by ethical design and shared governance. In particular, Simmons offers several foundational tactics, including maintaining focused cohorts of trusted sources updated less frequently but more deeply, rather than broad skimming. This can be followed by scheduling "deep-work" windows to engage with major advancements without interruption and employing customizable AI agents with human-defined criteria to surface only high-relevance updates. Simmons raises the urgent need for curricula on "information singularity literacy" to prepare the next generation for emerging phenomena and calls stakeholders to co-design shared standards for AI-mediated information flows. In the meantime, the author recommends that individuals, organizations, and societies to proactively deploy new cognitive infrastructures, combining human judgment with AI curation.

Following these analyses, one could derive that the two singularities are related. The inability of humans to keep up with the information deluge creates pressure to develop more AI assistance. Conversely, a technological singularity can help *solve* the information singularity for itself since a superintelligence could process far more data than we can, but it might deepen our dependence on AI. Hence, one can argue that the information singularity can be seen as a precursor and contributor to the technological singularity and, therefore, will arrive before a true AI singularity. In the next sections, we examine how current trends in AI and QIS might drive us toward these singularities and whether and how those technologies could also help manage the foreseen crisis.

8.3 How AI Might Lead to Information Singularity

Modern AI is a double-edged sword with regard to the information explosion. On the one hand, AI technologies dramatically *accelerate the generation of new information*. On the other hand, AI offers powerful tools for *processing and filtering* information. The net effect on the *information singularity balance* (information in vs. information processed) is a critical question. In the next sections, we analyze several ways AI contributes to or might ultimately trigger an information singularity.

8.3.1 Exponential Knowledge Discovery

AI is increasingly used to automate or assist scientific research, data analysis, and innovation. ML algorithms can sift through massive datasets to find patterns and insights that humans might miss. As these AI tools improve, they can produce *new knowledge faster than human researchers can absorb*. In effect, AI augments the *knowledge doubling rate* of humanity. If one human researcher can only read, say, 200 papers a year, but an AI system can read and summarize *2 million* papers, then the pace of scientific advancement can surge ahead of human comprehension. This scenario is not hypothetical—it is already beginning. Observers note that even AI specialists struggle to keep up: *"As someone who is pretty good at keeping up with AI, I can barely keep up...*

no one has the whole picture now" (Simmons, 2025). Breakthroughs in AI, such as LLMs, among others, are coming out on a monthly or even weekly basis, causing *"cognitive whiplash"* for experts trying to update their mental models (Simmons, 2025). This suggests we are approaching the threshold where *even the leading minds in a field cannot absorb new developments in real time,* a clear marker of an impending information singularity.

8.3.2 Diminishing Human Attention and Expertise

Human conscious cognitive throughput appears to be constrained, and recent estimates suggest on the order of 10 bits per second (Zheng & Meister, 2025). Since our brains can only process a limited number of bits/second, beyond that limit, performance degrades. AI systems, however, effectively increase the rate of information production far beyond human capabilities. This creates a widening gap between information supply and human attention. One vivid illustration can be found in the global Internet infrastructure. In March 2020, the Frankfurt Internet Exchange (DE-CIX) recorded a data throughput peak exceeding 9 terabits per second, which was a new world record at the time (DE-CIX, 2020). Given human biological constraints, even if the entire population were to process that information simultaneously, the total conscious throughput would amount to less than one percent of that data stream.

Schmachtenberger (2022) claims that there would no longer be an expert in any complex domain, because even within narrow specialties, the volume of papers, results, and data points will exceed what any individual can review. For example, in medicine, hundreds of thousands of new research articles are published each year. No doctor can read them all, so they increasingly rely on AI literature discovery tools or reviews, which themselves may miss things. According to Simmons (2025), since the knowledge landscape shifts monthly, and even specialists may feel like beginners in their own field, we have effectively hit an information singularity for that domain. This erosion of expertise and situational awareness is a dangerous phenomenon. It could lead to flawed decisions and missed opportunities simply because critical information got lost in the flood or arrived too late to be understood. It also means that knowledge power shifts to those who control AI. If only an AI can truly assimilate the state of the art, then human judgment must defer to AI outputs. This dynamic is closely tied to the technological singularity, also referred to as AI dominance, but it can occur even with sub-superintelligent AI simply due to the scale of data.

8.3.3 AI-Generated Content Deluge

Beyond formal research, AI is enabling an explosion of *content creation.* Generative AI models can produce articles, essays, code, images, music, and videos on a scale. The result is that information is proliferating faster than ever, and much of it is machine-generated. For instance, an AI-driven news bot could generate thousands of news summaries per day, far beyond any human journalist's output. While some of this content is useful or entertaining, a vast quantity is simply adding to the noise: duplicate or low-quality information, spam, auto-generated marketing copy, etc.

In an information singularity state, valuable knowledge becomes a needle in a towering haystack of AI-produced text and media. Already, internet platforms are contending with surges of AI-generated content. The challenge is that *more content does not equal more clarity.* In fact, past a point, *more content can mean less accessible information*, as important signals get drowned in the noise. According to Schmachtenberger (2022), this leads to a loss of any shared factual basis—experts and laypeople alike end up siloed in custom information feeds, each feed curated or generated by algorithms, which in turn leads to a breakdown of *knowability.* As a result, one can only get what algorithms predict you want or need. In practical terms, it means that unless counterbalanced by equally powerful filtering and quality control, AI's prolific content generation hastens the approach of a critical overload point. In turn, for society, information singularity could manifest as *continuous instability*—frequent shocks of misinformation, constant shifts in what is considered true or important, and an inability to form long-term plans because the factual ground is always moving.

Following these analyses, one could infer that the two singularities are related and their interplay suggests a conceptual feedback loop. That is, the inability of human cognition and institutions to keep pace with exponential data growth intensifies demand for AI-mediated processing, which in turn accelerates pathways toward technological singularity. Yet, this same trajectory positions AI as a potential resolution mechanism for the information singularity, albeit at the cost of deepened systemic reliance.

8.3.4 Race or Slowdown?

The AI2027 project encapsulates this tension vividly, offering two imagined futures—a *race* and a *slowdown*—that frame humanity's choices in approaching the information singularity (AI2027, 2025).

The race scenario envisions relentless competition, where states, corporations, and research entities drive forward without pause. Here, AI systems recursively improve themselves, quantum computing removes computational bottlenecks, and the explosion of data reaches incomprehensible magnitudes. This trajectory could lead to profound advancements—solving grand challenges in medicine, energy, and climate—but it also risks bypassing ethical safeguards, regulatory preparedness, and societal consensus. History has shown that untempered technological acceleration often magnifies inequality and destabilizes governance, and in the context of AI and quantum-driven information systems, such risks scale exponentially (AI2027, 2025; Braga & Logan, 2019).

Conversely, the slowdown scenario posits a deliberate deceleration, embedding governance mechanisms, ethical oversight, and institutional resilience within our technological trajectory. This path acknowledges that while innovation is vital, unchecked progress risks surpassing our ability to comprehend, control, and contextualize it. A managed slowdown allows time for standards, legal frameworks, and social adaptation to mature—preventing runaway systems while still benefiting from transformative gains. Rather than stalling progress, this model seeks to synchronize technological change with human capacity for responsible stewardship (AI2027, 2025; Plebe & Perconti, 2013).

Following the previous section, we are confronted with a dichotomy emblematic of our technological age—the potential for acceleration versus the imperative for restraint. On the one hand, AI, by *accelerating knowledge production, automating content creation, and outpacing human cognitive limits*, generates the problem by propelling us toward information singularity. On the other hand, it is also the primary tool we have to address it—a paradox we explore further below. But first, we consider the role of QIS in this picture, since quantum technology may amplify these trends even further or offer new mitigation avenues.

8.4 The Role of QIS

QIS, encompassing quantum computing, quantum communication, and quantum sensing, is recognized as the next scientific and technological frontier field with the potential to transform how information is processed and transmitted (OECD, 2024, 2025). The advent of QIS naturally raises the question of whether it could trigger or accelerate an information singularity or instead help humanity cope with ever-increasing data volumes through more powerful processing. As discussed in the following subsections, the answer is nuanced.

8.4.1 Quantum Computing

On the one hand, quantum computers could significantly speed up the production and analysis of information. Although these devices are not universal accelerators, there is already clear evidence that they outperform classical supercomputers on carefully chosen tasks (Arute et al., 2019; Zlokapa et al., 2023). For example, as discussed in Chapter 7, Shor's algorithm factors integers in polynomial time, vastly outperforming the best-known classical algorithms for large-number factoring, and Grover's algorithm provides a quadratic speed-up for unstructured search. Such breakthroughs could unlock new domains of scientific knowledge by enabling the simulation of complex chemical reactions, the discovery of novel materials, and the modeling of intricate biological interactions at unprecedented speed (Dalzell et al., 2023). This, in turn, would dramatically accelerate how knowledge enters the global pool. Hence, in this respect, QIS could tighten the innovation feedback loop and amplify the pace of discovery, potentially contributing to the accelerating trajectory of the information singularity.

Some futurists have even speculated that achieving quantum supremacy—solving problems infeasible for classical computers—is a milestone on the way to a kind of quantum singularity, wherein our computational capability takes a leap forward. For example, Romero (2025) draws a parallel between the sudden, world-changing impact of ChatGPT in late 2022 and an anticipated quantum singularity. He argues that just as generative AI leapfrogged expectations, emerging quantum processors could similarly surprise the broader community and usher in practical quantum advantage. That, in turn, could propel AI development into a new phase, hastening both the technological and information singularities timeline.

On the other hand, scholars emphasize that quantum computation, though transformative, remains bounded by physical and informational constraints, such as formidable challenges of decoherence and fault-tolerant scaling. Hence, most real-world problems still cannot simply inherit these theoretical gains (Hoefler et al., 2023; Peral-García et al., 2024). These scholars scrutinize the widespread belief that quantum computing will catalyze artificial superintelligence (ASI) by delivering hypercomputational capabilities with computations beyond the power of any classical Turing machine, which in turn can trigger a rapid *intelligence explosion*. For example, Grabowska and Gunia (2024) note that while some assume quantum mechanics inherently allows hypercomputation, enabling an unbounded leap in AI capability, in fact, although quantum supremacy demonstrates superiority over classical machines on specific tasks, it does not equate to the ability to compute functions that are fundamentally incomputable by classical means. That means that quantum computing cannot solve non-Turing-computable problems. Hence, since a quantum system is confined to a finite-dimensional Hilbert space, it cannot store or process infinite information, and regardless of achieving polynomial or exponential speed-ups on certain tasks, it will remain within the class of Turing-computable functions (Grover, 1997; Shor, 1997). While most of AI progress hinges on conceptual and algorithmic breakthroughs, including model architecture, learning paradigms, and algorithmic innovation, quantum hardware alone cannot realize the technological singularity or directly spawn ASI. The central challenge of superintelligence lies in areas where quantum hardware offers an aid rather than a panacea.

At the same time, since quantum speed-ups can accelerate AI training or optimization subroutines, Grabowska and Gunia (2024) acknowledge two plausible avenues where quantum computing could indirectly aid ASI. These are a) *quantum-accelerated optimization*, where advanced neural-architecture search could achieve incremental performance gains by faster solving of combinatorial subproblems, and b) *quantum-enhanced simulations*, where superior simulations of physical, chemical, or biological systems could open new scientific insights (Kim et al., 2023; Lee et al., 2023; Weidman et al., 2024), indirectly fueling AI by expanding the knowledge base. Yet, these remain far from guaranteeing a recursive self-improvement loop or a true intelligence explosion.

8.4.2 Quantum Communications

Quantum communication, as part of a QIS ecosystem, underpins how quantum devices, networks, and distributed processors interact. Thus, quantum communication extends the discussion about the role of QIS in information singularity by taking it from *processing* to *moving and sharing* quantum information. Modern quantum key distribution (QKD) has crossed the ~1000 km mark in optical fiber via twin-field protocols (Liu et al., 2023), and comprehensive reviews map the path to long-haul quantum networks using quantum repeaters (Azuma et al., 2023). These long-distance quantum networks enable the reliable transmission of quantum information over continental or even global scales. Recent proposals go further, unifying sensing and communication so that entanglement distribution both secures a link and enhances remote parameter estimation under quantum integrated sensing and communication (Liu et al., 2024). These developments suggest that future quantum networks could help distribute specialized workloads, such as secure multi-party simulation or federated learning with quantum resources, increasing both bandwidth efficiency and security. In the long term, the emergence of a quantum internet could transform the topology of global information systems, allowing secure, high-fidelity data exchange and potentially reshaping how distributed AI and scientific infrastructures operate (OECD, 2025).

8.4.3 Quantum Sensing

Beyond computation and communication, quantum sensing represents another pillar of QIS poised to transform how humanity observes the physical world. As discussed in Chapter 7, quantum sensors already enable breakthroughs in precision navigation, mineral exploration, biomedical imaging, and fundamental physics experiments. As networks of quantum sensors expand, they will produce high-resolution, high-frequency data streams about phenomena that were previously beyond detection. The result will be an explosion of new empirical data across fields such as astronomy, geophysics, materials science, climate observation, and more. Hence, often under-appreciated, quantum sensors constitute another source and driver of information growth. As discussed above, since quantum sensors can share infrastructure with quantum communication systems, while quantum encryption doesn't increase volume by itself, trust in security could encourage even more data to be sent. Hence, far from merely helping to cope with big data, quantum sensing may actually amplify the information flood by opening new observational frontiers and *feeding the information explosion* by encouraging even more pervasive digitization.

Taken together, the combined advances in quantum computing, communication, and sensing reveal an ambiguous yet profound duality. On one hand, QIS promises extraordinary computational and analytical power that might help to cope with exploding information by faster analyzing and filtering it. On the other hand, it enables the generation of even more information through accelerated discovery and new data sources. In this sense, the net effect of QIS is likely to become an *amplifier* of the trajectory we are already on. If AI and data creation are growing exponentially, QIS could push parts of that curve even steeper. While alone, it does not guarantee technological singularity or infinite intelligence, it plausibly steepens the trajectory of knowledge growth and compresses the timescales. Hence, even without infinity, a quantum-fueled surge in scientific output could suffice to *bring the inflection point of an information singularity closer.*

8.4.4 Quantum AI

Quantum technologies accelerate computations and extend the bandwidth, precision, and fidelity of information flow, but they remain inert conduits until paired with agents that can extract semantic value from the immense quantum-enabled data streams. Hence, the true transformative potential of QIS becomes evident only when its physical infrastructure converges with systems capable of autonomous cognition and interpretation. This integration creates a new inflection point. Once quantum infrastructures feed directly into learning and reasoning architectures, the bottleneck of human comprehension gives way to machine-mediated analysis operating at the same quantum-level scale. Consequently, the rate of knowledge expansion becomes constrained not by physical throughput alone, but by the adaptive capacity of algorithms to interpret, generalize, and act upon information. In this light, the emergence of Quantum Artificial Intelligence (QAI) represents a cognitive extension of the quantum revolution by transforming QIS from a powerful analytical substrate into an active, co-evolving agent within the knowledge-creation process.

According to Klusch et al. (2024), QAI embodies a bidirectional synthesis between quantum computing and artificial intelligence. On one side, quantum processors promise to accelerate AI through speed-ups in optimization, search, and simulation. On the other, AI techniques enhance quantum systems themselves by optimizing circuit calibration, error mitigation, and adaptive control. This mutual reinforcement forms a recursive positive feedback loop in which advances in one domain amplify progress in the other, creating a dynamic often regarded as the *catalyst of accelerating technological change.*

This dynamic, wherein technological capability improvements increase the rate of further improvements, and the concept of an *ultraintelligent machine* that could design better machines, has been known since the middle of the 1960s, as discussed previously in this chapter. We also discussed Vinge's (1993) vision, suggesting that once such feedback outpaces human cognitive capacity, it could precipitate *technological singularity*. Kurzweil (2004) formalized these concepts as the *Law of Accelerating Returns,* arguing that each generation of technology enhances the tools used to create its successor, producing super-exponential growth. From an economic perspective, this corresponds to the theory of *general-purpose technologies (GPTs),* which drive long-run growth by spreading innovation complementarities across sectors (Bresnahan & Trajtenberg, 1995). However, not all scholars predict indefinite acceleration. Research on innovation productivity indicates that idea generation may face increasing difficulty over time, leading to diminishing marginal returns and requiring major paradigm shifts to sustain progress (Bloom et al., 2020).

As discussed in Chapter 7, the QIS progress remains bounded by tangible constraints such as noisy intermediate-scale quantum (NISQ) hardware with a limited number of qubits, short coherence times, and more. As a result, the current landscape of QAI is dominated by hybrid architectures, combining classical pre- and post-processing with quantum subroutines. These systems deliver measurable advantages for specific tasks such as combinatorial optimization or pattern recognition, yet they fall short of enabling an unrestricted computational leap.

Taken together, we contextualize the QIS ↔ AI feedback loop as a contemporary instantiation of the same autocatalytic mechanism underlying past technological transformations. Whether this loop results in a managed evolution of complexity or a phase transition toward an information singularity depends on how effectively reinforcing dynamics, such as learning acceleration and hardware improvement, outpace countervailing forces like resource constraints and the escalating cost of discovery.

This grounded perspective tempers singularity narratives that envision a sudden *quantum take-off.* In light of the above, we believe that QAI could be seen as a distributed accelerator producing localized surges of capability across specialized domains rather than a global explosion of intelligence. Thus, the convergence of QIS and QAI reframes the path toward information singularity as neither an abrupt discontinuity nor a deterministic inevitability. Instead, it appears as a progressive steepening of the information-growth curve driven by the coupling of quantum-enabled infrastructures with intelligent systems capable of autonomous meaning-making. The interplay between physical acceleration through QIS and semantic acceleration through AI suggests that the singularity, if it occurs, will emerge not from a single technological threshold but from the sustained entanglement of computation, cognition, and communication across quantum and classical domains. It's conceivable that by the 2030s, specialized quantum accelerators could be part of AI data centers, helping train massive models or solve optimization problems orders of magnitude faster. There are startups and research groups already exploring quantum machine learning, though it's in early stages. In the next sections, we discuss how we might get prepared to *manage or respond to* an information singularity, especially by harnessing advanced information systems built on AI and QIS, rather than being overwhelmed by them.

8.5 Are We Ready?

Every major leap in how we handle information has reshaped society from the ground up. The printing press sparked literacy movements and the creation of new schools. The rise of telegraphs, telephones, and other industrial-era communications demanded fresh skills and entire bureaucracies to manage them. But these shifts happened over decades or even centuries, giving people time to adjust. The singularity scenario is different. It compresses those adaptations into years, sometimes months. As Chapter 6 discussed, AI-driven information systems collapse what used to be a step-by-step process, collecting, storing, processing, and sharing, into an almost instant feedback loop. That means we are not just trying to understand what machines tell us; we also have to judge whether their output can be trusted in a world full of misinformation, synthetic media, and opaque algorithms.

In this environment, digital literacy is not enough if it is only about knowing how to use tools. We also need epistemic literacy, the skill to question AI's conclusions, recognize when it makes mistakes, and place its outputs in the wider social and political context. The challenge is not just technical. It is about how we think and what we choose to believe. History offers another sobering parallel. Industrial automation replaced physical labor but eventually created new industries and jobs. This time, AI-enhanced systems are going after cognitive work itself, jobs that once seemed safe from automation. Without serious investment in reskilling and rethinking education, we risk splitting into two worlds: one inhabited by a tech-fluent elite, and another made up of those left out of the algorithmic economy.

The AI2027 *race versus slowdown* framework offers a way to think about this. In the past, our responses to disruptive technologies swung between letting them run wild, like the early, unregulated days of the internet, and cracking down too late, as happened after the Cambridge Analytica scandal. Neither extreme worked well. For the systems we are building now, we'll need something different—managed transitions. That could mean safe "sandbox" environments for testing high-impact technologies, combined with international coordination to manage shared risks, much like the IAEA helped guide nuclear development while trying to prevent catastrophe. But AI and quantum systems evolve in recursive, self-improving ways, so the governance around them must be equally adaptive, with constant monitoring built into the regulatory framework itself.

History tells us we can navigate moments of upheaval. We've done it before, changing laws, ethics, and institutions along the way. But next-generation systems bring more speed, autonomy, and complexity than ever before, compressing our window for adaptation. Coping is possible, but only if we act in advance, blending lessons from the past with forward-looking governance, building ethics into the core of these systems, and preparing society as quickly as technology advances. If we do not, we risk waking up to find the decisions have already been made without us. The question is not just whether we can cope but whether we can move fast enough to stay co-authors of our future rather than becoming mere passengers in it (AI2027, 2025).

8.5.1 Can Next-Generation Information Systems Cope?

The convergence of AI, quantum technologies, and advanced IS intensifies an enduring question: can humanity and its institutions adapt quickly enough to manage next-generation information systems and the march toward an information singularity? This challenge is not merely technological but civilizational, requiring an understanding of historical precedents and their limitations when projected into an era defined by autonomous, self-optimizing systems. As seen throughout this book, from the historical progression of information practices (Chapter 2) to the rise of cyberspace and digital sovereignty (Chapters 2–3), and through the challenges of contemporary IS (Chapters 4–6), every technological leap has demanded societal restructuring, yet none has approached the scale or speed of the transformation now underway.

However, the current trajectory differs fundamentally. Previous revolutions in information systems, whether writing, printing, or networked computing, were largely linear, offering time for adaptation. By contrast, AI-integrated IS and quantum-enabled infrastructures evolve non-linearly, with recursive improvements that compress the interval between disruption and adaptation. Governance that lags even modestly risks irrelevance, as decisions once reserved for human oversight are delegated to opaque, autonomous systems operating at speeds beyond human comprehension. Unlike past eras where regulation caught up, here the pace of transformation risks exceeding the temporal capacity of law and policy.

Ethics in prior technological transitions often followed rather than preceded innovation. As Chapter 2 illustrated, ancient scribal cultures and early bureaucratic systems employed information control to consolidate political power long before codified ethical constraints emerged. Similarly, during the Industrial Revolution, labor exploitation and social upheaval were only gradually mitigated by legal reforms. Information systems in the digital age followed a comparable pattern: widespread data commodification and surveillance capitalism developed far in advance of privacy laws like the GDPR or the Digital Services Act.

In the singularity context, however, this reactive model is untenable. When AI-driven IS autonomously generates knowledge, disseminates decisions, and even participates in self-improvement cycles, ethical lag becomes existentially risky. The "ethics-by-design" paradigm discussed in previous chapters must thus be institutionalized as a proactive requirement, not merely as aspirational soft law. The precedent is analogous to bioethics in molecular biology: after the Asilomar Conference of 1975, scientists imposed moratoria and safeguards on recombinant DNA research to pre-empt catastrophic misuse (Hurlbut, 2025). A similar anticipatory model must govern AI and quantum IS, embedding ethical checks at both the technical and institutional levels.

Furthermore, one cannot discuss ethics without discussing security risks as well as environmental threats, as covered in Chapters 6 and 7. The security risks associated with next-generation information systems stem from both novel threats and the magnification of existing vulnerabilities. Quantum computing poses a major danger by rendering current cryptographic standards obsolete, potentially compromising financial, governmental, and industrial infrastructures. At the same time, AI-driven offensive capabilities, including autonomous malware, adaptive cyberattacks, and sophisticated disinformation campaigns, threaten to overwhelm human-led defense mechanisms. These risks extend to cyber-physical systems, such as smart grids and autonomous vehicles, where breaches could result in real-world harm. The global nature of information networks amplifies these challenges, as fragmented cybersecurity frameworks and uneven adoption of post-quantum measures create exploitable weak links. To mitigate these escalating risks, anticipatory governance must prioritize quantum-safe encryption, AI-enabled defensive tools, and internationally harmonized cybersecurity standards capable of keeping pace with rapidly evolving threats.

The environmental risks of next-generation information systems are driven primarily by the massive energy and resource demands of AI and quantum computing. Training advanced AI models and operating hyperscale data centers consume vast amounts of electricity and water, contributing significantly to carbon emissions and placing strain on local ecosystems. Additionally, the production and disposal of specialized hardware, reliant on rare earth minerals and complex supply chains, exacerbate ecological degradation and electronic waste challenges, particularly in regions lacking effective recycling infrastructure. As AI and QIS workloads scale, their energy intensity risks creating a self-reinforcing cycle of computational demand and environmental impact, necessitating the integration of sustainable practices such as renewable-powered data centers, carbon accounting for large-scale computational projects, and circular economy models for hardware design and reuse.

8.5.2 Information Singularity Readiness Maturity Model

Addressing information singularity is a challenge that deserves careful attention. One way to manage it is to treat this challenge as a readiness problem driven by AI- and QIS-specific considerations, such as AI trustworthiness at scale and the impact of QIS on the security and architecture stack. To do so, we propose an Information Singularity Readiness Maturity Model (ISRMM) that outlines an *organization's readiness* for AI and the quantum era. The model enables assessment of whether an organization can safely scale AI-enabled autonomy, including high-velocity decision cycles, agentic workflows, and model-driven operations, as well as execute disruptive security transitions such as post-quantum cryptography (PQC).

The ISRMM design is inspired by the Cybersecurity Capacity Maturity Model (CCMM) from Oxford University's Global Cyber Security Capacity Centre, which operationalizes complex socio-technical capabilities through staged maturity, from the start-up to the dynamic stage, and emphasizes benchmarking via observable indicators and improvement planning, rather than aspirational commitments (GCSCC, 2021). While CCMM focuses on building the ability of organizations to respond and grow capacity in the face of a changing cybersecurity landscape, we adapt it to the challenge of changing IS environments, whether they are social or technical, which has never been more important than in the age of quantum computing and AI.

The Capability Maturity Model's (CMM) approach is not new, and it can be traced, among others, to the frameworks and standards that contain, among others, the process capability assessment framework (ISO, 2019) and enterprise process improvement (CMMI, n.d.). In 2025, these also include the AI system impact assessment (ISO, 2025), the Artificial Intelligence Risk Management Framework (NIST, 2023), the NIST's transition plan for post-quantum standards (Moody et al., 2024), and more. Similar to CCMM

(GCSCC, 2021) and additional models like ISO/IEC 21827 (ISO, 2008) and ISO/IEC 33020 (ISO, 2019), the ISRMM has six stages (0-5), which range from opacity to adaptive assurance. We defined the stages of the ISRMM so that they present both expectations and verifiable artifacts to allow both the identification of the current posture and what is required for sequential evolution.

At Level 0 (Unprepared/Opaque), AI tools and automation proliferate without reliable visibility into models, data flows, or cryptographic dependencies. Level 1 (Ad hoc/Reactive) introduces scattered controls, but primarily as after-the-fact responses to incidents or events following the AI and quantum technologies deployment. Level 2 (Managed/Repeatable) establishes baseline discipline, systematic inventories (including models, vendors, and cryptography), and repeatable lifecycle checkpoints so that AI and business decisions are no longer improvised. We believe that in the mid-2020s, many companies can be placed in these two and aspire to develop to the next level. Level 3 (Defined/Governance-by-design) marks the key architectural shift—obligations such as auditability, traceability, and bounded autonomy are engineered into systems as design properties, and crypto-agility is treated as an architectural requirement rather than a project. Level 4 (Measured/Continuously verified) operationalizes assurance through continuous monitoring (drift, abuse, and integrity), routine auditing, and rehearsed transitions, including PQC migration drills. Finally, Level 5 (Adaptive/Anticipatory) assumes persistent uncertainty, and organizations use scenario planning and trigger-based decision points to update controls as models, regulations, and cryptographic assumptions change, enabling them to capture AI- and QIS-enabled acceleration while actively minimizing technical and regulatory debt. It is important to emphasize that the ISRMM model is conceptual—it provides a structured framing and planning utility to guide assessment and transition design, rather than a validated measurement instrument or universal scoring standard. Table 8.1 presents the ISRMM.

This maturity ladder, presented in Table 8.1, might be used as a conceptual diagnostic and sequencing tool. Organizations can locate their current posture by identifying the highest level for which the “minimum expectations” and artifacts are consistently present across critical systems, then treat the next level as a bounded set of implementation targets. Progression should not be interpreted as just capability scoring but as more governable autonomy, the ability to accelerate decision-making while preserving evidence, control, and accountability, including under disruptive transitions such as PQC migration.

Table 8.1 The Information Singularity Readiness Maturity Model (ISRMM)

Level	Maturity label	Core posture	What "good" looks like at this level (minimum expectations)	Typical evidence/ artifacts
0	Unprepared (Opaque)	Acceleration without control	AI/automation is informal; limited visibility into models, data flows, and decision logic; cryptographic dependencies are largely unknown; governance is not embedded in design.	No reliable inventories (assets/ models/vendors/ cryptography); weak logs; ad hoc vendor tools; fragmented policies with no enforcement.
1	Ad hoc (Reactive)	Controls following AI-deployment	Basic rules exist but are inconsistent; responses are event-driven; obligations are discussed but not engineered into systems; PQC/ quantum risk is not yet programmatically addressed.	Post-incident patches; partial documentation; scattered approvals; inconsistent controls; sporadic risk memos.
2	Managed (Repeatable)	Standardized basics	Central registers exist (assets/data/models/ vendors/crypto); repeatable lifecycle checkpoints for higher-risk AI use; baseline security and evaluation practices; initial PQC awareness and crypto dependency mapping.	Inventories and registers; baseline evaluations (security/privacy/ bias); documented change control; minimum logging standard; cryptography inventory.
3	Defined (Governance-by-design)	Governance as architecture	Duties become system properties: auditability, traceability, controllability, and resilience are designed in; structured human oversight; crypto-agility is an architectural requirement; PQC migration is planned for critical systems.	Reference architectures; control mappings; audit-ready evidence trails; responsibility assignment / role mapping; approval & exception workflows; crypto-agility design patterns; PQC transition plan.

(*continued*)

Table 8.1 (continued)

Level	Maturity label	Core posture	What "good" looks like at this level (minimum expectations)	Typical evidence/ artifacts
4	Measured (Continuously verified)	Continuous assurance	Continuous monitoring for drift, integrity, abuse, and policy compliance; routine internal/external audit cadence; regular red-team/abuse testing; PQC pilots and migration rehearsals in realistic environments.	Monitoring dashboards; alert/ runbook suite; periodic red-team and abuse tests; audit packages; "crypto change" runbooks; PQC pilot reports + performance/ interoperability metrics.
5	Adaptive (Anticipatory)	Designed for uncertainty	Scenario-based planning with decision checkpoints; controls adapt to regulatory/ technical change (including quantum-era cryptography); autonomy is expanded only with evidence and bounded risk; technical/regulatory debt is actively managed.	Scenario playbooks; trigger-based governance updates; continuous capability investment; cross-border compliance engineering; board-level KPIs and risk reporting; continuous PQC validation for critical paths.

8.6 The Way Ahead: Future Trends and Applications

As discussed in previous sections, QAI fuses complementary strengths of AI and quantum technologies, creating a recursive positive feedback loop in which advances in one domain amplify progress in the other. This synergy matters for IS because the most difficult problems in real organizations are often combinatorial, random, or high-dimensional, like routing, scheduling, portfolio/risk optimization, anomaly detection in enormous streams, and learning under data sparsity, where pure quantum strength is not enough. While Quantum Neural Networks (QNN) and quantum-enhanced learning can compress state spaces and explore solution landscapes more efficiently, near- and mid-term QAI will probably be hybrid, with classical pipelines orchestrating quantum subroutines for the parts of a workload that map well to quantum advantage, while the rest remains classical (Klusch et al., 2024).

QAI can become invisible to end-users if it is done and implemented correctly, just as web and cloud-based technologies now stream information for users and are barely felt. The usability risk is explainability, of course, as quantum subroutines can be opaque. IS must therefore wrap QAI with classical guardrails, model cards, sensitivity analyses, and policy constraints so outputs remain auditable and contestable.

The near-term win is solution quality per unit or time on optimization and sampling tasks. That is, we write this as we consider seamless integration and optimization. Regardless of risks, security concerns, biases, and other related problems, we can assume that we will see targeted pilot programs and experiments in the near term where quantum-inspired and hybrid methods yield incremental gains in scheduling, routing, and risk analytics. Although the long-term gains remain uncertain, once QAI is scalable, fault-tolerant systems should emerge, and QAI could reshape how IS handles real-time adaptive planning, merging sensing, prediction, and optimization into a continuously learning, constraint-aware core. Thus, the bottom line is—QAI is not a replacement for IS—it is an enhancement.

8.7 Conclusions

This book began with a simple observation and an audacious claim. The observation is that information systems have ceased to be backstage infrastructure; they are now the stage on which economies, polities, and cultures are performed. We are accelerating toward an information singularity, a phase change driven by the mutual reinforcement of AI and QIS, in which the cost of deriving, moving, and acting on knowledge trends toward zero while the consequences of doing so trend toward infinity. Managing that future is not a matter of adding one more module to an ERP or fine-tuning a model; it is a civic, organizational, and scientific stewardship challenge.

Across the chapters, we traced how IS emerged, professionalized, fragmented, and recombined and how TPS, MIS, DSS, ESS/EIS, ERP, CRM, SCM, and BI converged into an increasingly integrated, data-centric fabric, globally connected. We showed how AI, now agentic AI, tool-using, and workflow-orchestrating, has transformed that fabric from a set of reports into a living process that perceives, decides, and acts. We examined how governance frameworks from GDPR and the EU AI Act to NIST's AI RMF are catching up and how cyber sovereignty, cross-border data flows, and platform power complicate any simple compliance playbook. We mapped the risk surface, bots that now comprise the majority of traffic, memetic disinformation at machine scale, opaque recommender systems, and brittle dependencies in global digital supply chains and argued that resilience, assurance, and accountability must be engineered into the stack, not bolted on.

Looking ahead, QAI is poised to amplify both the promise and the peril. By marrying AI's pattern-learning with quantum's parallelism, QAI makes tractable problems that were formerly intractable, like combinatorial optimization across supply chains, sub-second risk re-pricing under market stress, privacy-preserving analytics via quantum-secure protocols, and training of richer, more expressive models with enhanced data due to enhanced sensing that can explore solution spaces classical systems cannot. In practical terms, this matters for core IS classes as TPS and MIS gain near-real-time anomaly detection and reconciliation at scale, reducing fraud and leakage while compressing close cycles. DSS or ESS/EIS, as well as BI, shifts from retrospective dashboards to prescriptive, counterfactual simulation, evaluating *what if* across millions of policies, prices, or routes simultaneously. ERP, CRM, and SCMs will likely move from plan-then-execute to the sense-predict-replan loops that rebalance inventory, logistics, and production under volatile constraints.

But QAI also pressures the control plane we rely on, as post-quantum cryptography must be adopted before *harvest now, decrypt later* attacks mature; data governance must anticipate models that can infer more from less; and auditability must extend to probabilistic, non-deterministic pipelines. What, then, should responsible stewards of information systems do now? First, we assume, based on the body of knowledge provided in this book, that we must ensure autonomy is safe for AI and further on for QAI. We should treat models and agents as safety-critical subsystems when they decide, act, or transact. Require provenance like data lineage and policy lineage; separation of duties of model, policy, and actuator; dual-control on irreversible actions; and continuous verification, e.g., detect-and-disable on drift or anomaly—we must assure systems can fail safely and securely.

Second, we should ensure governance—something most countries failed to do with cyberspace/the internet. We should translate policy frameworks into machine-readable controls enforced at run time with data contracts, PII tagging, purpose binding, retention automation, and attestations embedded in pipelines. In essence, *paper compliance* must be replaced with evidence-producing systems because, in cross-border disputes and audits, evidence wins. This, of course, is one of the more difficult problems to address, as every major country, international organization, and even technology giant, sees priorities differently.

Third, architecture for post-quantum and privacy must be a default with protection of data and the development of PCQ standards and protocols but also with risk management and even access control, not just for human users but also for agentic users. As discussed in Chapter 5, there might be a legal basis for granting AI agents some rights, just like a private company, and with rights, they must have great responsibility. Future IS, enhanced with QIS and AI, must also be resilient enough to handle chaotic production or research lifecycles. This real-world use is what will likely stall the technological adaptation the most.

Thus, our fourth point is literacy. The field's future belongs to hybrid professionals who are fluent across data, models, processes, and law. That is, what good is technology if no one knows how to use it? In this regard, one applicable aspect that should be explored further is the changing role of IS professionals under AI and QIS acceleration. Traditional IS professionals focused on systems analysis and design, database management, some programming, and business fundamentals. In addition, they often served as translators between technological capability, organizational strategy, legal compliance, and ethical oversight. In AI- and QIS-driven environments, IS professionals must supervise data quality, model integration and explainability, and bias monitoring and assess cryptographic resilience, infrastructure readiness, and new forms of computational risk. Thus, their future role can be perceived as a socio-technical architect and governance actor responsible for aligning disruptive systems with organizational goals and ethical and regulatory demands, as well as societal values (World Economic Forum, 2025).

As IS and AI, as well as QIS, develop further, we also suggest the need for a theory that will attempt to explain and predict the socio-technical behavior of IS users. We explored this socio-technical behavior in Chapters 2 and 3, and similarities, of course, arise. However, we emphasize the need to adapt such approaches to the new forthcoming IS, enhanced with QIS, AI, and eventually with QAI. This socio-technical behavior remains a key topic for future exploration.

In the paragraphs above, we mentioned many *should* and *must be*, but these are not just luxury thoughts because the alternative is a future in which organizations optimize locally while destabilizing globally, like, for instance, with social media platforms nowadays, and in which cryptography lags behind attackers. This is also a future in which *efficient* systems silently encode bias and amplify harm and in which legal fragmentation makes cross-border operations fragile and expensive or even illegal. Stewardship, as our final approach, asks more of us, but it also confers strategic advantage. Firms that can prove their systems are safe, fair, private, and reliable will win trust, talent, and, eventually, market access. States that align innovation policy with interoperable safeguards will attract investment without forfeiting rights.

The final lesson of this book is that *managing information singularity is less about predicting the end state and more about shaping the trajectory*. The history of IS reminds us that our field thrives when it builds shared language, portable methods, and testable evidence. The present teaches that agentic AI can turn intent into action across the enterprise if we bind it wisely. The near future hints that QAI will unlock new classes of solutions only if we harden the cryptographic and governance foundations first. If we do these things patiently, rigorously, and together, the information singularity will be less a point of crisis and more a horizon we can navigate. The systems we design will not only be more intelligent; they will be more humane. And that, finally, is the measure that matters.

References

AI2027. (2025). *AI2027*. https://ai-2027.com

Ali, M. (2023). *Information systems research: Foundations, design and theory*. Palgrave Macmillan. https://doi.org/10.1007/978-3-031-25470-3

Arute, F., Arya, K., Babbush, R., Bacon, D., Bardin, J. C., Barends, R., ... Neven, H. (2019). Quantum supremacy using a programmable superconducting processor. *Nature, 574*(7779), 505–510. https://doi.org/10.1038/s41586-019-1666-5

Azuma, K., Economou, S. E., Elkouss, D., Hilaire, P., Jiang, L., Lo, H.-K., & Tzitrin, I. (2023). Quantum repeaters: From quantum networks to the quantum internet. *Reviews of Modern Physics, 95*(4), 045006. https://doi.org/10.1103/RevModPhys.95.045006

Bloom, N., Jones, C. I., Van Reenen, J., & Webb, M. (2020). Are ideas getting harder to find? *American Economic Review, 110*(4), 1104–1144. https://doi.org/10.1257/aer.20180338

Braga, A., & Logan, R. K. (2019). AI and the singularity: A fallacy or a great opportunity? *Information, 10*(2), Article 73. https://doi.org/10.3390/info10020073

Bresnahan, T. F., & Trajtenberg, M. (1995). General purpose technologies: Engines of growth? *Journal of Econometrics, 65*(1), 83–108. https://doi.org/10.1016/0304-4076(94)01598-T

CMMI Institute. (n.d.). *CMMI*. https://cmmiinstitute.com/cmmi

Dalzell, A. M., McArdle, S., Berta, M., Bienias, P., Chen, C.-F., Gilyén, A., Hann, C. T., Kastoryano, M. J., Khabiboulline, E. T., Kubica, A., Salton, G., Wang, S.,

& Brandão, F. G. S. L. (2023). *Quantum algorithms: A survey of applications and end-to-end complexities*. arXiv. https://arxiv.org/abs/2310.03011

DE-CIX. (2020, March 11). *DE-CIX sets a new world record: More than 9 terabits per second data throughput at Frankfurt Internet Exchange* [Press release]. https://www.de-cix.net/en/about-de-cix/media/press-releases/de-cix-sets-a-new-world-record

Gafni, R., Kantsepolsky, B., & Sherman, S. (2026). Biases and ethical considerations in AI-driven knowledge management. In M. Russ & M. Lytras (Eds.), *AI-driven knowledge management: Strategies for the modern business landscape* (pp. 1–18). Emerald Publishing. https://doi.org/10.1108/978-1-80592-391-620261013

GCSCC. (2021). *Cybersecurity capacity maturity model for nations (CMM)*. https://gcscc.ox.ac.uk/files/cmm2021editiondocpdf

Good, I. J. (1966). Speculations concerning the first ultraintelligent machine. In F. L. Alt & M. Rubinoff (Eds.), *Advances in computers* (Vol. 6, pp. 31–88). Academic Press. https://doi.org/10.1016/S0065-2458(08)60418-0

Grabowska, A., & Gunia, A. (2024). On quantum computing for artificial superintelligence. *European Journal for Philosophy of Science, 14*, Article 25. https://doi.org/10.1007/s13194-024-00584-7

Grover, L. K. (1997). Quantum mechanics helps in searching for a needle in a haystack. *Physical Review Letters, 79*(2), 325–328. https://doi.org/10.1103/PhysRevLett.79.325

Heylighen, F. (2007). *Accelerating socio-technological evolution: From ephemeralization and stigmergy to the global brain*. arXiv. https://arxiv.org/pdf/cs/0703004.pdf

Hoefler, T., Häner, T., & Troyer, M. (2023). *Disentangling hype from practicality: On realistically achieving quantum advantage*. arXiv. https://arxiv.org/abs/2307.00523

Hurlbut, J. B. (2025). Taking responsibility: Asilomar and its legacy. *Science, 387*(6733), 468–472. https://doi.org/10.1126/science.adv3132

IBM Corporation. (2010). *IBM big data success stories* [PDF]. https://public.dhe.ibm.com/software/data/sw-library/big-data/ibm-big-data-success.pdf

International Organization for Standardization, & International Electrotechnical Commission. (2019). *Information technology—Process assessment—Process measurement framework for assessment of process capability (ISO/IEC 33020:2019, 2nd ed.)*. International Organization for Standardization. https://www.iso.org/standard/78526.html

International Organization for Standardization. (2008). *ISO/IEC 21827:2008*. https://www.iso.org/standard/44716.html

International Organization for Standardization. (2025). *Information technology—Artificial intelligence (AI)—AI system impact assessment (ISO/IEC 42005:2025, 1st ed.)*. International Organization for Standardization. https://www.iso.org/standard/42005

Katkov, Y., Romanova, A., & Katkova, E. (2025). Economic security of agro-industrial organizations in the era of technological singularity: A hybrid model approach. *International Journal of Safety and Security Engineering, 15*(5), 997–1005. https://doi.org/10.18280/ijsse.150513

Kim, Y., Miško, J., Huggins, W., et al. (2023). Evidence for the utility of quantum computing before fault tolerance. *Nature, 618*(7965), 500–505. https://doi.org/10.1038/s41586-023-06096-3

Klusch, M., Lässig, J., Müssig, D., Macaluso, A., & Wilhelm, F. K. (2024). Quantum artificial intelligence: A brief survey. *KI—Künstliche Intelligenz, 38*(4), 257–276. https://doi.org/10.1007/s13218-024-00871-8

Kostikov, Y. (2022, July 21). How to prepare our minds for the information singularity? *TechTalks*. https://bdtechtalks.com/2022/07/21/brain-limits-individual-artificial-intelligence/

Kurzweil, R. (2004). The law of accelerating returns. In C. Teuscher (Ed.), *Alan Turing: Life and legacy of a great thinker* (pp. 381–416). Springer. https://doi.org/10.1007/978-3-662-05642-4_16

Kurzweil, R. (2005). *The singularity is near: When humans transcend biology*. Viking.

Lee, S., Lee, J., Zhai, H., Tong, Y., Dalzell, A. M., Kumar, A., ... Chan, G. K.-L. (2023). Evaluating the evidence for exponential quantum advantage in ground-state quantum chemistry. *Nature Communications, 14*, Article 1952. https://doi.org/10.1038/s41467-023-37587-6

Liu, Y., Zhang, W.-J., Jiang, C., Chen, J.-P., Zhang, C., Pan, W.-X., ... Pan, J.-W. (2023). Experimental twin-field quantum key distribution over 1000 km fiber distance. *Physical Review Letters, 130*, 210801. https://doi.org/10.1103/PhysRevLett.130.210801

Liu, Y.-C., Cheng, Y.-B., Pan, X.-B., Sun, Z.-Z., Pan, D., & Long, G.-L. (2024). Quantum integrated sensing and communication via entanglement. *Physical Review Applied, 22*(3), 034051. https://doi.org/10.1103/PhysRevApplied.22.034051

Moody, D., Perlner, R., Regenscheid, A., Robinson, A., & Cooper, D. (2024). *Transition to post-quantum cryptography standards* (NIST Internal Report 8547, Initial Public Draft). National Institute of Standards and Technology. https://doi.org/10.6028/NIST.IR.8547.ipd

Müller, V. C., & Bostrom, N. (2016). Future progress in artificial intelligence: A survey of expert opinion. In S. C. Lloyd (Ed.), *Fundamental issues of artificial intelligence* (pp. 555–572). Springer. https://doi.org/10.1007/978-3-319-26485-1_33

National Institute of Standards and Technology. (2023, January). *Artificial intelligence risk management framework (AI RMF 1.0)* (NIST AI 100-1). https://doi.org/10.6028/NIST.AI.100-1

Organisation for Economic Co-operation and Development. (2024, April 3). *Quantum technologies: Briefing document*. OECD Global Forum on Technology. https://www.oecd.org/content/dam/oecd/en/networks/global-forum-on-technology/global-forum-on-technology-quantum-technologies-brief-2024.pdf

Organisation for Economic Co-operation and Development. (2025, February 4). *Quantum technologies as a new paradigm for digital economies and societies*. https://www.oecd.org/content/dam/oecd/en/publications/reports/2025/02/quantum-technologies-as-a-new-paradigm-for-digital-economies-and-societies_0f18bb86/e6664d58-en.pdf

Pearlson, K. E., Saunders, C. S., & Galletta, D. F. (2024). *Managing and using information systems*: A strategic approach (8th ed.). Wiley.

Peral-García, D., Cruz-Benito, J., & García-Peñalvo, F. J. (2024). Systematic literature review: Quantum machine learning and its applications. *Computer Science Review, 51*, 100619. https://doi.org/10.1016/j.cosrev.2024.100619

Plebe, A., & Perconti, P. (2013). The slowdown hypothesis. In A. H. Eden, J. H. Moor, J. H. Søraker, & E. Steinhart (Eds.), *Singularity hypotheses: A scientific and philosophical assessment* (pp. 349–365). Springer. https://doi.org/10.1007/978-3-642-32560-1_17

Reinsel, D., Gantz, J., & Rydning, J. (2017, March). *Data age 2025: The digitization of the world—From edge to core* [White paper]. Seagate Technology. https://www.seagate.com/files/www-content/our-story/trends/files/Seagate-WP-DataAge2025-March-2017.pdf

Romero, L. (2025, January 18). Quantum computing could achieve singularity in 2025—A ChatGPT moment. *Forbes*. https://www.forbes.com/sites/luisromero/2025/01/18/quantum-computing-could-achieve-singularity-in-2025-a-chatgpt-moment/

Russell, S., & Norvig, P. (2021). *Artificial intelligence: A modern approach* (4th ed.). Pearson.

Schmachtenberger, D. (2022, July 21). *Homegrown Humans—Existential Risk* [Audio podcast episode transcript]. In J. Wheal (Host), *Homegrown Humans*. Civilization Emerging. https://civilizationemerging.com/media/homegrown-humans-existential-risk/

Shanahan, M. (2015). *The technological singularity*. MIT Press.

Shor, P. W. (1997). Polynomial-time algorithms for prime factorization and discrete logarithms on a quantum computer. *SIAM Journal on Computing, 26*(5), 1484–1509. https://doi.org/10.1137/S0097539795293172

Simmons, M. (2025, February 26). *Information singularity: What happens when even AI experts can't keep up with AI* [Blog post]. *Blockbuster Blueprint with Michael Simmons*. https://blockbuster.thoughtleader.school/p/information-singularity-what-happens

Solovyev, A. V. (2023). The problem of information singularity in the storage of digital data. In N. P. Artyukh et al. (Eds.), *Artificial intelligence application in networks and systems* (Lecture Notes in Networks and Systems, Vol. 482, pp. 101–105). Springer. https://doi.org/10.1007/978-3-031-35314-7_9

Ulam, S. (1958). Tribute to John von Neumann. *Bulletin of the American Mathematical Society, 64*(3, Pt. 2), 1–49. https://projecteuclid.org/euclid.bams/1183522369

Vinge, V. (1993). *The coming technological singularity: How to survive in the post-human era* (NASA Conference Publication No. 10129). NASA Lewis Research Center & Ohio Aerospace Institute. https://ntrs.nasa.gov/api/citations/19940022856/downloads/19940022856.pdf

Weidman, J. D., Sajjan, M., Mikolas, C., Stewart, Z. J., Pollanen, J., Kais, S., & Wilson, A. K. (2024). Quantum computing and chemistry. *Cell Reports Physical Science, 5*(9), 102105. https://doi.org/10.1016/j.xcrp.2024.102105

World Economic Forum. (2025). *Future of jobs report 2025*. https://reports.weforum.org/docs/WEF_Future_of_Jobs_Report_2025.pdf

Zheng, J., & Meister, M. (2025). The unbearable slowness of being: Why do we live at 10 bits/s? *Neuron, 113*(2), 192–204. https://doi.org/10.1016/j.neuron.2024.11.008

Zlokapa, A., Thomas, N., Villalonga, B., Mi, X., Anand, S., Niu, M. Y., ... Neven, H. (2023). Boundaries of quantum supremacy via random circuit sampling. *npj Quantum Information, 9*, Article 35. https://doi.org/10.1038/s41534-023-00703-x

Index

A
Access control 36, 40, 72, 98, 101, 102, 110, 111, 112, 114, 115, 116, 118, 128, 249
Accountability 4, 5, 7, 66, 70, 74, 78, 80, 93, 94, 98, 99, 101, 102, 111, 113, 115, 117, 118, 119, 122, 125, 126, 127, 128, 138, 150, 152, 160, 161, 162, 165, 166, 167, 170, 173, 174, 175, 177, 244, 248
Adaptive assurance 244
Adversarial testing 136, 175
Altair 19
Amazon Web Services (AWS) 42, 84
Analytical Engine 12, 13
Ancient civilization 11
Ancient civilizations 10, 11
Antikythera Mechanism 11
AppExchange 36
Apple II 19
Application Programming Interfaces (APIs) 35, 36, 40, 43, 44, 48, 149, 155
ARPANET 20, 21
Artificial intelligence (AI) 1, 2, 3, 4, 5, 6, 7, 8, 21, 37, 40, 41, 42, 46, 48, 49, 50, 52, 55, 56, 65, 67, 70, 71, 72, 73, 74, 75, 77, 80, 85, 86, 87, 93, 94, 97, 103, 108, 109, 119, 121, 122, 128, 135, 136, 137, 138, 139, 140, 141, 142, 143, 144, 145, 146, 147, 148, 149, 150, 151, 152, 153, 154, 155, 156, 157, 158, 159, 160, 161, 162, 163, 164, 165, 166, 167, 168, 169, 170, 171, 172, 173, 174, 175, 176, 177, 214, 225, 226, 227, 228, 229, 230, 231, 232, 233, 234, 235, 236, 237, 238, 239, 240, 241, 242, 243, 244, 245, 246, 247, 248, 249, 250
agentic AI 135, 136, 149, 150, 151, 155, 159, 166, 172, 175, 247, 250
Artificial General Intelligence (AGI) 139

B. Kantsepolsky, L. Topor, *Managing Information Singularity*,
https://doi.org/10.1007/978-3-032-26223-3

computer vision (CV) 138, 144, 146, 147, 153, 155, 158
deep learning 138, 143, 144, 145, 147, 148, 152, 161
expert systems 138, 141, 154
functional types 137, 140, 141
generative AI 67, 71, 72, 85, 103, 148, 159, 164, 168, 228, 233, 235
machine learning (ML) 4, 40, 56, 138, 142, 143, 153, 154, 156, 158, 162, 163, 170, 231, 232, 240
natural language processing (NLP) 137, 138, 145, 147, 152, 154, 155, 156, 158, 170, 176
natural language processing (NLP) 137, 138, 145, 147, 152, 154, 155, 156, 158, 170, 176
reinforcement learning 142, 143, 157, 158, 176
Asilomar Conference 242
Aspect, Alain 198, 199
ATM 34, 84
Audit trail 35, 36, 37, 136, 175
Augmented analytics 40
Autocatalytic mechanism 239
Automation bias 136, 175

B

Babbage, Charles 12
Bacic Combined Programming Language (BCPL) 18
Balanced scorecard 37
BASIC 19
BB84 protocol 195, 206
Bell inequalities 199
Bell Labs 14, 16
Bennett, Charles H. 194, 195, 197, 201, 202, 205, 206, 207, 208
Berners-Lee, Tim 21
Bias 3, 4, 5, 7, 66, 69, 70, 72, 73, 74, 75, 80, 86, 108, 119, 121, 122, 136, 143, 148, 151, 159, 160, 162, 163, 164, 166, 172, 173, 174, 175, 177, 203, 245, 247, 249
algorithmic discrimination 74, 75, 119, 162, 163, 177
fairness 55, 73, 80, 97, 98, 99, 120, 121, 122, 151, 163, 168, 174
Biases 173
Big data 26, 36, 46, 52, 103, 237
Black-body radiation 188
Blockchain 39, 93
Bohr, Niels 189
Bombe 13
Brassard, Gilles 195, 197, 201, 202, 205, 206
Bring Your Own Device (BYOD) 44, 53
Budapest Convention 72, 94, 96, 111, 125
Business intelligence (BI) 2, 34, 35, 36, 37, 38, 40, 56, 155, 158, 175, 247
analytics systems 40
dashboards and visualization 35, 36, 37, 38, 40, 158

C

California Consumer Privacy Act (CCPA) 80, 96, 101, 113, 114
Cambridge Analytica 66, 74, 76, 81, 82, 86, 122, 240
Canada 98, 101, 102, 105, 117
PIPEDA 98, 101, 102, 117
CCTV 147, 153
Channel capacity 194
ChatGPT 67, 77, 139, 140, 146, 148, 149, 164, 168, 235
Children's Online Privacy Protection Act (COPPA) 101, 121
China 69, 71, 75, 94, 96, 98, 102, 103, 105, 107, 115, 116, 117, 118, 123, 124, 128, 168, 198, 206

Cybersecurity Law 98, 102, 103, 117, 124
Data Security Law 102, 103
Personal Information Protection Law 102, 103, 118, 124
Clay tablets 10
Client-server 2, 26
CLOUD Act 94, 124, 126
Cloud computing 3, 26, 33, 42, 43, 44, 45, 52, 56, 115, 123
Cloud-native applications 43
COBOL 16, 19, 171
Coherence 8, 100, 193, 197, 199, 203, 204, 239
Colossus 13, 14
Combinatorial optimization 239, 248
Compatible Time-Sharing System (CTSS) 16, 17, 18
time-sharing 17
Complementarity 189
Compliance 7, 35, 37, 38, 43, 79, 81, 82, 83, 94, 96, 97, 98, 99, 100, 101, 104, 105, 106, 107, 108, 109, 110, 112, 113, 114, 115, 116, 117, 118, 119, 120, 123, 124, 128, 136, 150, 161, 166, 171, 173, 175, 177, 246, 248, 249
Compliance-as-architecture 6
Computer vision (CV) 138, 144, 146, 147, 153, 155, 158
Consumer safety 108, 109
Content management systems (CMS) 41
Contestable outputs 247
Continuous verification 2, 248
Convention 99, 104
Copilot 40, 148, 158, 164
Cross-border data transfers 102, 104, 115, 124
Crypto-agility 5, 8, 244, 245
Cryptographic agility 4
Cuneiform 10
Customer relationship management (CRM) 4, 34, 36, 39, 40, 42, 43, 135, 149, 150, 155, 157, 158, 175, 176, 247, 248
Cyberattack 84
Cyberattacks 72, 117, 119, 242
Cybercrime treaty 111
Cyber-physical systems 45, 46, 242
Cybersecurity 26, 49, 54, 55, 56, 67, 70, 72, 80, 83, 84, 85, 95, 96, 97, 98, 102, 103, 106, 107, 108, 109, 110, 111, 112, 113, 114, 115, 116, 117, 123, 125, 126, 127, 164, 201, 207, 214, 242, 243
Cybersecurity Capacity Maturity Model (CCMM) 243

D

Data authenticity 65, 67, 70, 72, 73, 85, 86, 87, 160
Data breaches 81, 82, 84, 101, 102, 110, 112, 113, 114, 177
Data falsification 72
Data governance 40, 108, 118, 171, 248
Data integrity 23, 36, 110, 160
Data lineage 136, 151, 166, 175, 248
Data localization 94, 96, 102, 104, 105, 115, 123, 124, 127
Data privacy 70, 71, 96, 98, 100, 116, 117, 138, 159
Data processing 2, 13, 14, 21, 22, 33, 45, 103, 108, 123
Data protection 55, 71, 76, 79, 87, 95, 96, 98, 106, 109, 113, 114, 115, 116, 117, 120, 122, 123, 126, 164
Data warehouse 37
Dataverse 39
de Broglie, Louis 189
Decision support systems (DSS) 4, 34, 35, 36, 37, 40, 41, 112, 119, 135,

155, 156, 157, 158, 175, 176, 247, 248
Decoherence 192, 196, 203, 207, 209, 235
Deep learning 138, 143, 144, 145, 147, 148, 152, 161
Deepfakes 72, 86, 148, 165, 229
Deep-work 230
Deployment pipelines 40
Deutsch, David 195, 199, 202, 203
Digital commons 127
Digital Markets Act (DMA) 66, 78, 79, 113, 114
Digital Services Act (DSA) 78, 79, 113, 114, 165, 242
Digital sovereignty 124, 127, 214, 241
Digital transformation 23, 26, 27, 33, 46, 53, 56
Disinformation 5, 67, 72, 79, 87, 94, 113, 166, 242, 248
Distributed computing 16

E

E-commerce 21, 40, 53, 55, 98, 113, 114, 117, 152
Edge computing 45
Einstein Discovery 156, 158
Einstein, Albert 157, 189, 192, 193
Elastic Compute Cloud (EC2) 42
Electronic Numerical Integrator and Computer (ENIAC) 14, 15
Energy consumption 16, 109, 125, 169
Energy quanta 188
Enigma 13
Entanglement 192, 193, 194, 195, 197, 198, 199, 201, 207, 208, 237, 239
Enterprise applications 34, 38, 39, 40, 44
Enterprise Resource Planning (ERP) 34, 38, 40, 56, 135, 149, 155, 160, 172, 175, 247, 248
Entropy 194, 195, 196
Environmental regulations 107, 108
Epistemic literacy 240
Ethernet 22
Ethics 70, 73, 77, 93, 94, 121, 122, 140, 156, 169, 226, 227, 241, 242
European Union AI Act 71, 80, 94, 97, 108, 121, 165, 177, 247
Executive Information Systems (EIS) 34, 37, 176, 247, 248
Executive Support Systems (ESS) 34, 37, 38, 41, 155, 157, 176, 247, 248
Expert systems 138, 141, 154
Explainability 4, 108, 119, 128, 161, 162, 174, 177, 247, 249
Explainable AI (XAI) 159, 161, 162
Export controls 107, 109

F

Fairness 55, 73, 80, 97, 98, 99, 120, 121, 122, 151, 163, 168, 174
Fault-tolerant quantum computing (FTQC) 204, 205
Fear of Missing Out (FOMO) 230
Federal Information Security Management Act (FISMA) 110, 114, 115, 125
Feedback loop 7, 155, 159, 162, 174, 226, 233, 235, 238, 239, 240, 246
Feynman, Richard 195, 201, 208, 209
Finance 4, 19, 35, 37, 38, 39, 50, 80, 81, 82, 85, 86, 98, 101, 102, 106, 107, 110, 112, 113, 117, 118, 119, 121, 141, 150, 153, 154, 157, 158, 162, 164, 168, 171, 172, 173, 242
First quantum revolution 16, 17, 107, 188, 190, 192, 193, 194, 198, 199, 211, 212
  atomic clocks 193, 198, 211, 212
  integrated circuits 188, 193

lasers 188, 193, 199
microprocessors 193
semiconductors 17, 107, 188, 192, 193, 199
transistors 16, 188, 193
FORTRAN 15, 16, 19
Fraud detection 114, 137, 142, 143, 144, 153, 156, 158, 163, 171

G

General Data Protection Regulation (GDPR) 3, 66, 69, 70, 78, 79, 80, 82, 95, 96, 98, 100, 101, 102, 105, 109, 111, 112, 113, 114, 115, 116, 117, 118, 119, 120, 121, 122, 123, 124, 164, 242, 247
Generative AI 67, 71, 72, 85, 103, 148, 159, 164, 168, 228, 233, 235
Global cooperation 98, 125
Global Cyber Security Capacity Centre (GCSCC) 243, 244
Global positioning system (GPS) 45, 193, 212
Google 42, 47, 76, 78, 84, 138, 144, 146, 152, 165, 198, 201, 203, 204, 205, 208, 211
Google Quantum AI 204
Governance 1, 7, 35, 54, 74, 80, 93, 94, 95, 97, 98, 103, 106, 107, 108, 109, 110, 112, 117, 118, 119, 120, 121, 122, 123, 125, 127, 128, 136, 150, 151, 152, 155, 159, 160, 161, 162, 165, 166, 170, 171, 172, 174, 175, 176, 177, 214, 226, 229, 230, 234, 241, 242, 244, 245, 246, 247, 248, 249
AI governance 7, 93, 103, 165, 166, 170, 171, 174, 176, 177, 230, 234, 241, 242, 247, 250
anticipatory governance 94, 128, 242

anticipatory governance 94, 128, 242

compliance and standards 7, 35, 106, 107, 118, 120
human oversight 1, 7, 108, 121, 155, 172, 241, 245
provenance and auditability 120, 128, 136, 150, 152, 160, 161, 162, 165, 166, 175, 248
risk management 8, 54, 109, 110, 119, 120, 125, 128, 153, 249
Governance-by-design 106, 128, 244, 245
Gramm-Leach-Bliley Act (GLBA) 101, 112, 117
Graphical user interface (GUI) 20

H

Hallucinations 148, 173
Harvest now, decrypt later 248
Healthcare 55, 76, 84, 98, 100, 101, 109, 111, 112, 117, 125, 138, 143, 153, 162, 171, 172, 173
Heisenberg limit 197
Heisenberg, Werner 189, 190, 191
Heylighen, Francis 228
Hieroglyphics 11
HIPAA 98, 100, 101, 111, 115, 117, 118
Honeywell 203, 204
Human oversight 1, 7, 108, 121, 155, 172, 241, 245
Human-AI cognitive partnership 230
Human-in-the-loop 5, 136, 151, 166, 175
Hybrid cloud 43
Hypertext Markup Language (HTML) 21
Hypertext Transfer Protocol (HTTP) 21, 85

I

IAEA 240

IBM 14, 15, 16, 18, 19, 20, 37, 38, 138, 139, 140, 141, 157, 198, 203, 204, 205, 229
IBM Cognos 37, 38, 157
IBM Quantum 204, 205
Idempotency 35
Immutable logs 136
Incident response 5, 103, 106, 109, 110, 115, 116, 125
Industrial Revolution 9, 12, 13, 242
Information cycle 1, 6, 8
Information literacy 72, 230, 240
Information singularity 1, 2, 6, 225, 226, 228, 229, 230, 231, 232, 233, 235, 236, 238, 239, 243, 244, 245, 246, 247, 248
  adaptive control 2, 238
  AI-generated content deluge 233
  continuous verification 2, 248
  exponential knowledge discovery 231
  human-AI cognitive partnership 230
  information cycle, compression of 1, 6
  information singularity literacy 230
  Information Singularity Readiness Maturity Model (ISRMM) 6, 243, 244, 245
  mutual reinforcement 238, 247
  positive feedback loops 226, 238, 246
  QIS-AI feedback loop 235, 239, 246
  relation to technological singularity 225, 226, 228, 229, 230, 231, 232, 233, 236, 238
  trusted sources and deep work 230
Information systems (IS) 1, 2, 4, 6, 7, 9, 10, 22, 23, 24, 25, 26, 27, 33, 34, 50, 52, 55, 65, 93, 162, 168, 169, 176, 188, 240, 246, 249
  academic field and schools of thought 24
  AI-enhanced 4, 162, 168, 169, 176, 240
  challenges and dilemmas 65
  common types of 34
  current state of 27, 33, 203
  education and skills 2, 7, 22, 24, 25, 26, 33, 52, 55, 240
  legal and regulatory frameworks 93
  quantum-era transformation 6, 246
  socio-technical nature of 249
Information theory 194, 196, 197, 198, 213
Infrastructure as a Service (IaaS) 42, 43
Integer BASIC 19
Integrated circuits 188, 193
Intelligence explosion 226, 227, 236
International Federation for Information Processing (IFIP) 25
Internet 2, 3, 9, 10, 20, 21, 22, 42, 43, 44, 45, 57, 66, 71, 73, 74, 75, 78, 84, 87, 107, 146, 164, 207, 208, 232, 233, 240, 248
Internet of Things (IoT) 42, 45, 46, 53, 75, 84, 103, 107, 108, 112
Interoperability 39, 46, 116, 120, 123, 124, 126, 127, 128, 246
IonQ 203, 204

J

Jurisdiction 39, 69, 70, 87, 94, 95, 97, 103, 104, 105, 111, 115, 116, 117, 118, 121, 122, 123, 124, 126, 127, 167, 175
Jurisdictions 96, 165
Just-in-time 39

K

Key performance indicators (KPIs) 35, 37, 38, 40, 49, 50, 156, 158, 246
Knowledge management systems (KMS) 41, 53, 229
Kostikov 228, 229, 233
Kurzweil, Ray 227, 238

L

Landauer, Rolf 194
Laser 18, 188, 193, 197, 199, 208
Least privilege 83, 116, 136, 151, 166, 175
Legal personhood 166, 167
Light quanta 189
Lineage views 40
LISP 19, 20
Lorenz cipher 13
Low-code 40, 158

M

Machine learning (ML) 4, 36, 40, 56, 73, 138, 142, 143, 144, 145, 148, 152, 153, 154, 156, 158, 163, 170, 231, 232
Magnetic resonance imaging (MRI) 147, 193
Mainframe computing 2, 9, 22, 26
Managed transitions 240
Management information systems (MIS) 4, 22, 25, 35, 36, 38, 41, 55, 135, 154, 155, 156, 175, 247, 248
Management Information Systems (MIS) 34
Matrix mechanics 190, 191
Metrology 197, 198, 199, 200, 201
Microprocessors 193
Microservices 43
Microsoft Dynamics 39, 156
Misinformation 72, 122, 168, 173, 233, 240
Mobile computing 2, 22, 33, 42, 82
Mobile Device Management (MDM) 44
Model cards 136, 166, 175, 247
Model flows 167
Multi-cloud 43
Multics 17
Mutual Legal Assistance Treaties (MLATs) 126

N

National security 74, 78, 82, 97, 102, 104, 106, 107, 109, 121, 124, 126
Natural language processing (NLP) 137, 138, 145, 147, 152, 154, 155, 156, 158, 170, 176
Network and Information Security (NIS) Directive 109, 112, 117, 125
NIST AI RMF 119, 166, 175, 247
NIST CSF 126
No-cloning theorem 195
Noisy Intermediate-Scale Quantum (NISQ) 203, 204, 205, 239

O

Omnichannel strategies 44
OpenAI 77, 138, 146, 148, 164
Operational technology (OT) 46
Order-to-cash 38, 39, 155
Organizational challenges 170
Over-reliance on AI 136, 160, 177

P

Paginated reports 40
Papyrus 11
Payment Card Industry Data Security Standard (PCI DSS) 35, 112, 119
Personal computer (PC) 19, 20, 22, 26, 106
Personal data 70, 71, 73, 75, 76, 78, 79, 81, 87, 96, 98, 99, 101, 102, 103, 104, 105, 109, 111, 114, 115, 117, 123, 126
Personal Information Protection and Electronic Documents Act (PIPEDA) 98, 101, 102, 117
Pervasive computing 44
Phoenicians 11
Photoelectric effect 189
Photons 189, 195, 199, 205, 206

Planck constant (h) 188, 189
Planck, Max 188, 189
Platform as a Service (PaaS) 43
Point-of-sale (POS) 34, 156
Policy challenges 86
Policy constraints 247
Positive feedback loop 226, 238, 246
Post-quantum cryptography (PQC) 207, 243, 244, 245, 246
Power BI 36, 39, 40, 158
Power Platform 39
Predictive analytics 36, 121, 136, 145, 154, 156, 157, 158
Printing press 12, 240
Privacy 3, 54, 55, 65, 66, 67, 69, 70, 71, 73, 74, 75, 76, 77, 78, 79, 80, 81, 82, 84, 86, 87, 94, 95, 96, 98, 99, 100, 101, 105, 111, 112, 113, 115, 116, 117, 118, 119, 121, 122, 123, 124, 126, 127, 128, 160, 163, 164, 167, 168, 171, 242, 245, 248, 249
  AI and 55
  laws and regulation 66, 70, 71, 95, 96, 100, 101, 242
Privacy Shield 115, 124
Private cloud 43
Procure-to-pay 38, 39
Project Genesis 165
Provenance 120, 128, 136, 150, 152, 160, 161, 162, 165, 166, 175, 248
Public cloud 43
Public sector 168, 171
Punch cards 15

Q

QIS-AI feedback loop 235, 239, 246
Qlik 158
Quanta 198, 199
Quantum 1.0 193
Quantum 2.0 194, 201
Quantum advantage 8, 204, 205, 213, 235, 247
Quantum AI (QAI) 238, 239, 246, 247, 248, 249, 250
Quantum coherence 192, 199
Quantum communication 197, 207, 208, 237
  quantum internet 207, 208, 237
  quantum teleportation 197, 207
Quantum communications 176, 199, 200, 213, 234, 236, 237
Quantum computing 197, 203, 204, 207, 234, 242
  current state of 27, 33, 203
  error correction 203, 204
  NISQ era 203, 204
  post-quantum implications 207, 242
  quantum volume 204
  role in information singularity 234
  superconducting qubits 204
  trapped ions 197, 203, 204, 208
Quantum error correction 203, 204
Quantum information science (QIS) 1, 4, 42, 176, 187, 194, 195, 196, 225, 226, 231, 233, 235, 243, 244, 247, 249
  channel capacity 194
  mutual information 194
  no-cloning theorem 195
  Shannon entropy 196
Quantum Internet 207, 208, 237
Quantum Key Distribution (QKD) 205, 206, 207, 213, 236
Quantum mechanics 7, 187, 188, 193, 194, 195, 199, 201, 202, 203, 213, 236
Quantum metrology 197
Quantum Neural Networks (QNN) 246
Quantum sensing 198, 199, 200, 208, 213, 234, 237
Quantum simulation 200, 213

Quantum supremacy 235, 236
Quantum theory 188, 189, 191, 199, 200
black-body radiation 188
complementarity 189
energy quanta 188
light quanta 189
photoelectric effect 189
Planck constant 188, 189
wave mechanics 191
wave-particle duality 189
Quantum volume 204
Quantum-enhanced learning 246
Quantum-safe encryption 242
Qubits 192, 195, 196, 197, 198, 201, 202, 203, 204, 205, 206, 207, 208, 239

R

Race or slowdown 234
Recommender systems 165, 248
Record-keeping 11, 12, 26, 157
Regulatory compliance 82, 118, 161
Reinforcement learning 142, 143, 157, 158, 176
RFID 45
Risk management 8, 54, 109, 110, 119, 120, 125, 128, 153, 249
Role-based access control 36, 40
Roomba 147
Row-level security 37
Russia 69, 71, 75, 84, 96, 103, 104, 105, 115, 123, 124, 161
personal data law 104, 105, 124

S

Safety regulations 107
Salesforce 36, 39, 42, 156, 157
Schmachtenberger, Daniel 228, 229, 232, 233
Schrems II 115, 124
Schrödinger, Erwin 189, 191, 192
Schumacher, Benjamin 196
Scientific management 12
Scorecards 37, 38, 40
Second quantum revolution 213
Section 230 165
Security 54, 57, 68, 69, 70, 82, 83, 84, 87, 94, 97, 98, 102, 103, 105, 106, 107, 109, 110, 111, 115, 116, 117, 120, 124, 125, 153, 164, 207, 230, 242
challenges to information systems 82
critical infrastructure 84, 102, 105, 107, 110, 115, 124, 125
cybersecurity law 98, 102, 103, 117, 124
quantum threats 54, 57, 68, 69, 70, 82, 83, 87, 94, 97, 106, 107, 109, 111, 115, 116, 117, 120, 125, 153, 164, 207, 230, 242
Semantic layer 37
Semantic models 149
Semiconductors 17, 107, 188, 192, 193, 199
Sensitivity analyses 247
Shanahan, Murray 226
Shannon entropy 196
Shannon, Claude 194, 195, 196, 213
Shor, Peter 196, 202
Shor's algorithm 202, 206, 235
Simmons 85, 229, 230, 231, 232
Single integrated platform 41
Single quanta 198
Slack 42
Slowdown scenario 234
Smart grids 211, 242
Social media 21, 35, 37, 47, 52, 53, 55, 65, 72, 77, 79, 81, 152, 249
Socio-technical systems 1, 2, 3, 6, 9, 10, 23, 24, 26, 50, 52, 120, 174, 188, 243, 249
Software as a Service (SaaS) 42, 43, 46

Standards 5, 8, 19, 40, 46, 71, 95, 97, 98, 99, 100, 103, 105, 106, 107, 109, 110, 112, 114, 115, 116, 118, 119, 120, 125, 126, 127, 128, 144, 165, 170, 171, 175, 177, 197, 206, 207, 210, 212, 214, 230, 234, 242, 243, 244, 245, 249
Stimulated emission 193
Stripe 35, 156
Sumerians 10
Superconducting qubits 204
Superintelligence 139, 227, 231, 236
Superposition 191, 192, 193, 194, 196, 199, 201
Supply chain management (SCM) 14, 34, 39, 135, 155, 158, 175, 176, 247, 248
Supply chain security 125
Sustainability 55, 122, 159, 169, 170, 177, 226
Symbolic AI 141

T

Tableau 36, 156, 158
Tallinn Manual 68, 95
Taylor, Frederick Winslow 12
Technological approaches 154
Technological singularity 225, 226, 227, 234, 236
  definitions of 226
  intelligence explosion 226, 227, 236
  race or slowdown 234
  relation to information singularity 225, 226
Telegraph 13, 240
Telephone 13, 240
Teleportation 197, 207
Timesharing 17
Traceability 4, 39, 108, 244, 245
Transaction processing systems (TPS) 34, 35, 36, 38, 40, 41
Transistors 16, 188, 193
Transmission Control Protocol/Internet Protocol (TCP/IP) 21
Transparency 3, 5, 7, 70, 74, 78, 79, 80, 82, 94, 98, 99, 102, 105, 108, 110, 113, 115, 116, 120, 121, 122, 126, 127, 128, 138, 141, 143, 158, 159, 161, 162, 165, 167, 171, 173, 174, 177
Trapped ions 197, 203, 204, 208
Trapped ions 197, 203, 204, 208
Trigger-based decision points 244
Trusted sources 230
Tunneling 192, 193
Turing, Alan 13, 137

U

Ulam, Stanislaw 226
Uncertainty bound 190
Uncertainty principle 189
UNCLOS analogy 94, 96, 127
UNESCO 25, 122
United Nations 77, 96, 105, 111, 125, 127, 187
United States 14, 15, 16, 20, 25, 69, 71, 74, 75, 76, 79, 81, 83, 86, 94, 96, 98, 100, 101, 106, 107, 110, 111, 112, 113, 114, 116, 121, 123, 124, 125, 126, 163, 165, 171, 200
  sectoral privacy laws 100, 101
UNIVAC 15, 16
Unix 17

V

Vacuum tubes 14, 15
Vendor lock-in 43
Vinge, Vernor 227, 228, 238
Virtualization 42
von Neumann, John 226

W
Water use 43, 46, 56, 109, 169, 242
Wave mechanics 191
Wave-particle duality 189
Wearables 45, 53, 108
Web browsers 21
Webhooks 35
What-if analysis 36, 38, 157
Willow processor 204
World War II 13, 14
World Wide Web (WWW) 21, 22

X
Xerox PARC 17